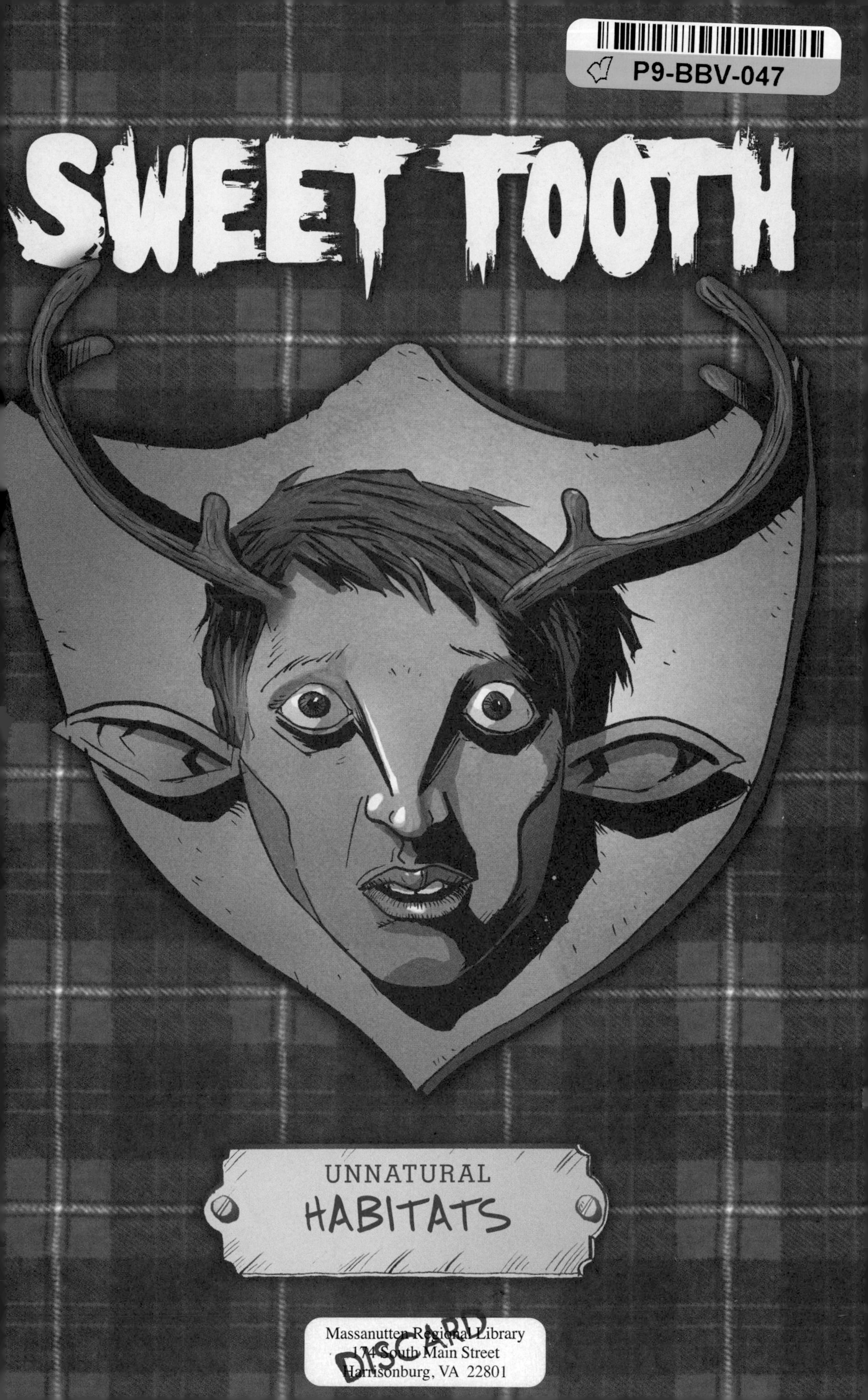
SWEET TOOTH
UNNATURAL
HABITATS

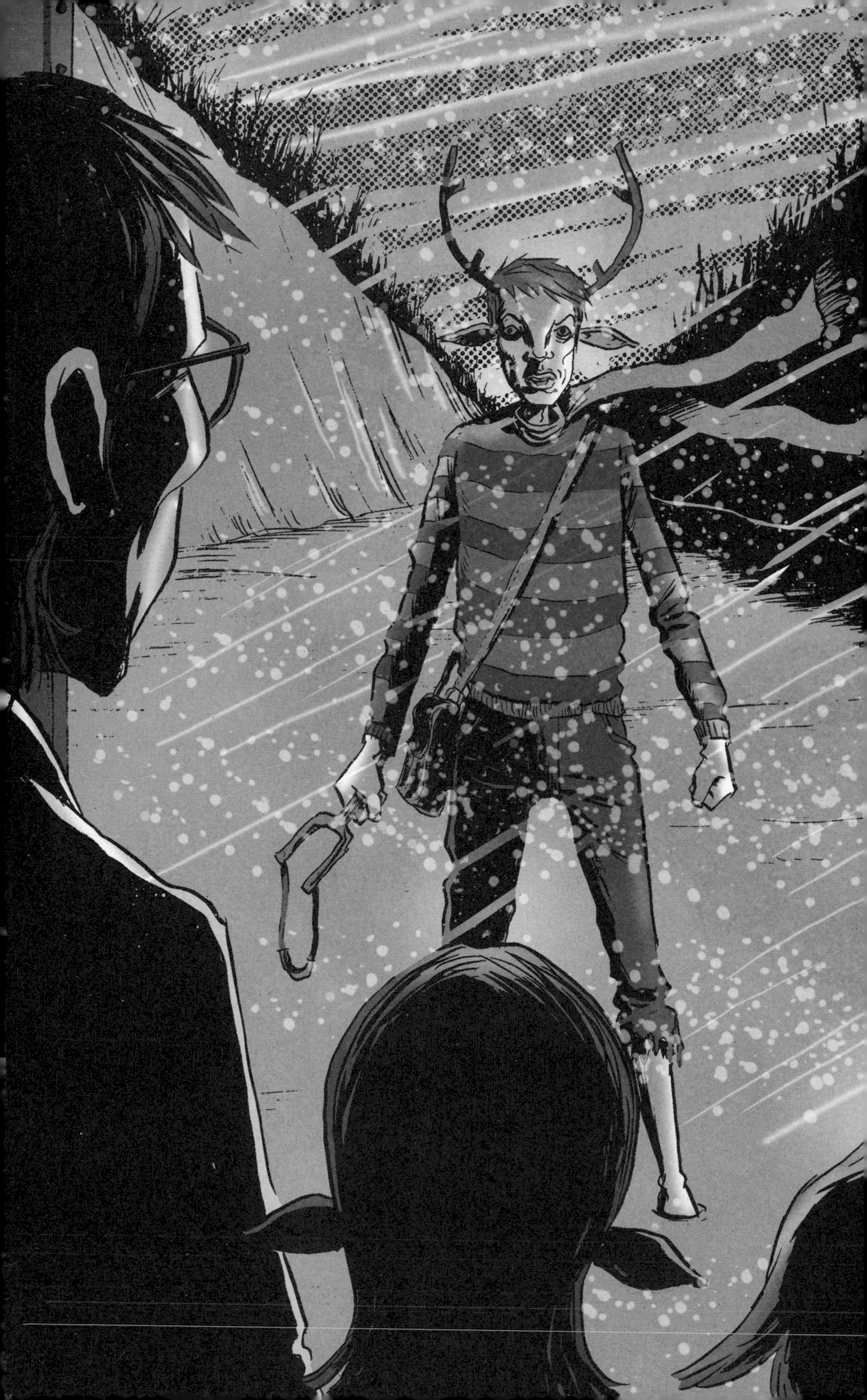

SWEET TOOTH

UNNATURAL HABITATS

JEFF LEMIRE
story & cover

MATT KINDT
art & color "THE TAXIDERMIST"

JEFF LEMIRE
art "UNNATURAL HABITATS"

JOSE VILLARUBIA
color "UNNATURAL HABITATS"

PAT BROSSEAU
CARLOS M. MANGUAL
letters

SWEET TOOTH
created by Jeff Lemire

SWEET TOOTH: UNNATURAL HABITATS Published by DC Comics. Cover and compilation Copyright © 2012 Jeff Lemire. All Rights Reserved.
Originally published in single magazine form in SWEET TOOTH 26-32 Copyright © 2011, 2012 Jeff Lemire. All Rights Reserved.
VERTIGO is a trademark of DC Comics. All characters, their distinctive likenesses and related elements featured in this
publication are trademarks of DC Comics. The stories, characters and incidents featured in this publication
are entirely fictional. DC Comics does not read or accept unsolicited ideas, stories or artwork.

DC Comics, 2900 W. Alameda Avenue, Burbank, CA 91505
Printed in the USA. Third Printing.
ISBN: 978-1-4012-3723-3

Library of Congress Cataloging-in-Publication Data

Lemire, Jeff.
Sweet tooth : unnatural habitats / Jeff Lemire, Matt Kindt.
p. cm.
"Originally published in single magazine form in Sweet Tooth 26-32."
ISBN 978-1-4012-3723-3 (alk. paper)
1. Graphic novels. I. Kindt, Matt. II. Title. III. Title: Unnatural habitats.
PN6733.L45S98 2012
741.5'973–dc23
2012023758

PREVIOUSLY

A decade ago a horrible disease raged across the world killing billions. Afterwards it spawned a new breed of human/animal hybrid children...the only children born since the plague.

GUS is one such hybrid. A young boy with a sweet soul, a sweeter tooth — and the features of a deer. After his father died and Gus finally left the seclusion of his forest home, Gus hooked up with a hulking and violent drifter named JEPPERD.

As they traveled, the two were joined by two more hybrid children — the sweet pig-girl WENDY and the lovable ground-hog boy BOBBY — as well as the children's former captors JOHNNY and DR. SINGH and rescued prostitutes LUCY and BECKY.

As they journeyed to Alaska, the group met WALTER FISH, a soft-spoken survivor with an extraordinary home. Walter had discovered the remains of an environmentalist commune, a self-sustaining stronghold with food, electricity and modern comforts not seen since before the plague.

While most of the travelers are content to make a permanent home with Walter, Singh wishes only to continue north on their quest to discover Gus's history (and perhaps the cause of the plague), and Jepperd urges the group not to trust Walter, believing their benefactor may not be as trustworthy as he seems.

But before things can be resolved with Walter, the story takes a brief interlude in Alaska, during the early 1900s, following a man known as "The Taxidermist," who will have a mysterious connection to Gus and all his friends...

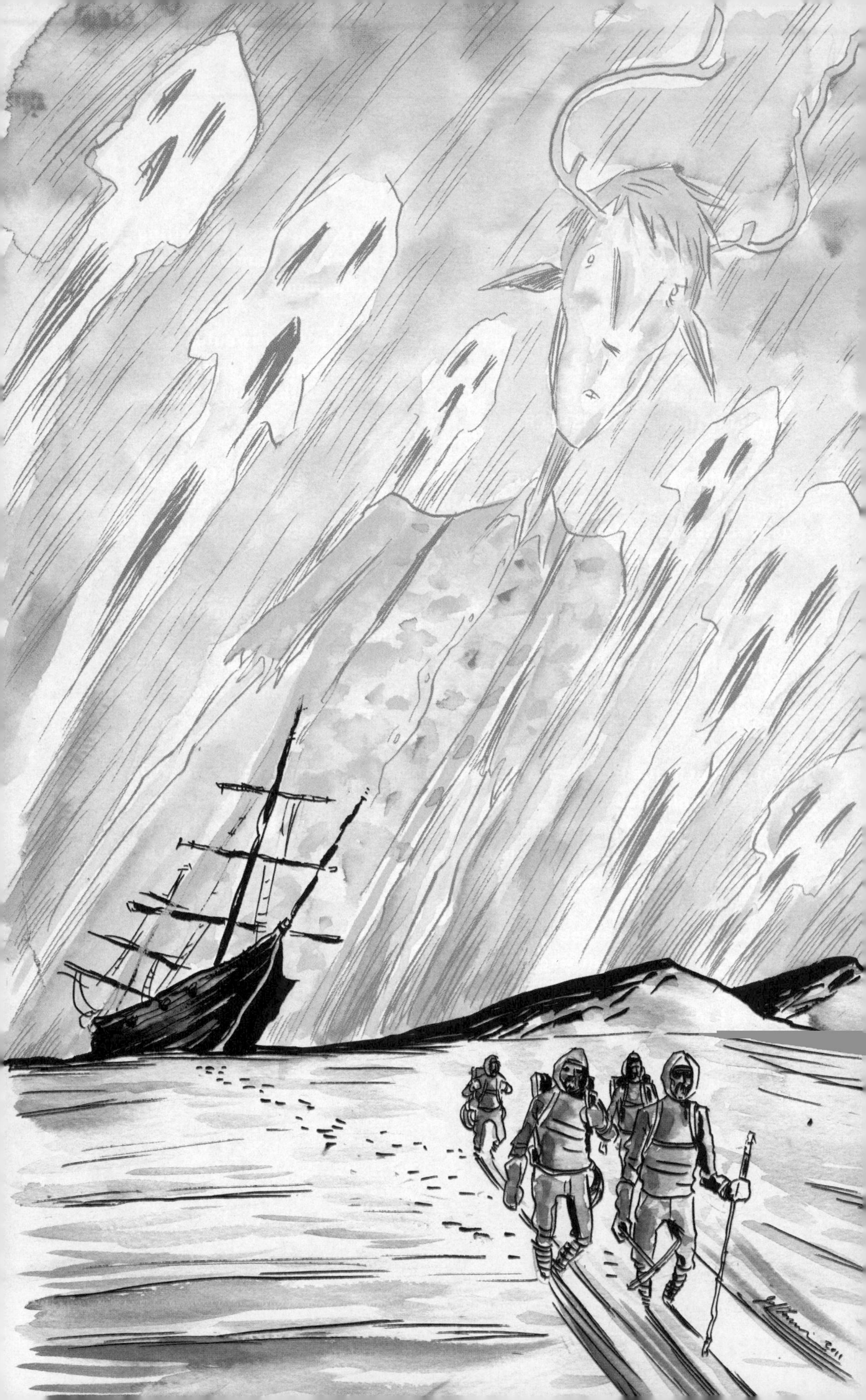

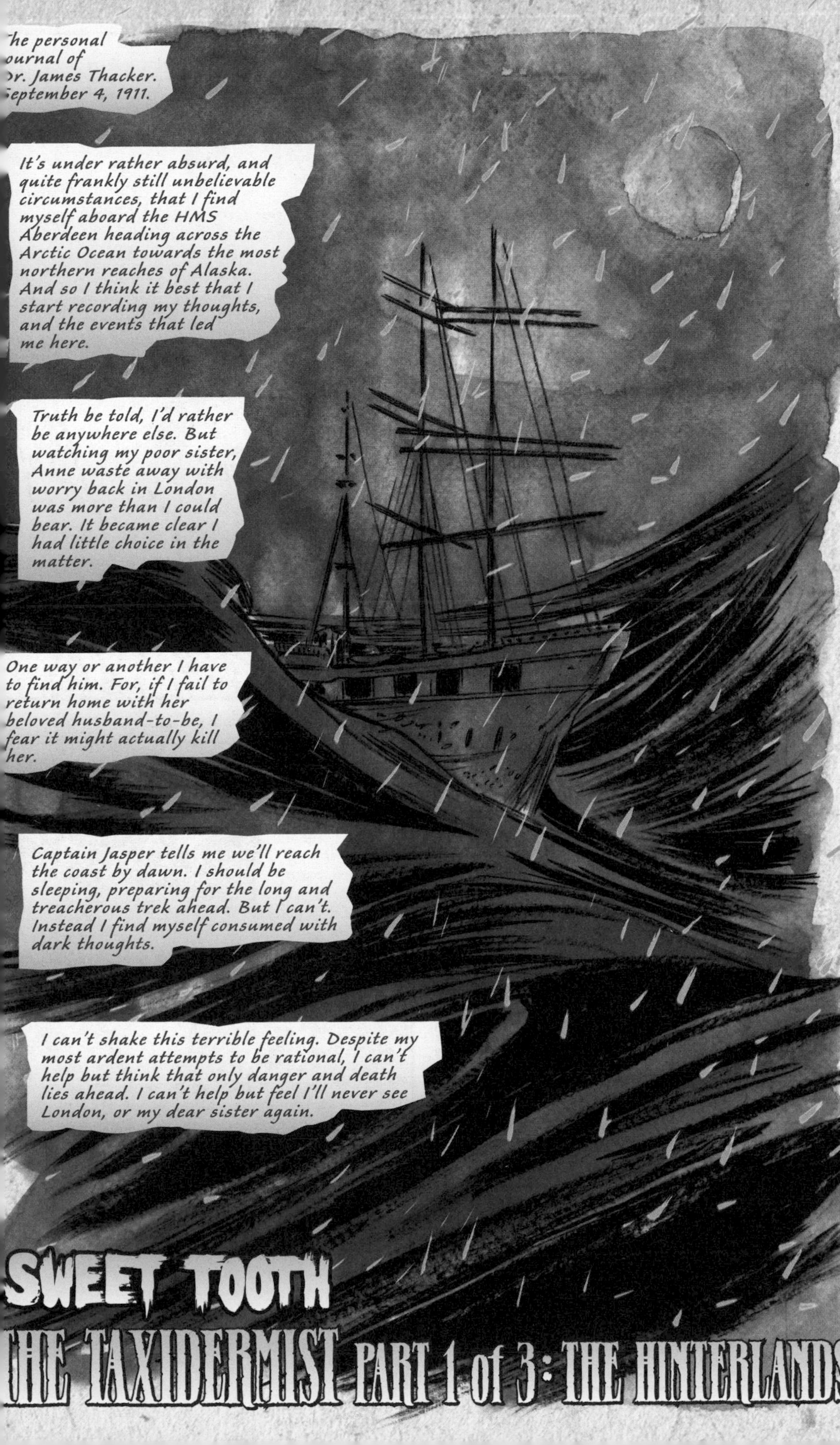
he personal ournal of r. James Thacker. eptember 4, 1911.
It's under rather absurd, and quite frankly still unbelievable circumstances, that I find myself aboard the HMS Aberdeen heading across the Arctic Ocean towards the most northern reaches of Alaska. And so I think it best that I start recording my thoughts, and the events that led me here.
Truth be told, I'd rather be anywhere else. But watching my poor sister, Anne waste away with worry back in London was more than I could bear. It became clear I had little choice in the matter.
One way or another I have to find him. For, if I fail to return home with her beloved husband-to-be, I fear it might actually kill her.
Captain Jasper tells me we'll reach the coast by dawn. I should be sleeping, preparing for the long and treacherous trek ahead. But I can't. Instead I find myself consumed with dark thoughts.
I can't shake this terrible feeling. Despite my most ardent attempts to be rational, I can't help but think that only danger and death lies ahead. I can't help but feel I'll never see London, or my dear sister again.
SWEET TOOTH
HE TAXIDERMIST PART 1 of 3: THE HINTERLANDS

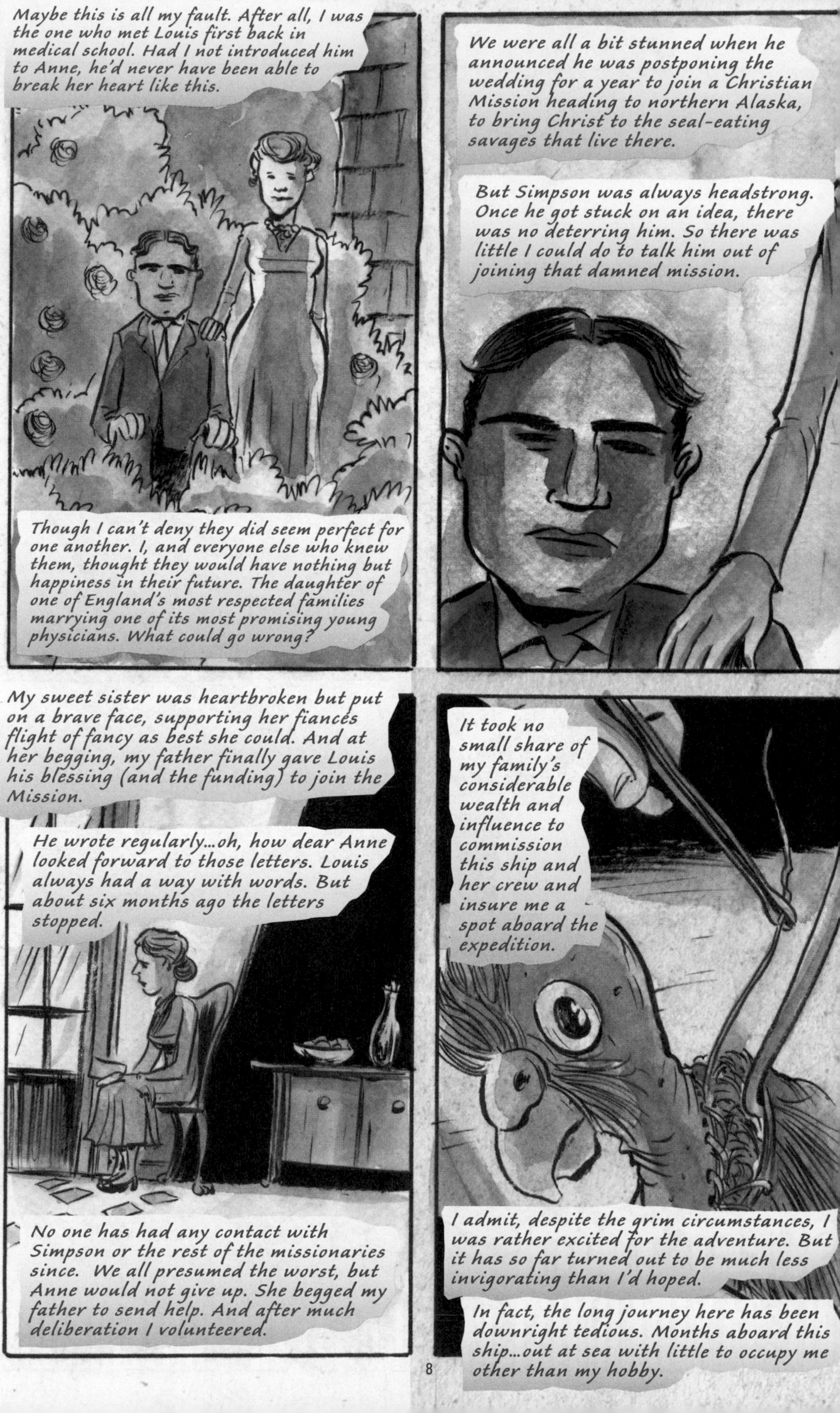
Maybe this is all my fault. After all, I was the one who met Louis first back in medical school. Had I not introduced him to Anne, he'd never have been able to break her heart like this.
Though I can't deny they did seem perfect for one another. I, and everyone else who knew them, thought they would have nothing but happiness in their future. The daughter of one of England's most respected families marrying one of its most promising young physicians. What could go wrong?
We were all a bit stunned when he announced he was postponing the wedding for a year to join a Christian Mission heading to northern Alaska, to bring Christ to the seal-eating savages that live there.
But Simpson was always headstrong. Once he got stuck on an idea, there was no deterring him. So there was little I could do to talk him out of joining that damned mission.
My sweet sister was heartbroken but put on a brave face, supporting her fiancés flight of fancy as best she could. And at her begging, my father finally gave Louis his blessing (and the funding) to join the Mission.
He wrote regularly...oh, how dear Anne looked forward to those letters. Louis always had a way with words. But about six months ago the letters stopped.
No one has had any contact with Simpson or the rest of the missionaries since. We all presumed the worst, but Anne would not give up. She begged my father to send help. And after much deliberation I volunteered.
It took no small share of my family's considerable wealth and influence to commission this ship and her crew and insure me a spot aboard the expedition.
I admit, despite the grim circumstances, I was rather excited for the adventure. But it has so far turned out to be much less invigorating than I'd hoped.
In fact, the long journey here has been downright tedious. Months aboard this ship...out at sea with little to occupy me other than my hobby.

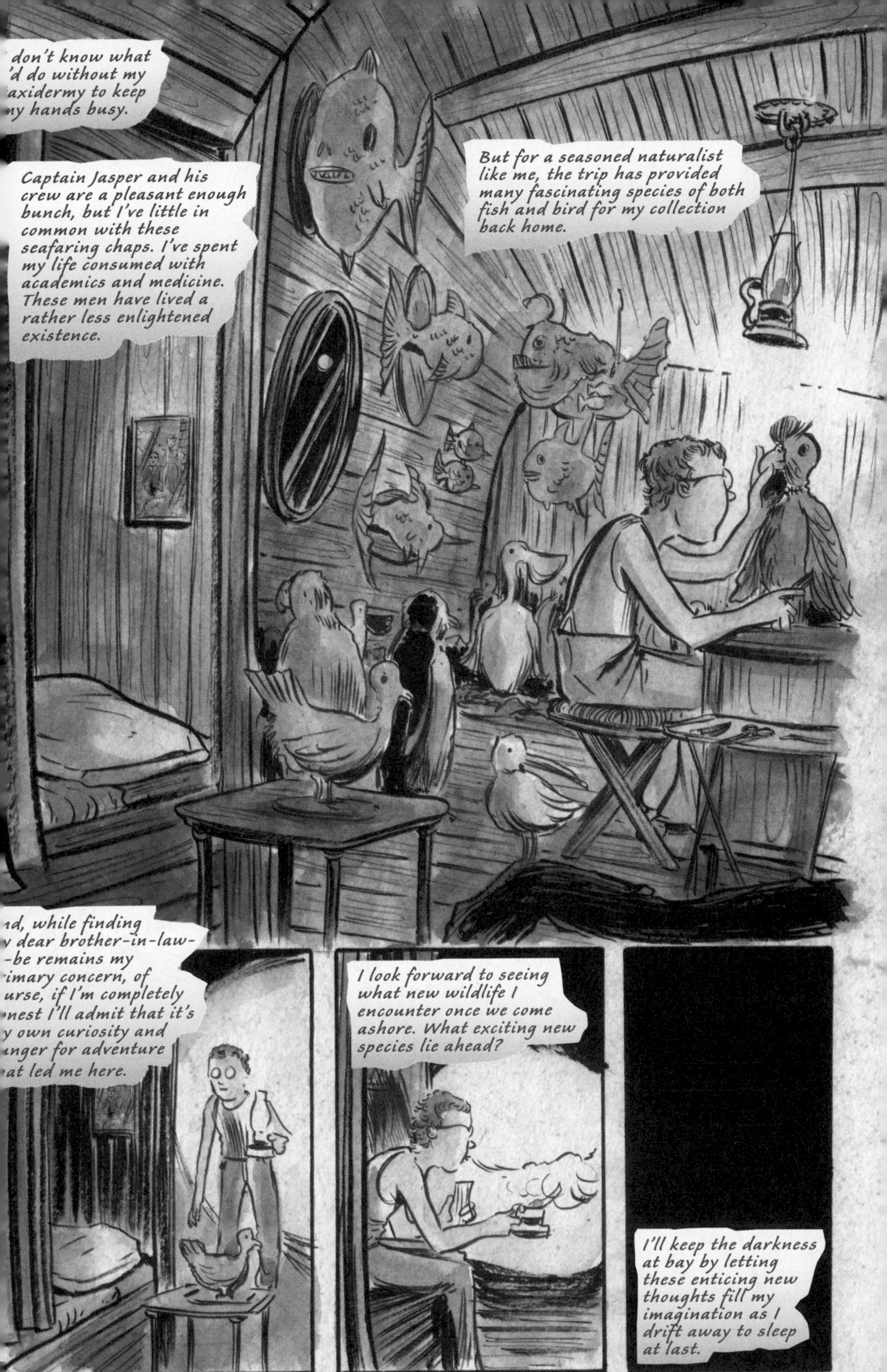
don't know what 'd do without my axidermy to keep ny hands busy.
Captain Jasper and his crew are a pleasant enough bunch, but I've little in common with these seafaring chaps. I've spent my life consumed with academics and medicine. These men have lived a rather less enlightened existence.
But for a seasoned naturalist like me, the trip has provided many fascinating species of both fish and bird for my collection back home.
id, while finding dear brother-in-law- -be remains my rimary concern, of urse, if I'm completely nest I'll admit that it's own curiosity and nger for adventure at led me here.
I look forward to seeing what new wildlife I encounter once we come ashore. What exciting new species lie ahead?
I'll keep the darkness at bay by letting these enticing new thoughts fill my imagination as I drift away to sleep at last.

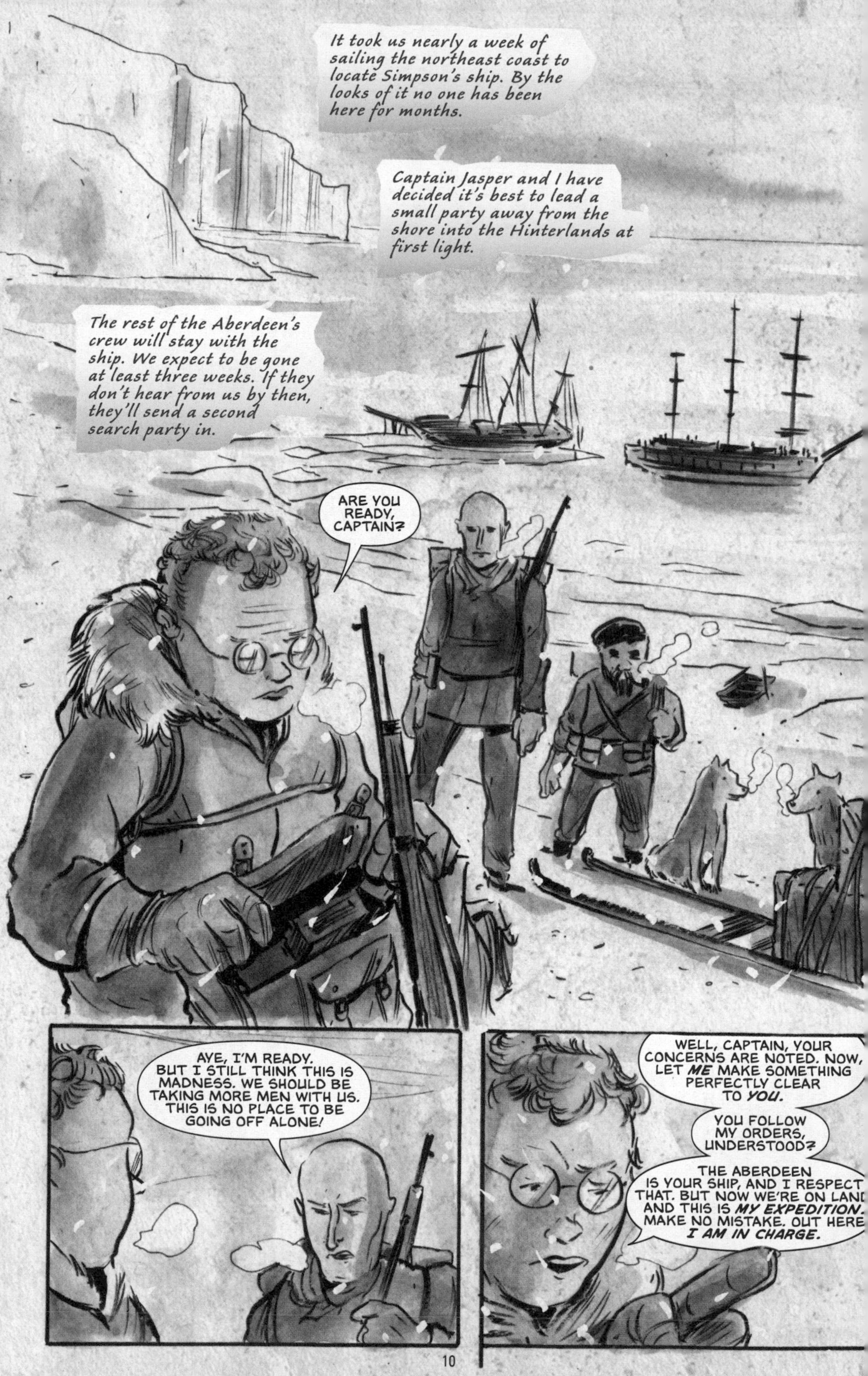
It took us nearly a week of sailing the northeast coast to locate Simpson's ship. By the looks of it no one has been here for months.
Captain Jasper and I have decided it's best to lead a small party away from the shore into the Hinterlands at first light.
The rest of the Aberdeen's crew will stay with the ship. We expect to be gone at least three weeks. If they don't hear from us by then, they'll send a second search party in.
ARE YOU READY, CAPTAIN?
AYE, I'M READY. BUT I STILL THINK THIS IS MADNESS. WE SHOULD BE TAKING MORE MEN WITH US. THIS IS NO PLACE TO BE GOING OFF ALONE!
WELL, CAPTAIN, YOUR CONCERNS ARE NOTED. NOW, LET *ME* MAKE SOMETHING PERFECTLY CLEAR TO *YOU*.
YOU FOLLOW MY ORDERS, UNDERSTOOD?
THE ABERDEEN IS YOUR SHIP, AND I RESPECT THAT. BUT NOW WE'RE ON LAND AND THIS IS ***MY EXPEDITION***. MAKE NO MISTAKE. OUT HERE ***I AM IN CHARGE***.

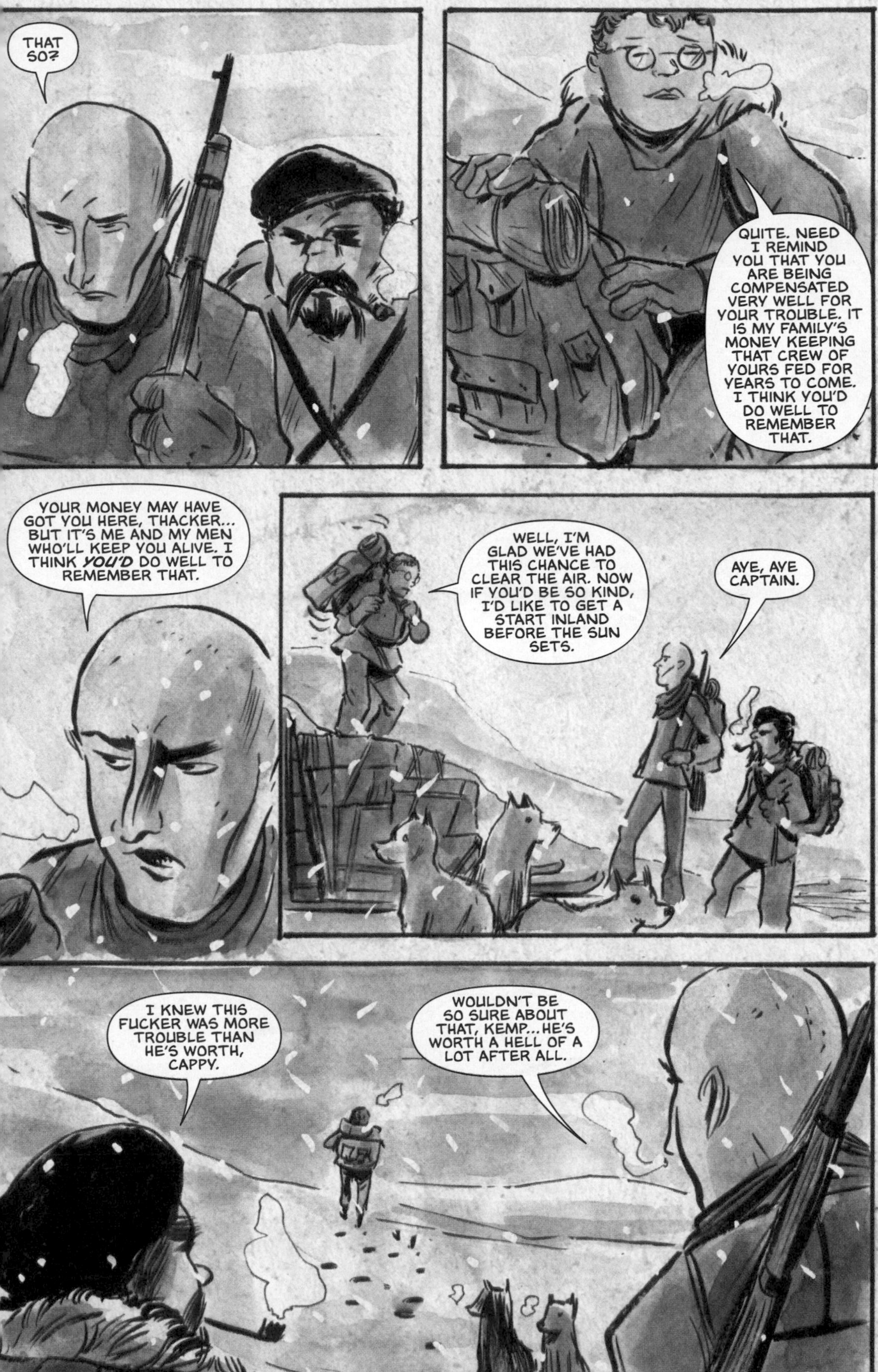
THAT SO?
QUITE. NEED I REMIND YOU THAT YOU ARE BEING COMPENSATED VERY WELL FOR YOUR TROUBLE. IT IS MY FAMILY'S MONEY KEEPING THAT CREW OF YOURS FED FOR YEARS TO COME. I THINK YOU'D DO WELL TO REMEMBER THAT.
YOUR MONEY MAY HAVE GOT YOU HERE, THACKER... BUT IT'S ME AND MY MEN WHO'LL KEEP YOU ALIVE. I THINK *YOU'D* DO WELL TO REMEMBER THAT.
WELL, I'M GLAD WE'VE HAD THIS CHANCE TO CLEAR THE AIR. NOW IF YOU'D BE SO KIND, I'D LIKE TO GET A START INLAND BEFORE THE SUN SETS.
AYE, AYE CAPTAIN.
I KNEW THIS FUCKER WAS MORE TROUBLE THAN HE'S WORTH, CAPPY.
WOULDN'T BE SO SURE ABOUT THAT, KEMP... HE'S WORTH A HELL OF A LOT AFTER ALL.

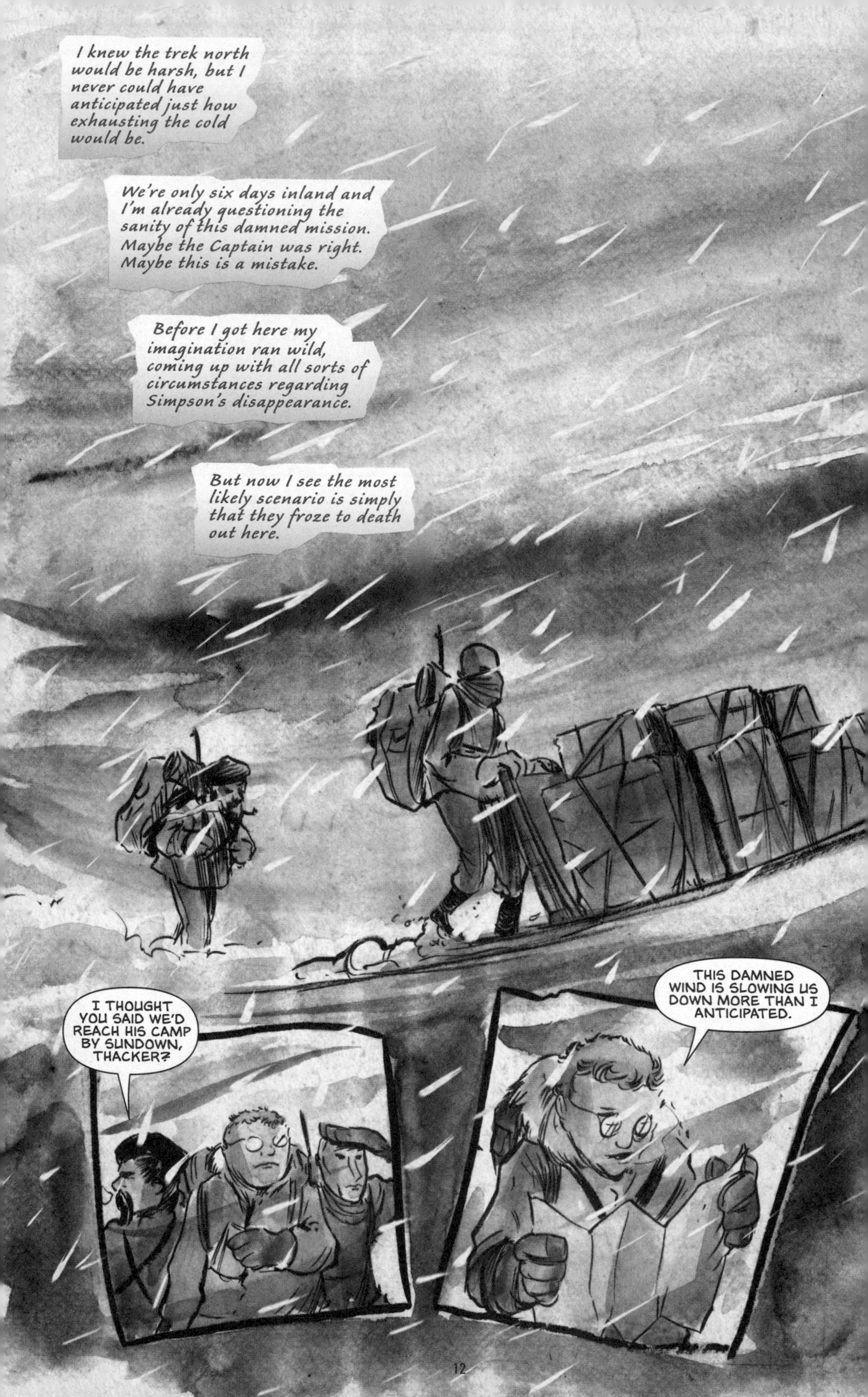
I knew the trek north would be harsh, but I never could have anticipated just how exhausting the cold would be.
We're only six days inland and I'm already questioning the sanity of this damned mission. Maybe the Captain was right. Maybe this is a mistake.
Before I got here my imagination ran wild, coming up with all sorts of circumstances regarding Simpson's disappearance.
But now I see the most likely scenario is simply that they froze to death out here.
I THOUGHT YOU SAID WE'D REACH HIS CAMP BY SUNDOWN, THACKER?
THIS DAMNED WIND IS SLOWING US DOWN MORE THAN I ANTICIPATED.

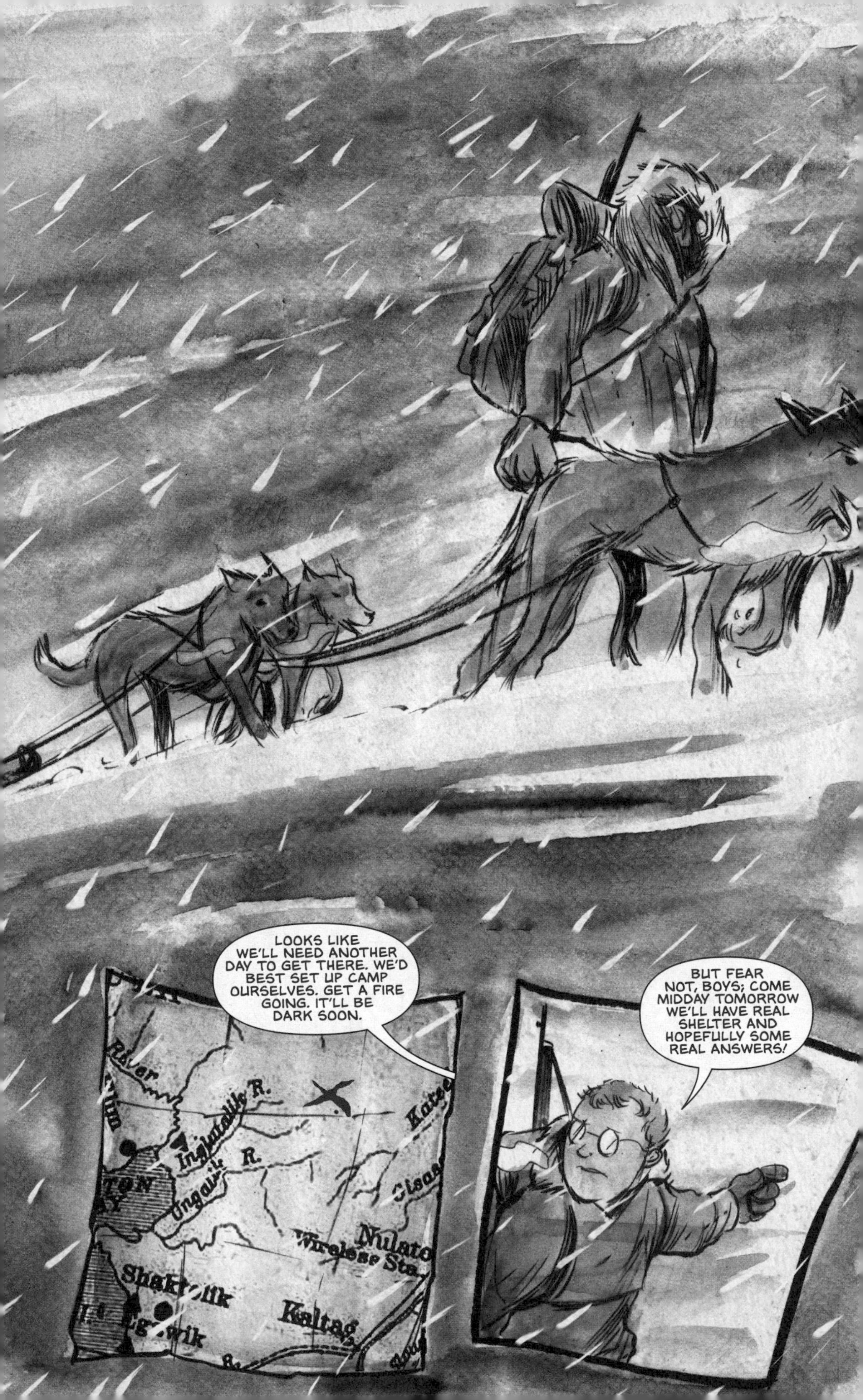
LOOKS LIKE WE'LL NEED ANOTHER DAY TO GET THERE. WE'D BEST SET UP CAMP OURSELVES. GET A FIRE GOING. IT'LL BE DARK SOON.
River
Inglutalik R.
R.
Nulato
Wireless Sta.
Kaltag
BUT FEAR NOT, BOYS; COME MIDDAY TOMORROW WE'LL HAVE REAL SHELTER AND HOPEFULLY SOME REAL ANSWERS!

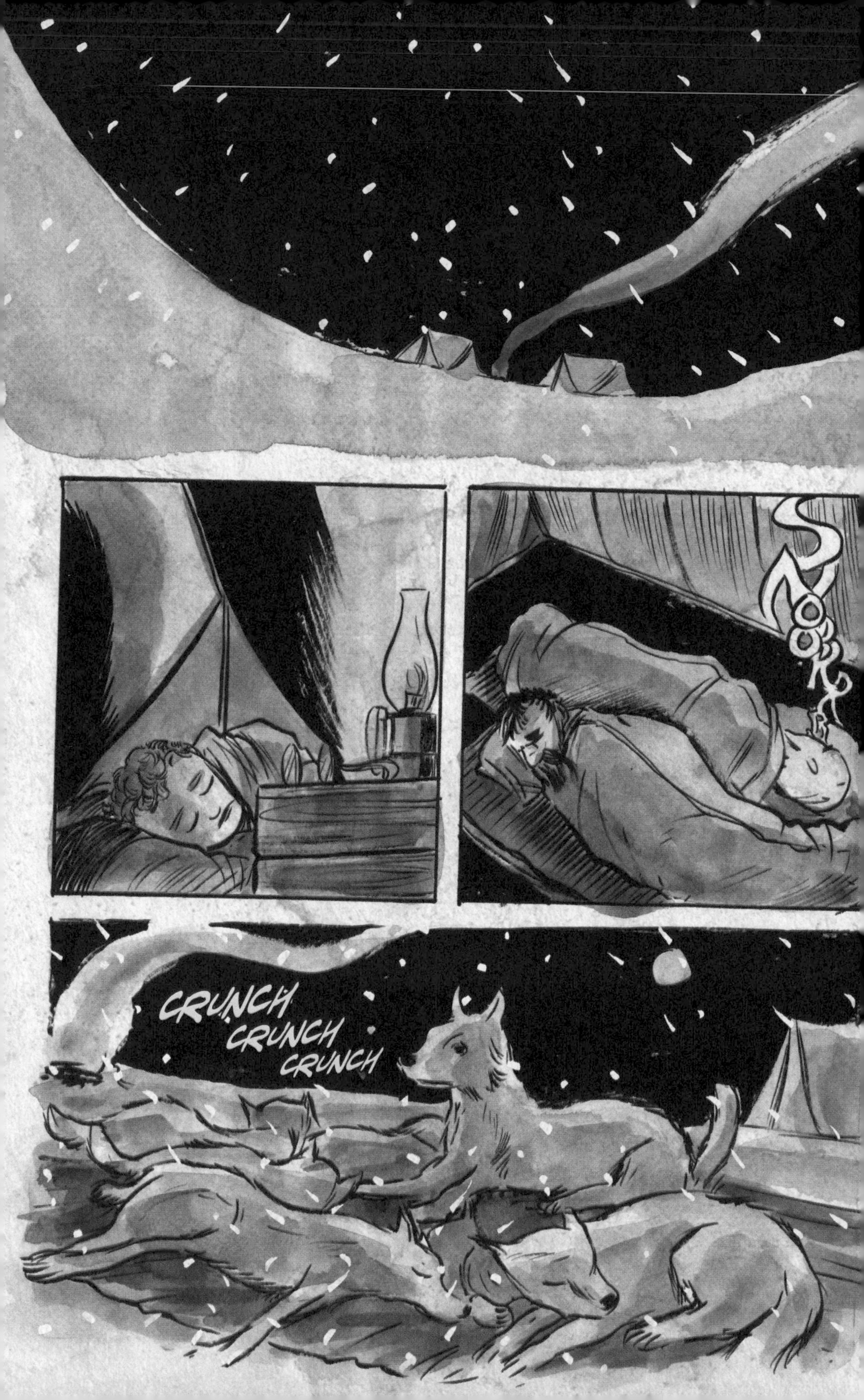
SNOORRR
CRUNCH
CRUNCH
CRUNCH

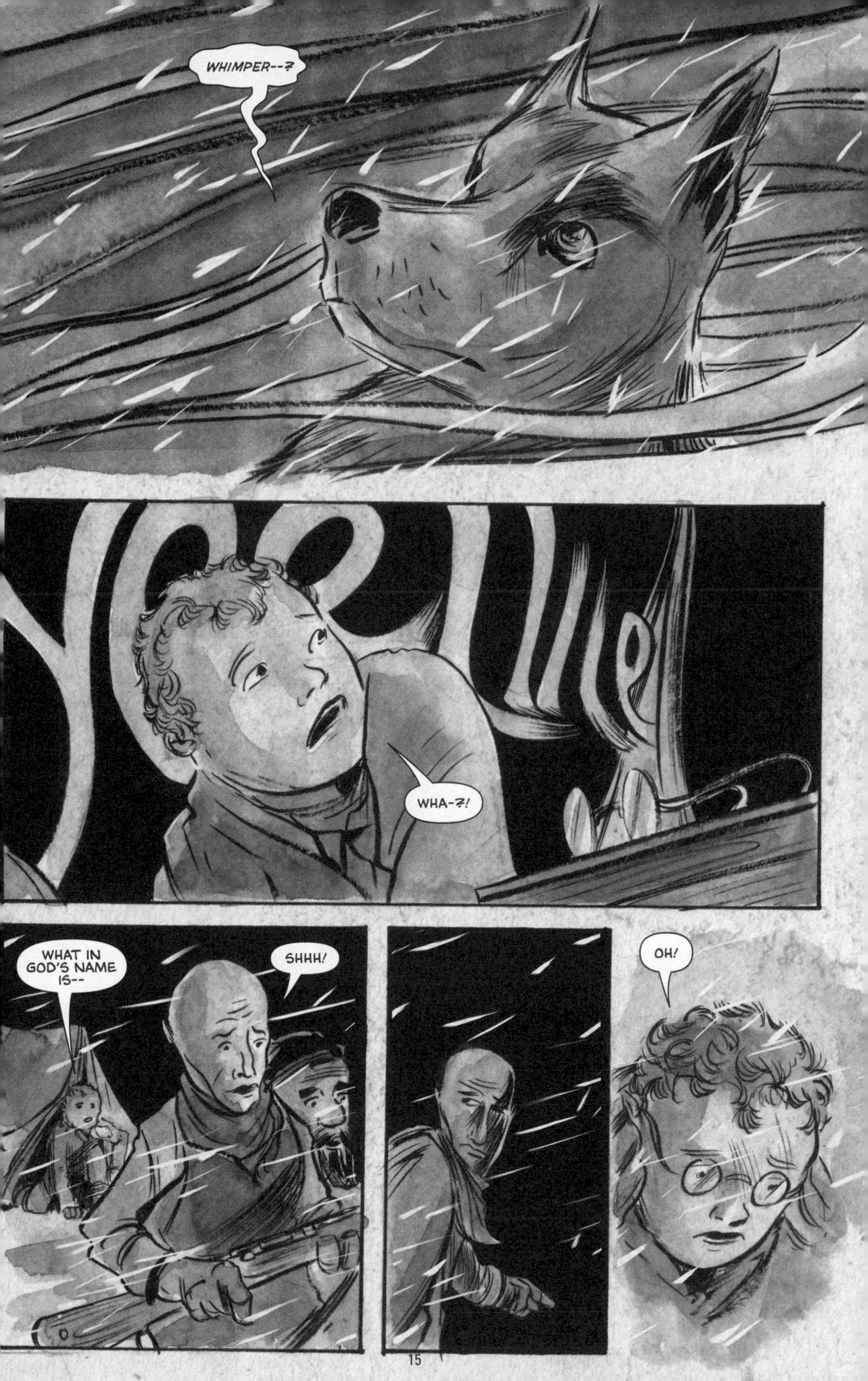
WHIMPER--?
WHA-?!
WHAT IN GOD'S NAME IS--
SHHH!
OH!

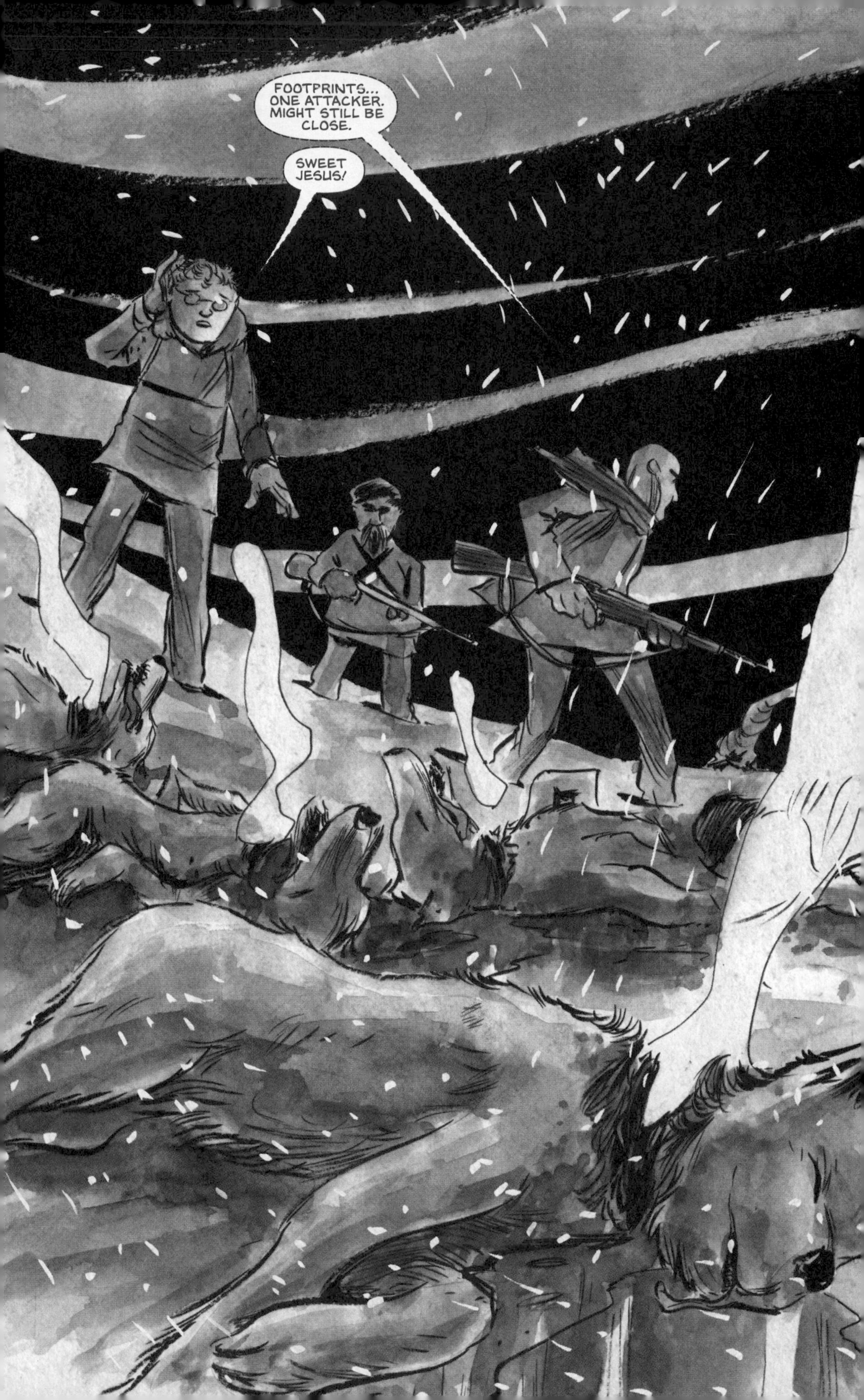
FOOTPRINTS... ONE ATTACKER. MIGHT STILL BE CLOSE.
SWEET JESUS!

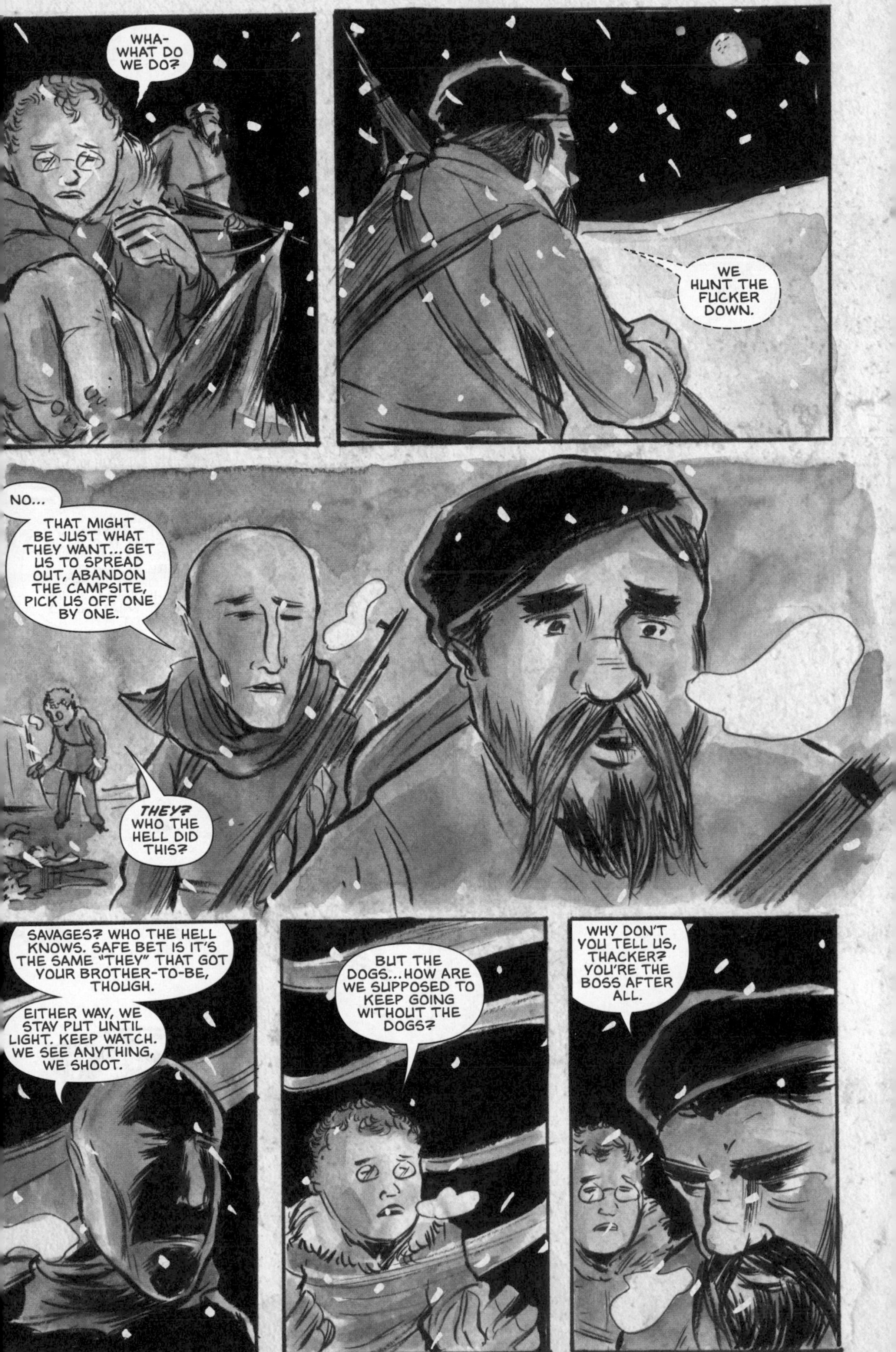
WHA- WHAT DO WE DO?
WE HUNT THE FUCKER DOWN.
NO...
THAT MIGHT BE JUST WHAT THEY WANT...GET US TO SPREAD OUT, ABANDON THE CAMPSITE, PICK US OFF ONE BY ONE.
THEY? WHO THE HELL DID THIS?
SAVAGES? WHO THE HELL KNOWS. SAFE BET IS IT'S THE SAME "THEY" THAT GOT YOUR BROTHER-TO-BE, THOUGH.
EITHER WAY, WE STAY PUT UNTIL LIGHT. KEEP WATCH. WE SEE ANYTHING, WE SHOOT.
BUT THE DOGS...HOW ARE WE SUPPOSED TO KEEP GOING WITHOUT THE DOGS?
WHY DON'T YOU TELL US, THACKER? YOU'RE THE BOSS AFTER ALL.

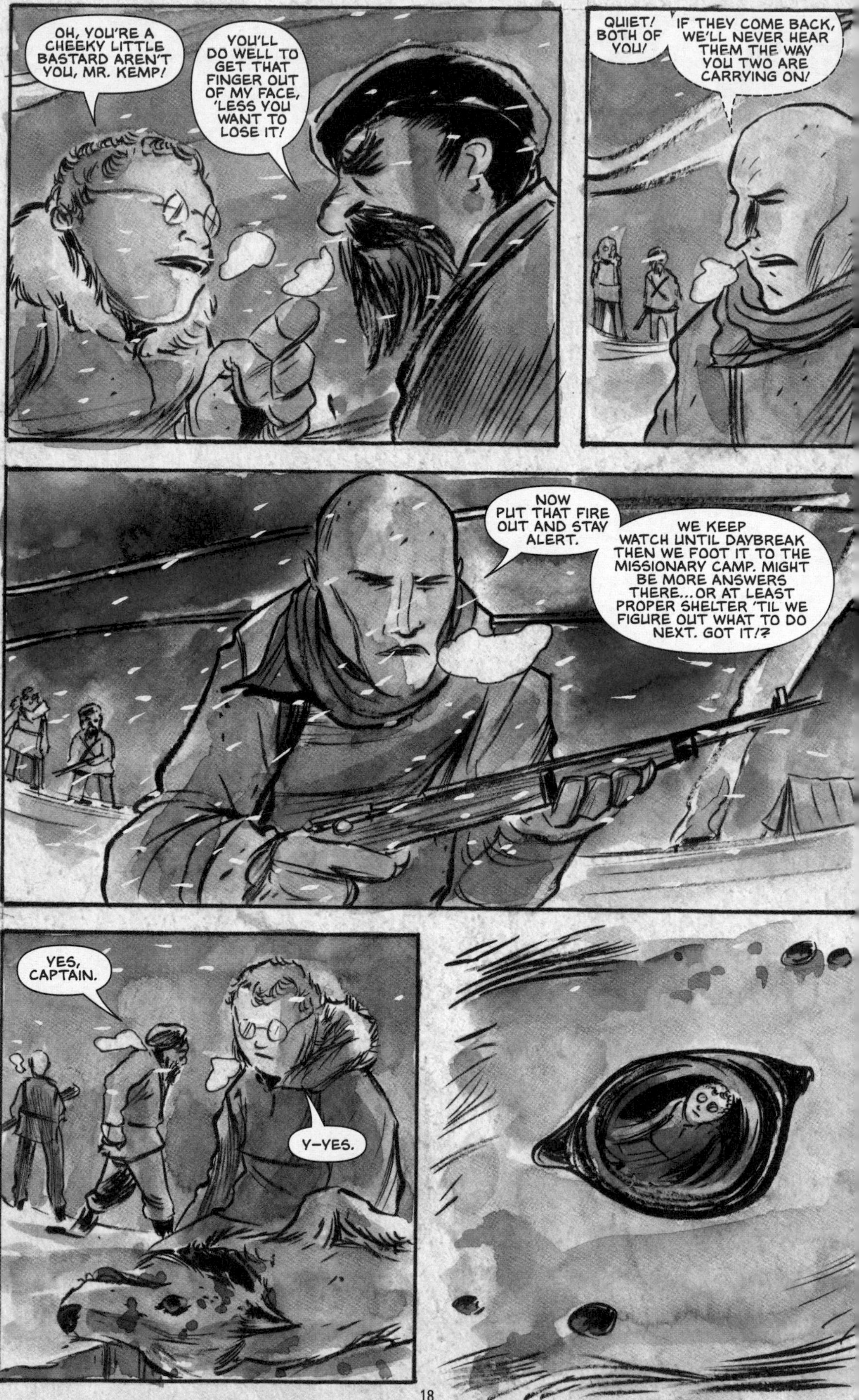
OH, YOU'RE A CHEEKY LITTLE BASTARD AREN'T YOU, MR. KEMP!
YOU'LL DO WELL TO GET THAT FINGER OUT OF MY FACE, 'LESS YOU WANT TO LOSE IT!
QUIET! BOTH OF YOU!
IF THEY COME BACK, WE'LL NEVER HEAR THEM THE WAY YOU TWO ARE CARRYING ON!
NOW PUT THAT FIRE OUT AND STAY ALERT.
WE KEEP WATCH UNTIL DAYBREAK THEN WE FOOT IT TO THE MISSIONARY CAMP. MIGHT BE MORE ANSWERS THERE...OR AT LEAST PROPER SHELTER 'TIL WE FIGURE OUT WHAT TO DO NEXT. GOT IT!?
YES, CAPTAIN.
Y-YES.

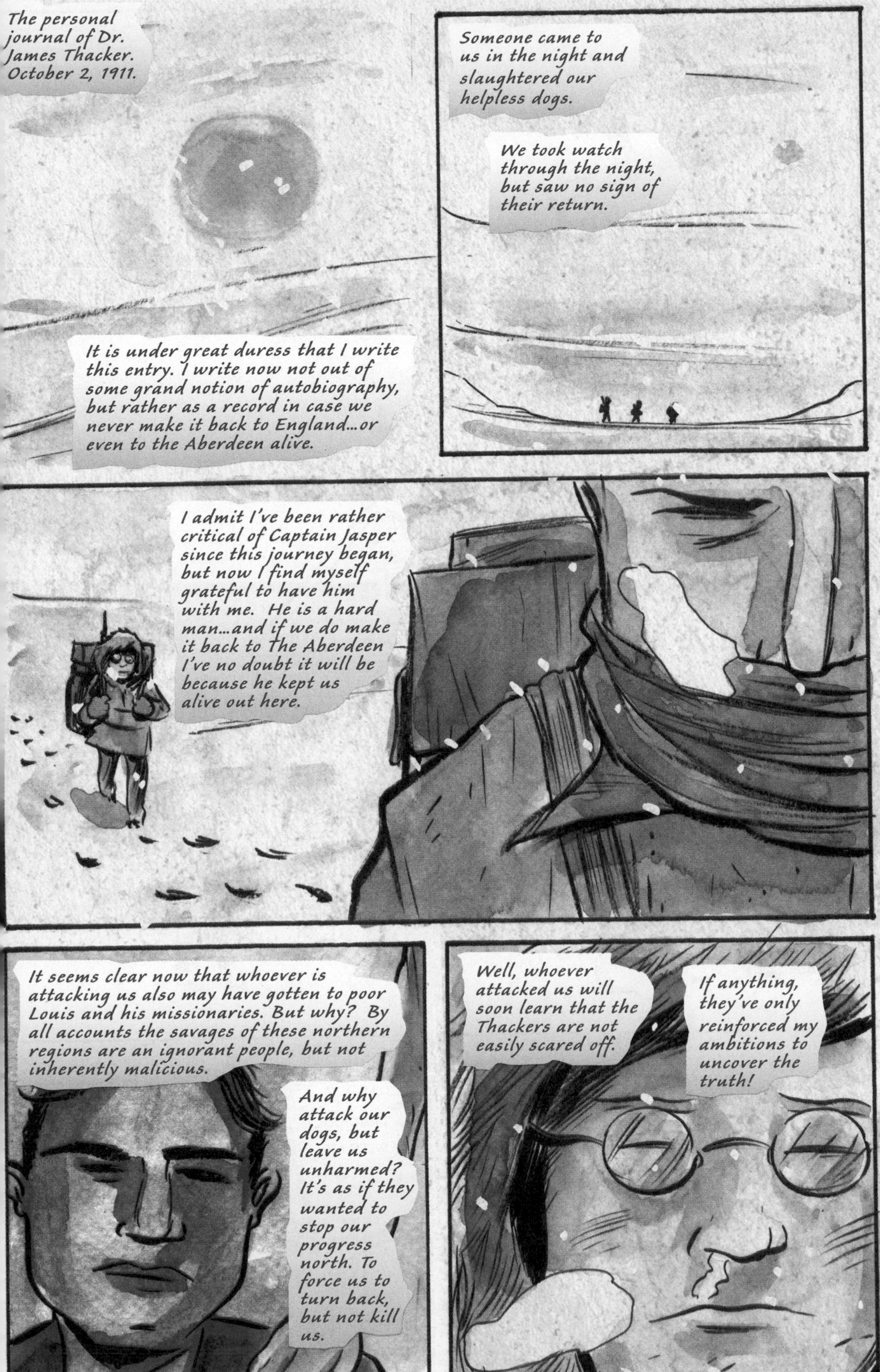
The personal journal of Dr. James Thacker. October 2, 1911.
It is under great duress that I write this entry. I write now not out of some grand notion of autobiography, but rather as a record in case we never make it back to England...or even to the Aberdeen alive.
Someone came to us in the night and slaughtered our helpless dogs.
We took watch through the night, but saw no sign of their return.
I admit I've been rather critical of Captain Jasper since this journey began, but now I find myself grateful to have him with me. He is a hard man...and if we do make it back to The Aberdeen I've no doubt it will be because he kept us alive out here.
It seems clear now that whoever is attacking us also may have gotten to poor Louis and his missionaries. But why? By all accounts the savages of these northern regions are an ignorant people, but not inherently malicious.
And why attack our dogs, but leave us unharmed? It's as if they wanted to stop our progress north. To force us to turn back, but not kill us.
Well, whoever attacked us will soon learn that the Thackers are not easily scared off.
If anything, they've only reinforced my ambitions to uncover the truth!

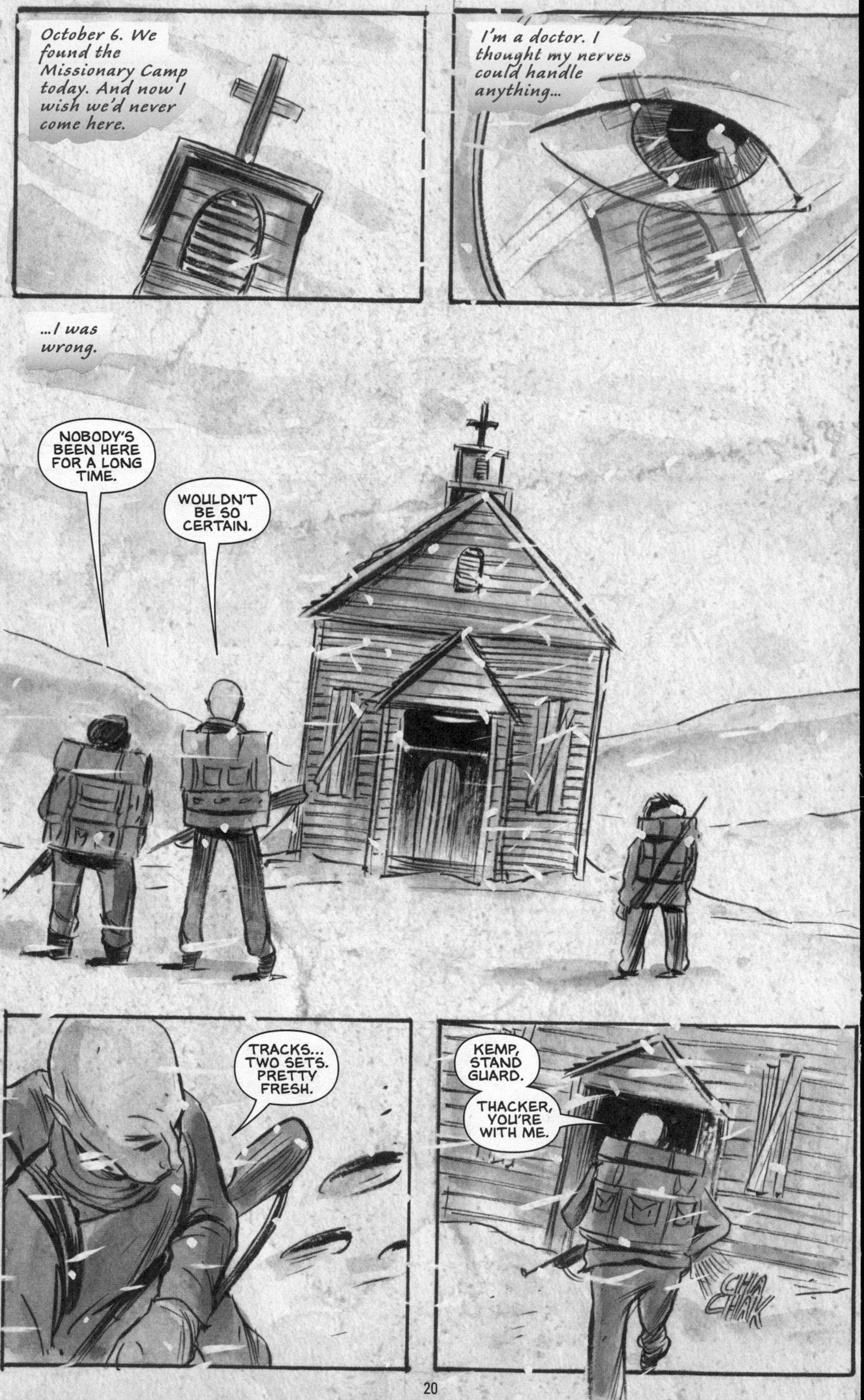
October 6. We found the Missionary Camp today. And now I wish we'd never come here.
I'm a doctor. I thought my nerves could handle anything...
...I was wrong.
NOBODY'S BEEN HERE FOR A LONG TIME.
WOULDN'T BE SO CERTAIN.
TRACKS... TWO SETS. PRETTY FRESH.
KEMP, STAND GUARD.
THACKER, YOU'RE WITH ME.
CHA CHAK

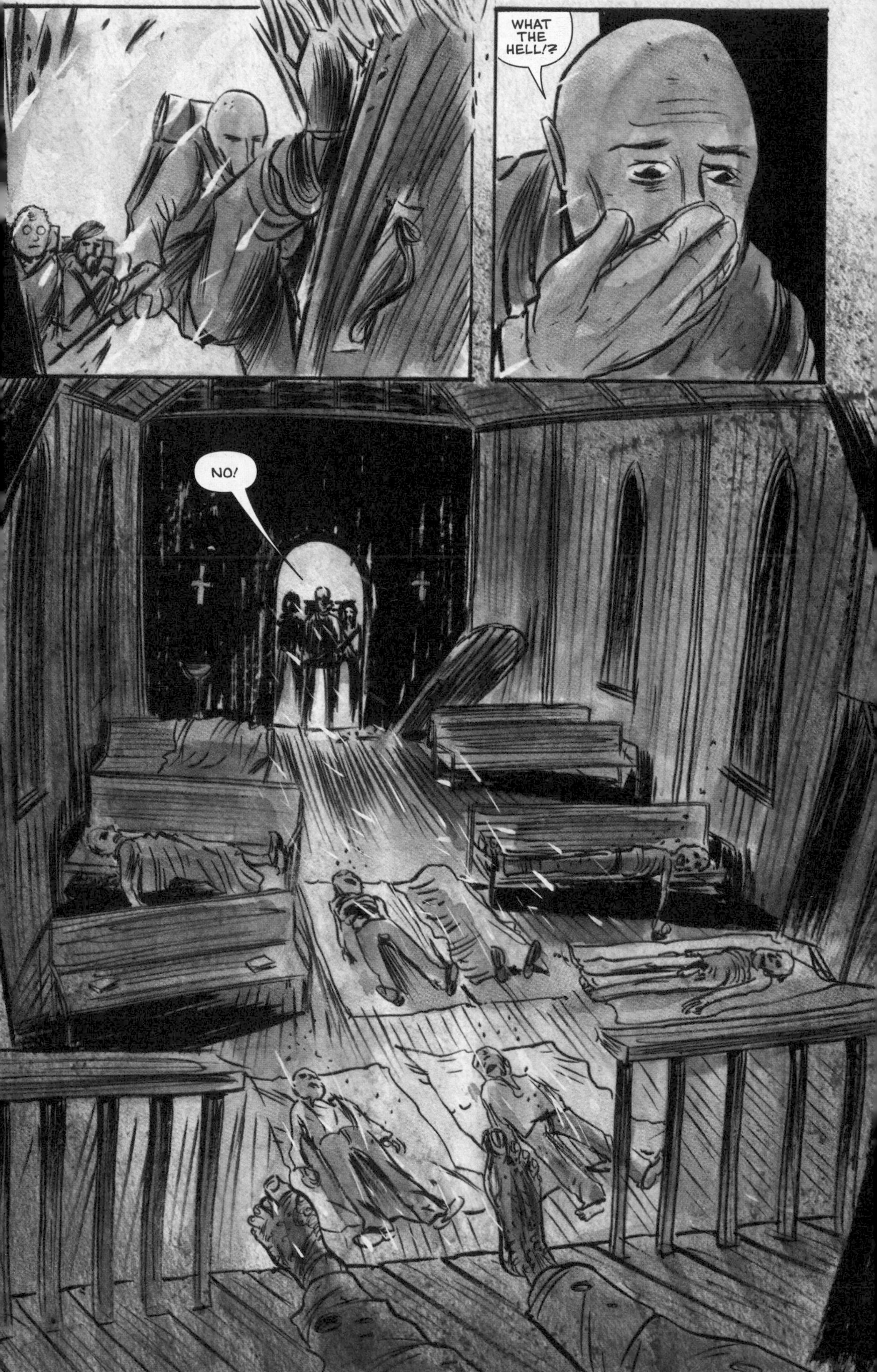
WHAT THE HELL!?
NO!

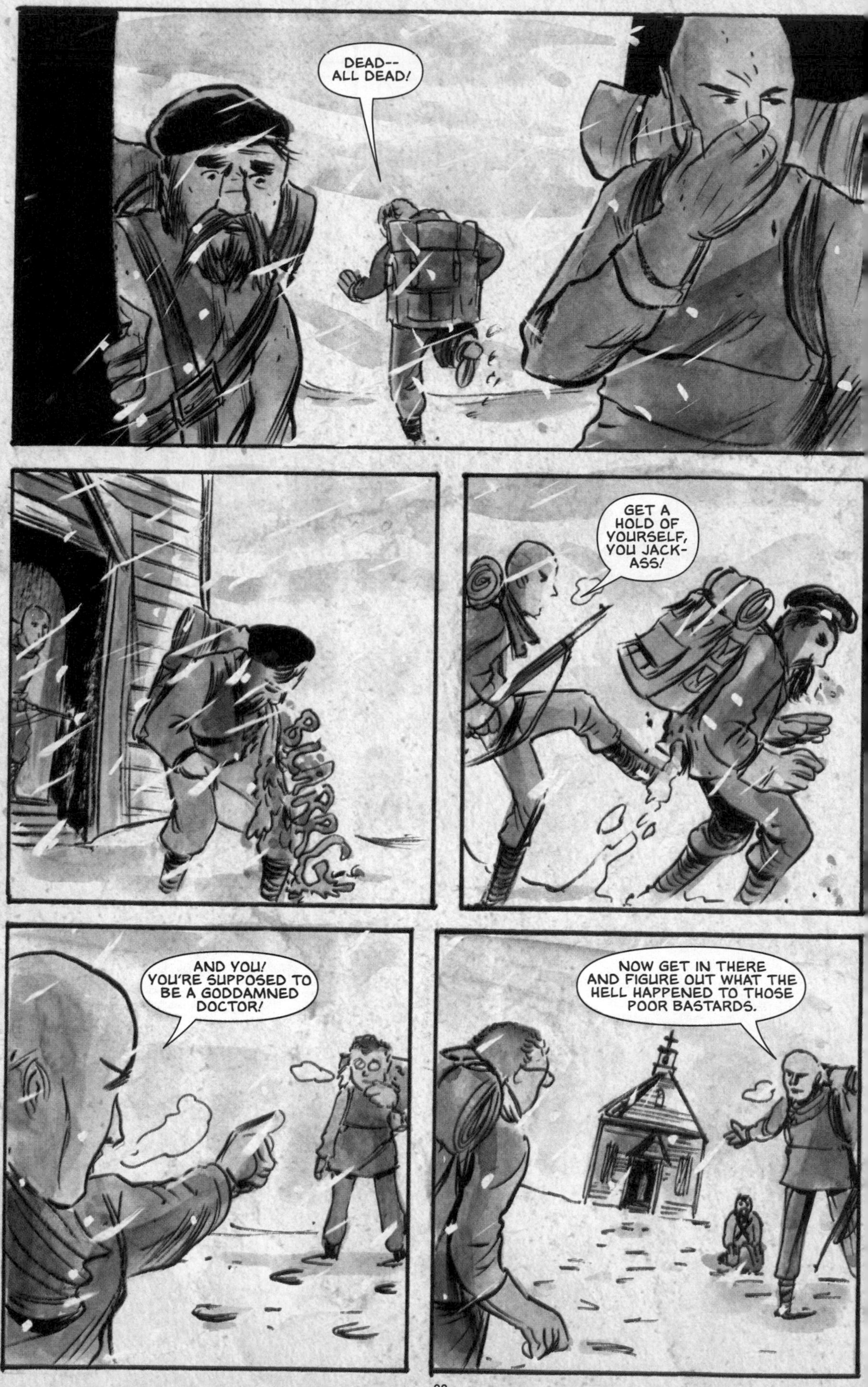
DEAD-- ALL DEAD!
GET A HOLD OF YOURSELF, YOU JACK-ASS!
AND YOU! YOU'RE SUPPOSED TO BE A GODDAMNED DOCTOR!
NOW GET IN THERE AND FIGURE OUT WHAT THE HELL HAPPENED TO THOSE POOR BASTARDS.

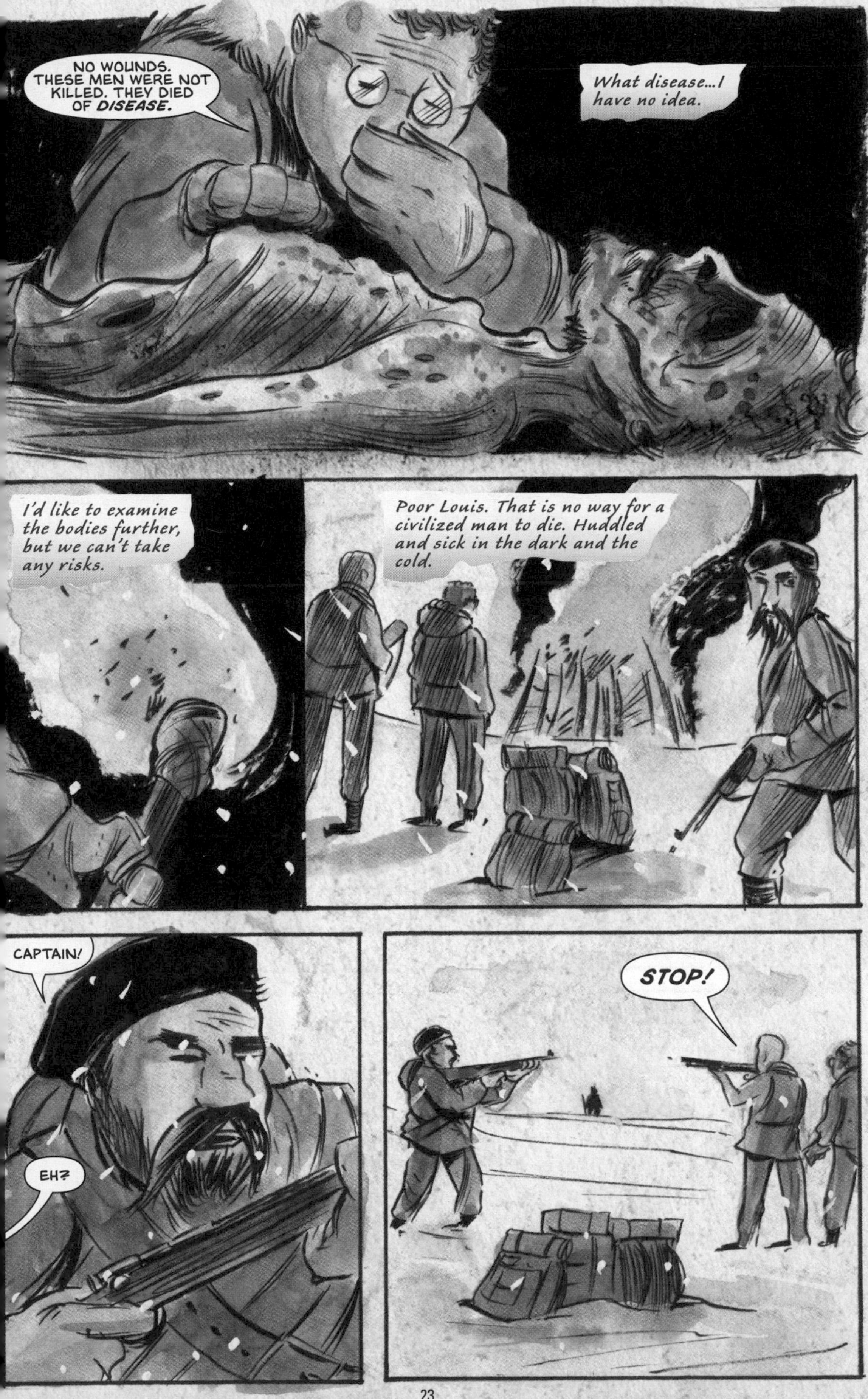
NO WOUNDS. THESE MEN WERE NOT KILLED. THEY DIED OF DISEASE.
What disease...I have no idea.
I'd like to examine the bodies further, but we can't take any risks.
Poor Louis. That is no way for a civilized man to die. Huddled and sick in the dark and the cold.
CAPTAIN!
EH?
STOP!

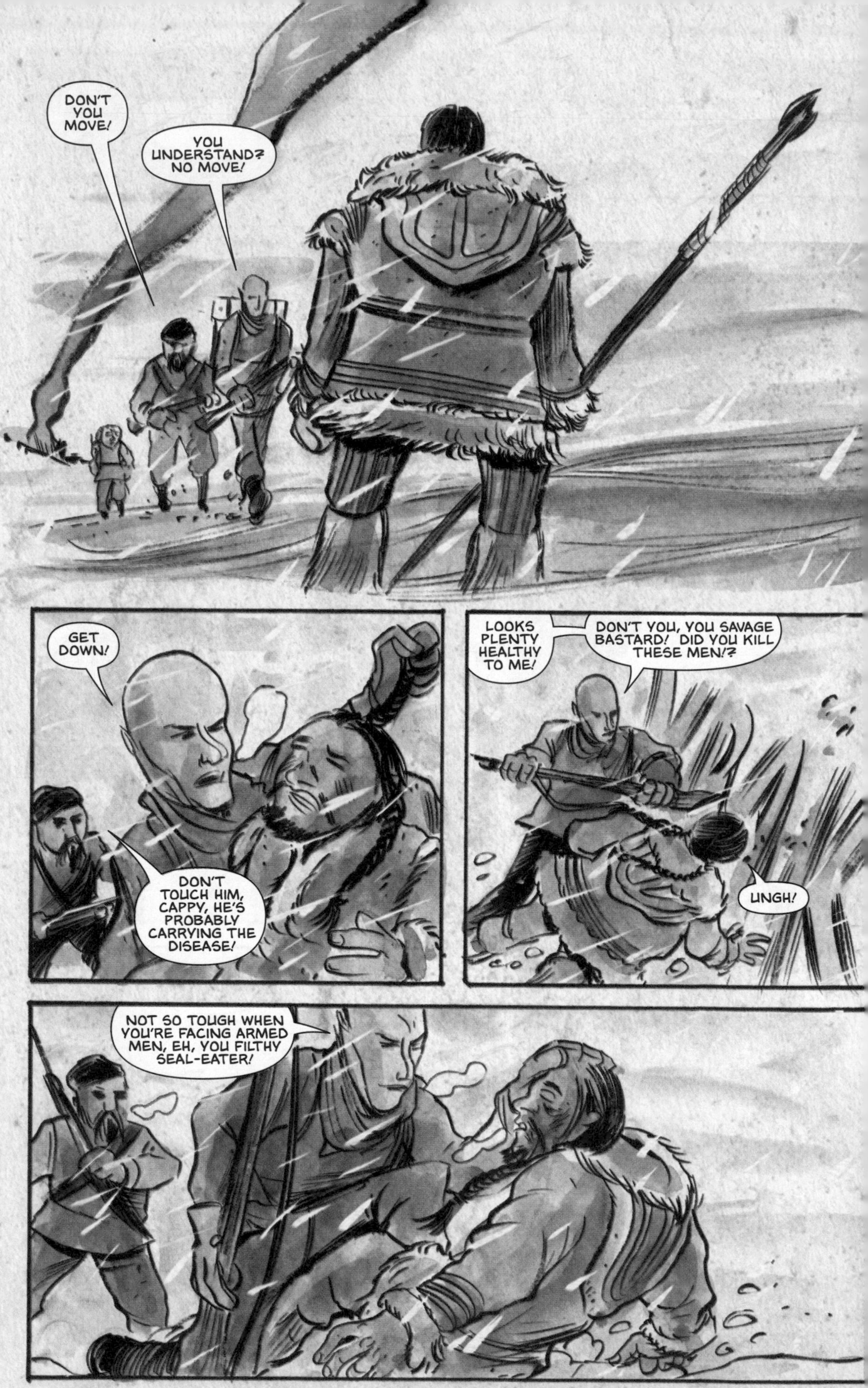
DON'T YOU MOVE!
YOU UNDERSTAND? NO MOVE!
GET DOWN!
DON'T TOUCH HIM, CAPPY, HE'S PROBABLY CARRYING THE DISEASE!
LOOKS PLENTY HEALTHY TO ME!
DON'T YOU, YOU SAVAGE BASTARD! DID YOU KILL THESE MEN!?
UNGH!
NOT SO TOUGH WHEN YOU'RE FACING ARMED MEN, EH, YOU FILTHY SEAL-EATER!

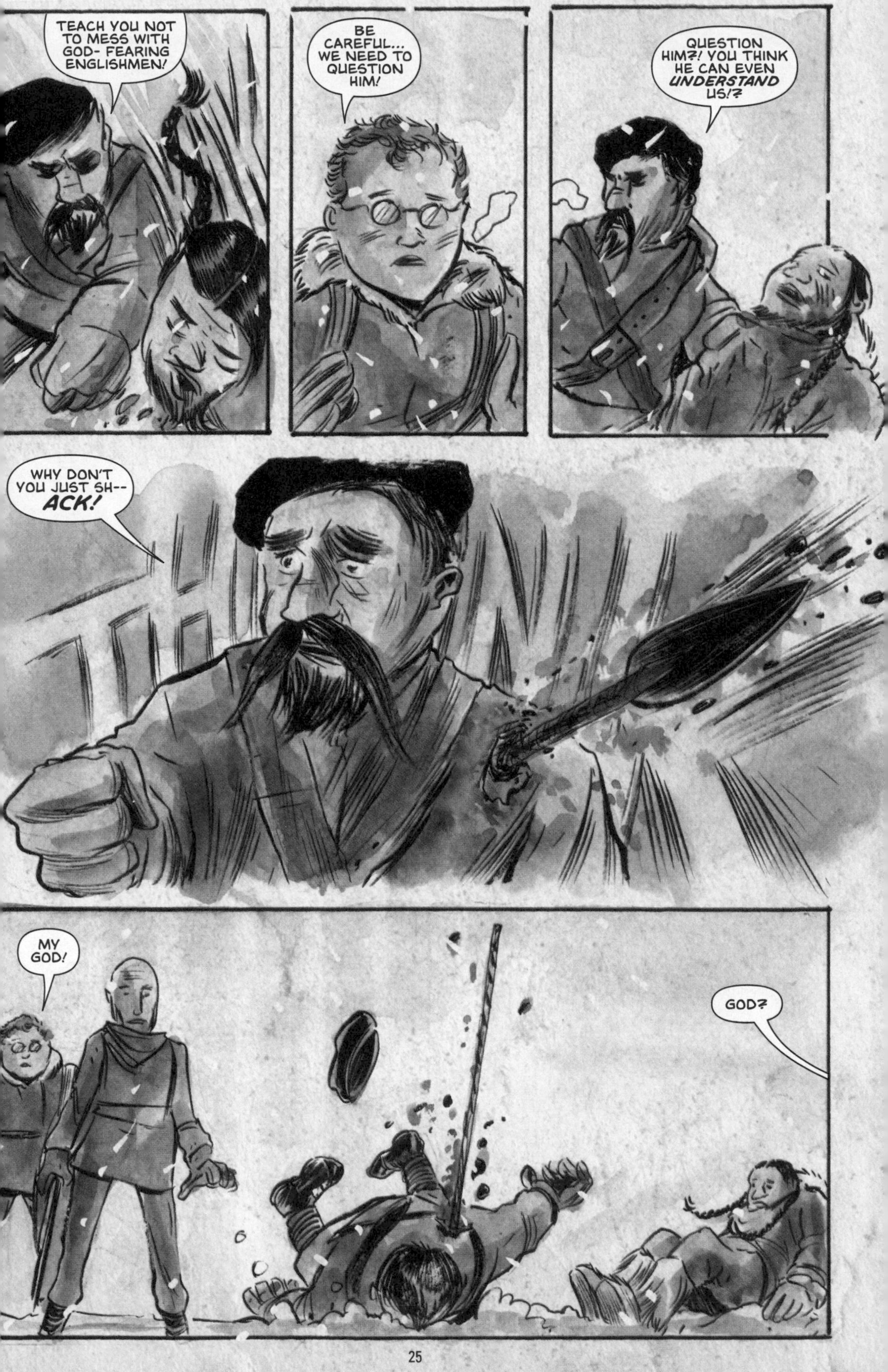
TEACH YOU NOT TO MESS WITH GOD- FEARING ENGLISHMEN!
BE CAREFUL... WE NEED TO QUESTION HIM!
QUESTION HIM?! YOU THINK HE CAN EVEN UNDERSTAND US!?
WHY DON'T YOU JUST SH-- ACK!
MY GOD!
GOD?

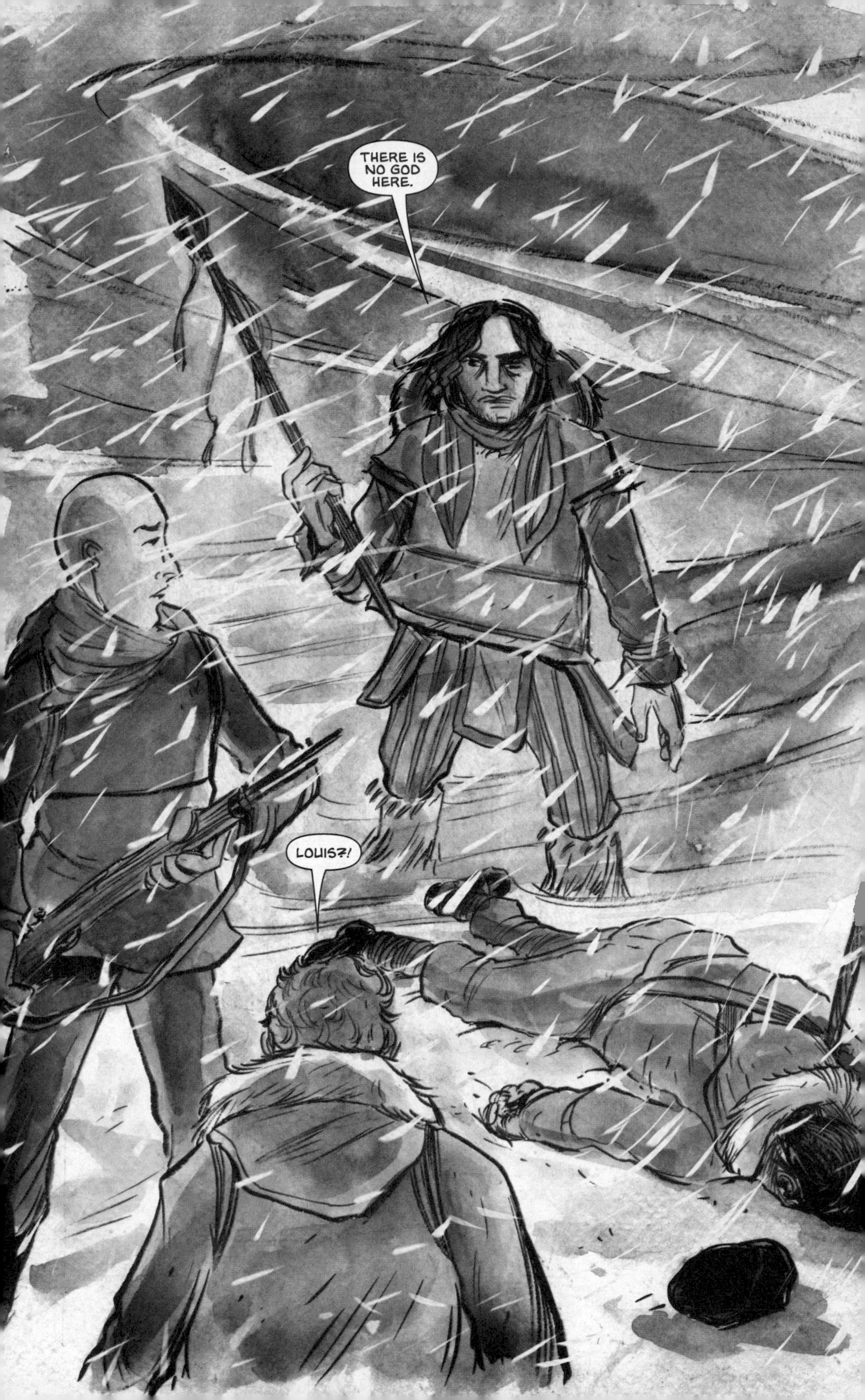
THERE IS NO GOD HERE.
LOUIS?!

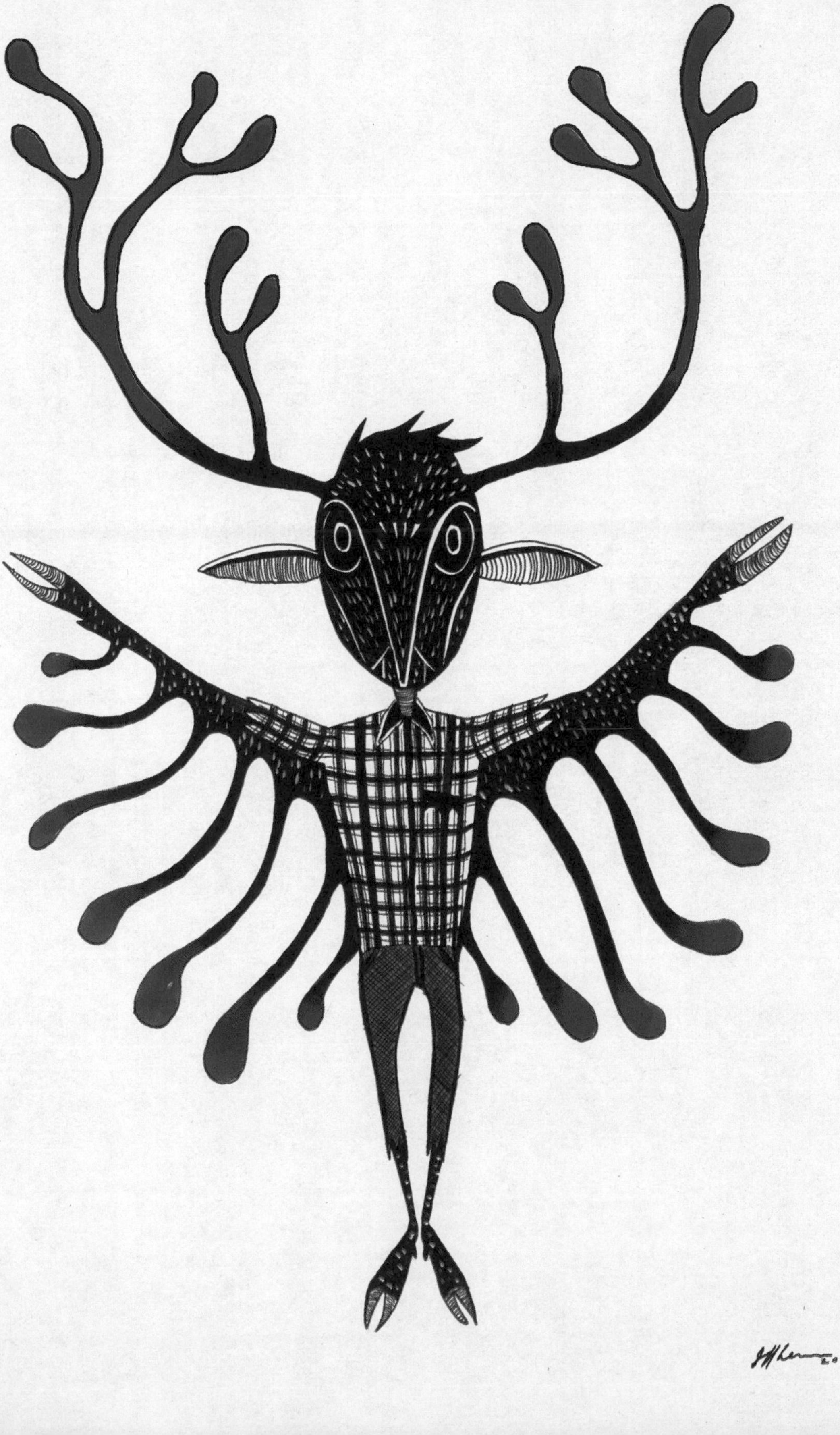

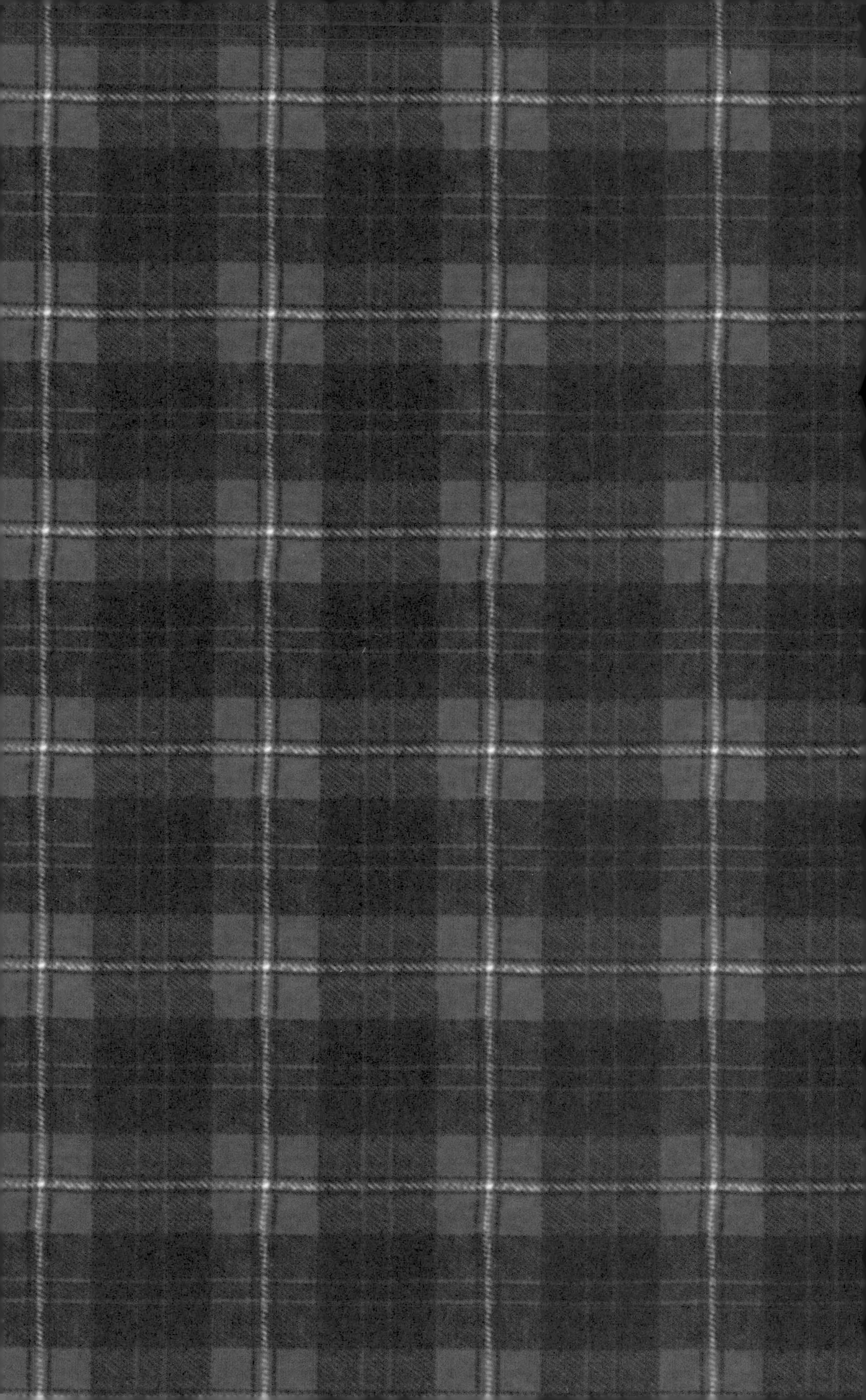

THE TAXIDERMIST PART 2 of 3: TABOOS

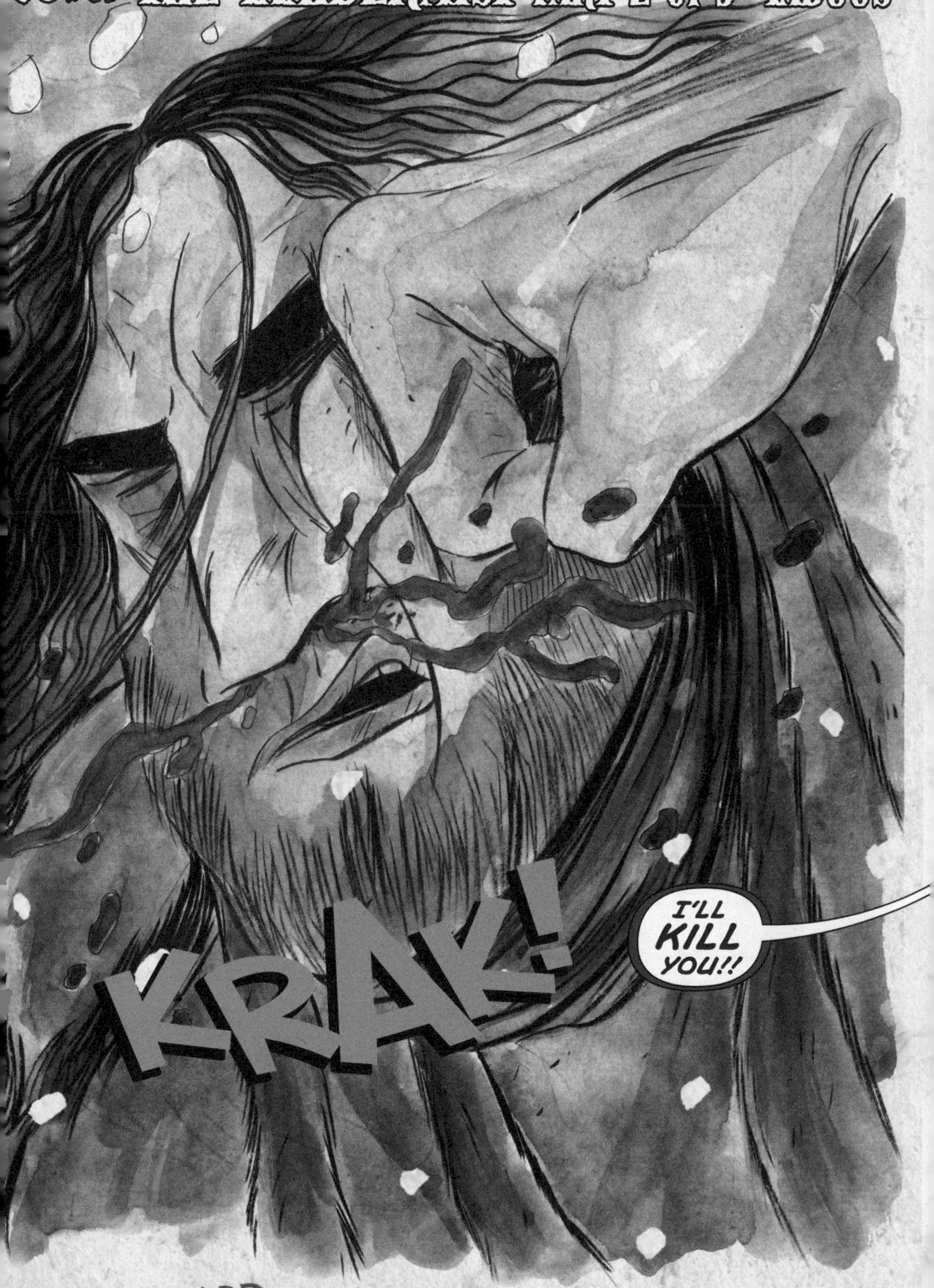
KRAK!
I'LL KILL YOU!!

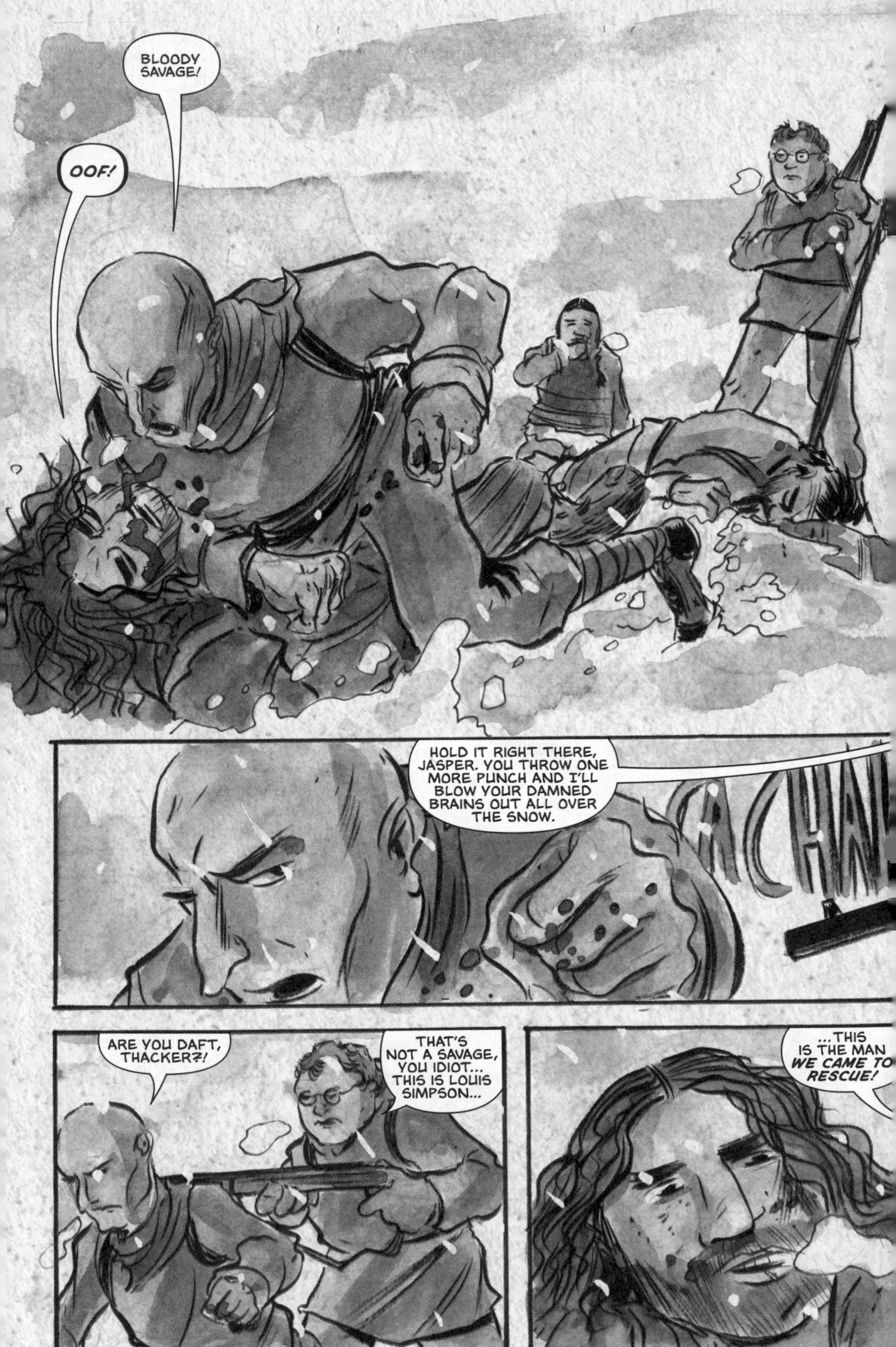
BLOODY SAVAGE!
OOF!
HOLD IT RIGHT THERE, JASPER. YOU THROW ONE MORE PUNCH AND I'LL BLOW YOUR DAMNED BRAINS OUT ALL OVER THE SNOW.
ARE YOU DAFT, THACKER?!
THAT'S NOT A SAVAGE, YOU IDIOT... THIS IS LOUIS SIMPSON...
...THIS IS THE MAN *WE CAME TO RESCUE!*

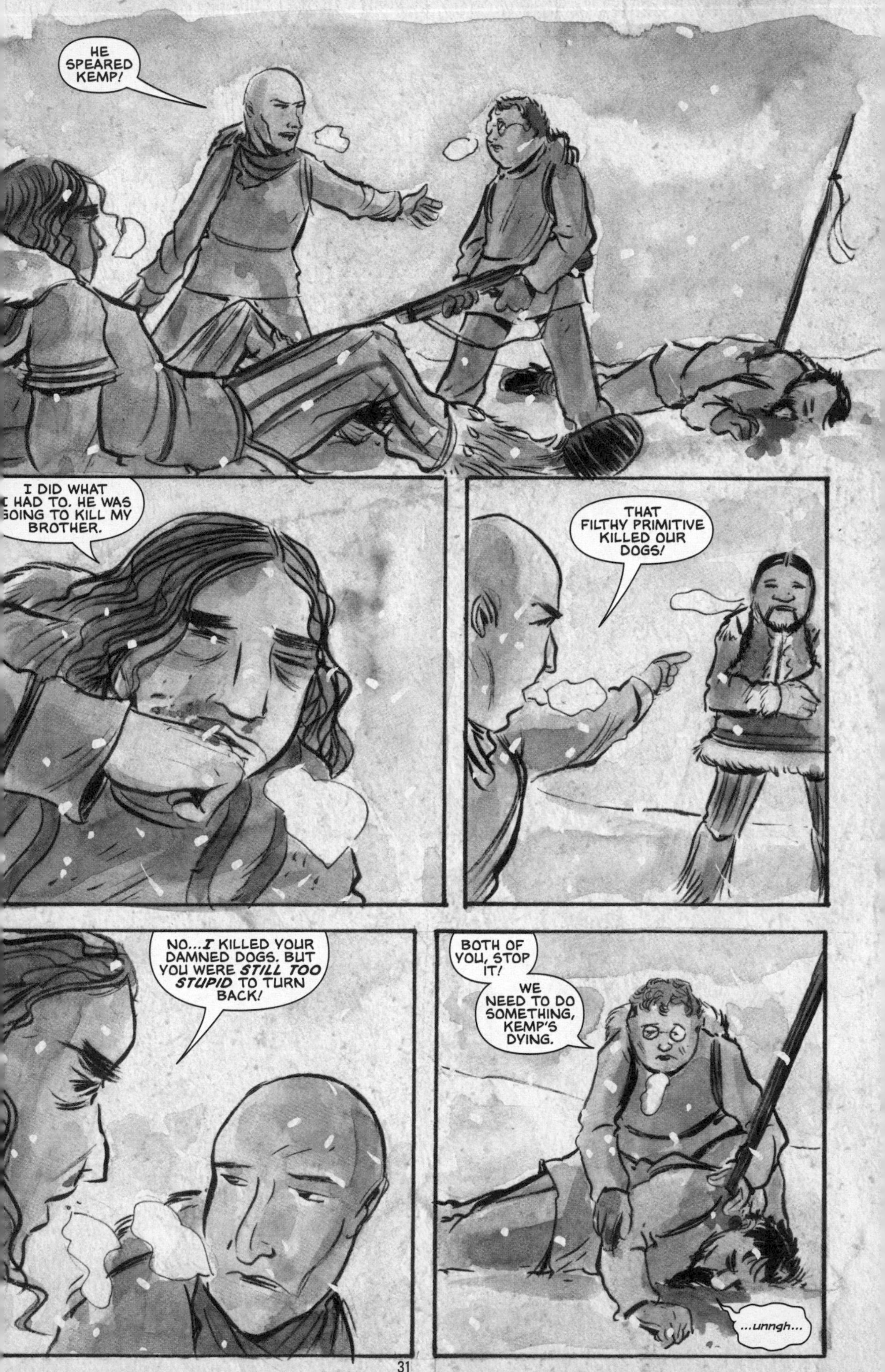
HE SPEARED KEMP!
I DID WHAT I HAD TO. HE WAS GOING TO KILL MY BROTHER.
THAT FILTHY PRIMITIVE KILLED OUR DOGS!
NO...I KILLED YOUR DAMNED DOGS. BUT YOU WERE STILL TOO STUPID TO TURN BACK!
BOTH OF YOU, STOP IT!
WE NEED TO DO SOMETHING, KEMP'S DYING.
...unngh...

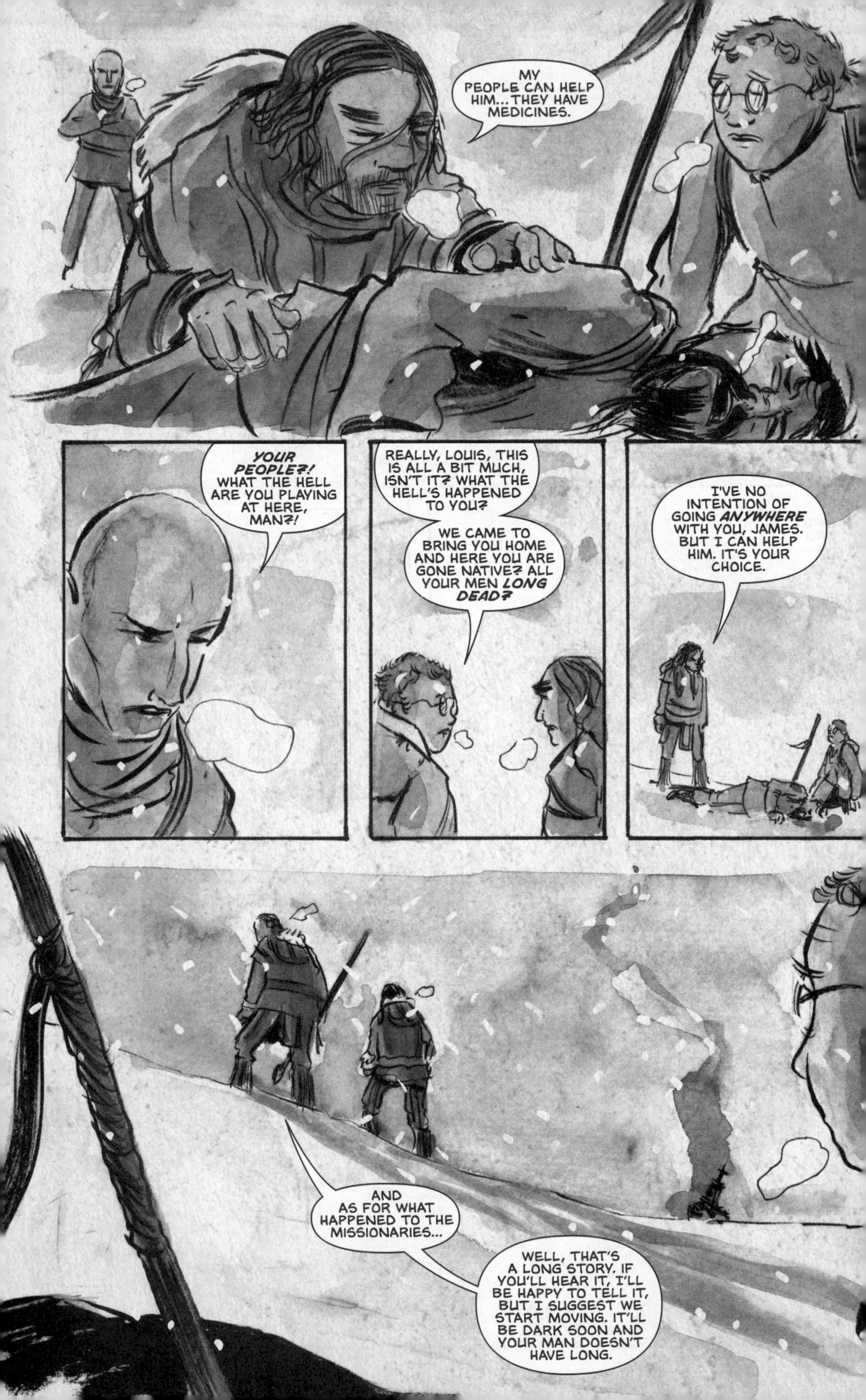
MY PEOPLE CAN HELP HIM... THEY HAVE MEDICINES.
YOUR PEOPLE?! WHAT THE HELL ARE YOU PLAYING AT HERE, MAN?!
REALLY, LOUIS, THIS IS ALL A BIT MUCH, ISN'T IT? WHAT THE HELL'S HAPPENED TO YOU?
WE CAME TO BRING YOU HOME AND HERE YOU ARE GONE NATIVE? ALL YOUR MEN LONG DEAD?
I'VE NO INTENTION OF GOING ANYWHERE WITH YOU, JAMES. BUT I CAN HELP HIM. IT'S YOUR CHOICE.
AND AS FOR WHAT HAPPENED TO THE MISSIONARIES...
WELL, THAT'S A LONG STORY. IF YOU'LL HEAR IT, I'LL BE HAPPY TO TELL IT, BUT I SUGGEST WE START MOVING. IT'LL BE DARK SOON AND YOUR MAN DOESN'T HAVE LONG.

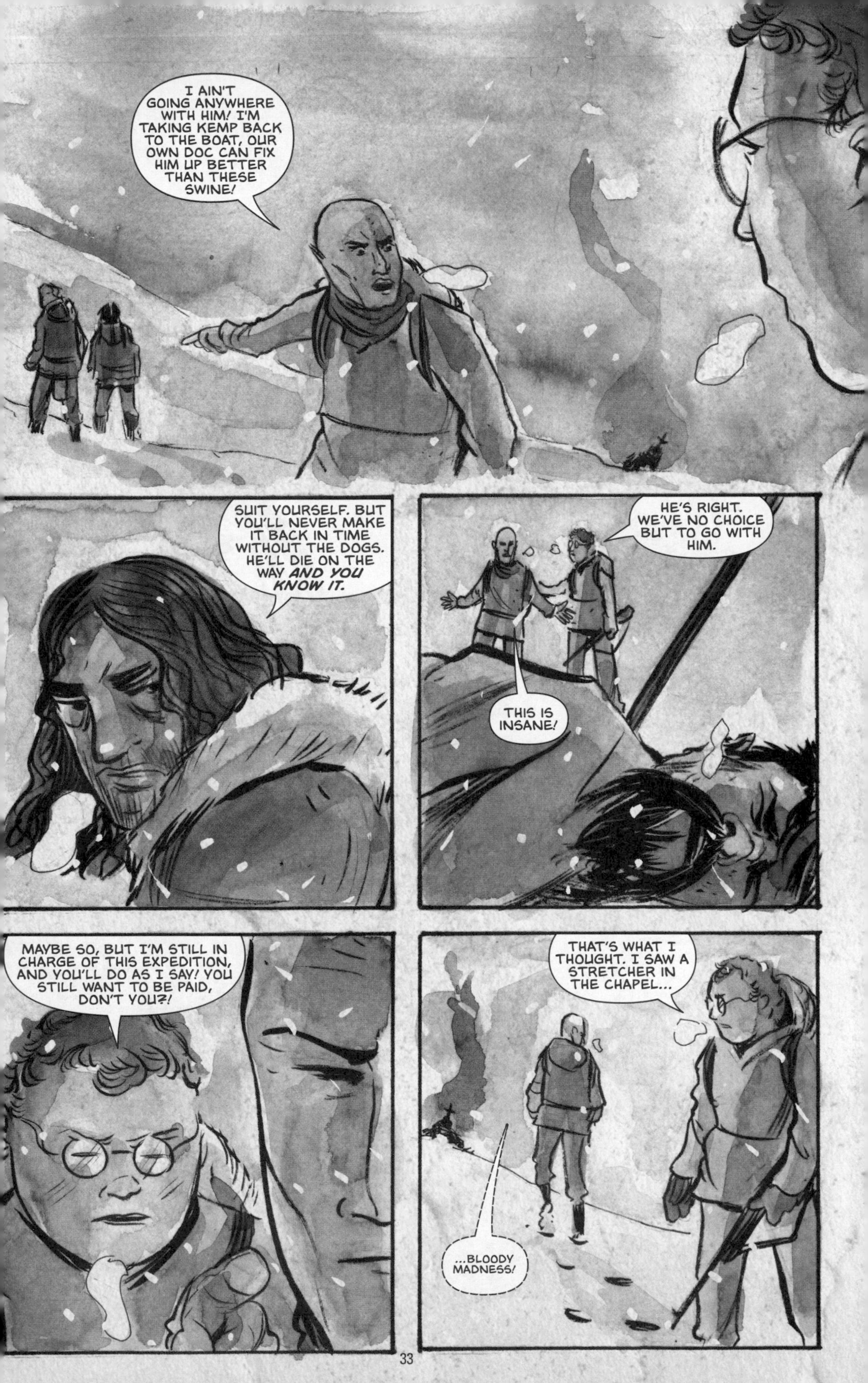
I AIN'T GOING ANYWHERE WITH HIM! I'M TAKING KEMP BACK TO THE BOAT, OUR OWN DOC CAN FIX HIM UP BETTER THAN THESE SWINE!
SUIT YOURSELF. BUT YOU'LL NEVER MAKE IT BACK IN TIME WITHOUT THE DOGS. HE'LL DIE ON THE WAY *AND YOU KNOW IT.*
HE'S RIGHT. WE'VE NO CHOICE BUT TO GO WITH HIM.
THIS IS INSANE!
MAYBE SO, BUT I'M STILL IN CHARGE OF THIS EXPEDITION, AND YOU'LL DO AS I SAY! YOU STILL WANT TO BE PAID, DON'T YOU?!
THAT'S WHAT I THOUGHT. I SAW A STRETCHER IN THE CHAPEL...
...BLOODY MADNESS!

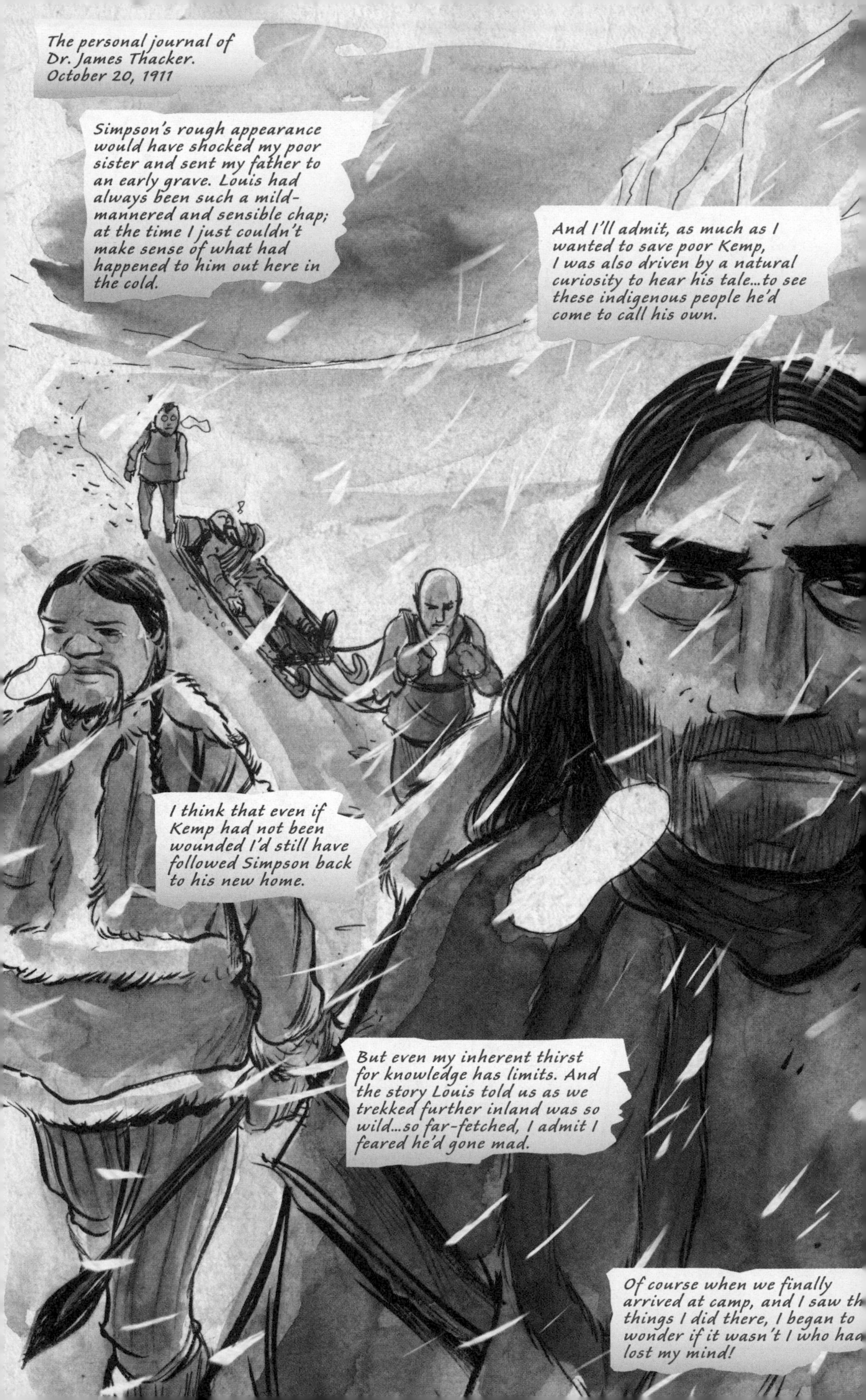
The personal journal of
Dr. James Thacker.
October 20, 1911
Simpson's rough appearance would have shocked my poor sister and sent my father to an early grave. Louis had always been such a mild-mannered and sensible chap; at the time I just couldn't make sense of what had happened to him out here in the cold.
And I'll admit, as much as I wanted to save poor Kemp, I was also driven by a natural curiosity to hear his tale...to see these indigenous people he'd come to call his own.
I think that even if Kemp had not been wounded I'd still have followed Simpson back to his new home.
But even my inherent thirst for knowledge has limits. And the story Louis told us as we trekked further inland was so wild...so far-fetched, I admit I feared he'd gone mad.
Of course when we finally arrived at camp, and I saw th things I did there, I began to wonder if it wasn't I who ha lost my mind!

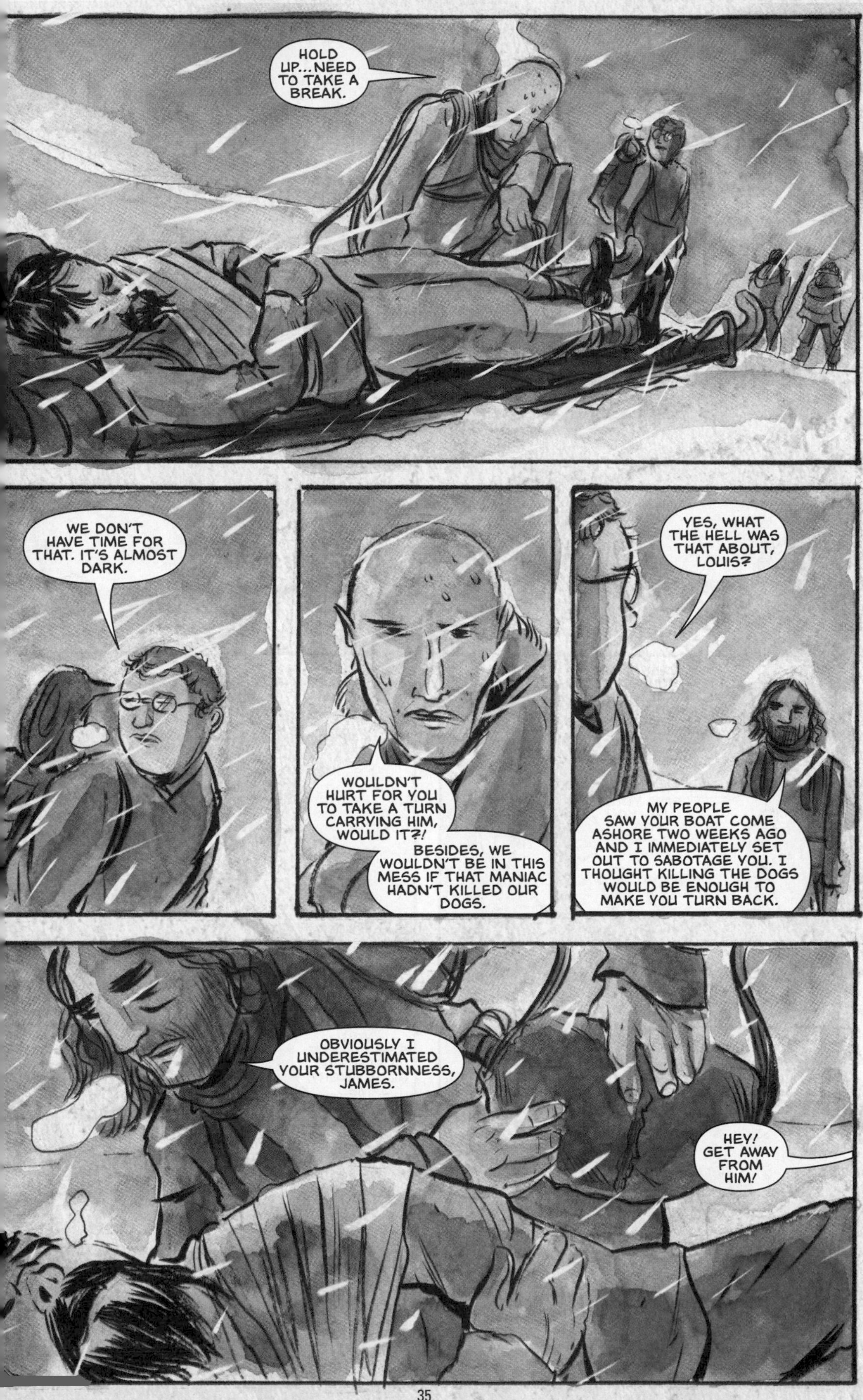
HOLD UP...NEED TO TAKE A BREAK.
WE DON'T HAVE TIME FOR THAT. IT'S ALMOST DARK.
WOULDN'T HURT FOR YOU TO TAKE A TURN CARRYING HIM, WOULD IT?!
BESIDES, WE WOULDN'T BE IN THIS MESS IF THAT MANIAC HADN'T KILLED OUR DOGS.
YES, WHAT THE HELL WAS THAT ABOUT, LOUIS?
MY PEOPLE SAW YOUR BOAT COME ASHORE TWO WEEKS AGO AND I IMMEDIATELY SET OUT TO SABOTAGE YOU. I THOUGHT KILLING THE DOGS WOULD BE ENOUGH TO MAKE YOU TURN BACK.
OBVIOUSLY I UNDERESTIMATED YOUR STUBBORNNESS, JAMES.
HEY! GET AWAY FROM HIM!

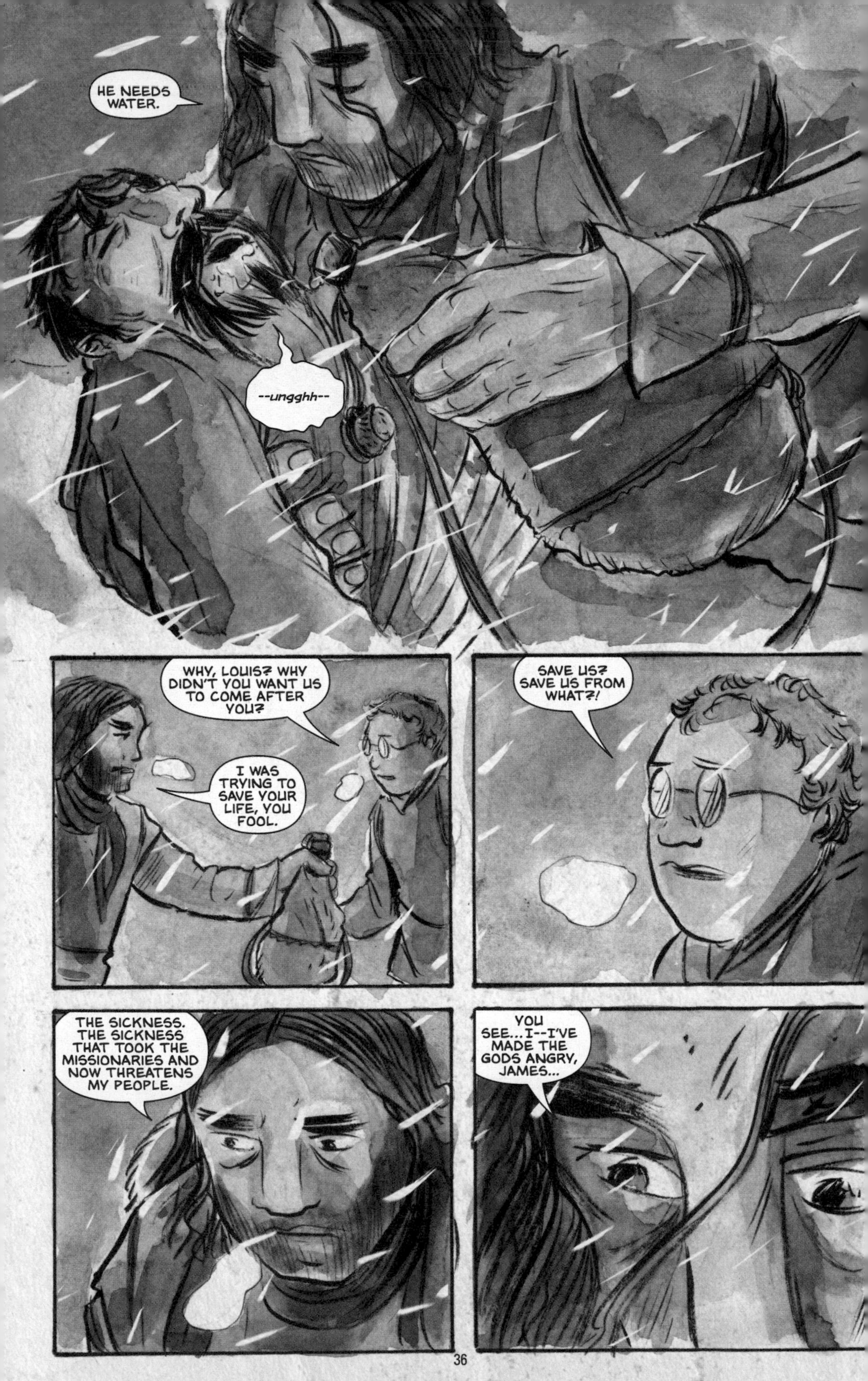
HE NEEDS WATER.
--ungghh--
WHY, LOUIS? WHY DIDN'T YOU WANT US TO COME AFTER YOU?
I WAS TRYING TO SAVE YOUR LIFE, YOU FOOL.
SAVE US? SAVE US FROM WHAT?!
THE SICKNESS. THE SICKNESS THAT TOOK THE MISSIONARIES AND NOW THREATENS MY PEOPLE.
YOU SEE... I--I'VE MADE THE GODS ANGRY, JAMES...

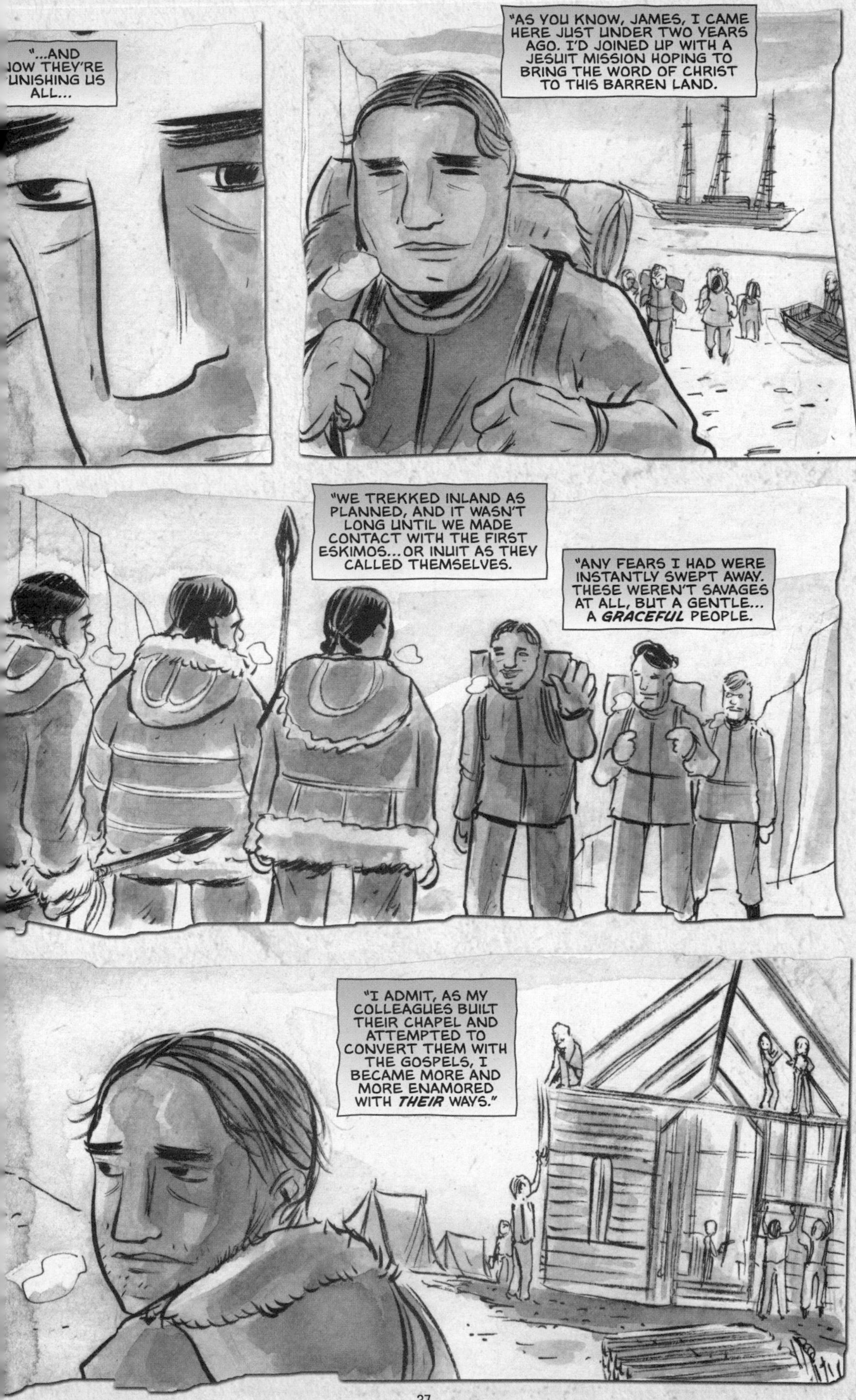
“...AND IOW THEY'RE UNISHING US ALL...
“AS YOU KNOW, JAMES, I CAME HERE JUST UNDER TWO YEARS AGO. I'D JOINED UP WITH A JESUIT MISSION HOPING TO BRING THE WORD OF CHRIST TO THIS BARREN LAND.
“WE TREKKED INLAND AS PLANNED, AND IT WASN'T LONG UNTIL WE MADE CONTACT WITH THE FIRST ESKIMOS...OR INUIT AS THEY CALLED THEMSELVES.
“ANY FEARS I HAD WERE INSTANTLY SWEPT AWAY. THESE WEREN'T SAVAGES AT ALL, BUT A GENTLE... A *GRACEFUL* PEOPLE.
“I ADMIT, AS MY COLLEAGUES BUILT THEIR CHAPEL AND ATTEMPTED TO CONVERT THEM WITH THE GOSPELS, I BECAME MORE AND MORE ENAMORED WITH *THEIR* WAYS.”

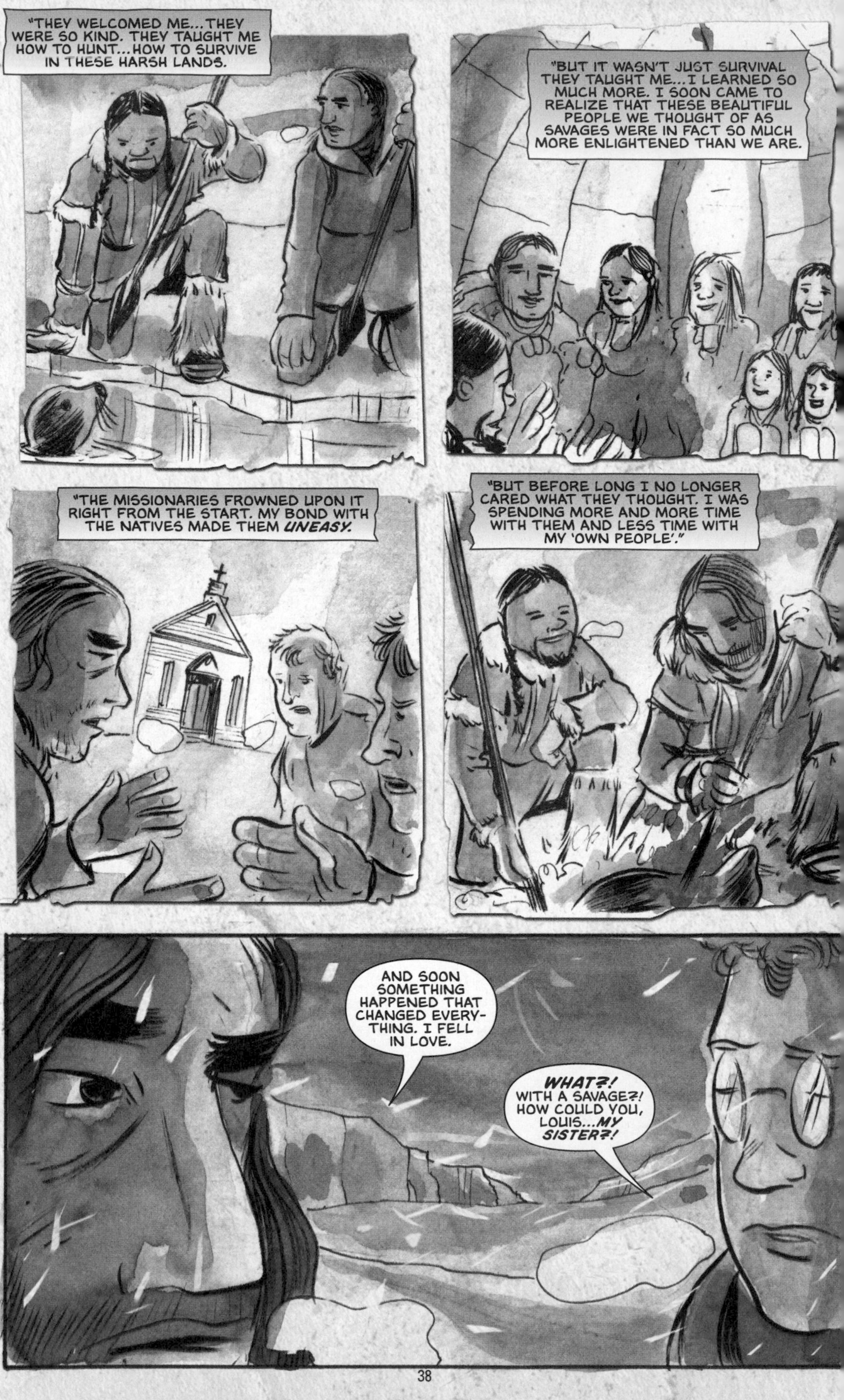
"THEY WELCOMED ME... THEY WERE SO KIND. THEY TAUGHT ME HOW TO HUNT... HOW TO SURVIVE IN THESE HARSH LANDS.
"BUT IT WASN'T JUST SURVIVAL THEY TAUGHT ME... I LEARNED SO MUCH MORE. I SOON CAME TO REALIZE THAT THESE BEAUTIFUL PEOPLE WE THOUGHT OF AS SAVAGES WERE IN FACT SO MUCH MORE ENLIGHTENED THAN WE ARE.
"THE MISSIONARIES FROWNED UPON IT RIGHT FROM THE START. MY BOND WITH THE NATIVES MADE THEM *UNEASY.*
"BUT BEFORE LONG I NO LONGER CARED WHAT THEY THOUGHT. I WAS SPENDING MORE AND MORE TIME WITH THEM AND LESS TIME WITH MY 'OWN PEOPLE'."
AND SOON SOMETHING HAPPENED THAT CHANGED EVERYTHING. I FELL IN LOVE.
WHAT?! WITH A SAVAGE?! HOW COULD YOU, LOUIS... ***MY SISTER?!***

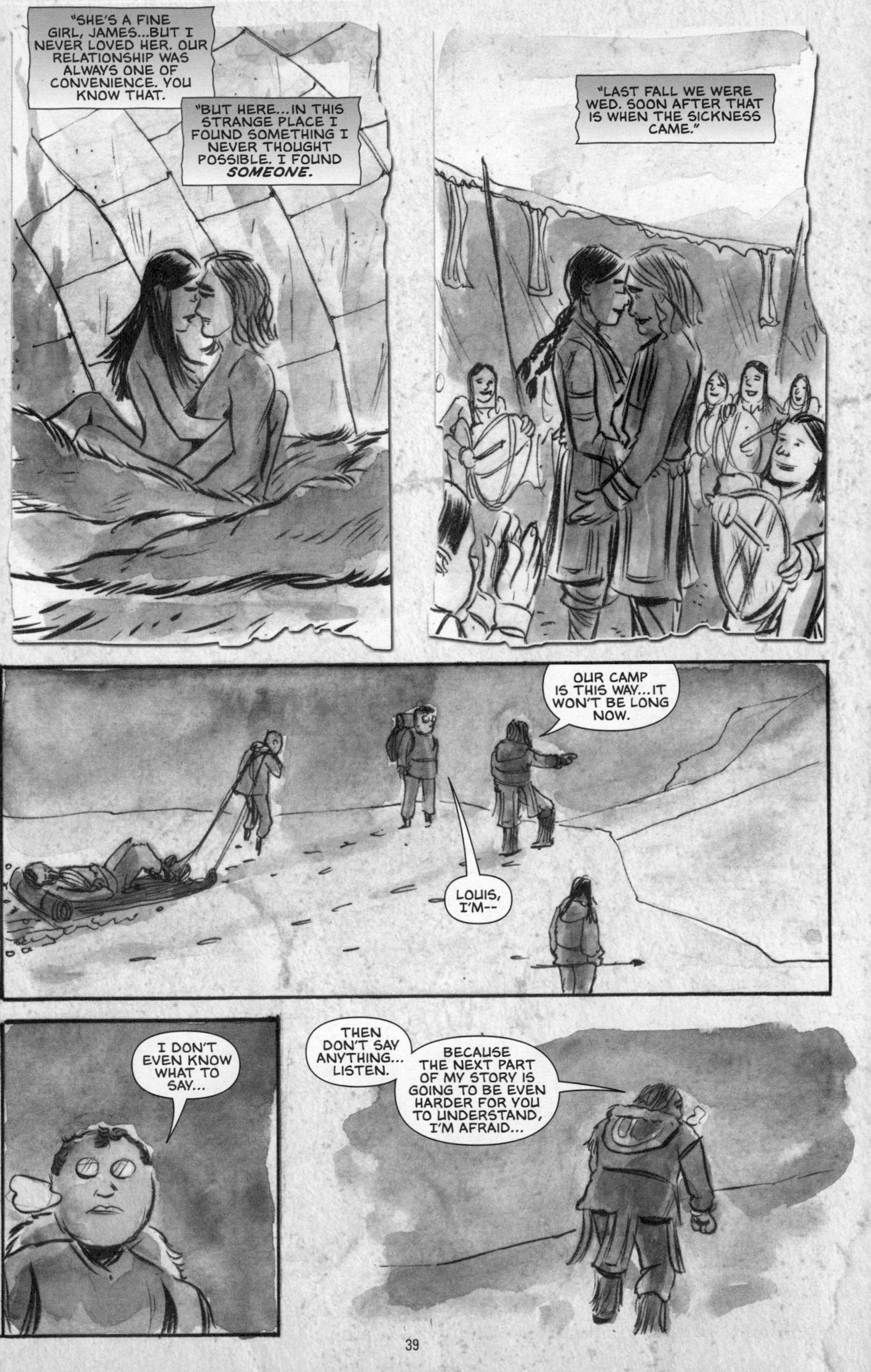
"SHE'S A FINE GIRL, JAMES...BUT I NEVER LOVED HER. OUR RELATIONSHIP WAS ALWAYS ONE OF CONVENIENCE. YOU KNOW THAT.
"BUT HERE...IN THIS STRANGE PLACE I FOUND SOMETHING I NEVER THOUGHT POSSIBLE. I FOUND *SOMEONE*.
"LAST FALL WE WERE WED. SOON AFTER THAT IS WHEN THE SICKNESS CAME."
OUR CAMP IS THIS WAY...IT WON'T BE LONG NOW.
LOUIS, I'M--
I DON'T EVEN KNOW WHAT TO SAY...
THEN DON'T SAY ANYTHING... LISTEN.
BECAUSE THE NEXT PART OF MY STORY IS GOING TO BE EVEN HARDER FOR YOU TO UNDERSTAND, I'M AFRAID...

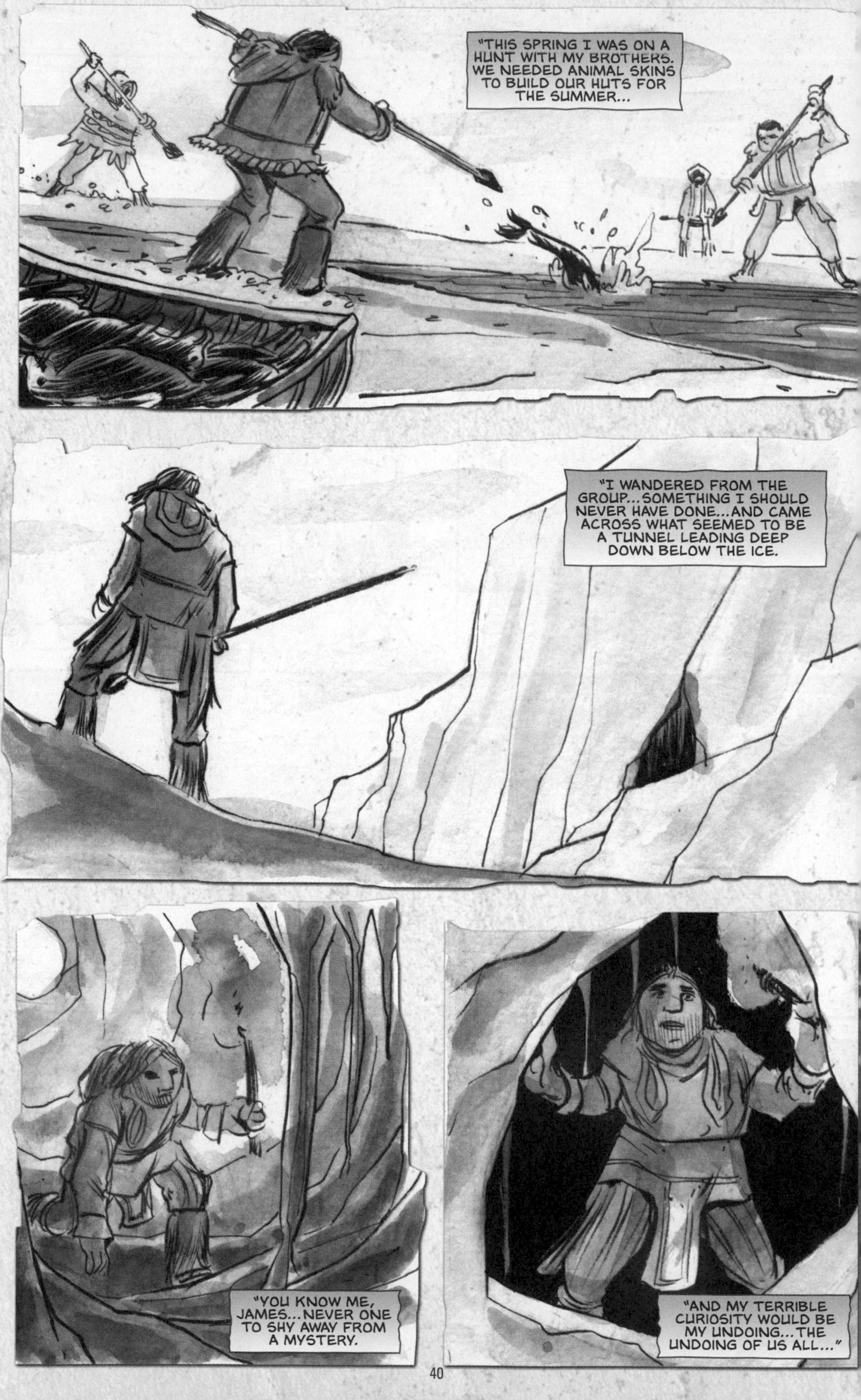
"THIS SPRING I WAS ON A HUNT WITH MY BROTHERS. WE NEEDED ANIMAL SKINS TO BUILD OUR HUTS FOR THE SUMMER...
"I WANDERED FROM THE GROUP...SOMETHING I SHOULD NEVER HAVE DONE...AND CAME ACROSS WHAT SEEMED TO BE A TUNNEL LEADING DEEP DOWN BELOW THE ICE.
"YOU KNOW ME, JAMES...NEVER ONE TO SHY AWAY FROM A MYSTERY.
"AND MY TERRIBLE CURIOSITY WOULD BE MY UNDOING...THE UNDOING OF US ALL..."

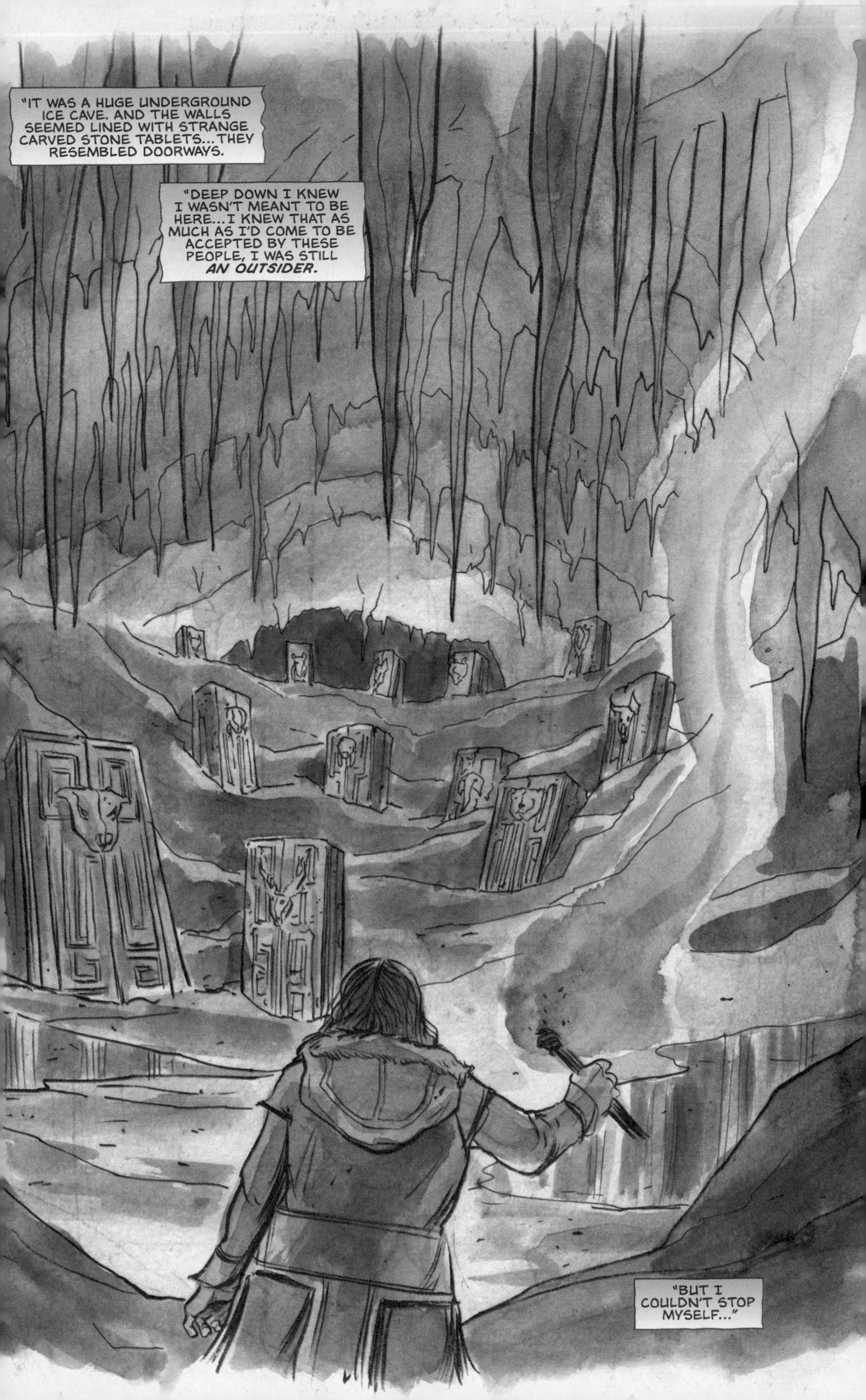
"IT WAS A HUGE UNDERGROUND ICE CAVE. AND THE WALLS SEEMED LINED WITH STRANGE CARVED STONE TABLETS...THEY RESEMBLED DOORWAYS.
"DEEP DOWN I KNEW I WASN'T MEANT TO BE HERE...I KNEW THAT AS MUCH AS I'D COME TO BE ACCEPTED BY THESE PEOPLE, I WAS STILL *AN OUTSIDER.*
"BUT I COULDN'T STOP MYSELF..."

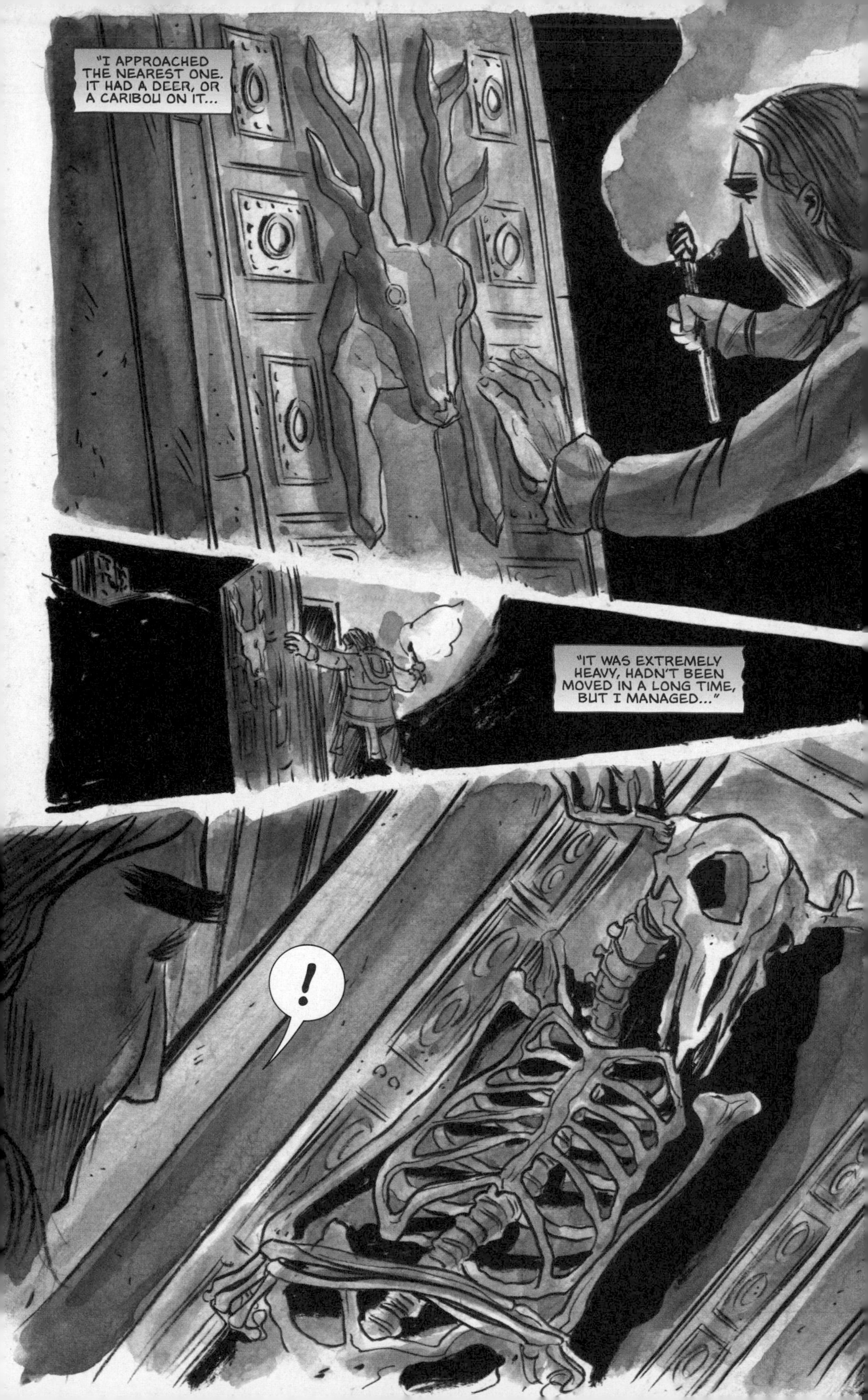
"I APPROACHED THE NEAREST ONE. IT HAD A DEER, OR A CARIBOU ON IT...
"IT WAS EXTREMELY HEAVY, HADN'T BEEN MOVED IN A LONG TIME, BUT I MANAGED..."
!

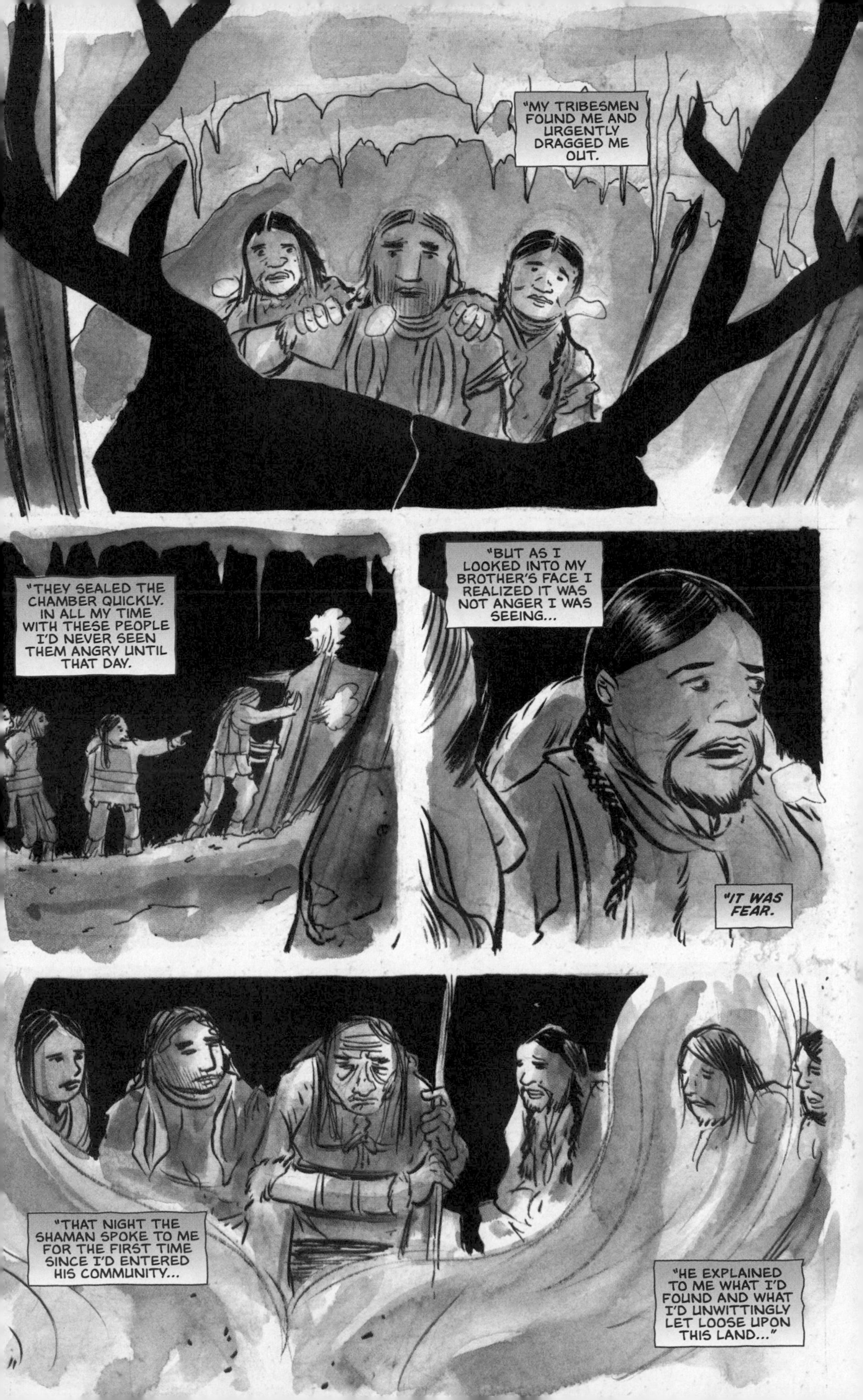
"MY TRIBESMEN FOUND ME AND URGENTLY DRAGGED ME OUT.
"THEY SEALED THE CHAMBER QUICKLY. IN ALL MY TIME WITH THESE PEOPLE I'D NEVER SEEN THEM ANGRY UNTIL THAT DAY.
"BUT AS I LOOKED INTO MY BROTHER'S FACE I REALIZED IT WAS NOT ANGER I WAS SEEING...
"IT WAS FEAR.
"THAT NIGHT THE SHAMAN SPOKE TO ME FOR THE FIRST TIME SINCE I'D ENTERED HIS COMMUNITY...
"HE EXPLAINED TO ME WHAT I'D FOUND AND WHAT I'D UNWITTINGLY LET LOOSE UPON THIS LAND..."

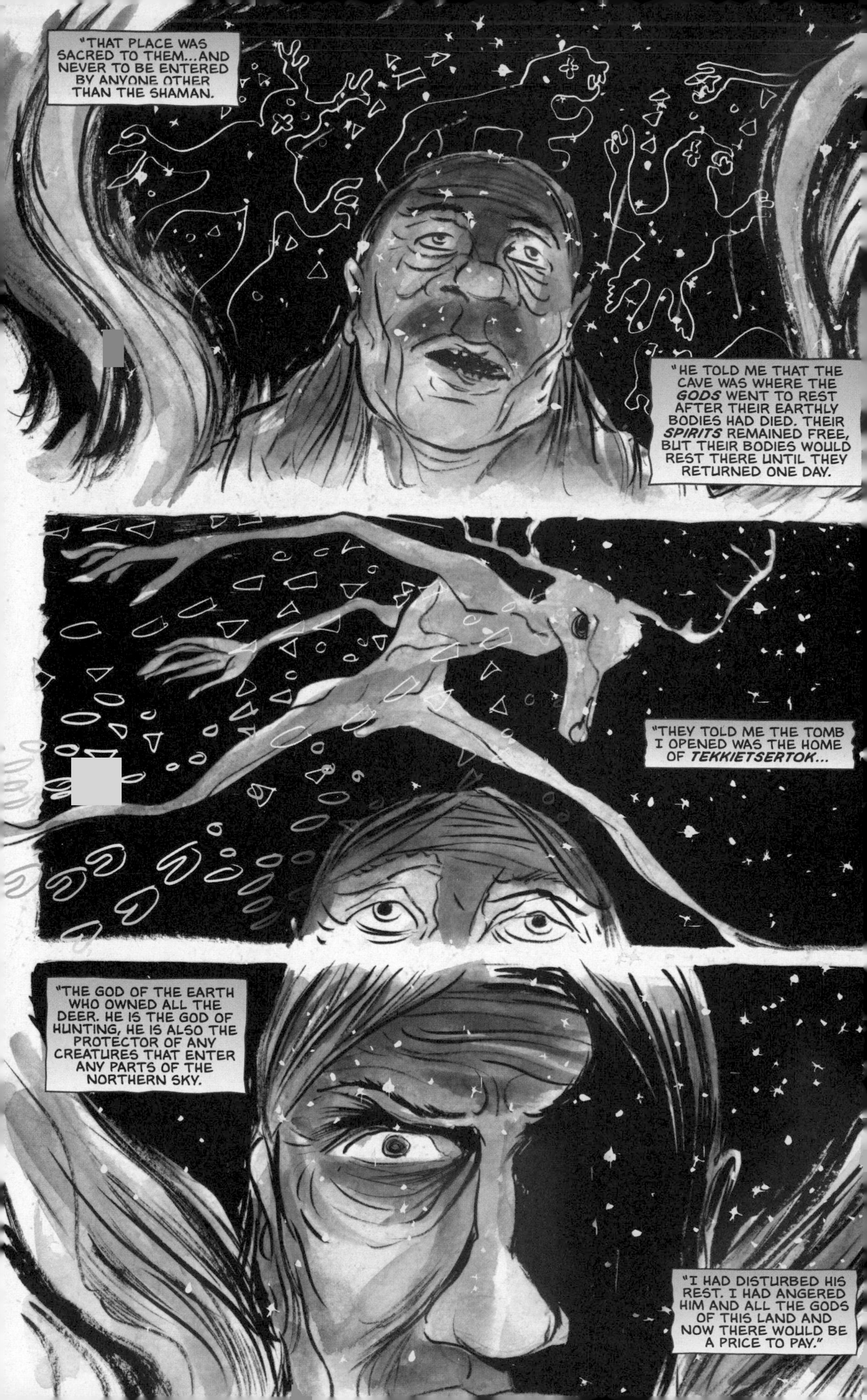
"THAT PLACE WAS SACRED TO THEM...AND NEVER TO BE ENTERED BY ANYONE OTHER THAN THE SHAMAN.
"HE TOLD ME THAT THE CAVE WAS WHERE THE *GODS* WENT TO REST AFTER THEIR EARTHLY BODIES HAD DIED. THEIR *SPIRITS* REMAINED FREE, BUT THEIR BODIES WOULD REST THERE UNTIL THEY RETURNED ONE DAY.
"THEY TOLD ME THE TOMB I OPENED WAS THE HOME OF *TEKKIETSERTOK*...
"THE GOD OF THE EARTH WHO OWNED ALL THE DEER. HE IS THE GOD OF HUNTING, HE IS ALSO THE PROTECTOR OF ANY CREATURES THAT ENTER ANY PARTS OF THE NORTHERN SKY.
"I HAD DISTURBED HIS REST. I HAD ANGERED HIM AND ALL THE GODS OF THIS LAND AND NOW THERE WOULD BE A PRICE TO PAY."

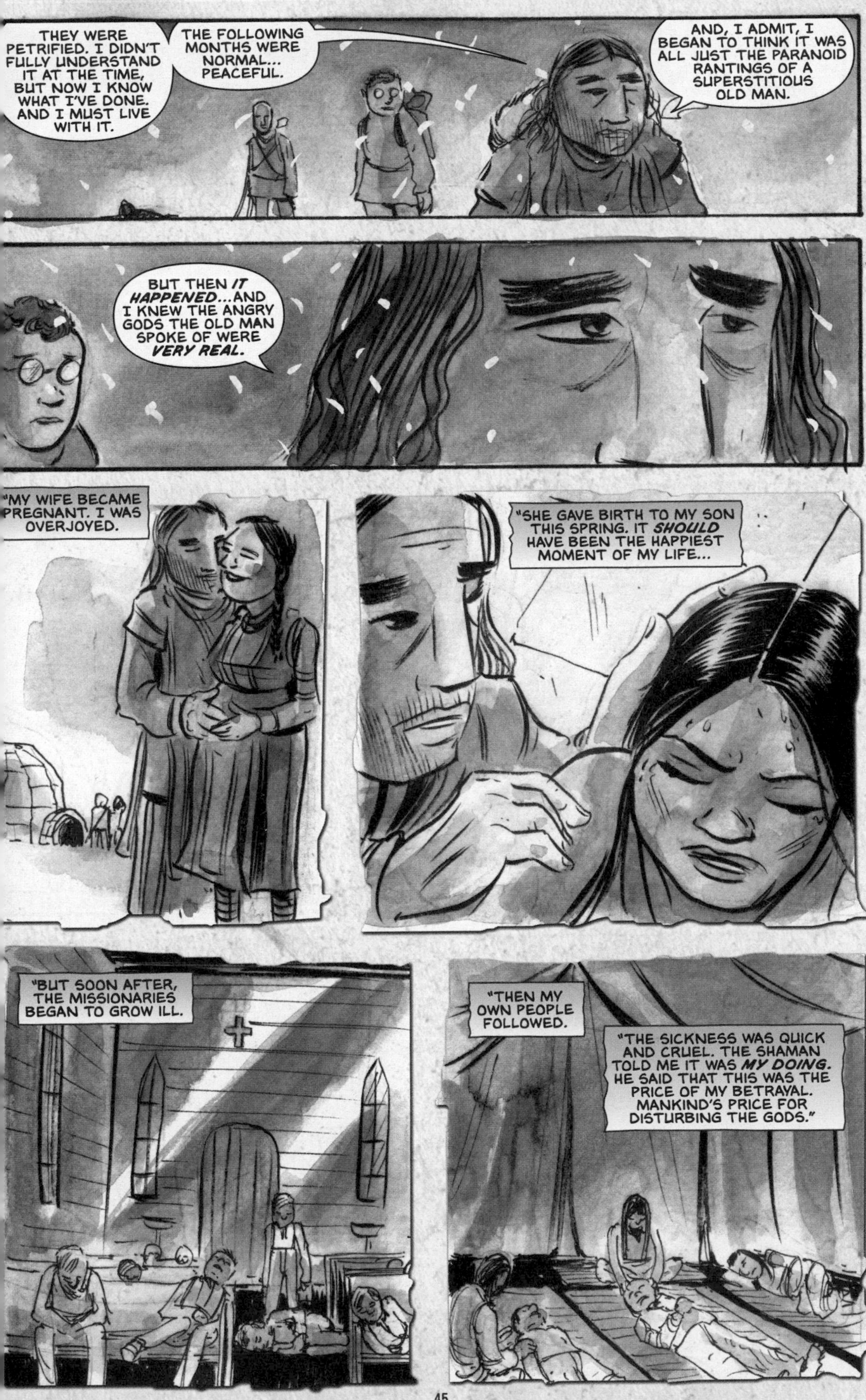
THEY WERE PETRIFIED. I DIDN'T FULLY UNDERSTAND IT AT THE TIME, BUT NOW I KNOW WHAT I'VE DONE. AND I MUST LIVE WITH IT.
THE FOLLOWING MONTHS WERE NORMAL... PEACEFUL.
AND, I ADMIT, I BEGAN TO THINK IT WAS ALL JUST THE PARANOID RANTINGS OF A SUPERSTITIOUS OLD MAN.
BUT THEN *IT HAPPENED*...AND I KNEW THE ANGRY GODS THE OLD MAN SPOKE OF WERE *VERY REAL.*
"MY WIFE BECAME PREGNANT. I WAS OVERJOYED.
"SHE GAVE BIRTH TO MY SON THIS SPRING. IT *SHOULD* HAVE BEEN THE HAPPIEST MOMENT OF MY LIFE...
"BUT SOON AFTER, THE MISSIONARIES BEGAN TO GROW ILL.
"THEN MY OWN PEOPLE FOLLOWED.
"THE SICKNESS WAS QUICK AND CRUEL. THE SHAMAN TOLD ME IT WAS *MY DOING.* HE SAID THAT THIS WAS THE PRICE OF MY BETRAYAL. MANKIND'S PRICE FOR DISTURBING THE GODS."

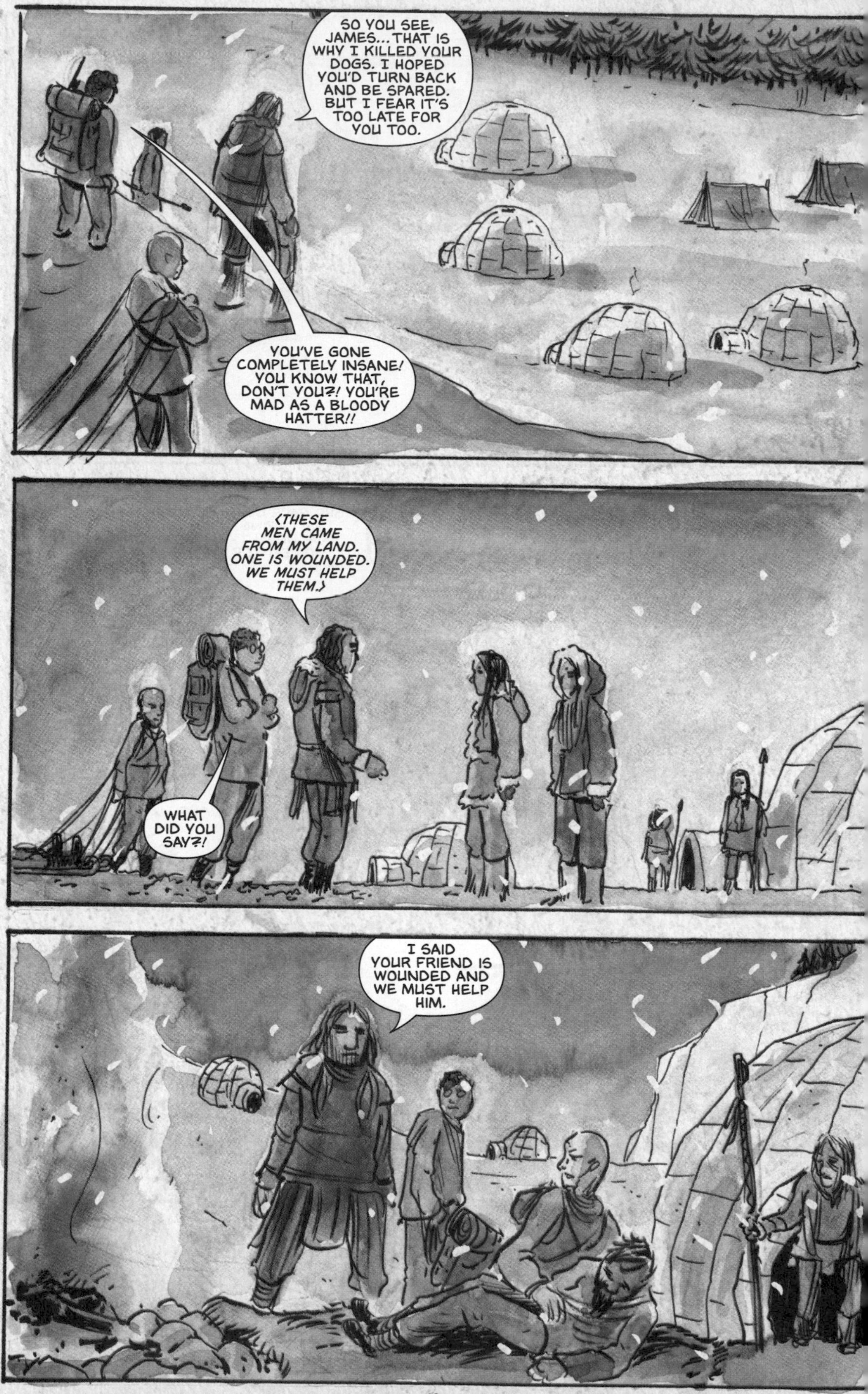
SO YOU SEE, JAMES... THAT IS WHY I KILLED YOUR DOGS. I HOPED YOU'D TURN BACK AND BE SPARED. BUT I FEAR IT'S TOO LATE FOR YOU TOO.
YOU'VE GONE COMPLETELY INSANE! YOU KNOW THAT, DON'T YOU?! YOU'RE MAD AS A BLOODY HATTER!!
<THESE MEN CAME FROM MY LAND. ONE IS WOUNDED. WE MUST HELP THEM.>
WHAT DID YOU SAY?!
I SAID YOUR FRIEND IS WOUNDED AND WE MUST HELP HIM.

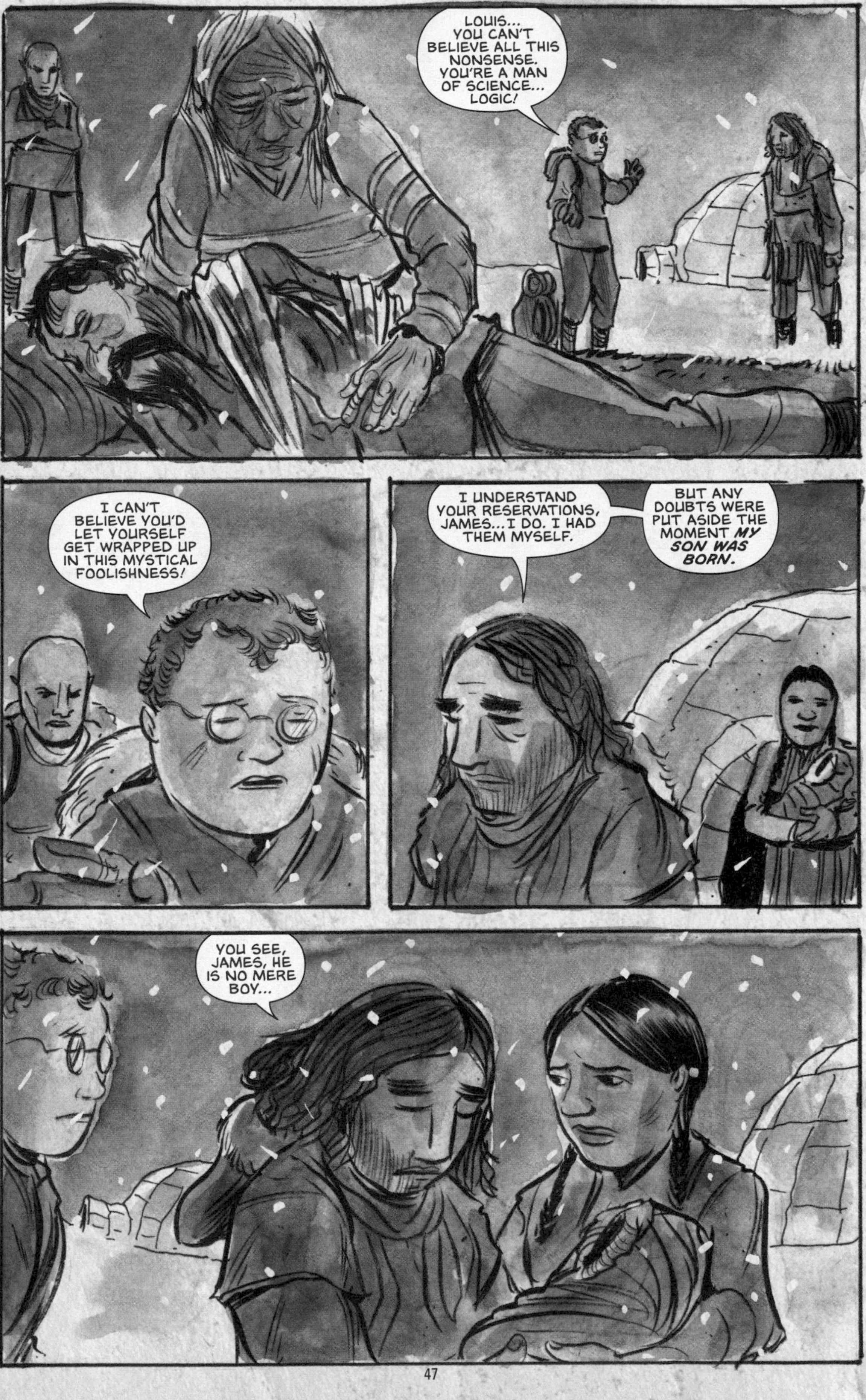
LOUIS... YOU CAN'T BELIEVE ALL THIS NONSENSE. YOU'RE A MAN OF SCIENCE... LOGIC!
I CAN'T BELIEVE YOU'D LET YOURSELF GET WRAPPED UP IN THIS MYSTICAL FOOLISHNESS!
I UNDERSTAND YOUR RESERVATIONS, JAMES... I DO. I HAD THEM MYSELF.
BUT ANY DOUBTS WERE PUT ASIDE THE MOMENT *MY SON WAS BORN.*
YOU SEE, JAMES, HE IS NO MERE BOY...

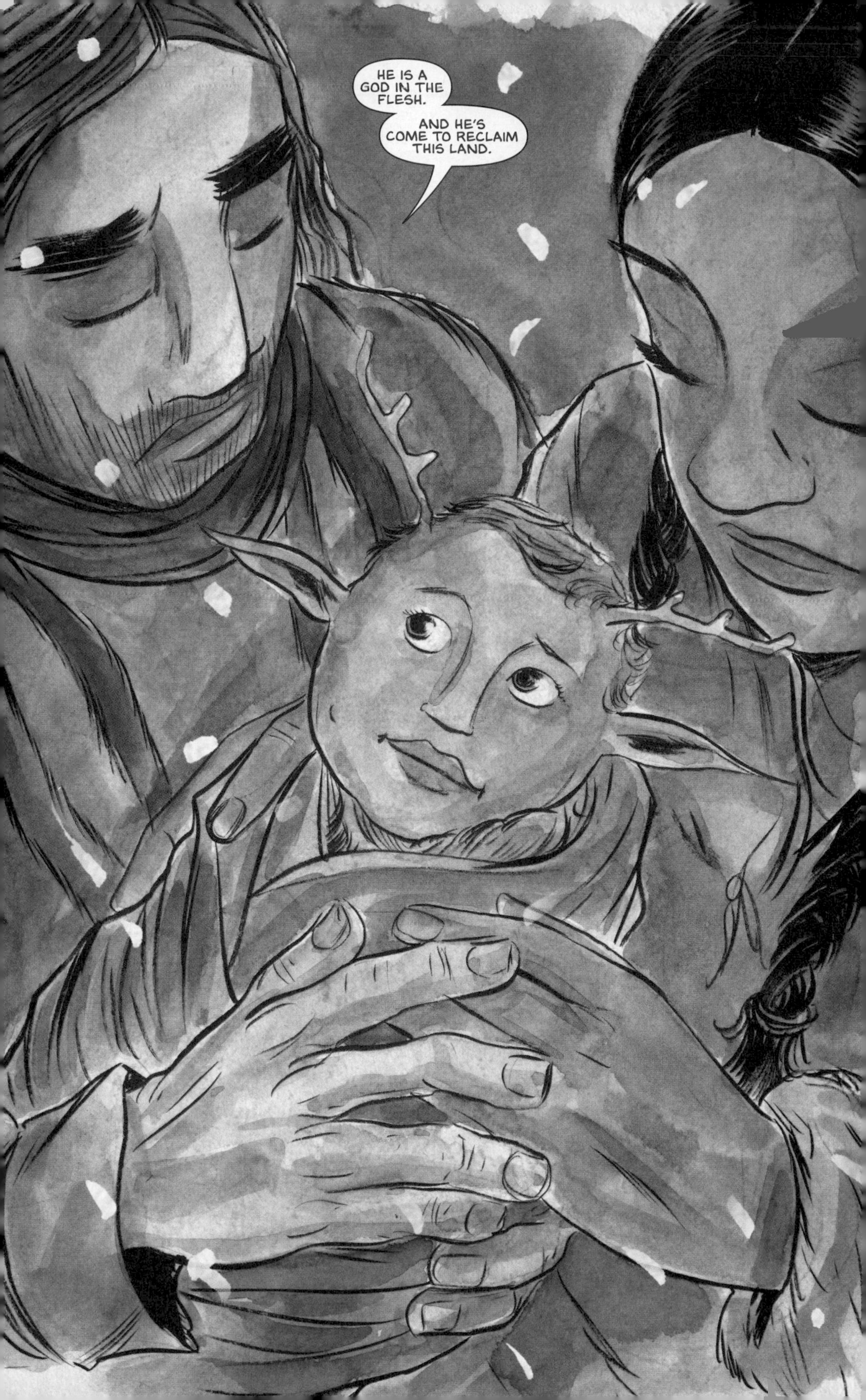
HE IS A GOD IN THE FLESH.
AND HE'S COME TO RECLAIM THIS LAND.

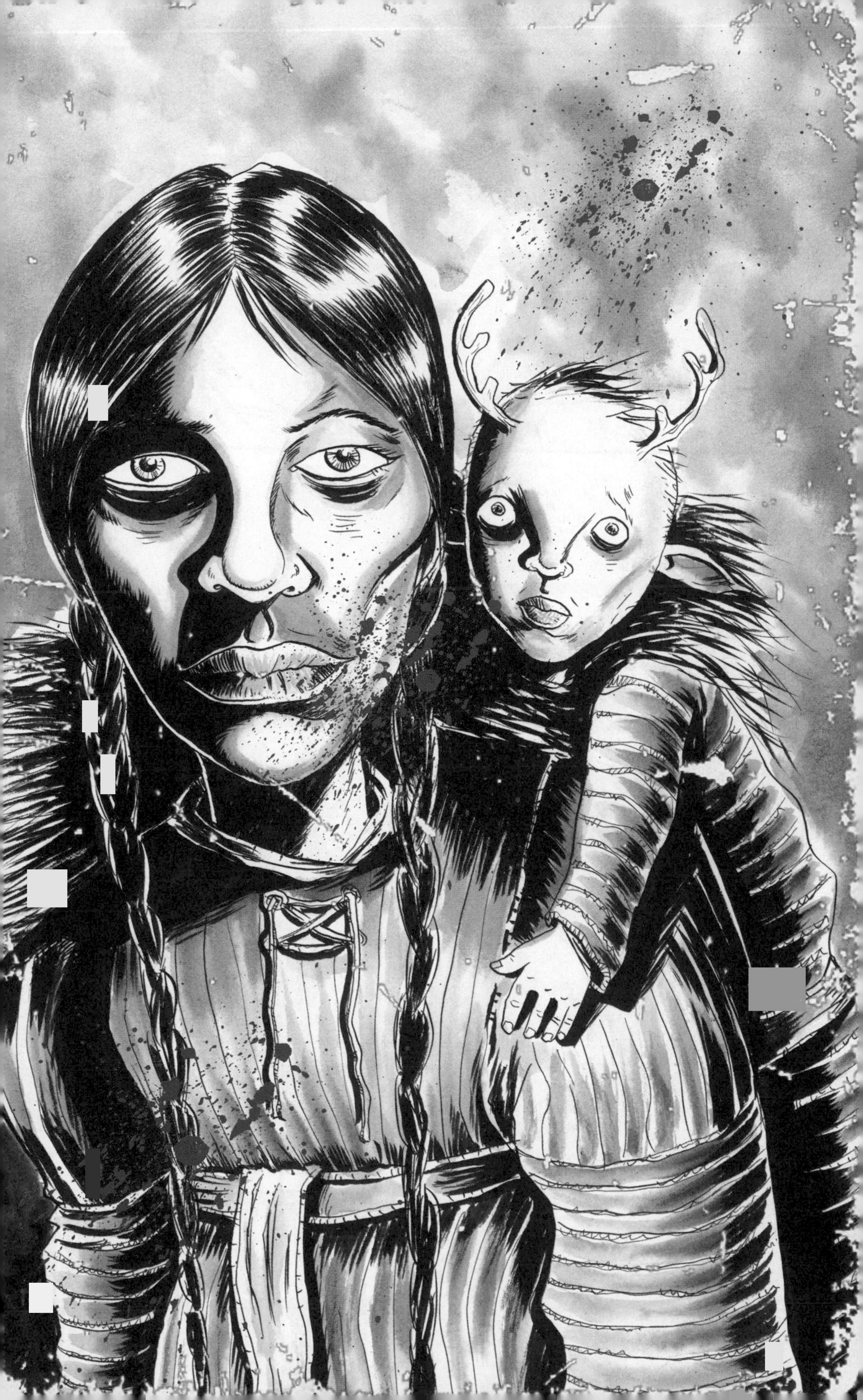

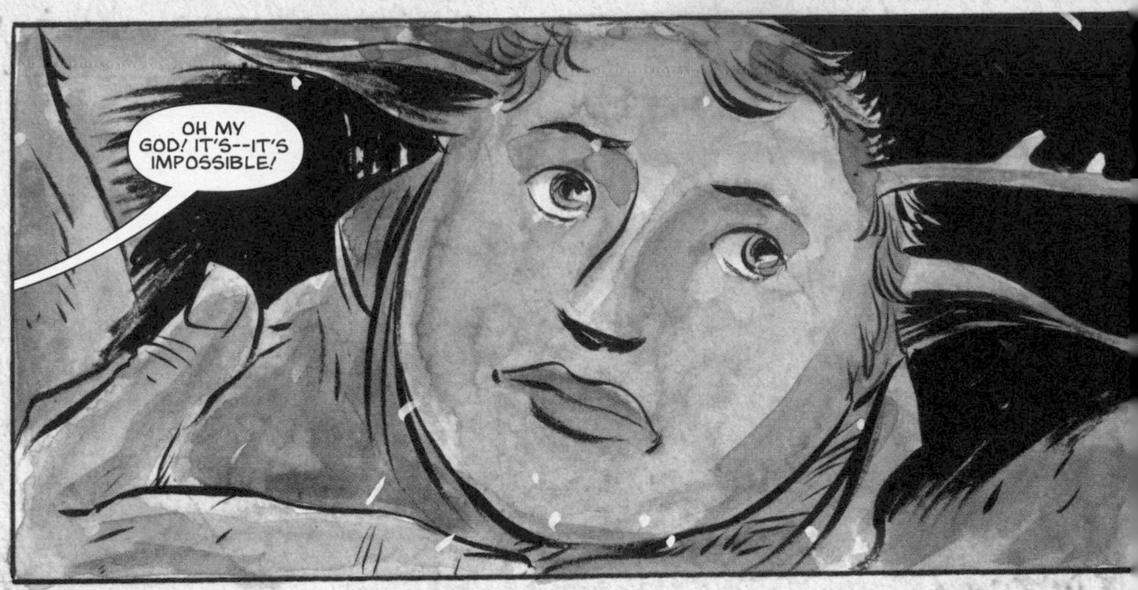
OH MY GOD! IT'S--IT'S IMPOSSIBLE!

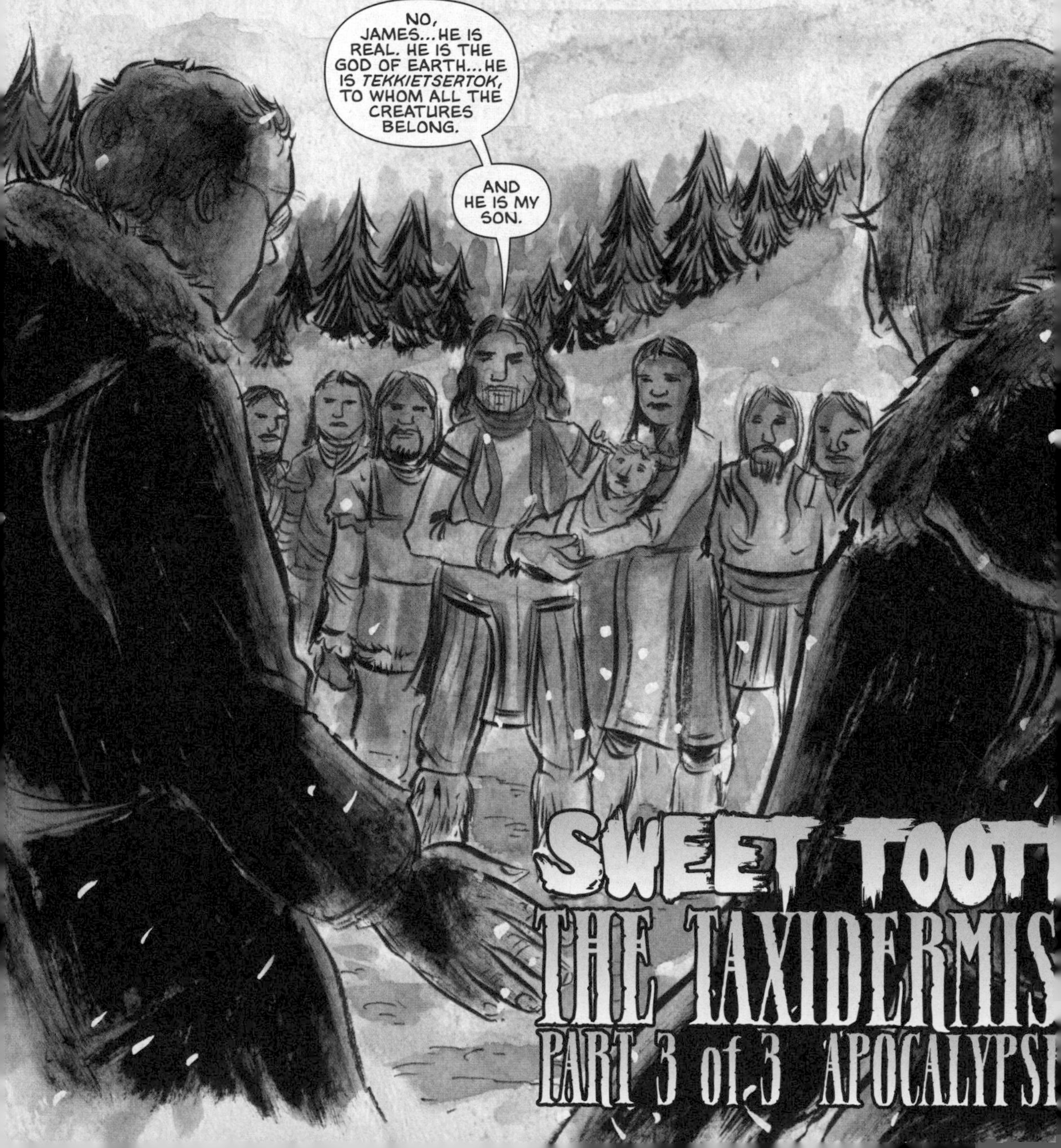
NO, JAMES...HE IS REAL. HE IS THE GOD OF EARTH...HE IS *TEKKIETSERTOK*, TO WHOM ALL THE CREATURES BELONG.
AND HE IS MY SON.
SWEET TOOT
THE TAXIDERMIS
PART 3 of 3 APOCALYPS

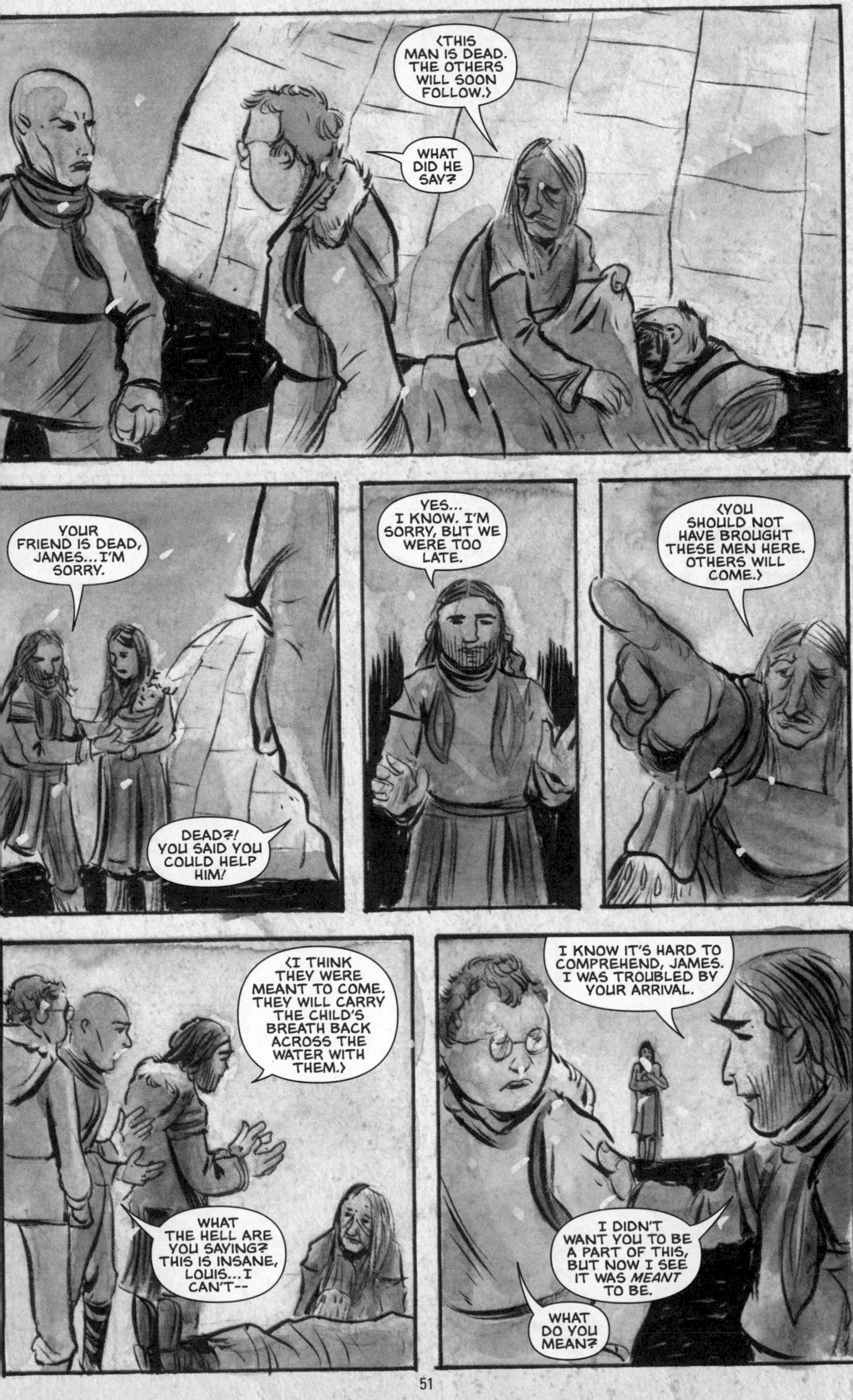
‹THIS MAN IS DEAD. THE OTHERS WILL SOON FOLLOW.›
WHAT DID HE SAY?
YOUR FRIEND IS DEAD, JAMES... I'M SORRY.
DEAD?! YOU SAID YOU COULD HELP HIM!
YES... I KNOW. I'M SORRY, BUT WE WERE TOO LATE.
‹YOU SHOULD NOT HAVE BROUGHT THESE MEN HERE. OTHERS WILL COME.›
‹I THINK THEY WERE MEANT TO COME. THEY WILL CARRY THE CHILD'S BREATH BACK ACROSS THE WATER WITH THEM.›
WHAT THE HELL ARE YOU SAYING? THIS IS INSANE, LOUIS... I CAN'T--
I KNOW IT'S HARD TO COMPREHEND, JAMES. I WAS TROUBLED BY YOUR ARRIVAL.
I DIDN'T WANT YOU TO BE A PART OF THIS, BUT NOW I SEE IT WAS *MEANT* TO BE.
WHAT DO YOU MEAN?

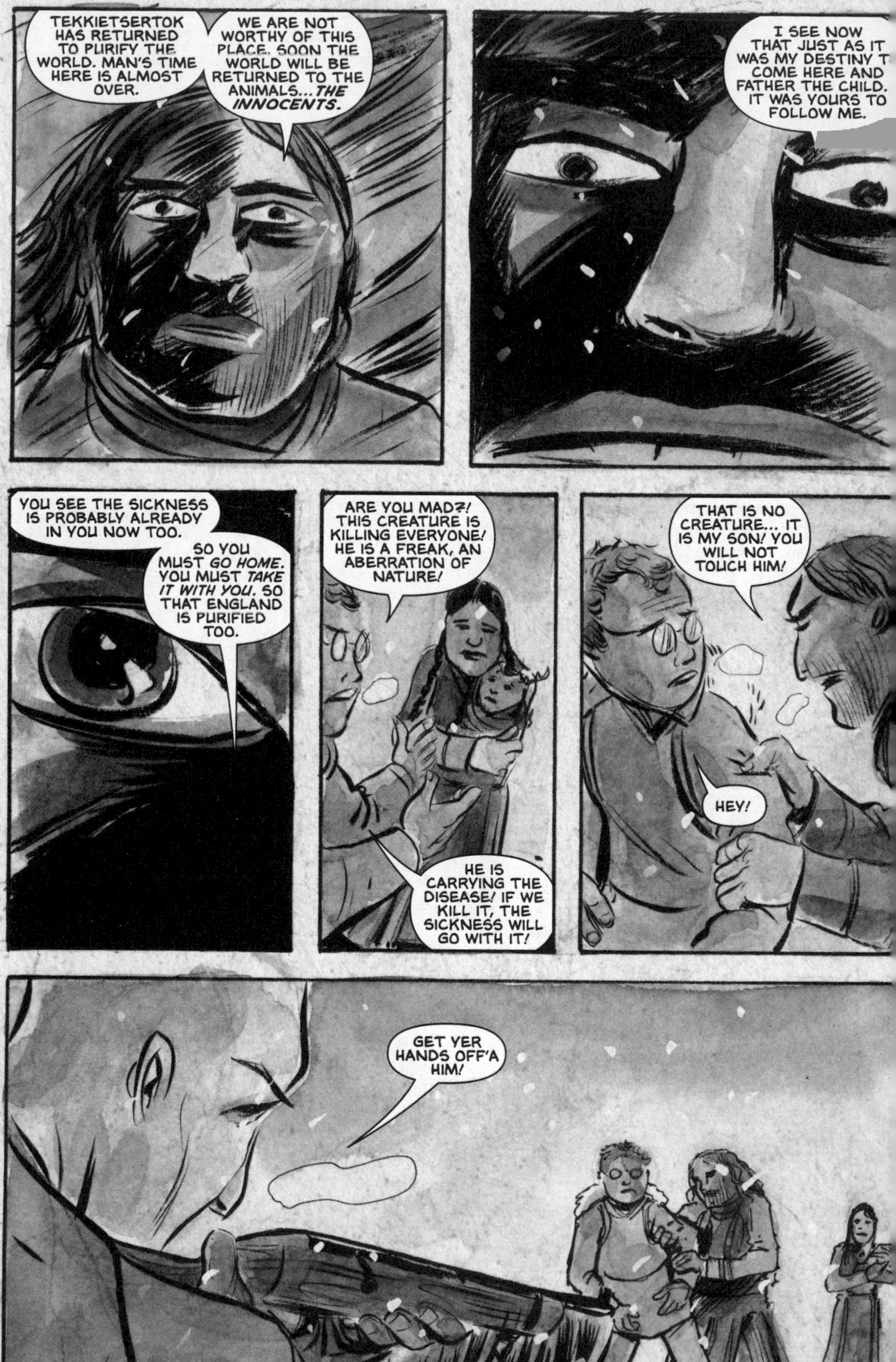
TEKKIETSERTOK HAS RETURNED TO PURIFY THE WORLD. MAN'S TIME HERE IS ALMOST OVER.
WE ARE NOT WORTHY OF THIS PLACE. SOON THE WORLD WILL BE RETURNED TO THE ANIMALS... *THE INNOCENTS.*
I SEE NOW THAT JUST AS IT WAS MY DESTINY T COME HERE AND FATHER THE CHILD. IT WAS YOURS TO FOLLOW ME.
YOU SEE THE SICKNESS IS PROBABLY ALREADY IN YOU NOW TOO.
SO YOU MUST *GO HOME.* YOU MUST *TAKE IT WITH YOU.* SO THAT ENGLAND IS PURIFIED TOO.
ARE YOU MAD?! THIS CREATURE IS KILLING EVERYONE! HE IS A FREAK, AN ABERRATION OF NATURE!
HE IS CARRYING THE DISEASE! IF WE KILL IT, THE SICKNESS WILL GO WITH IT!
THAT IS NO CREATURE... IT IS MY SON! YOU WILL NOT TOUCH HIM!
HEY!
GET YER HANDS OFF'A HIM!

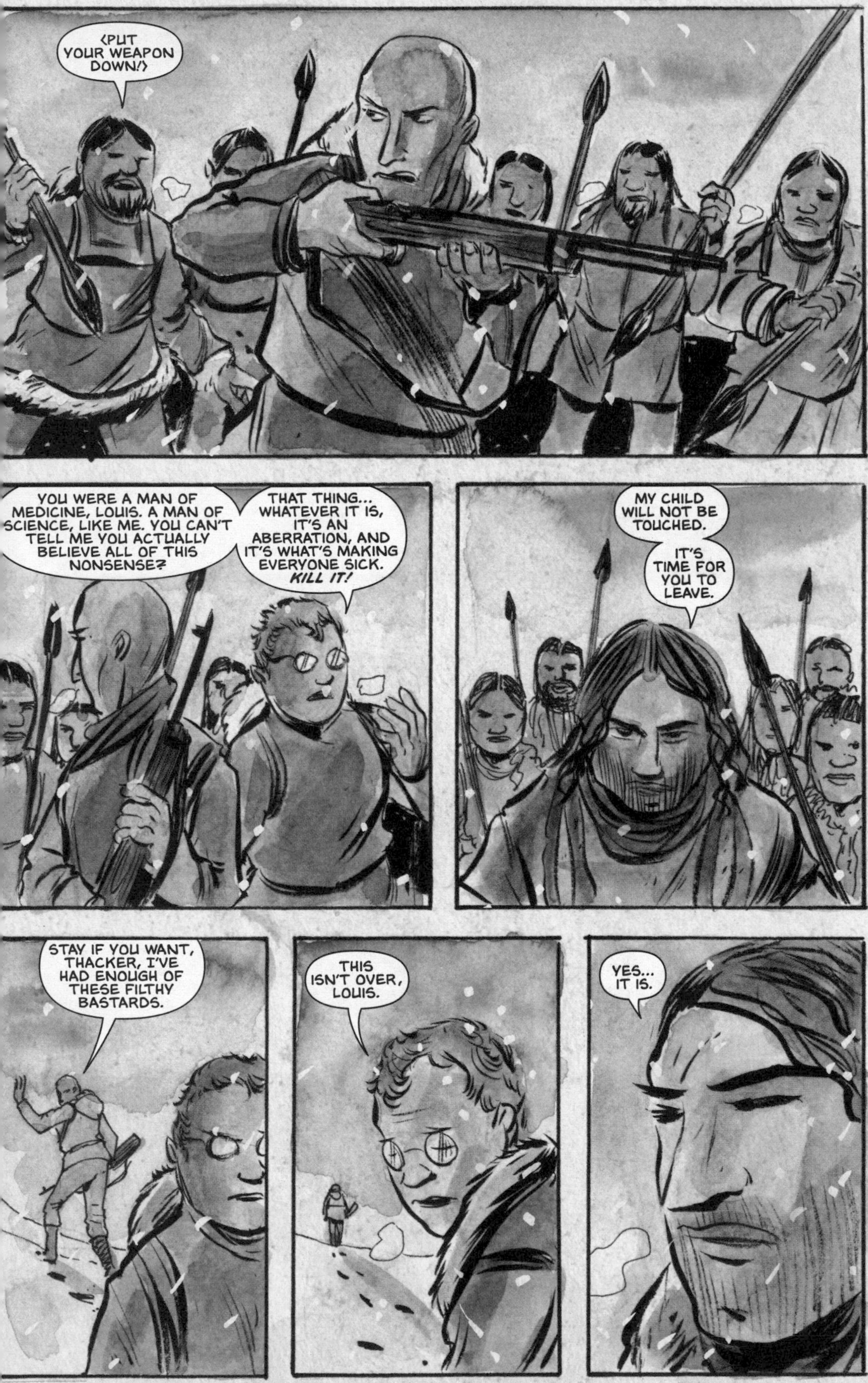

<PUT YOUR WEAPON DOWN!>
YOU WERE A MAN OF MEDICINE, LOUIS. A MAN OF SCIENCE, LIKE ME. YOU CAN'T TELL ME YOU ACTUALLY BELIEVE ALL OF THIS NONSENSE?
THAT THING... WHATEVER IT IS, IT'S AN ABERRATION, AND IT'S WHAT'S MAKING EVERYONE SICK. KILL IT!
MY CHILD WILL NOT BE TOUCHED.
IT'S TIME FOR YOU TO LEAVE.
STAY IF YOU WANT, THACKER, I'VE HAD ENOUGH OF THESE FILTHY BASTARDS.
THIS ISN'T OVER, LOUIS.
YES... IT IS.

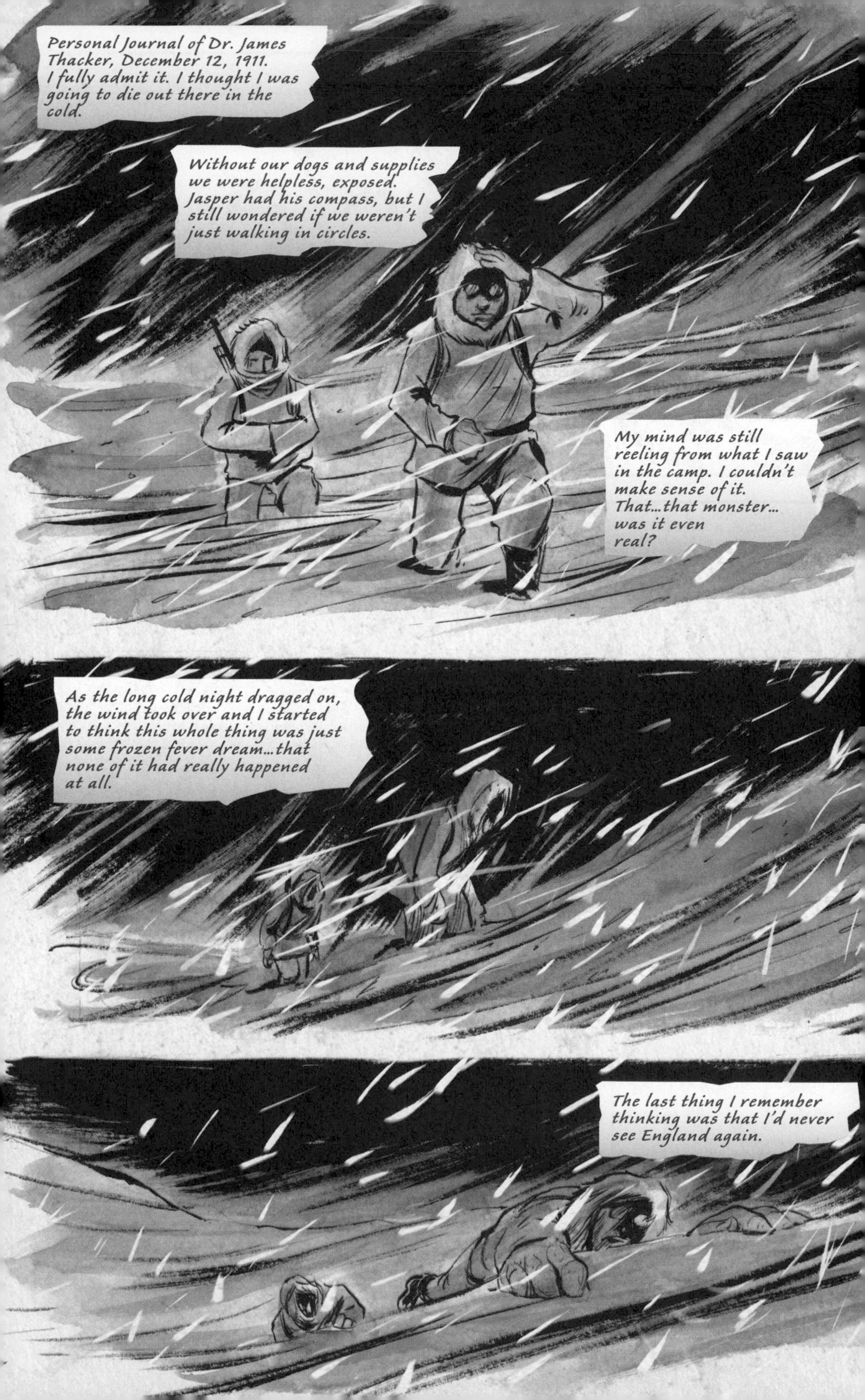
Personal Journal of Dr. James Thacker, December 12, 1911. I fully admit it. I thought I was going to die out there in the cold.
Without our dogs and supplies we were helpless, exposed. Jasper had his compass, but I still wondered if we weren't just walking in circles.
My mind was still reeling from what I saw in the camp. I couldn't make sense of it. That...that monster... was it even real?
As the long cold night dragged on, the wind took over and I started to think this whole thing was just some frozen fever dream...that none of it had really happened at all.
The last thing I remember thinking was that I'd never see England again.

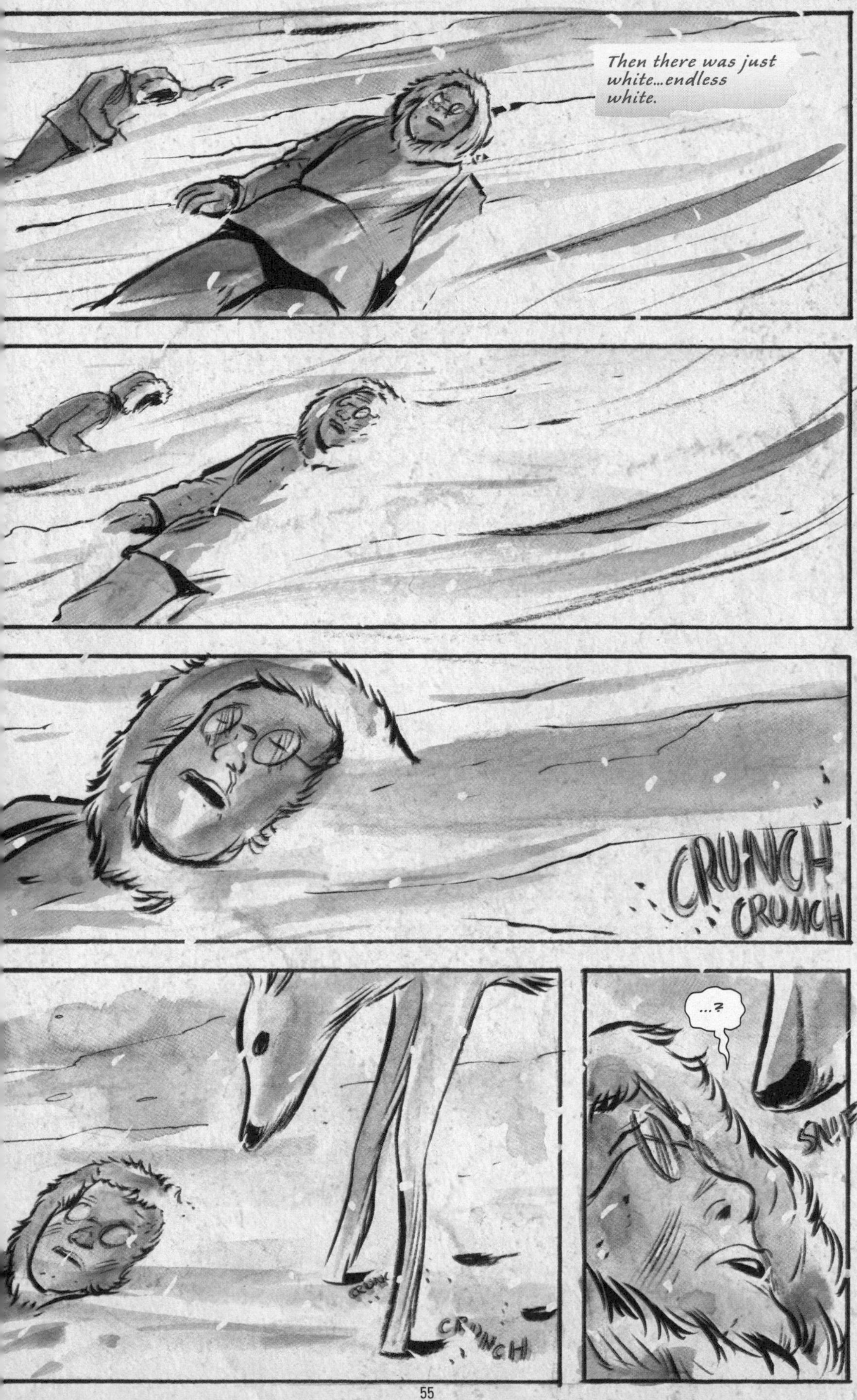
Then there was just white...endless white.
CRUNCH
CRUNCH
CRUNK
CRUNCH
...?
SNIFF

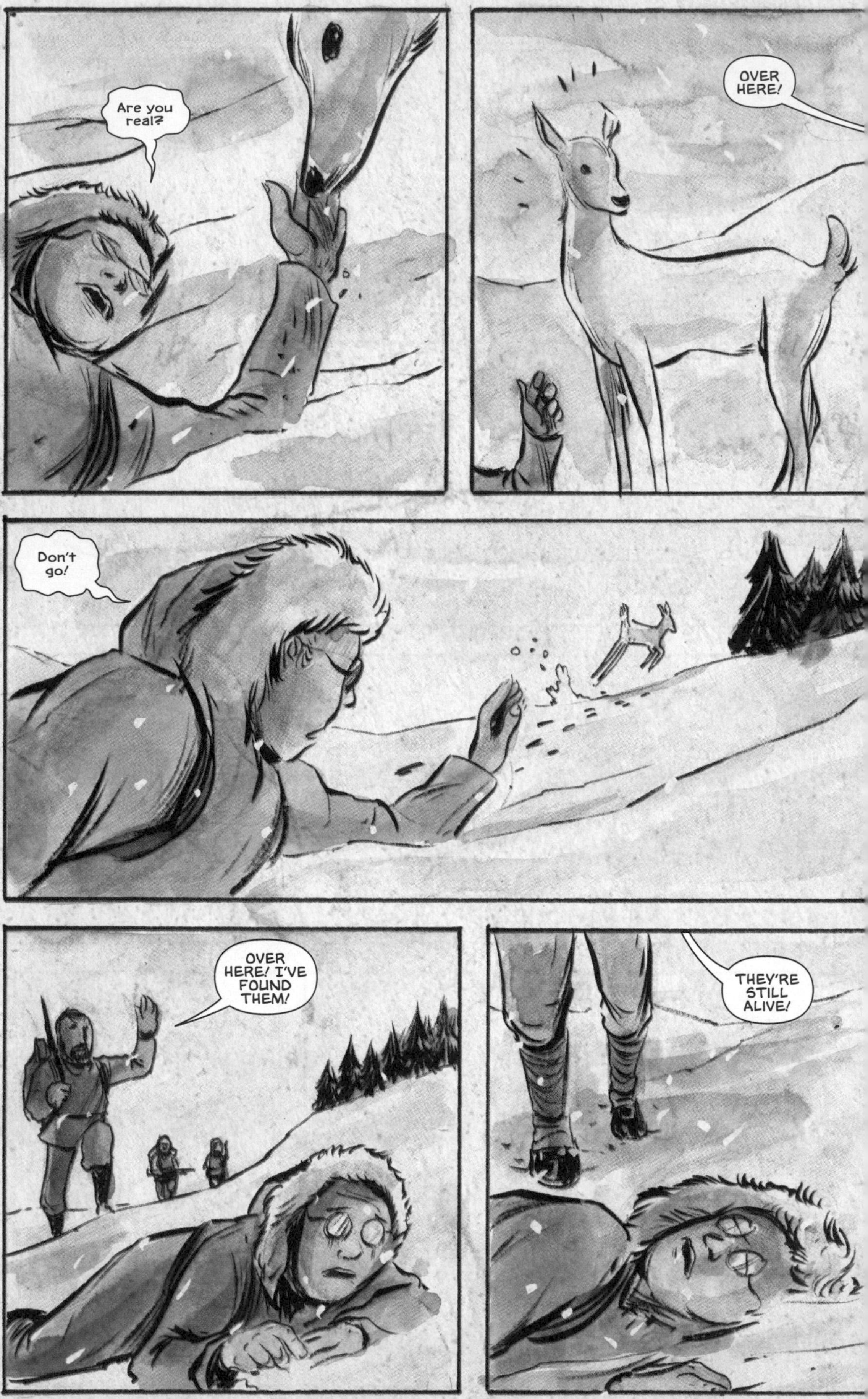
Are you real?
OVER HERE!
Don't go!
OVER HERE! I'VE FOUND THEM!
THEY'RE STILL ALIVE!

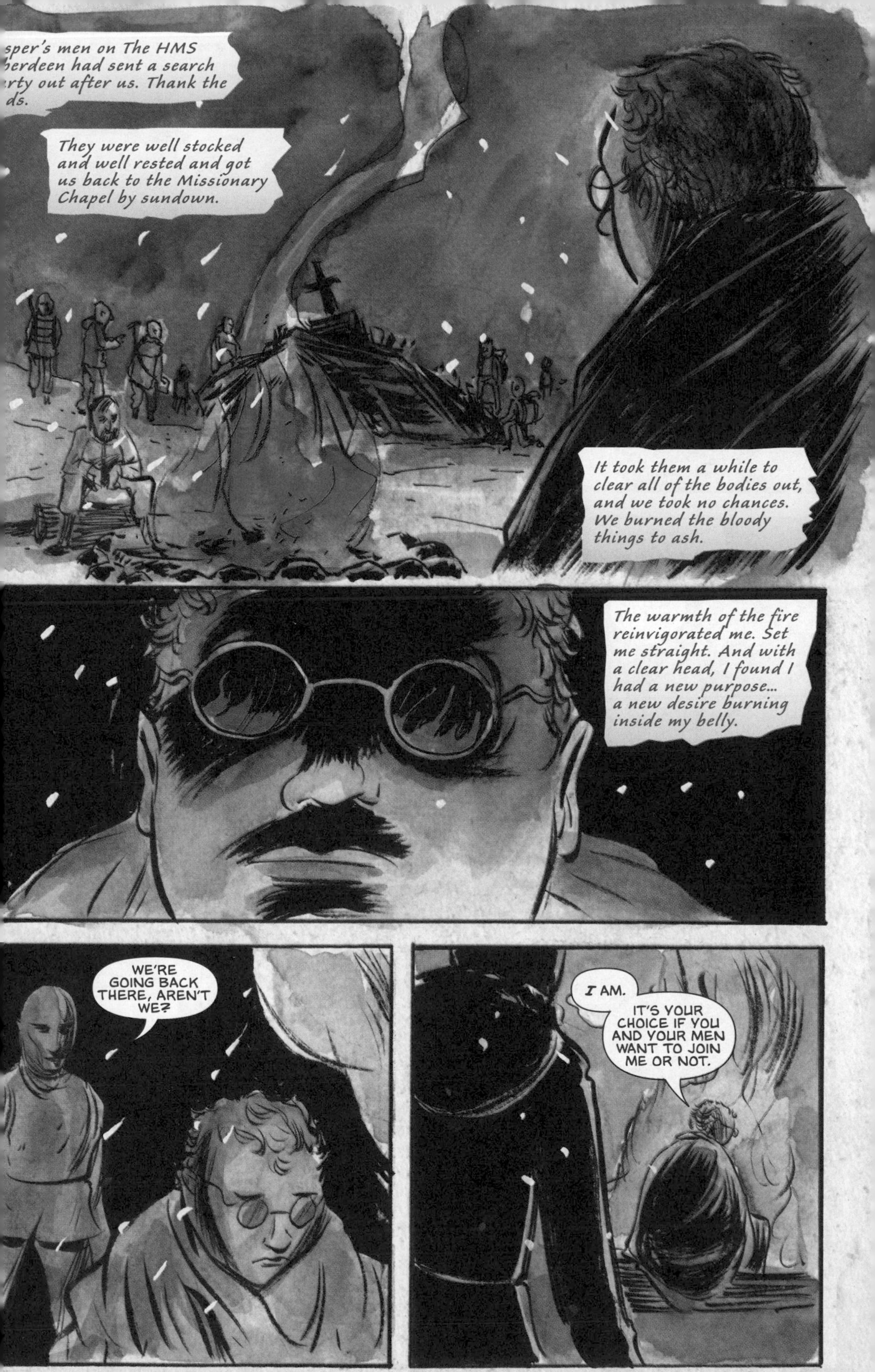
sper's men on The HMS
berdeen had sent a search
rty out after us. Thank the
ds.
They were well stocked and well rested and got us back to the Missionary Chapel by sundown.
It took them a while to clear all of the bodies out, and we took no chances. We burned the bloody things to ash.
The warmth of the fire reinvigorated me. Set me straight. And with a clear head, I found I had a new purpose... a new desire burning inside my belly.
WE'RE GOING BACK THERE, AREN'T WE?
I AM.
IT'S YOUR CHOICE IF YOU AND YOUR MEN WANT TO JOIN ME OR NOT.

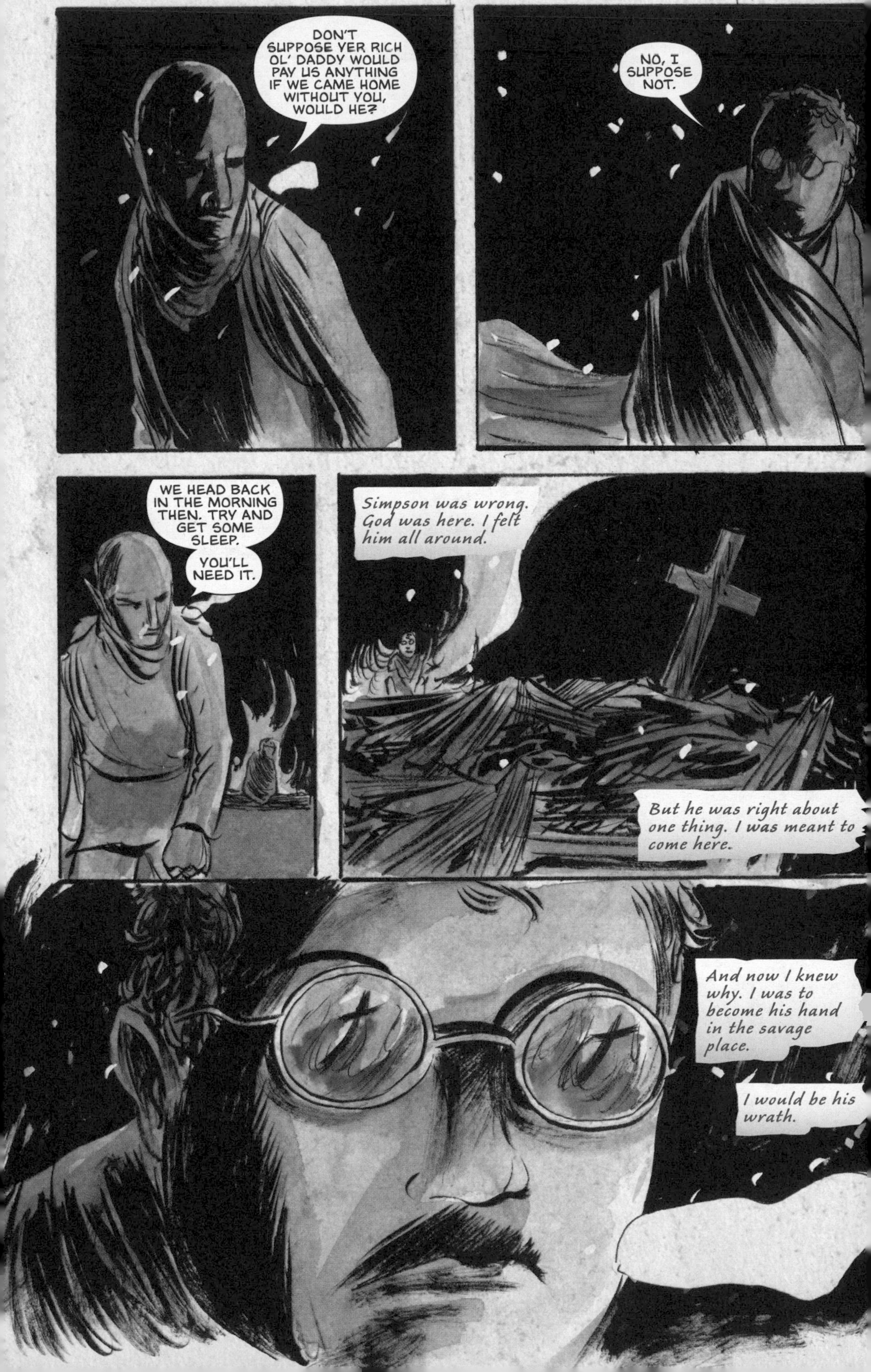
DON'T SUPPOSE YER RICH OL' DADDY WOULD PAY US ANYTHING IF WE CAME HOME WITHOUT YOU, WOULD HE?
NO, I SUPPOSE NOT.
WE HEAD BACK IN THE MORNING THEN. TRY AND GET SOME SLEEP.
YOU'LL NEED IT.
Simpson was wrong. God was here. I felt him all around.
But he was right about one thing. I was meant to come here.
And now I knew why. I was to become his hand in the savage place.
I would be his wrath.

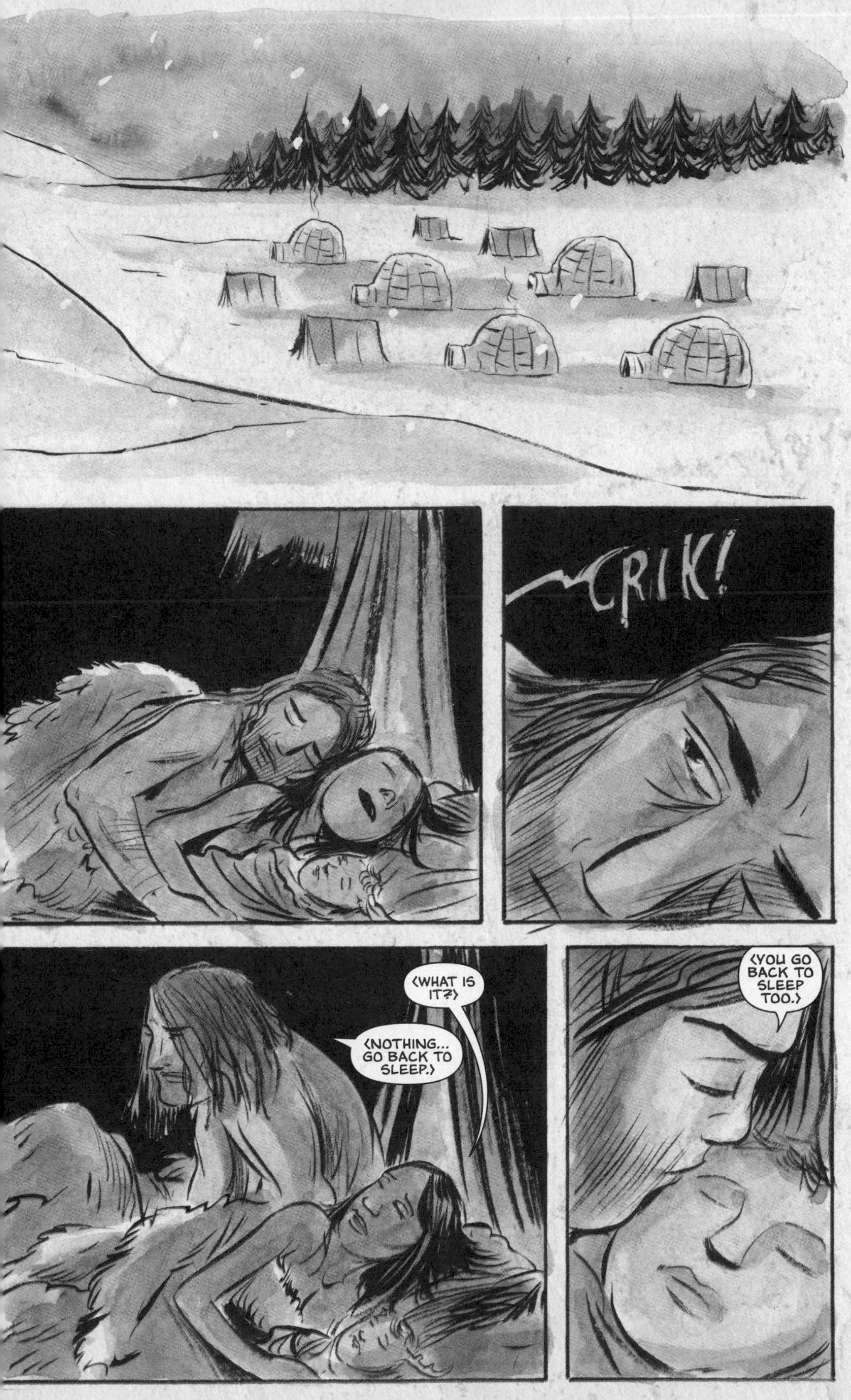
CRIK!
‹WHAT IS IT?›
‹NOTHING... GO BACK TO SLEEP.›
‹YOU GO BACK TO SLEEP TOO.›

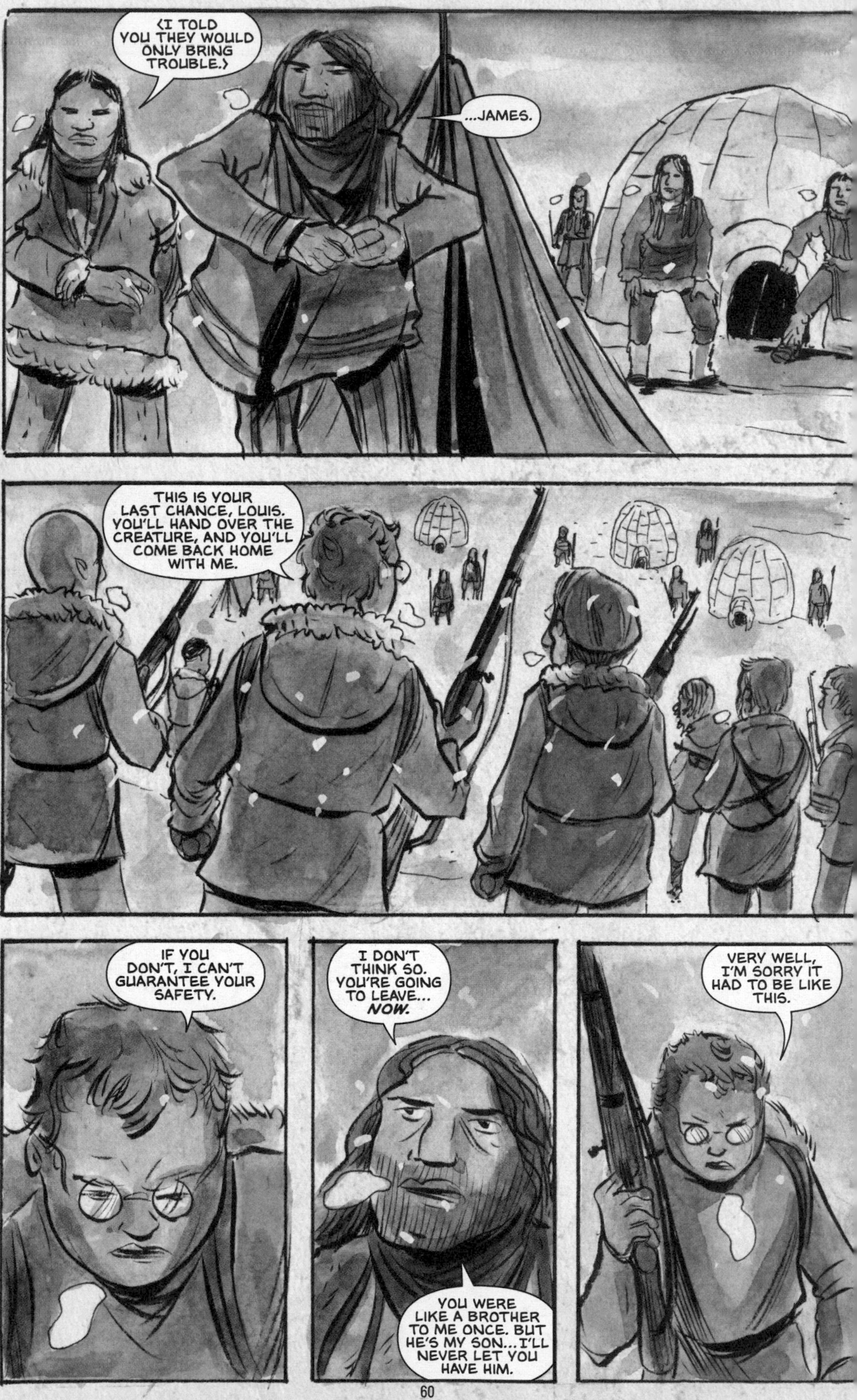

<I TOLD YOU THEY WOULD ONLY BRING TROUBLE.>
...JAMES.
THIS IS YOUR LAST CHANCE, LOUIS. YOU'LL HAND OVER THE CREATURE, AND YOU'LL COME BACK HOME WITH ME.
IF YOU DON'T, I CAN'T GUARANTEE YOUR SAFETY.
I DON'T THINK SO. YOU'RE GOING TO LEAVE... ***NOW.***
YOU WERE LIKE A BROTHER TO ME ONCE. BUT HE'S MY SON... I'LL NEVER LET YOU HAVE HIM.
VERY WELL, I'M SORRY IT HAD TO BE LIKE THIS.

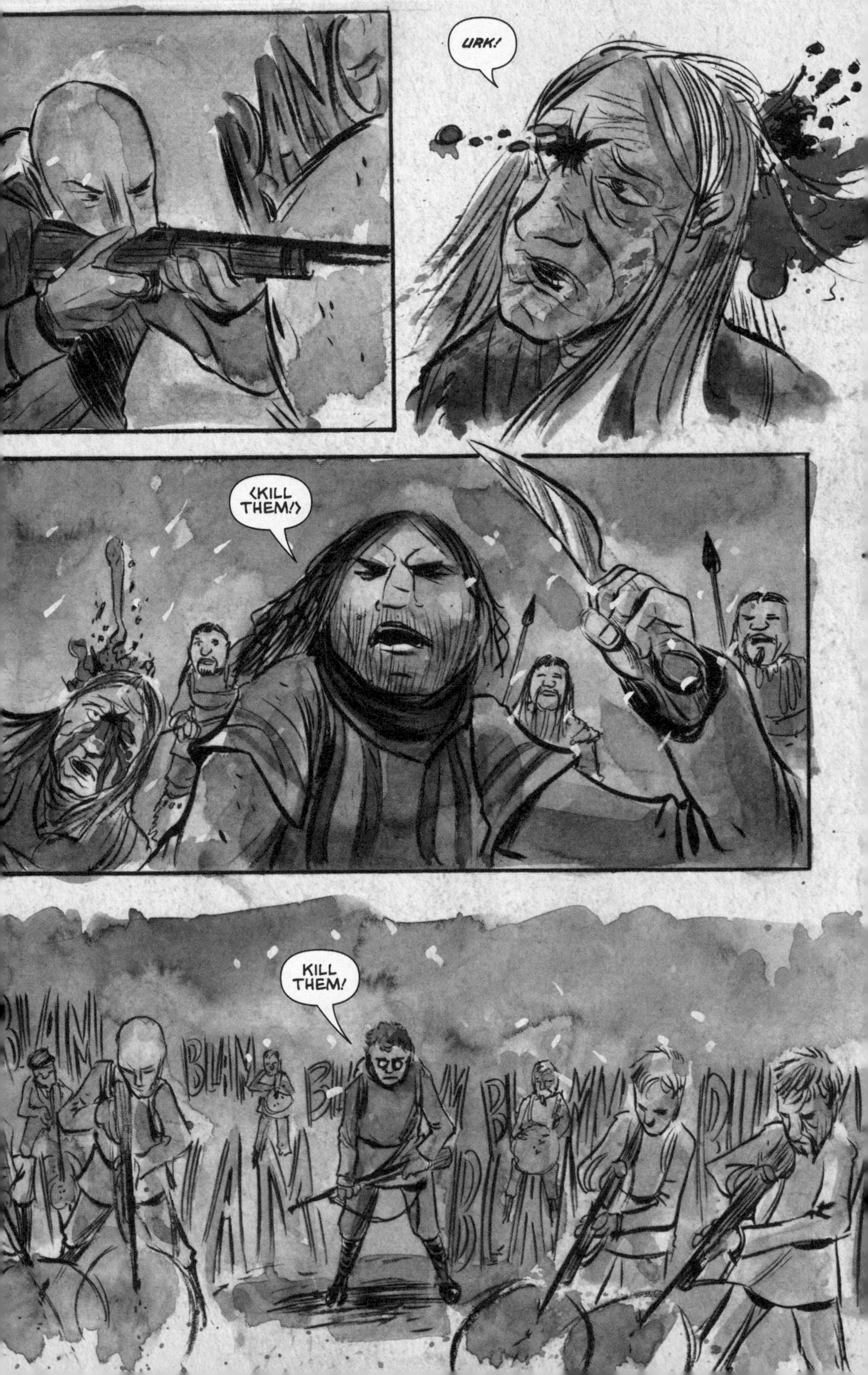
PANG
URK!
<KILL THEM!>
KILL THEM!
BLAM BLAM BLAM BLAM BLAM BLAM BLAM BLAM

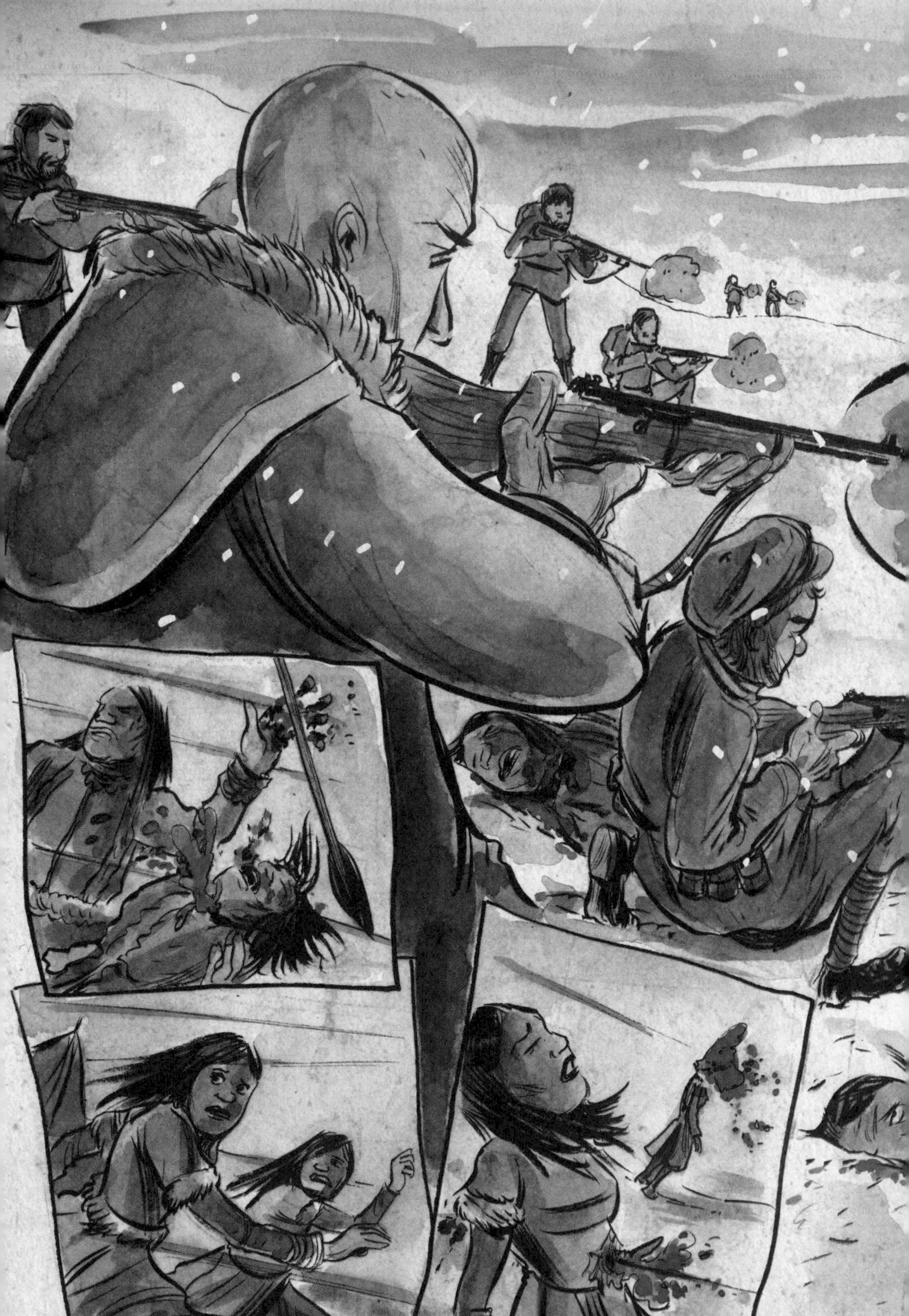

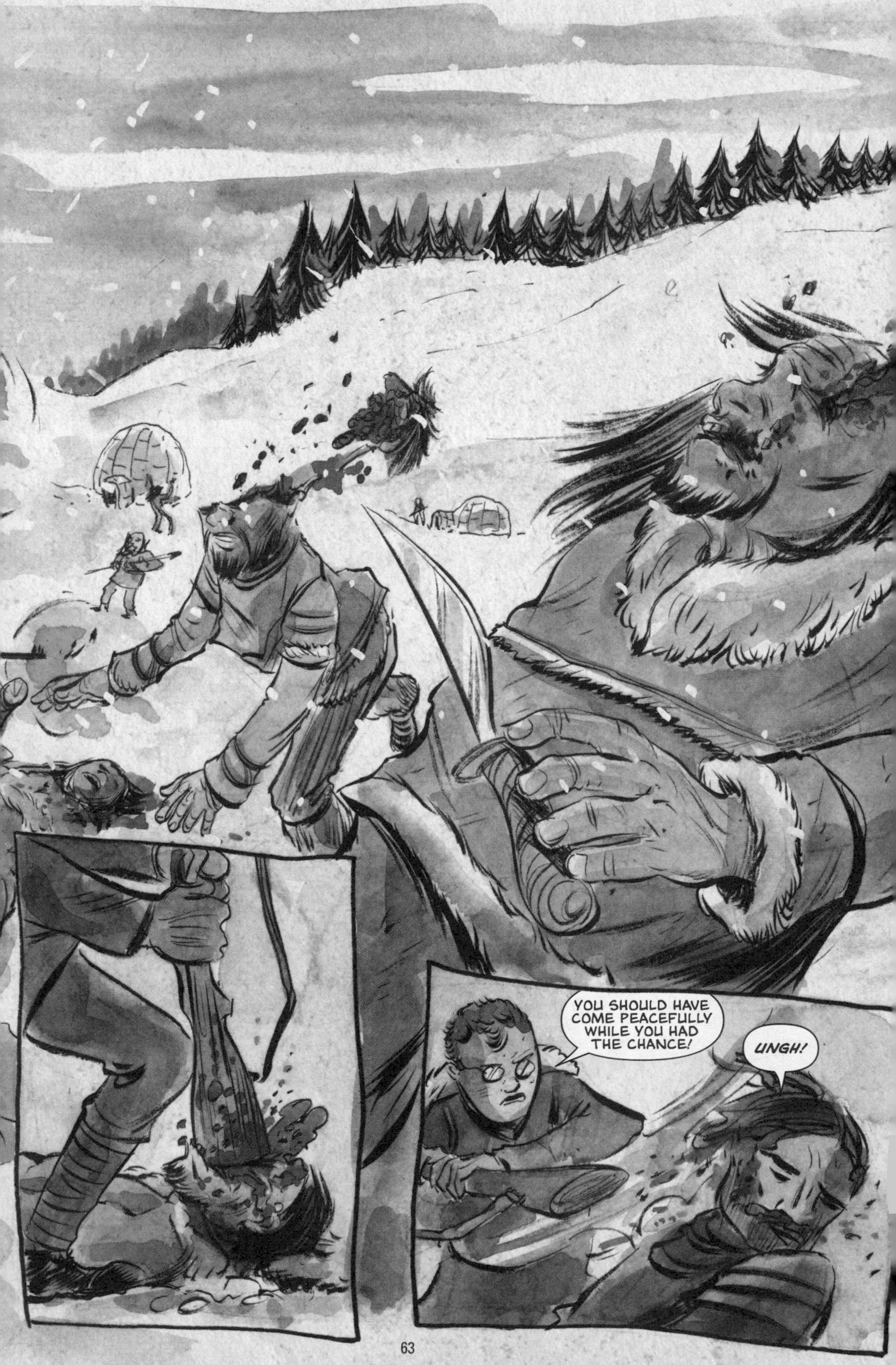
YOU SHOULD HAVE COME PEACEFULLY WHILE YOU HAD THE CHANCE!
UNGH!

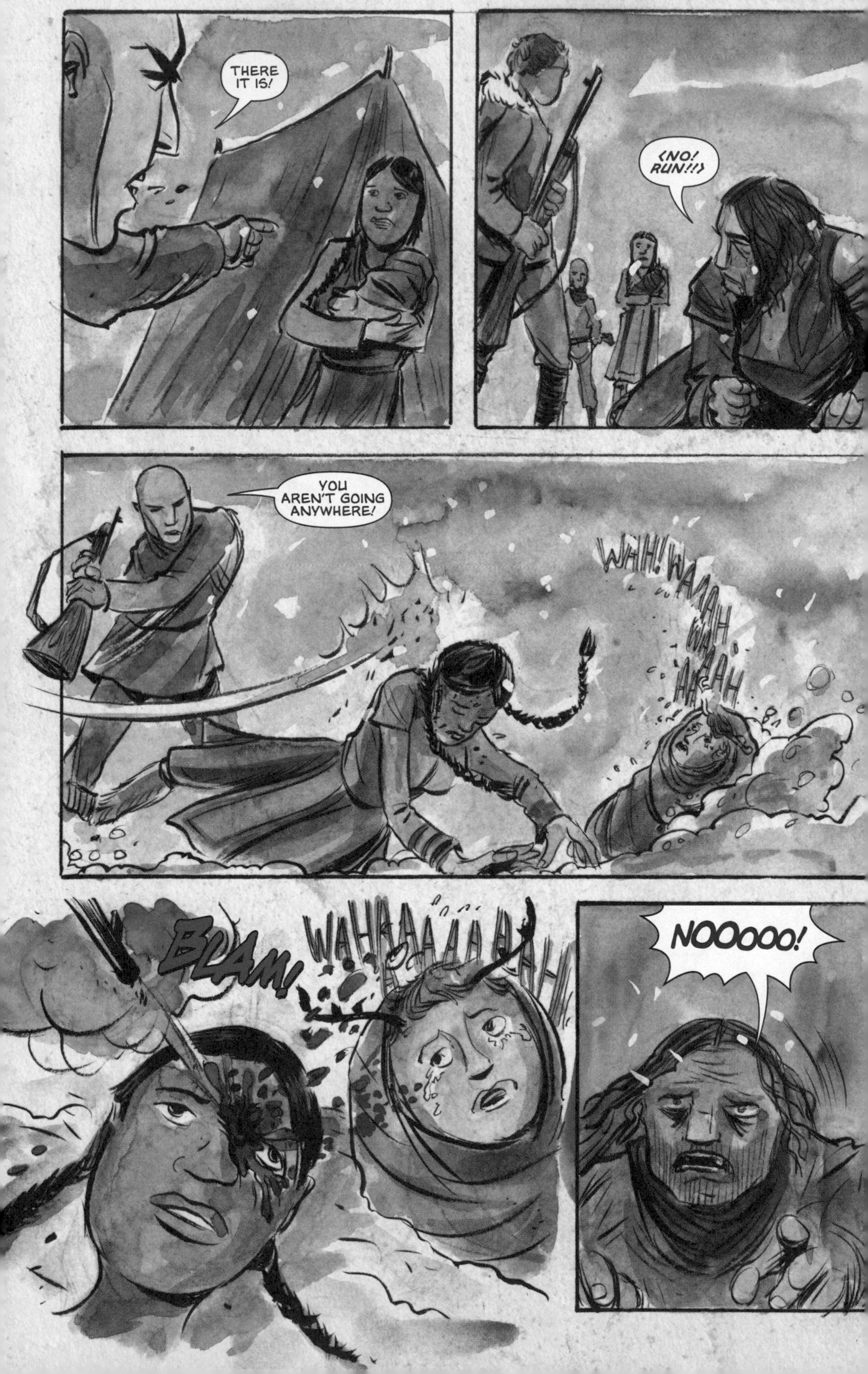
THERE IT IS!
‹NO! RUN!!!›
YOU AREN'T GOING ANYWHERE!
WHH! WAAAH WAAAH AHAAH
BLAM!
WAHAAAAAAAAH
NOOOOO!

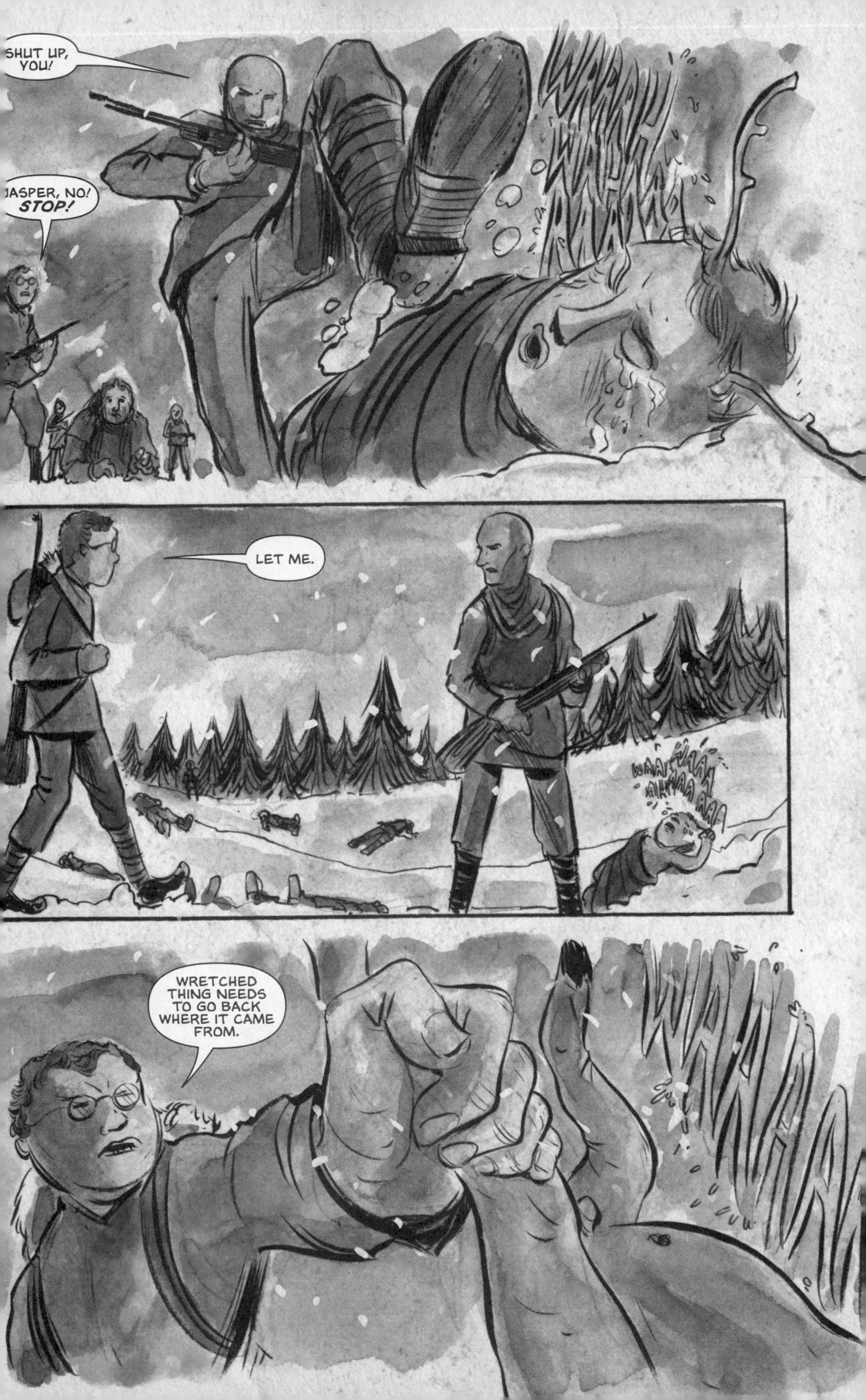
SHUT UP, YOU!
JASPER, NO! STOP!
LET ME.
WRETCHED THING NEEDS TO GO BACK WHERE IT CAME FROM.

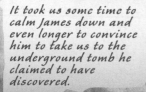

It took us some time to calm James down and even longer to convince him to take us to the underground tomb he claimed to have discovered.

But in the end he had little choice.

It was there... right where he said it was.

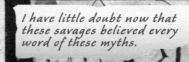

I have little doubt now that these savages believed every word of these myths.

But where they saw gods...I saw the truth...

...I saw demons.

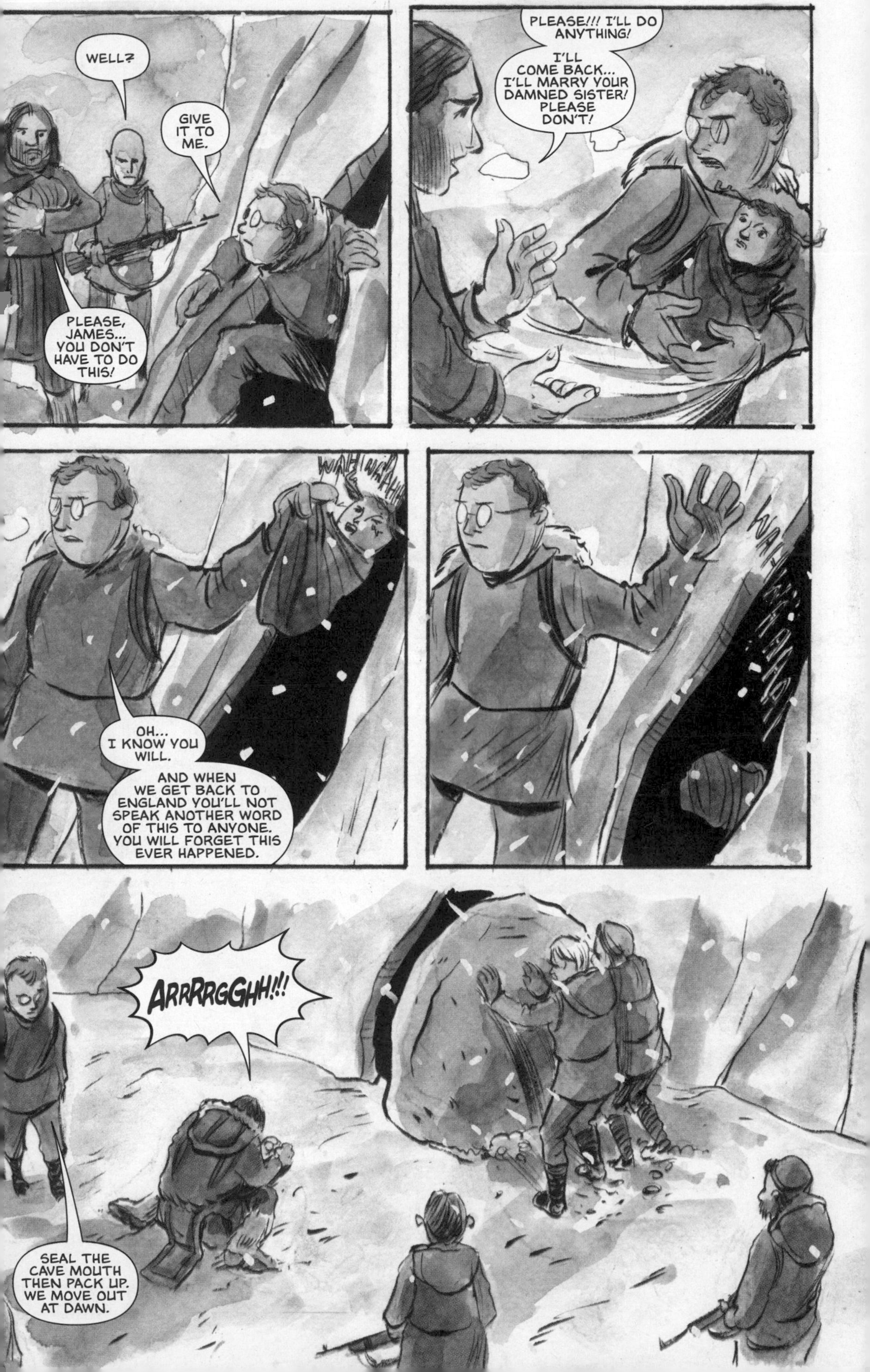

WELL?
GIVE IT TO ME.
PLEASE, JAMES... YOU DON'T HAVE TO DO THIS!
PLEASE!!! I'LL DO ANYTHING!
I'LL COME BACK... I'LL MARRY YOUR DAMNED SISTER! PLEASE DON'T!
OH... I KNOW YOU WILL.
AND WHEN WE GET BACK TO ENGLAND YOU'LL NOT SPEAK ANOTHER WORD OF THIS TO ANYONE. YOU WILL FORGET THIS EVER HAPPENED.
ARRRRGGHH!!!
SEAL THE CAVE MOUTH THEN PACK UP. WE MOVE OUT AT DAWN.

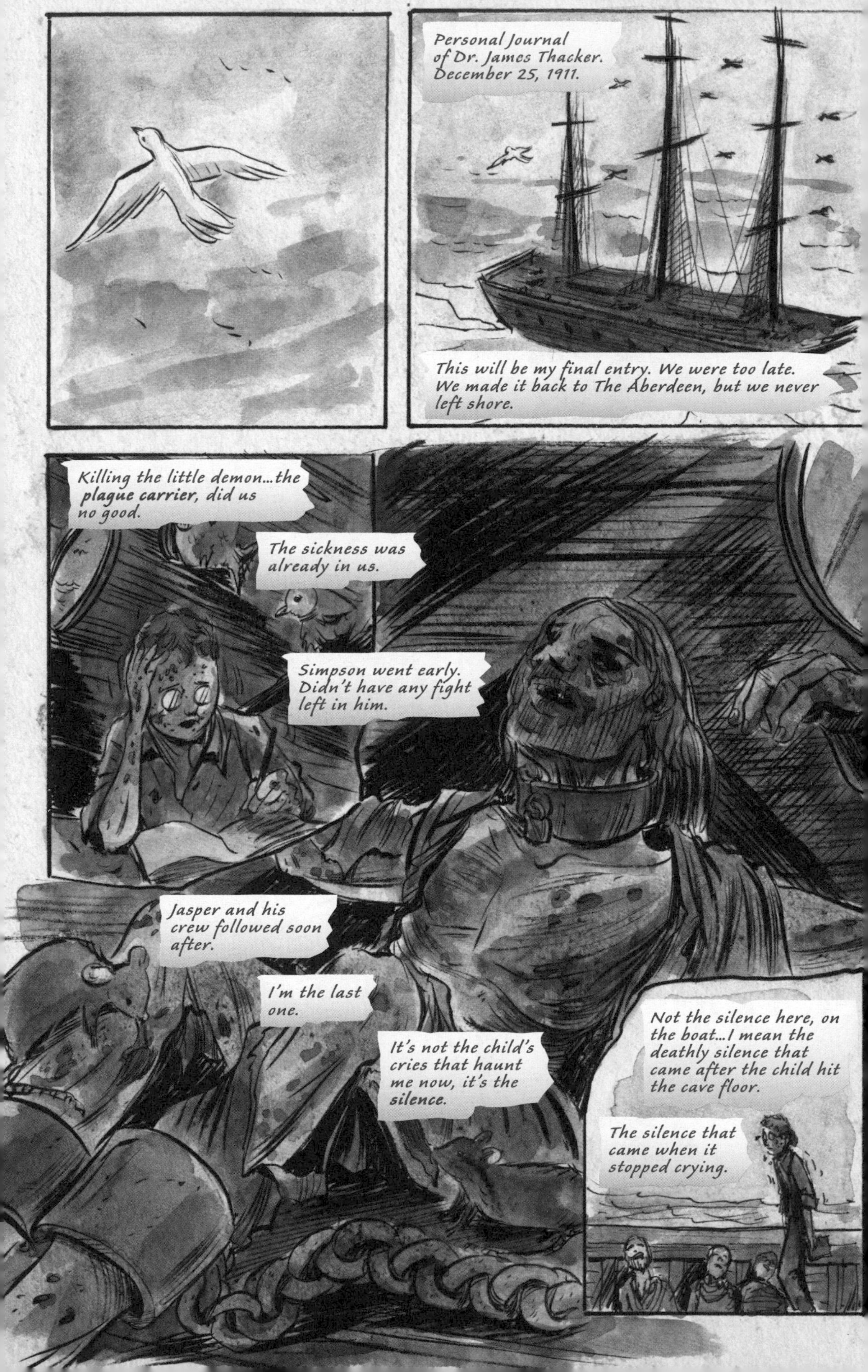
Personal Journal of Dr. James Thacker. December 25, 1911.
This will be my final entry. We were too late. We made it back to The Aberdeen, but we never left shore.
Killing the little demon...the plague carrier, did us no good.
The sickness was already in us.
Simpson went early. Didn't have any fight left in him.
Jasper and his crew followed soon after.
I'm the last one.
It's not the child's cries that haunt me now, it's the silence.
Not the silence here, on the boat...I mean the deathly silence that came after the child hit the cave floor.
The silence that came when it stopped crying.

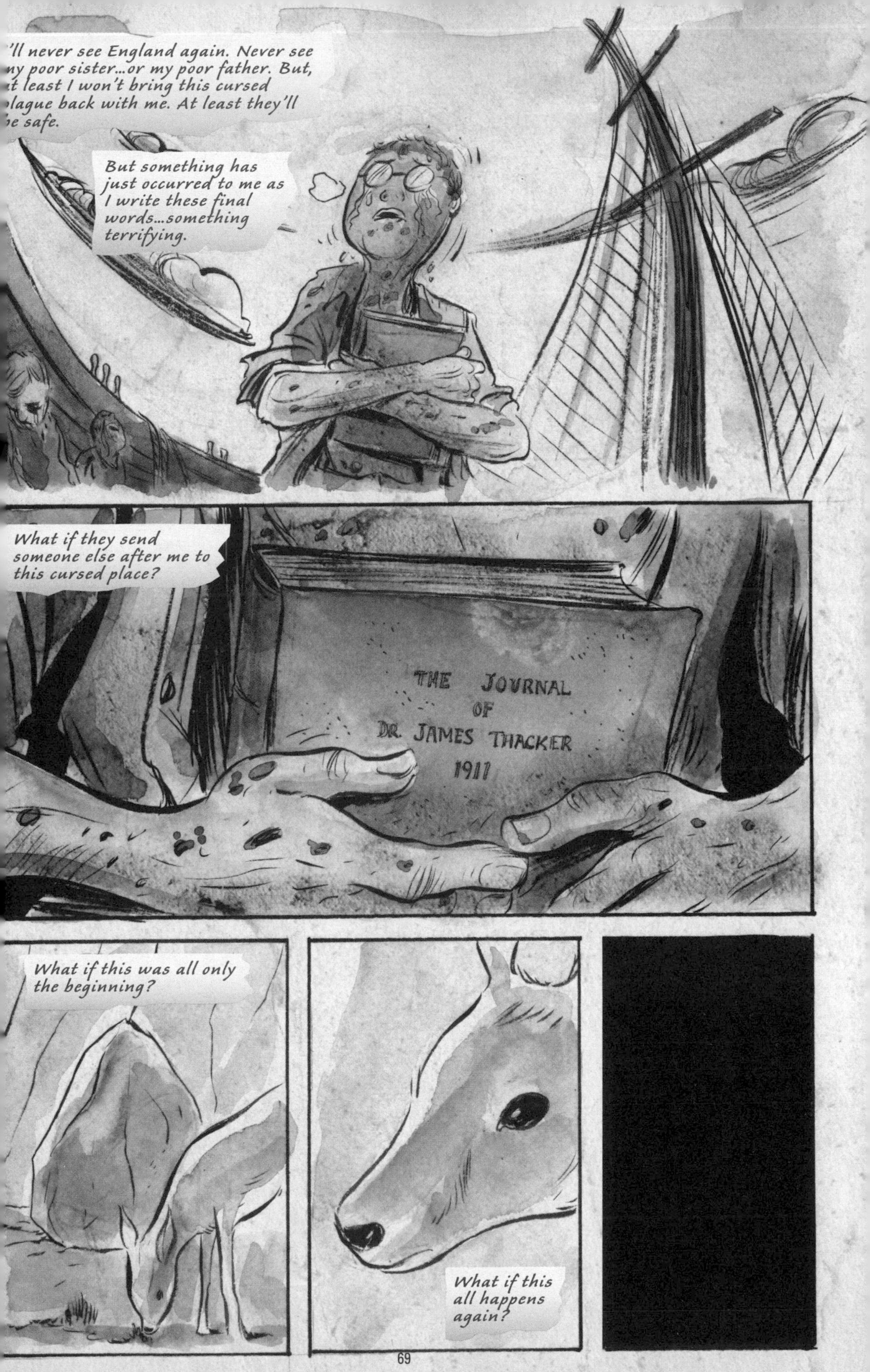
'll never see England again. Never see ny poor sister...or my poor father. But, t least I won't bring this cursed lague back with me. At least they'll e safe.
But something has just occurred to me as I write these final words...something terrifying.
What if they send someone else after me to this cursed place?
THE JOURNAL OF DR. JAMES THACKER 1911
What if this was all only the beginning?
What if this all happens again?

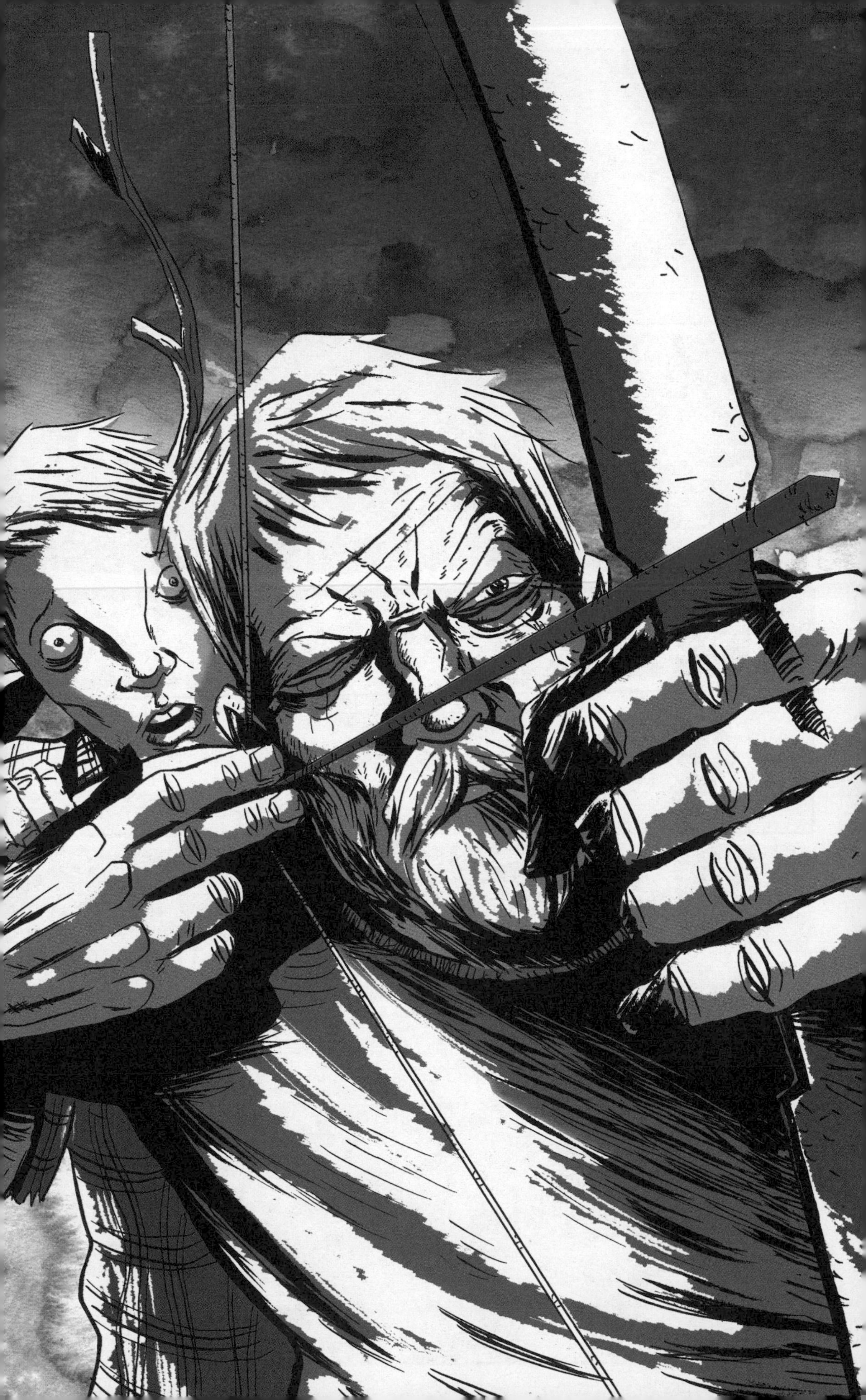

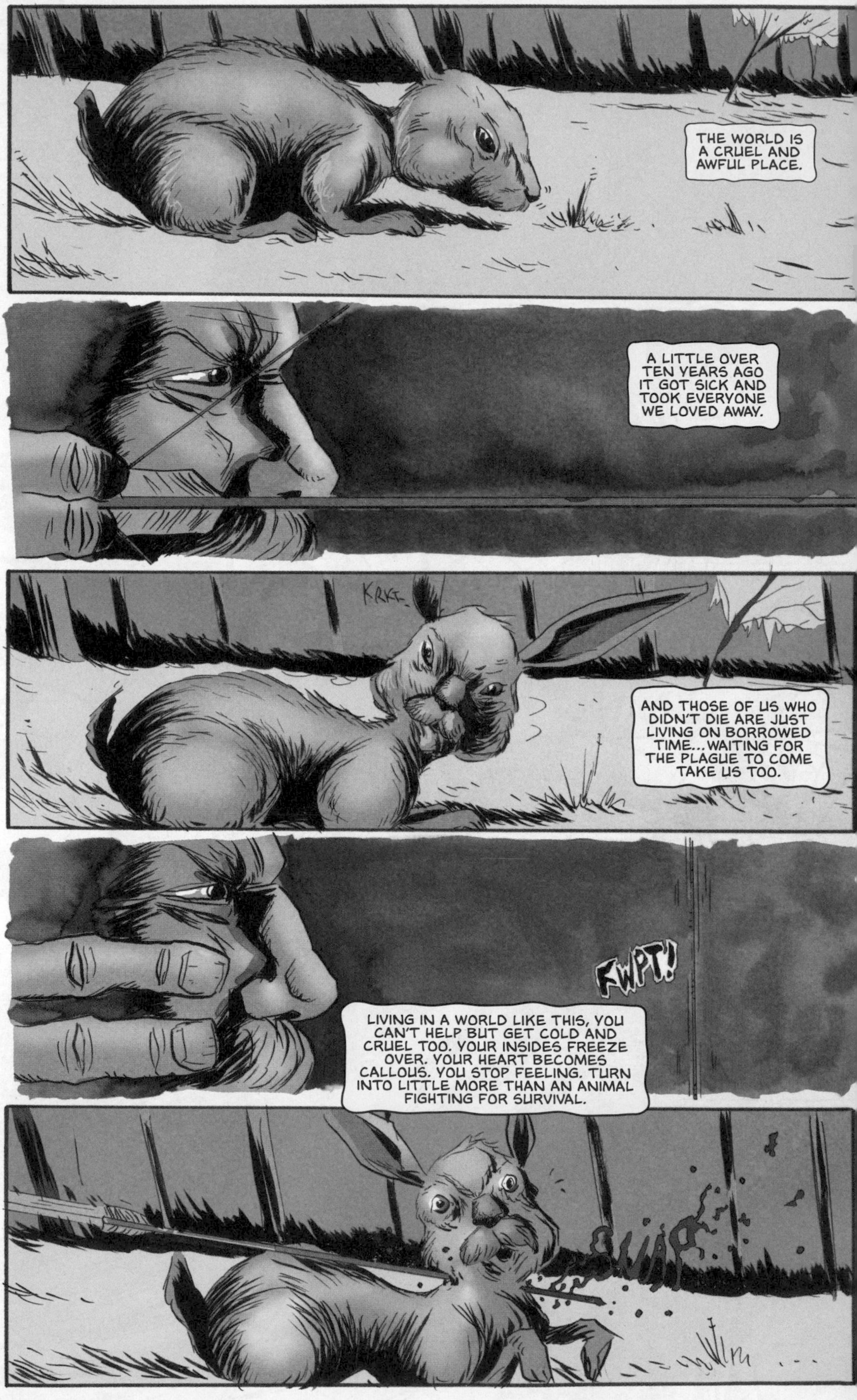
THE WORLD IS A CRUEL AND AWFUL PLACE.
A LITTLE OVER TEN YEARS AGO IT GOT SICK AND TOOK EVERYONE WE LOVED AWAY.
KRKT
AND THOSE OF US WHO DIDN'T DIE ARE JUST LIVING ON BORROWED TIME...WAITING FOR THE PLAGUE TO COME TAKE US TOO.
FWPT!
LIVING IN A WORLD LIKE THIS, YOU CAN'T HELP BUT GET COLD AND CRUEL TOO. YOUR INSIDES FREEZE OVER. YOUR HEART BECOMES CALLOUS. YOU STOP FEELING. TURN INTO LITTLE MORE THAN AN ANIMAL FIGHTING FOR SURVIVAL.
SNAP

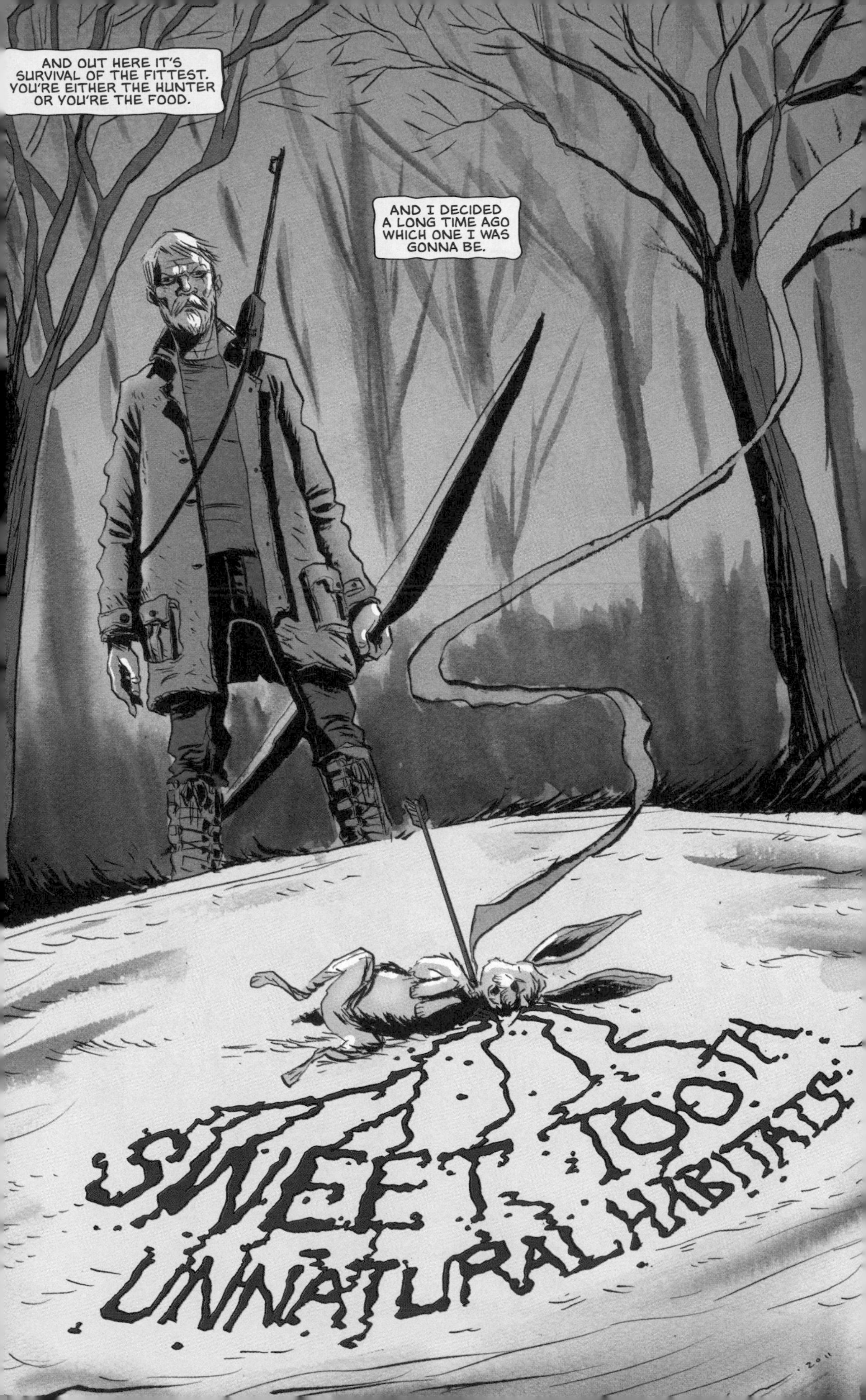
AND OUT HERE IT'S SURVIVAL OF THE FITTEST. YOU'RE EITHER THE HUNTER OR YOU'RE THE FOOD.
AND I DECIDED A LONG TIME AGO WHICH ONE I WAS GONNA BE.
SWEET TOOTH
UNNATURAL HABITATS

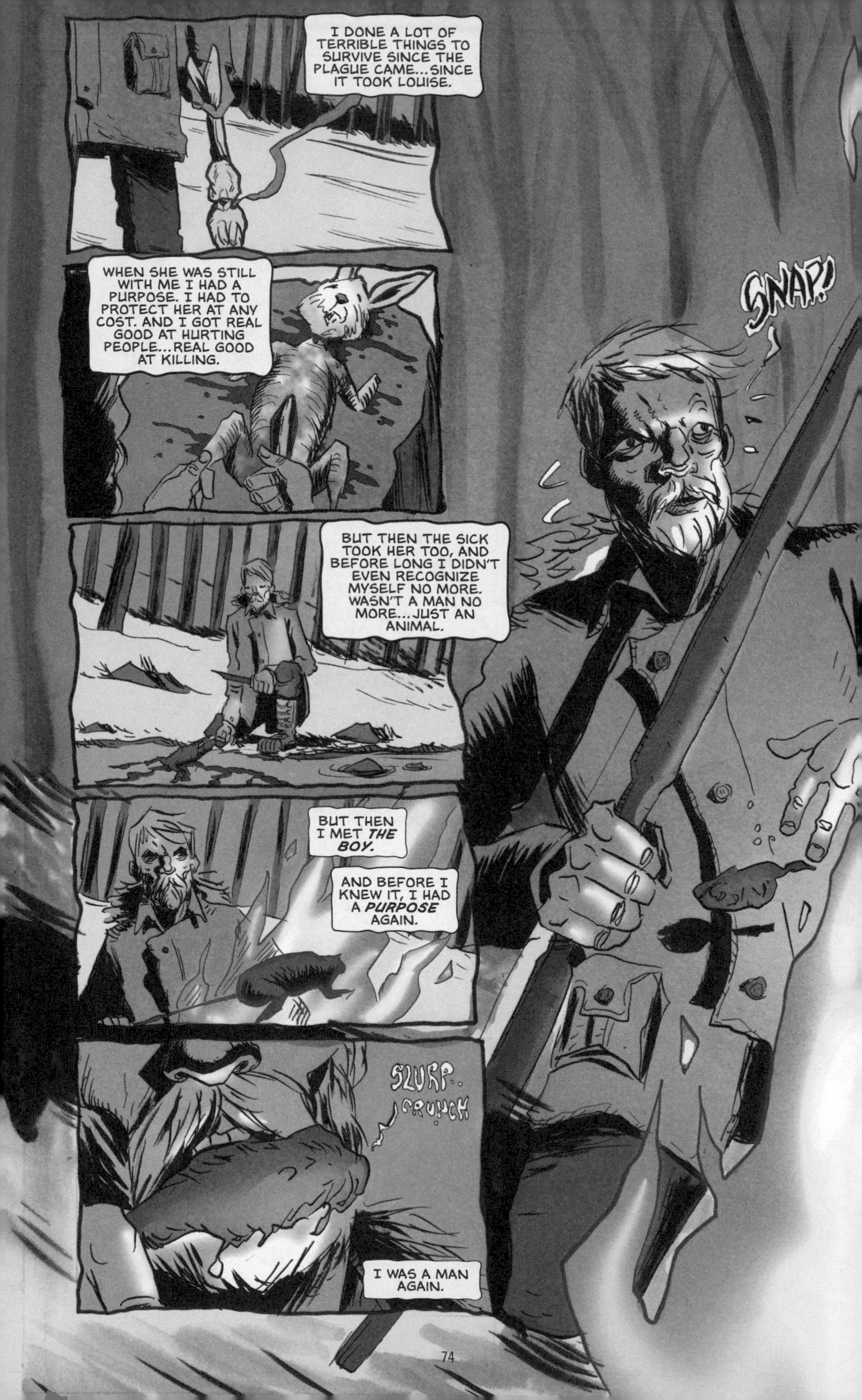
I DONE A LOT OF TERRIBLE THINGS TO SURVIVE SINCE THE PLAGUE CAME... SINCE IT TOOK LOUISE.
WHEN SHE WAS STILL WITH ME I HAD A PURPOSE. I HAD TO PROTECT HER AT ANY COST. AND I GOT REAL GOOD AT HURTING PEOPLE... REAL GOOD AT KILLING.
SNAP!
BUT THEN THE SICK TOOK HER TOO, AND BEFORE LONG I DIDN'T EVEN RECOGNIZE MYSELF NO MORE. WASN'T A MAN NO MORE... JUST AN ANIMAL.
BUT THEN I MET *THE BOY.*
AND BEFORE I KNEW IT, I HAD A *PURPOSE* AGAIN.
SLURP..
CRUNCH
I WAS A MAN AGAIN.

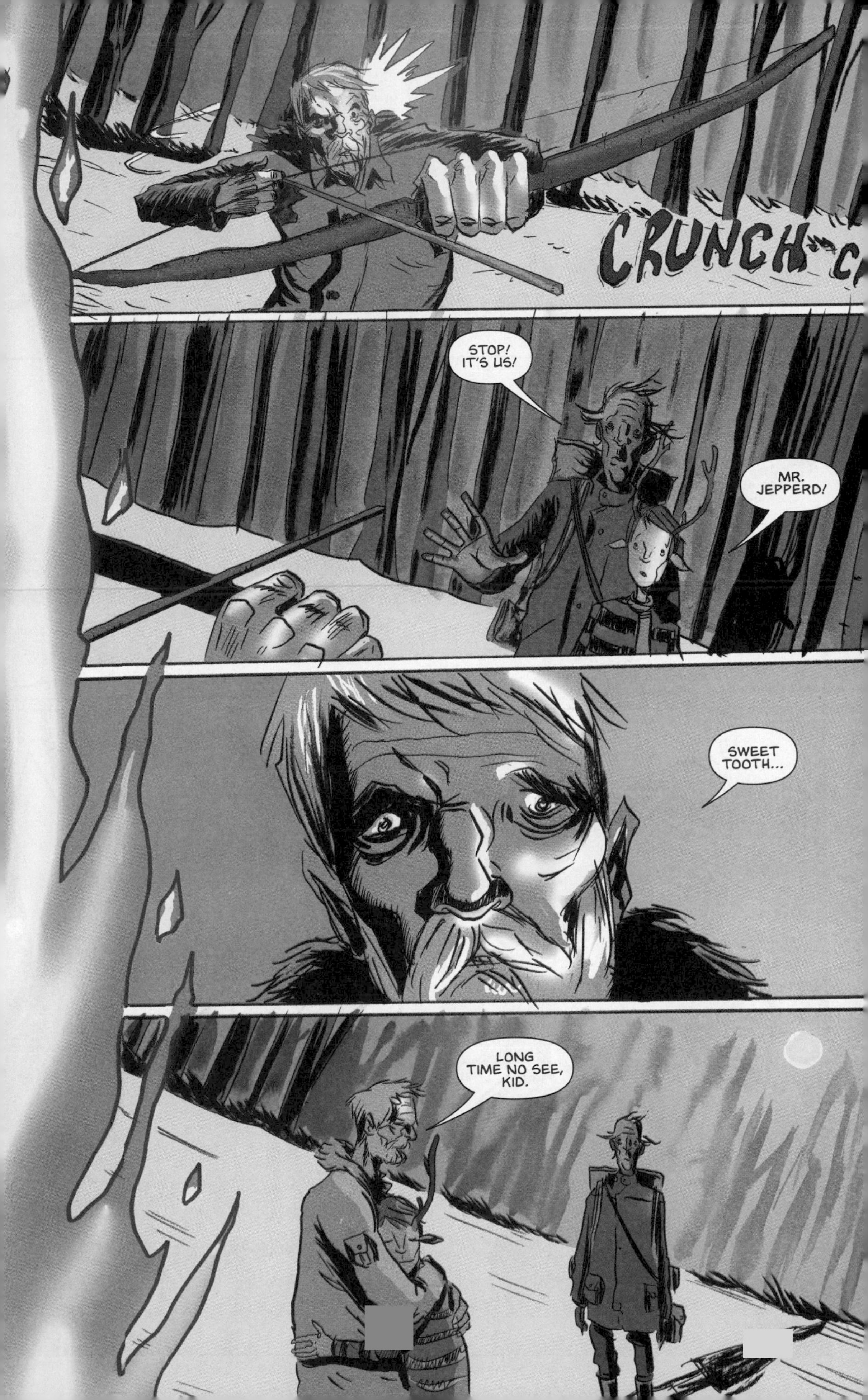
CRUNCH
STOP! IT'S US!
MR. JEPPERD!
SWEET TOOTH...
LONG TIME NO SEE, KID.

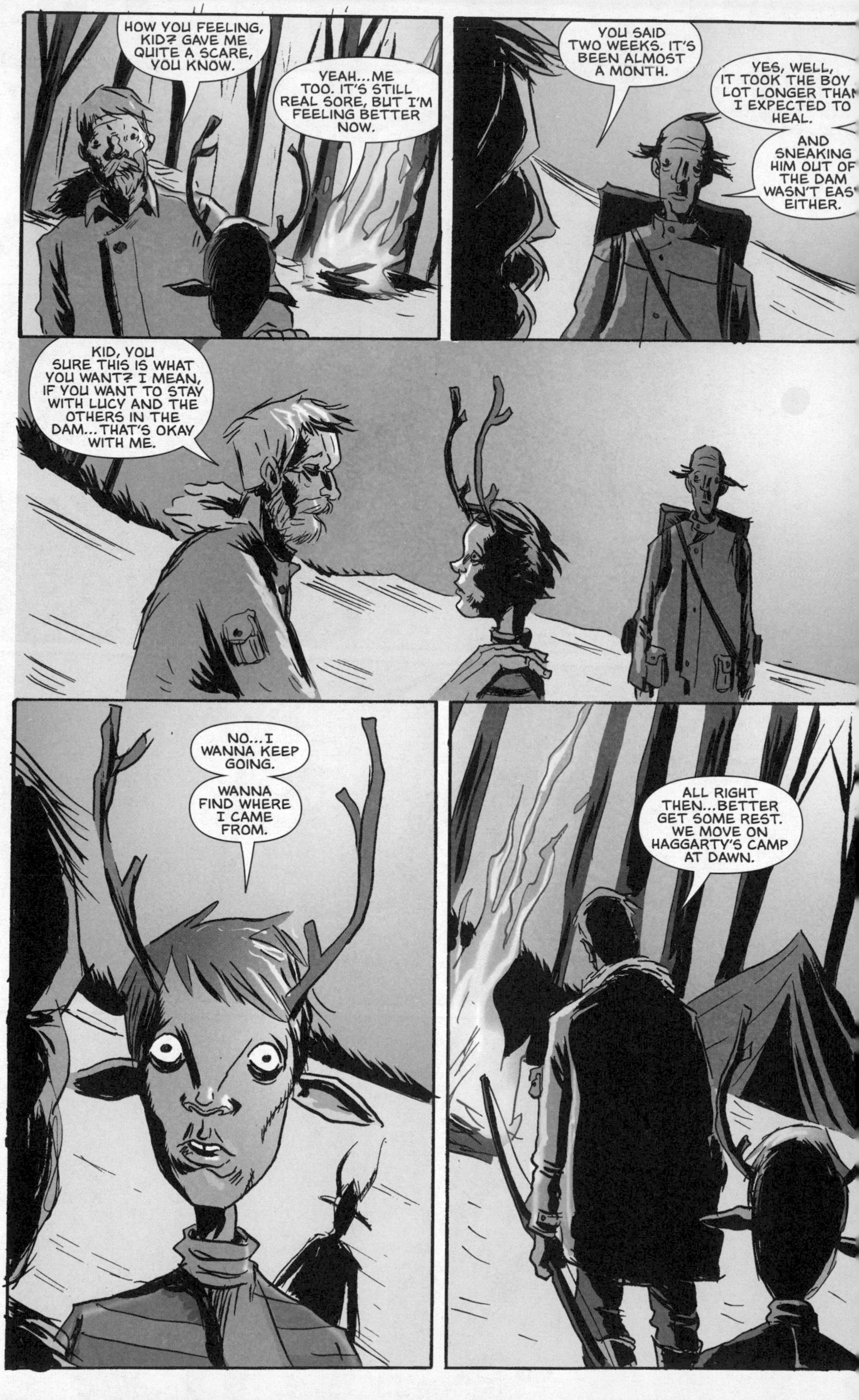
HOW YOU FEELING, KID? GAVE ME QUITE A SCARE, YOU KNOW.
YEAH... ME TOO. IT'S STILL REAL SORE, BUT I'M FEELING BETTER NOW.
YOU SAID TWO WEEKS. IT'S BEEN ALMOST A MONTH.
YES, WELL, IT TOOK THE BOY LOT LONGER THAN I EXPECTED TO HEAL.
AND SNEAKING HIM OUT OF THE DAM WASN'T EAS EITHER.
KID, YOU SURE THIS IS WHAT YOU WANT? I MEAN, IF YOU WANT TO STAY WITH LUCY AND THE OTHERS IN THE DAM... THAT'S OKAY WITH ME.
NO... I WANNA KEEP GOING.
WANNA FIND WHERE I CAME FROM.
ALL RIGHT THEN... BETTER GET SOME REST. WE MOVE ON HAGGARTY'S CAMP AT DAWN.

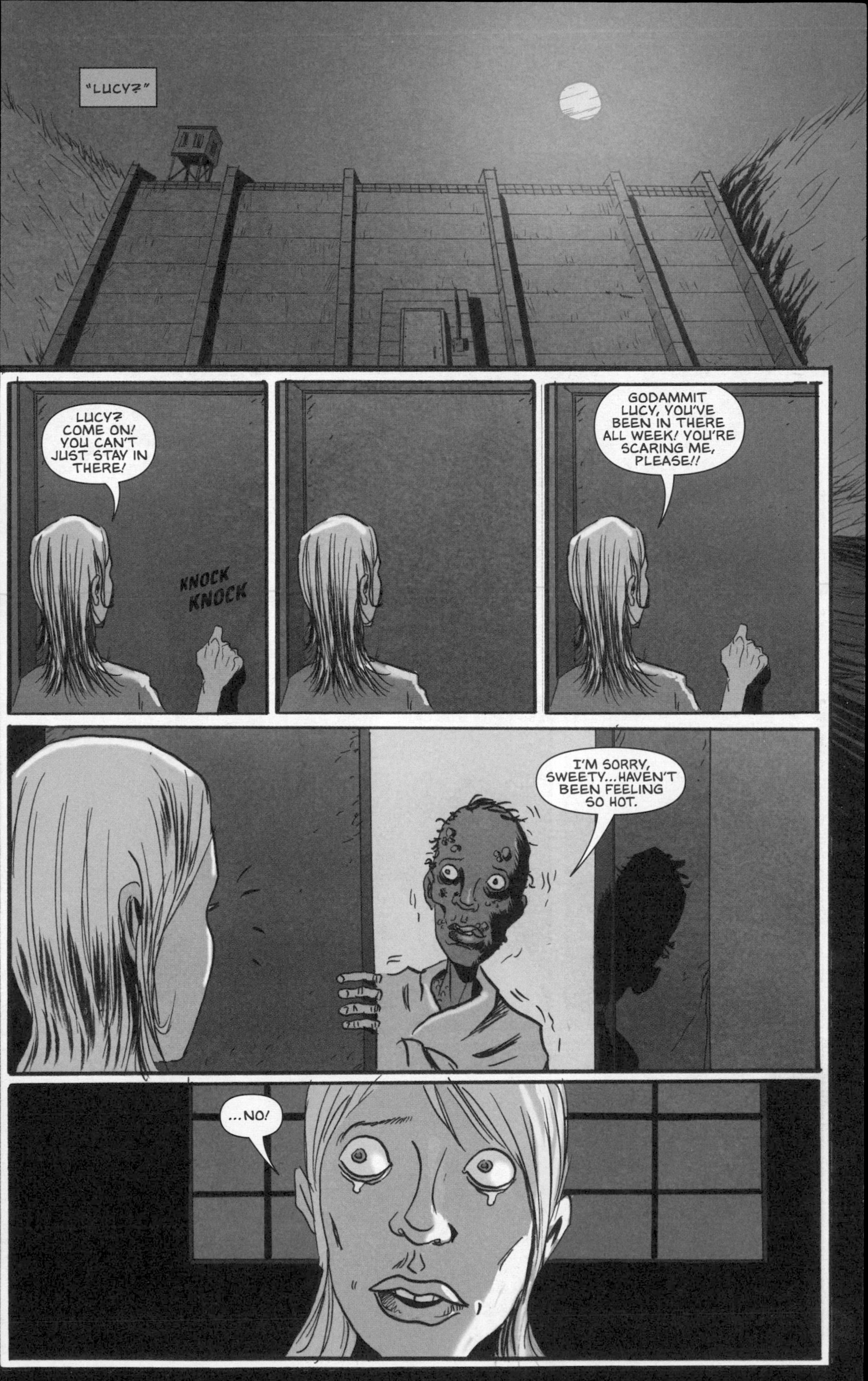
"LUCY?"
LUCY? COME ON! YOU CAN'T JUST STAY IN THERE!
KNOCK KNOCK
GODAMMIT LUCY, YOU'VE BEEN IN THERE ALL WEEK! YOU'RE SCARING ME, PLEASE!!
I'M SORRY, SWEETY...HAVEN'T BEEN FEELING SO HOT.
...NO!

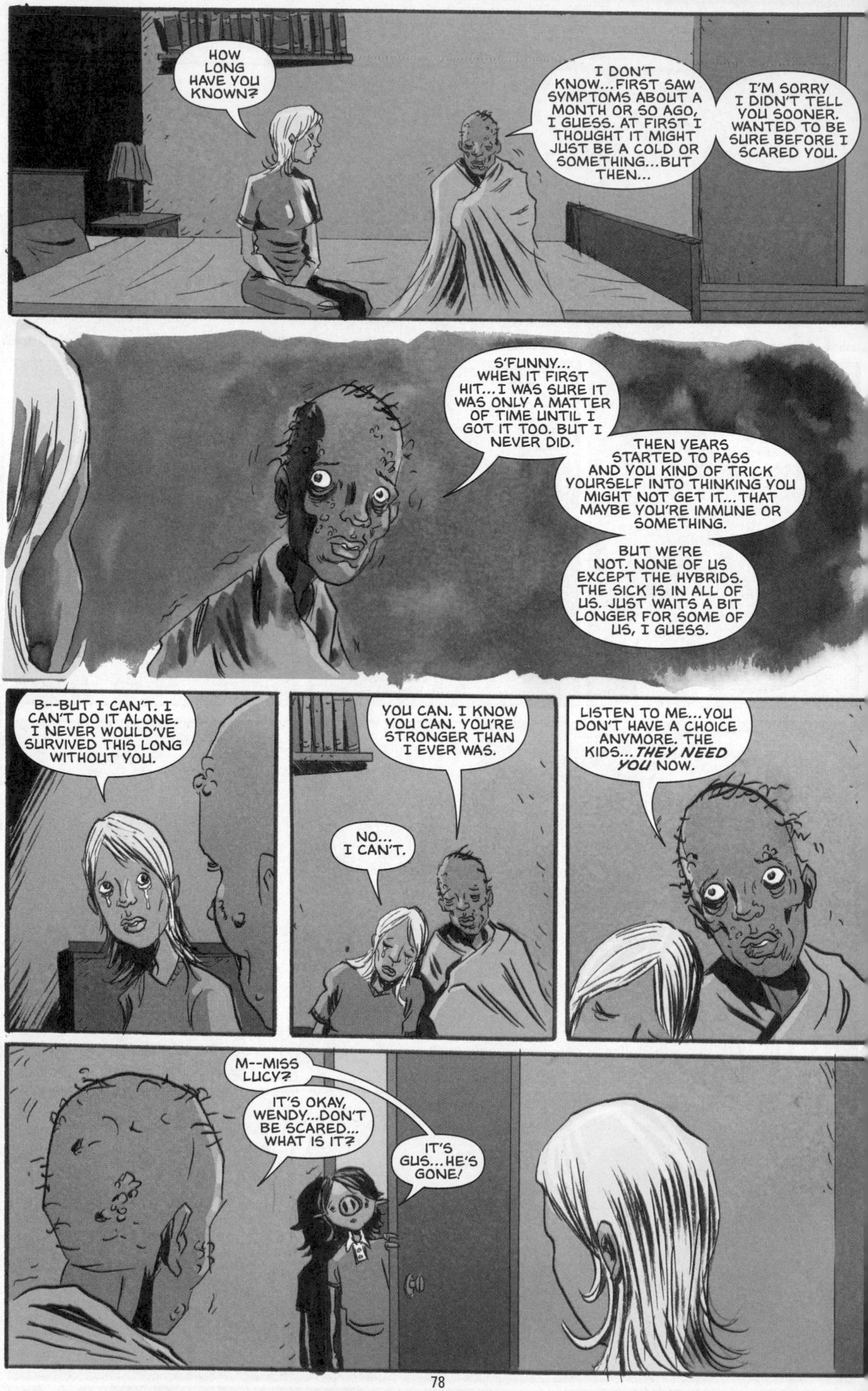
HOW LONG HAVE YOU KNOWN?
I DON'T KNOW...FIRST SAW SYMPTOMS ABOUT A MONTH OR SO AGO, I GUESS. AT FIRST I THOUGHT IT MIGHT JUST BE A COLD OR SOMETHING...BUT THEN...
I'M SORRY I DIDN'T TELL YOU SOONER. WANTED TO BE SURE BEFORE I SCARED YOU.
S'FUNNY... WHEN IT FIRST HIT...I WAS SURE IT WAS ONLY A MATTER OF TIME UNTIL I GOT IT TOO. BUT I NEVER DID.
THEN YEARS STARTED TO PASS AND YOU KIND OF TRICK YOURSELF INTO THINKING YOU MIGHT NOT GET IT...THAT MAYBE YOU'RE IMMUNE OR SOMETHING.
BUT WE'RE NOT. NONE OF US EXCEPT THE HYBRIDS. THE SICK IS IN ALL OF US. JUST WAITS A BIT LONGER FOR SOME OF US, I GUESS.
B--BUT I CAN'T. I CAN'T DO IT ALONE. I NEVER WOULD'VE SURVIVED THIS LONG WITHOUT YOU.
YOU CAN. I KNOW YOU CAN. YOU'RE STRONGER THAN I EVER WAS.
NO... I CAN'T.
LISTEN TO ME...YOU DON'T HAVE A CHOICE ANYMORE. THE KIDS...THEY NEED YOU NOW.
M--MISS LUCY?
IT'S OKAY, WENDY...DON'T BE SCARED... WHAT IS IT?
IT'S GUS...HE'S GONE!

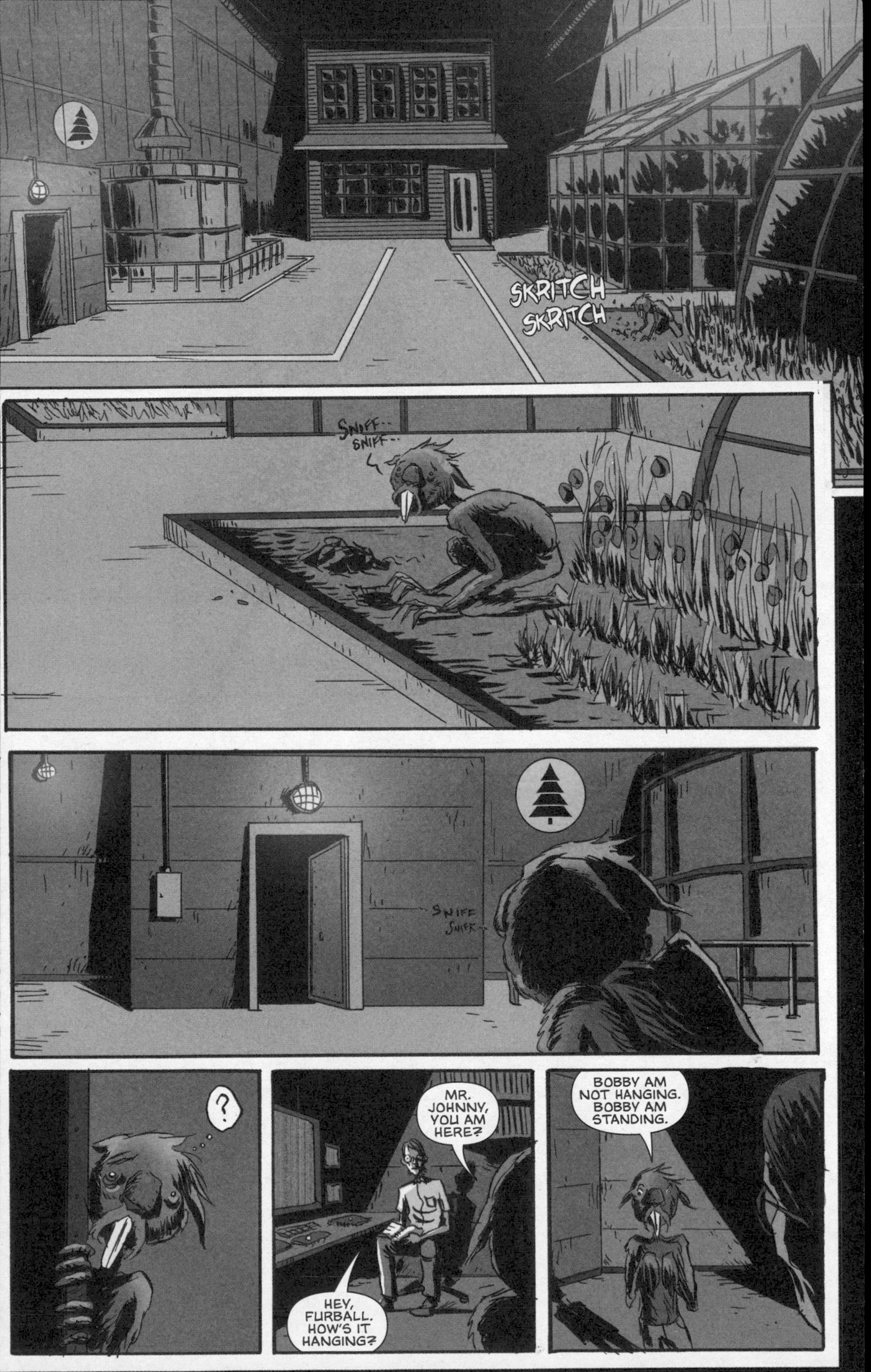
SKRITCH
SKRITCH
SNIFF..
SNIFF..
SNIFF
SNIFF..
?
MR. JOHNNY, YOU AM HERE?
HEY, FURBALL. HOW'S IT HANGING?
BOBBY AM NOT HANGING. BOBBY AM STANDING.

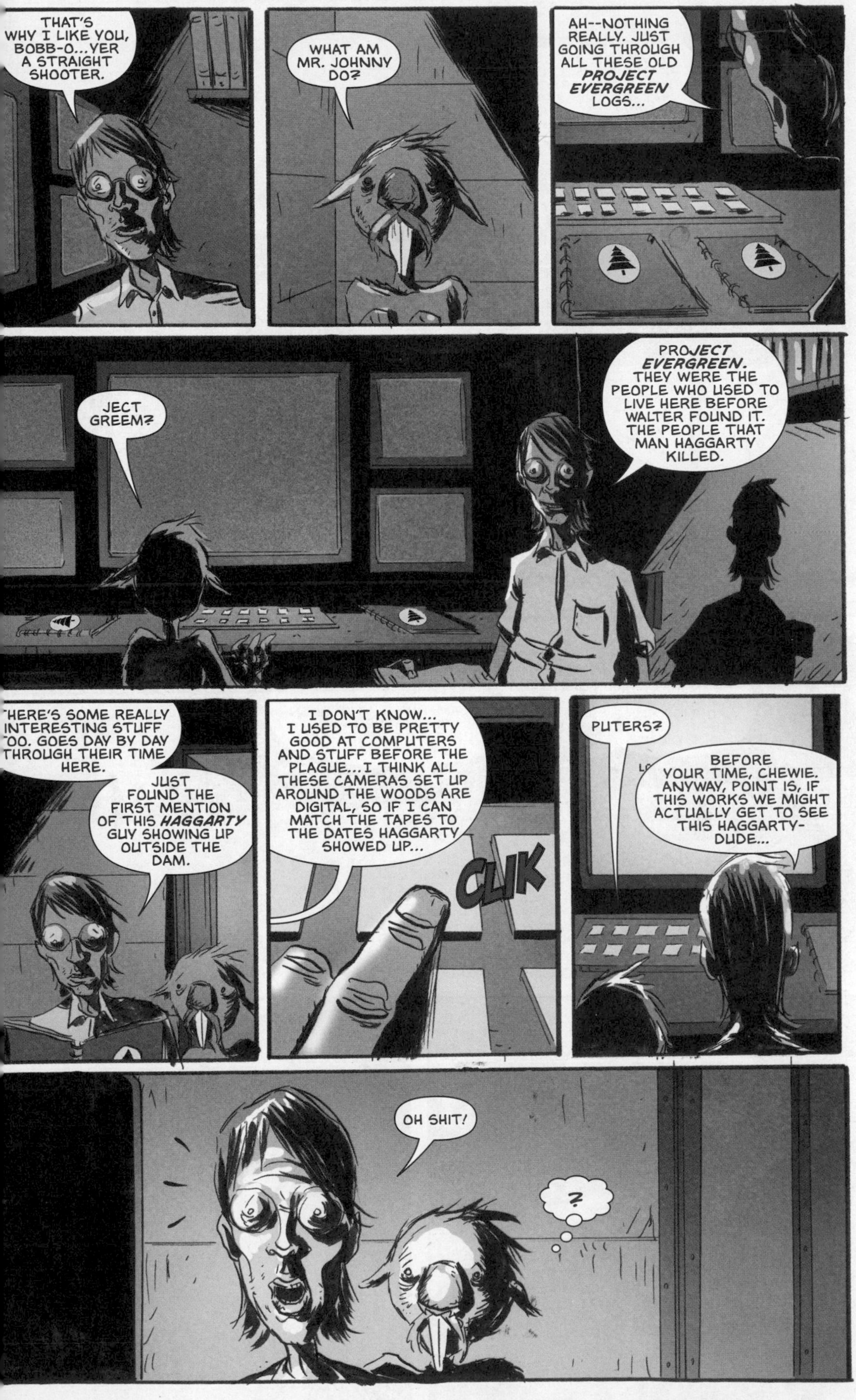
THAT'S WHY I LIKE YOU, BOBB-O...YER A STRAIGHT SHOOTER.
WHAT AM MR. JOHNNY DO?
AH--NOTHING REALLY. JUST GOING THROUGH ALL THESE OLD *PROJECT EVERGREEN* LOGS...
JECT GREEM?
PROJECT *EVERGREEN.* THEY WERE THE PEOPLE WHO USED TO LIVE HERE BEFORE WALTER FOUND IT. THE PEOPLE THAT MAN HAGGARTY KILLED.
THERE'S SOME REALLY INTERESTING STUFF TOO. GOES DAY BY DAY THROUGH THEIR TIME HERE.
JUST FOUND THE FIRST MENTION OF THIS *HAGGARTY* GUY SHOWING UP OUTSIDE THE DAM.
I DON'T KNOW... I USED TO BE PRETTY GOOD AT COMPUTERS AND STUFF BEFORE THE PLAGUE... I THINK ALL THESE CAMERAS SET UP AROUND THE WOODS ARE DIGITAL, SO IF I CAN MATCH THE TAPES TO THE DATES HAGGARTY SHOWED UP...
CLIK
PUTERS?
BEFORE YOUR TIME, CHEWIE. ANYWAY, POINT IS, IF THIS WORKS WE MIGHT ACTUALLY GET TO SEE THIS HAGGARTY-DUDE...
OH SHIT!
?

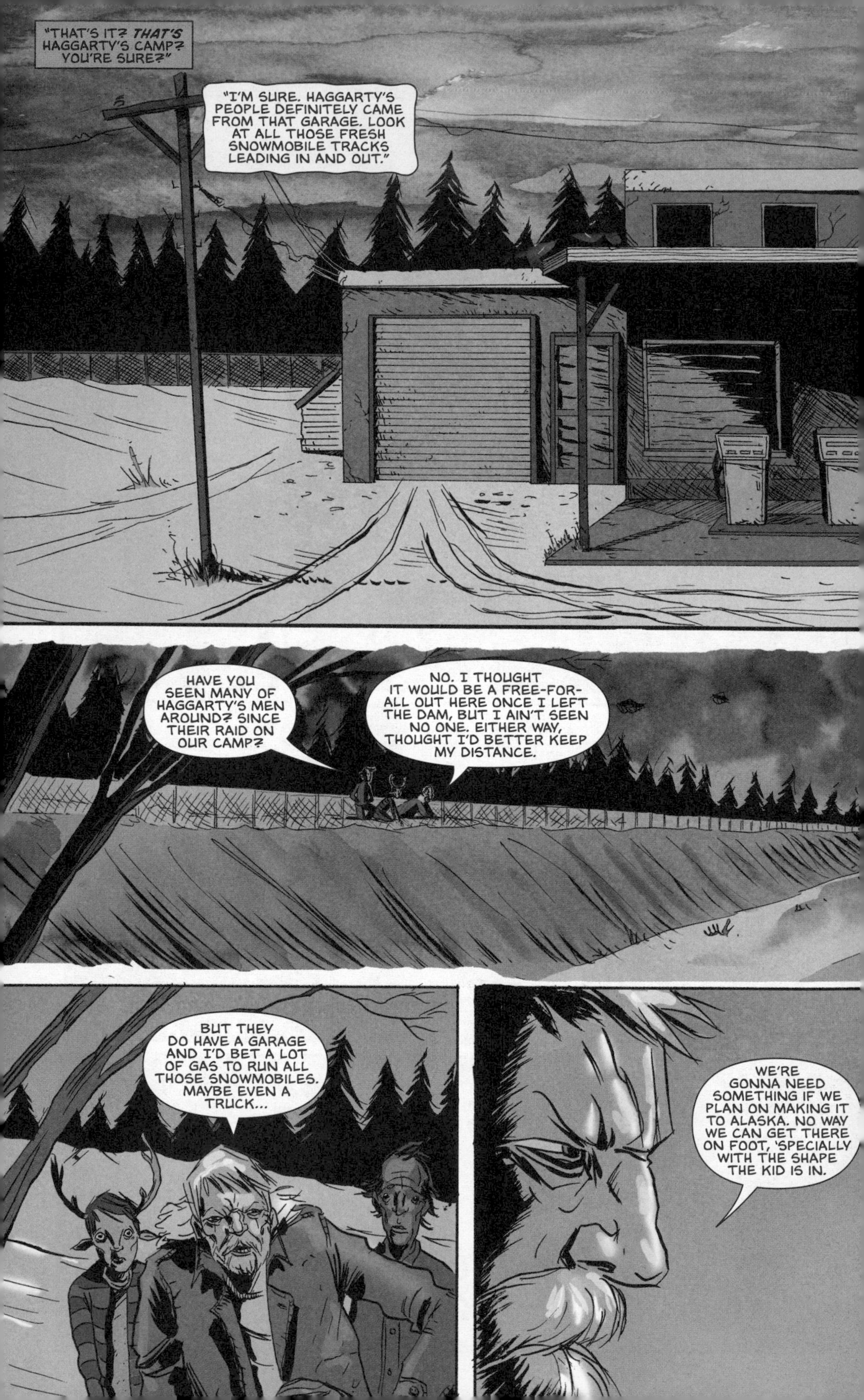
"THAT'S IT? THAT'S HAGGARTY'S CAMP? YOU'RE SURE?"
"I'M SURE. HAGGARTY'S PEOPLE DEFINITELY CAME FROM THAT GARAGE. LOOK AT ALL THOSE FRESH SNOWMOBILE TRACKS LEADING IN AND OUT."
HAVE YOU SEEN MANY OF HAGGARTY'S MEN AROUND? SINCE THEIR RAID ON OUR CAMP?
NO. I THOUGHT IT WOULD BE A FREE-FOR-ALL OUT HERE ONCE I LEFT THE DAM, BUT I AIN'T SEEN NO ONE. EITHER WAY, THOUGHT I'D BETTER KEEP MY DISTANCE.
BUT THEY DO HAVE A GARAGE AND I'D BET A LOT OF GAS TO RUN ALL THOSE SNOWMOBILES. MAYBE EVEN A TRUCK...
WE'RE GONNA NEED SOMETHING IF WE PLAN ON MAKING IT TO ALASKA. NO WAY WE CAN GET THERE ON FOOT, 'SPECIALLY WITH THE SHAPE THE KID IS IN.

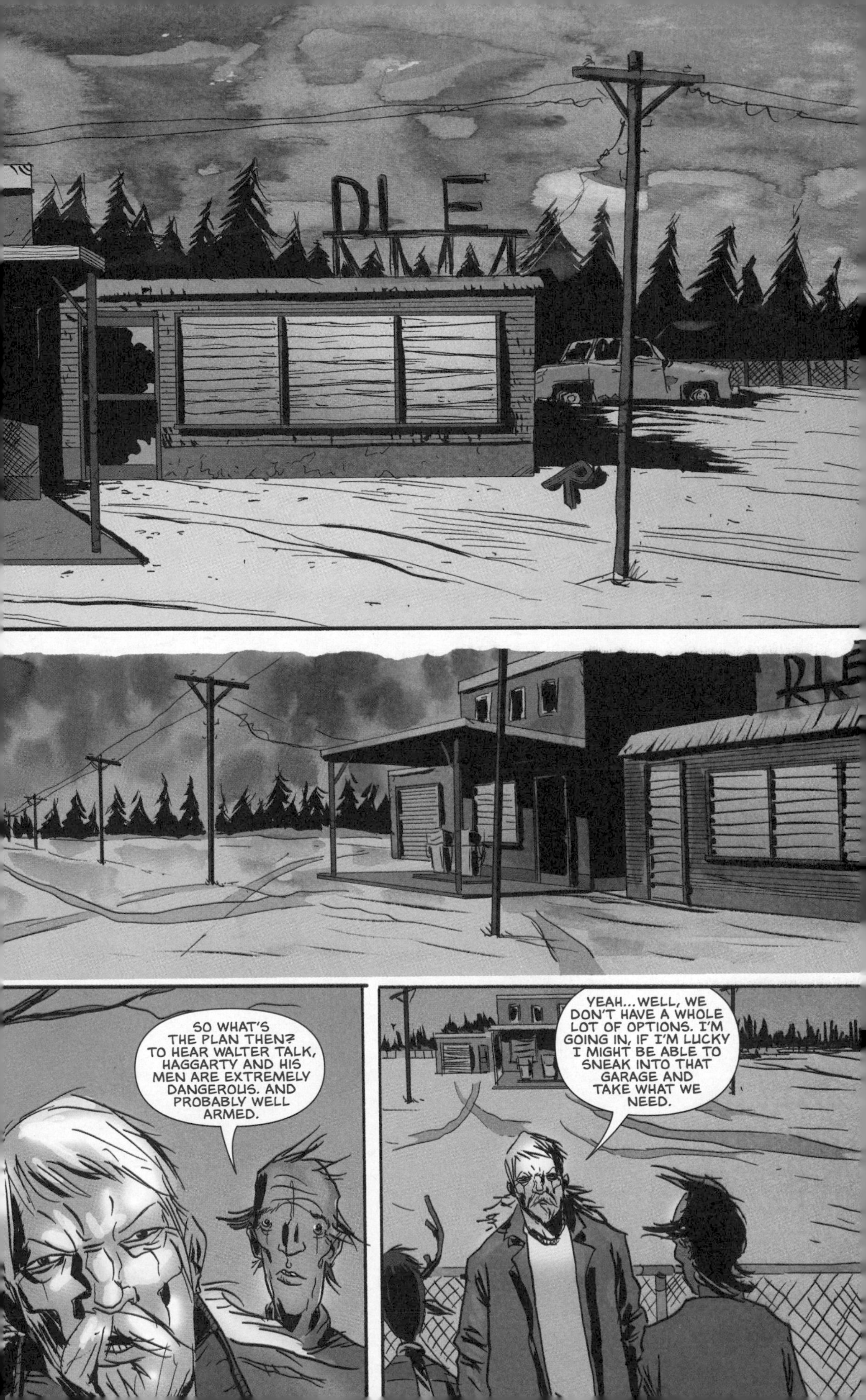
DLE
SO WHAT'S THE PLAN THEN? TO HEAR WALTER TALK, HAGGARTY AND HIS MEN ARE EXTREMELY DANGEROUS. AND PROBABLY WELL ARMED.
YEAH... WELL, WE DON'T HAVE A WHOLE LOT OF OPTIONS. I'M GOING IN, IF I'M LUCKY I MIGHT BE ABLE TO SNEAK INTO THAT GARAGE AND TAKE WHAT WE NEED.

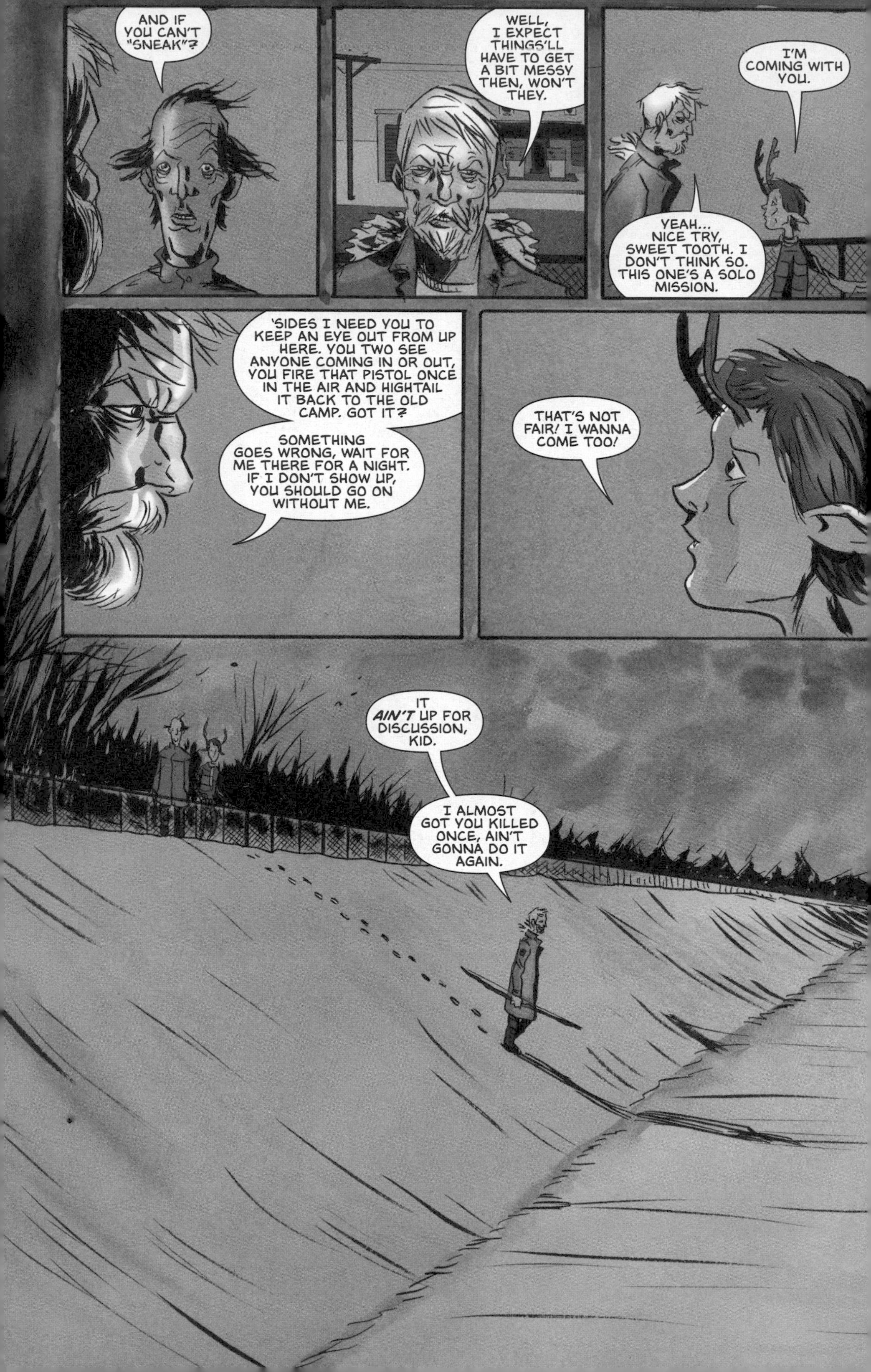
AND IF YOU CAN'T "SNEAK"?
WELL, I EXPECT THINGS'LL HAVE TO GET A BIT MESSY THEN, WON'T THEY.
I'M COMING WITH YOU.
YEAH... NICE TRY, SWEET TOOTH. I DON'T THINK SO. THIS ONE'S A SOLO MISSION.
'SIDES I NEED YOU TO KEEP AN EYE OUT FROM UP HERE. YOU TWO SEE ANYONE COMING IN OR OUT, YOU FIRE THAT PISTOL ONCE IN THE AIR AND HIGHTAIL IT BACK TO THE OLD CAMP. GOT IT?
SOMETHING GOES WRONG, WAIT FOR ME THERE FOR A NIGHT. IF I DON'T SHOW UP, YOU SHOULD GO ON WITHOUT ME.
THAT'S NOT FAIR! I WANNA COME TOO!
IT *AIN'T* UP FOR DISCUSSION, KID.
I ALMOST GOT YOU KILLED ONCE, AIN'T GONNA DO IT AGAIN.

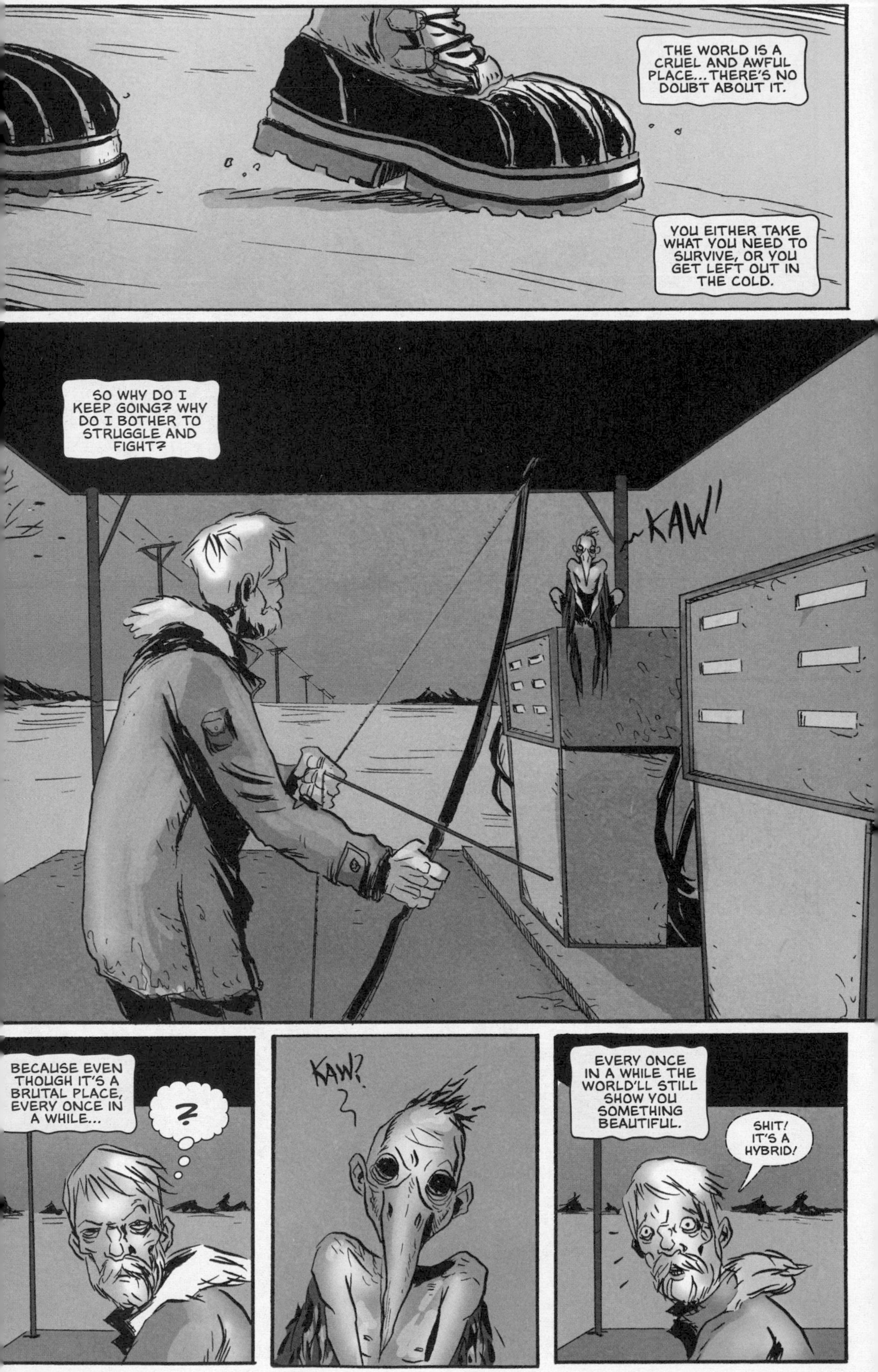
THE WORLD IS A CRUEL AND AWFUL PLACE...THERE'S NO DOUBT ABOUT IT.
YOU EITHER TAKE WHAT YOU NEED TO SURVIVE, OR YOU GET LEFT OUT IN THE COLD.
SO WHY DO I KEEP GOING? WHY DO I BOTHER TO STRUGGLE AND FIGHT?
KAW
BECAUSE EVEN THOUGH IT'S A BRUTAL PLACE, EVERY ONCE IN A WHILE...
?
KAW?
EVERY ONCE IN A WHILE THE WORLD'LL STILL SHOW YOU SOMETHING BEAUTIFUL.
SHIT! IT'S A HYBRID!

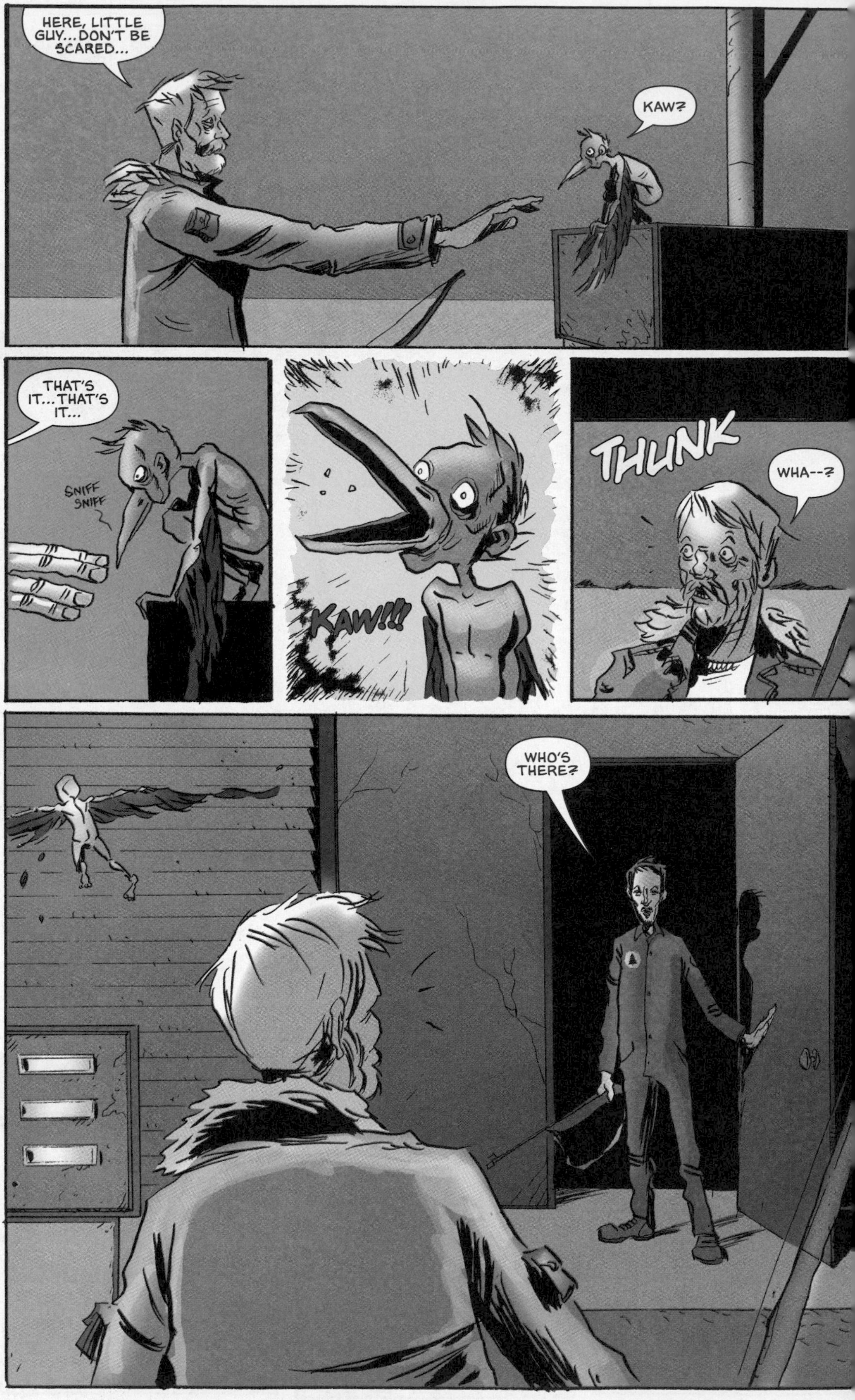
HERE, LITTLE GUY... DON'T BE SCARED...
KAW?
THAT'S IT... THAT'S IT...
SNIFF SNIFF
KAW!!!
THUNK
WHA--?
WHO'S THERE?

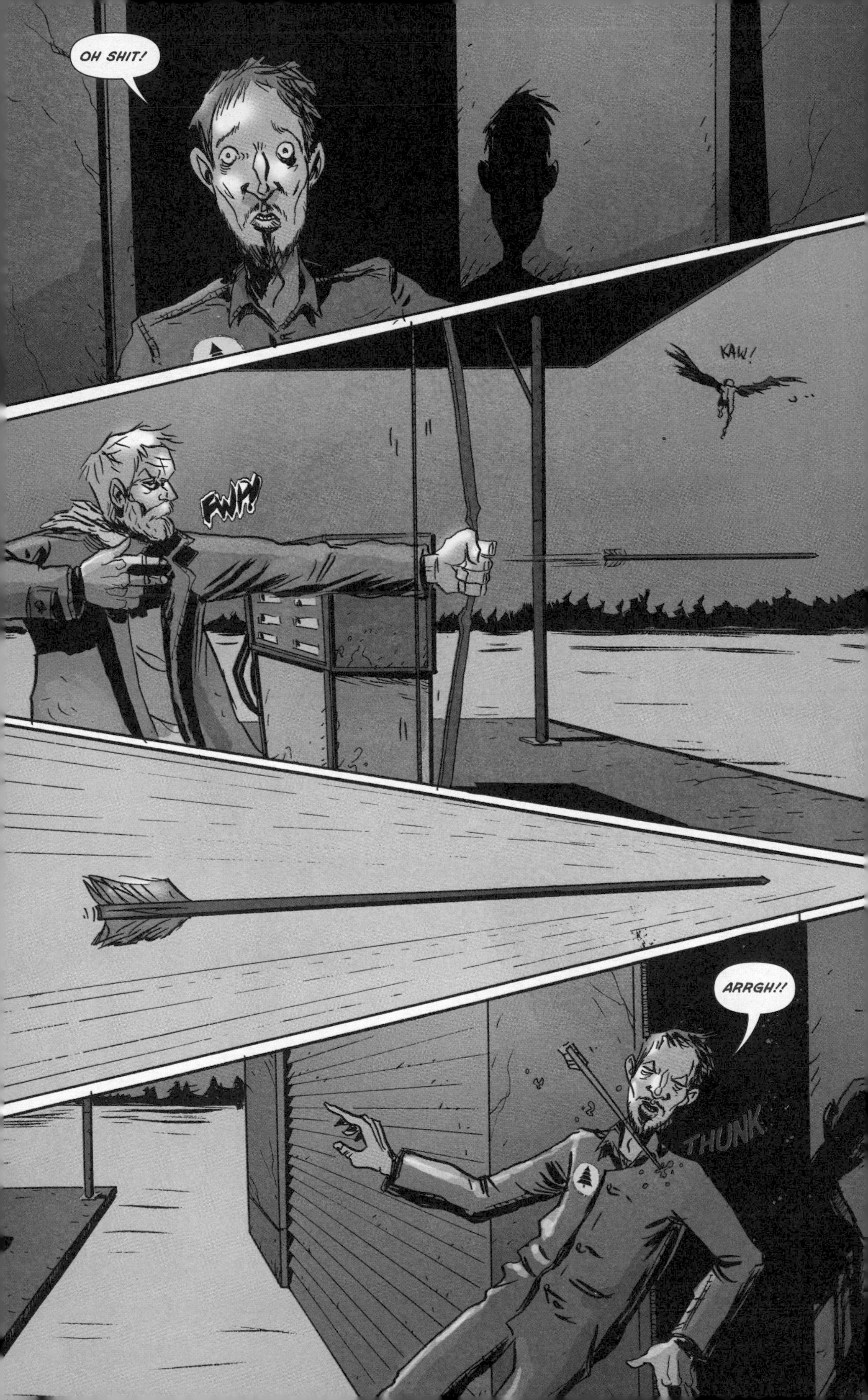
OH SHIT!
KAW!
FWIP!
ARRGH!!
THUNK

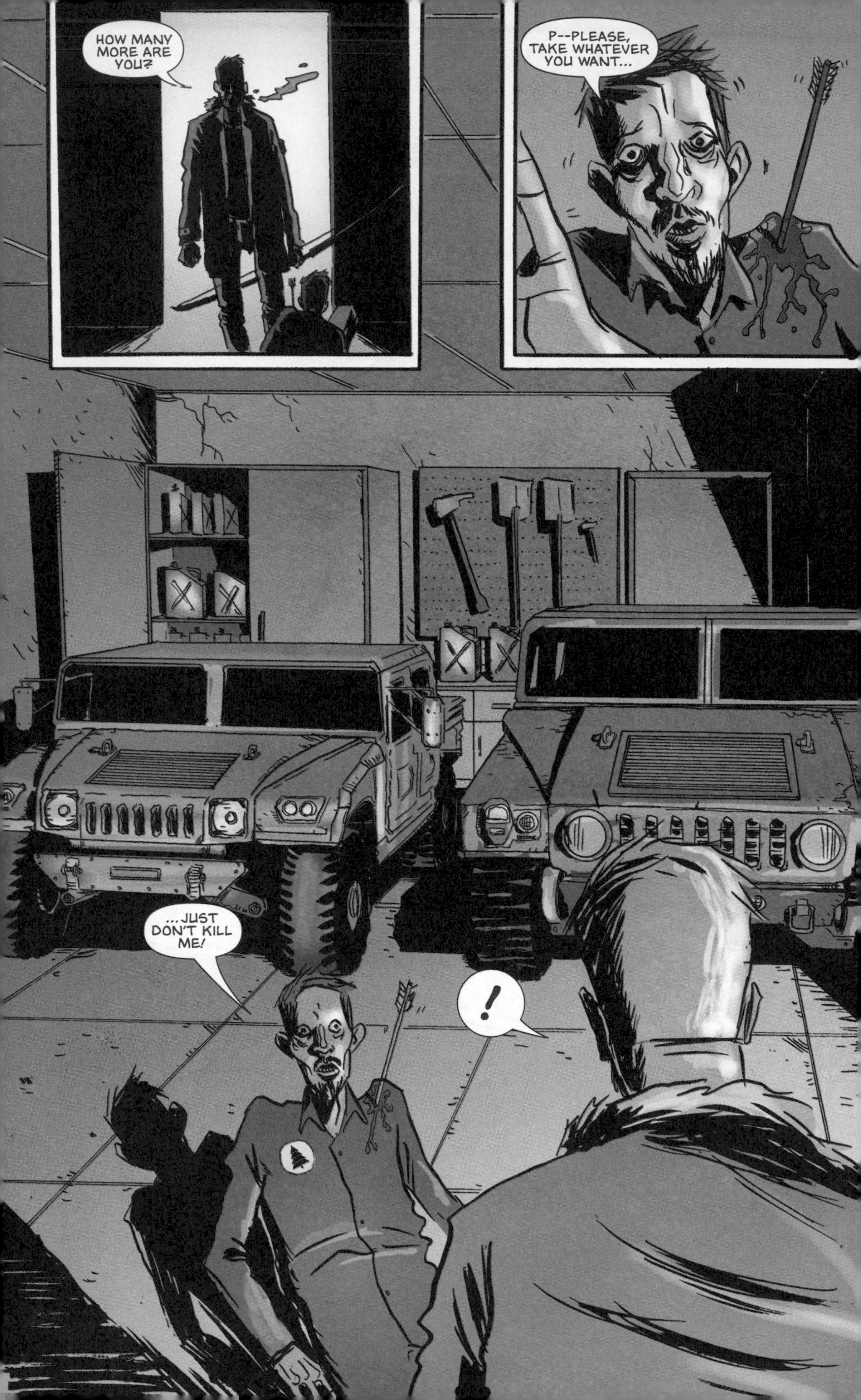
HOW MANY MORE ARE YOU?
P--PLEASE, TAKE WHATEVER YOU WANT...
...JUST DON'T KILL ME!
!

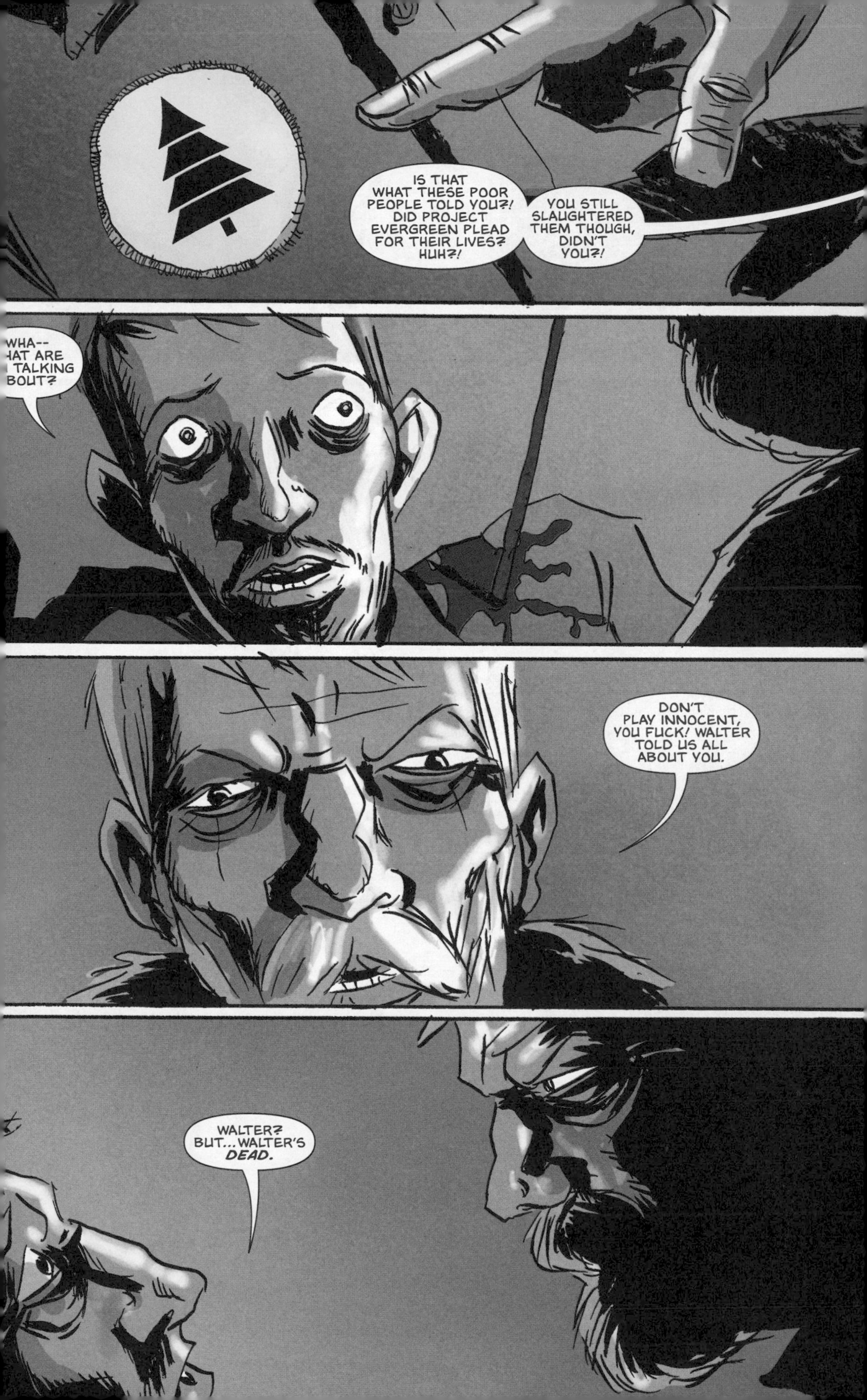
IS THAT WHAT THESE POOR PEOPLE TOLD YOU?! DID PROJECT EVERGREEN PLEAD FOR THEIR LIVES? HUH?!
YOU STILL SLAUGHTERED THEM THOUGH, DIDN'T YOU?!
WHA-- HAT ARE TALKING BOUT?
DON'T PLAY INNOCENT, YOU FUCK! WALTER TOLD US ALL ABOUT YOU.
WALTER? BUT... WALTER'S *DEAD.*

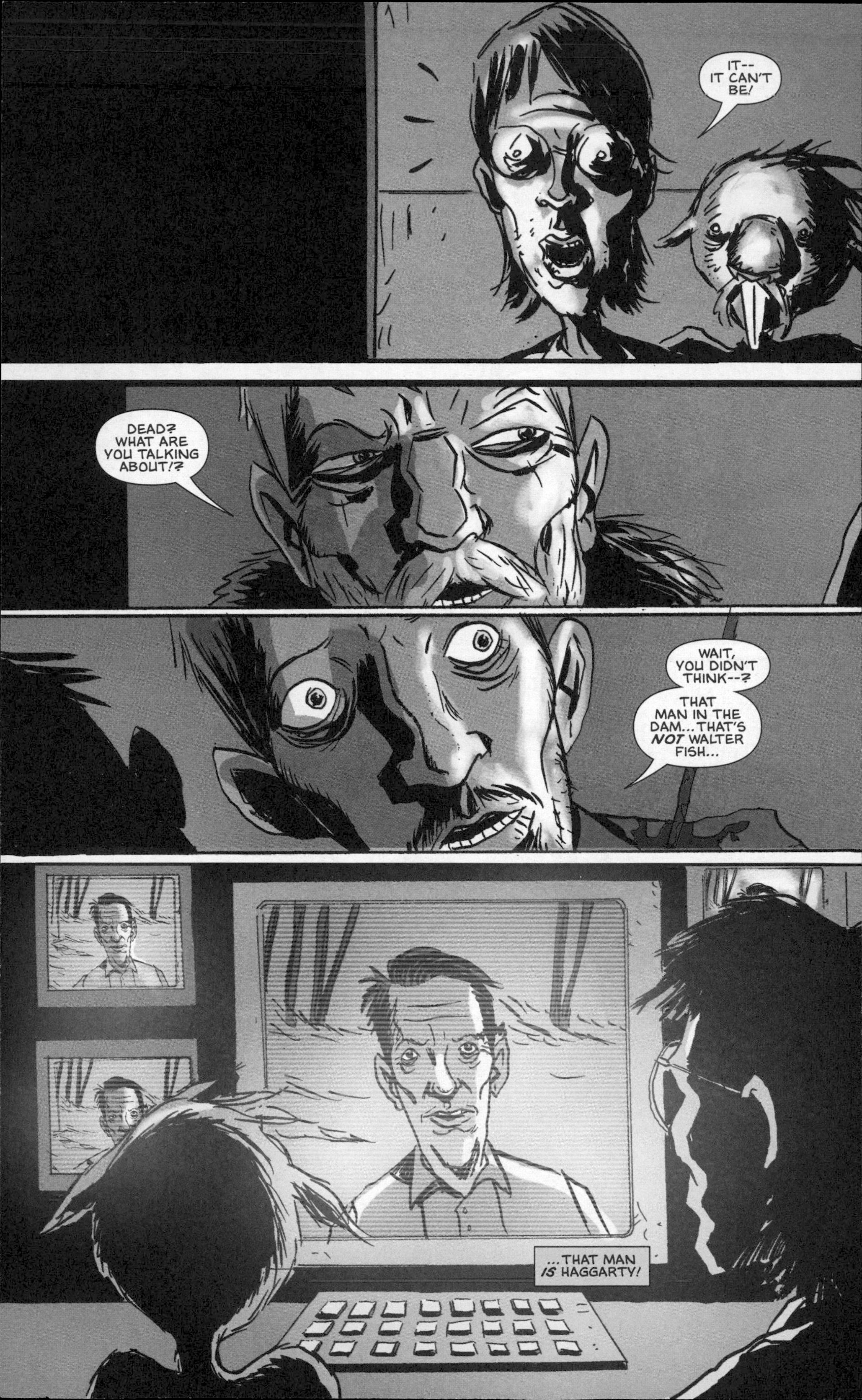
IT--
IT CAN'T
BE!
DEAD? WHAT ARE YOU TALKING ABOUT!?
WAIT, YOU DIDN'T THINK--?
THAT MAN IN THE DAM... THAT'S *NOT* WALTER FISH...
...THAT MAN *IS* HAGGARTY!

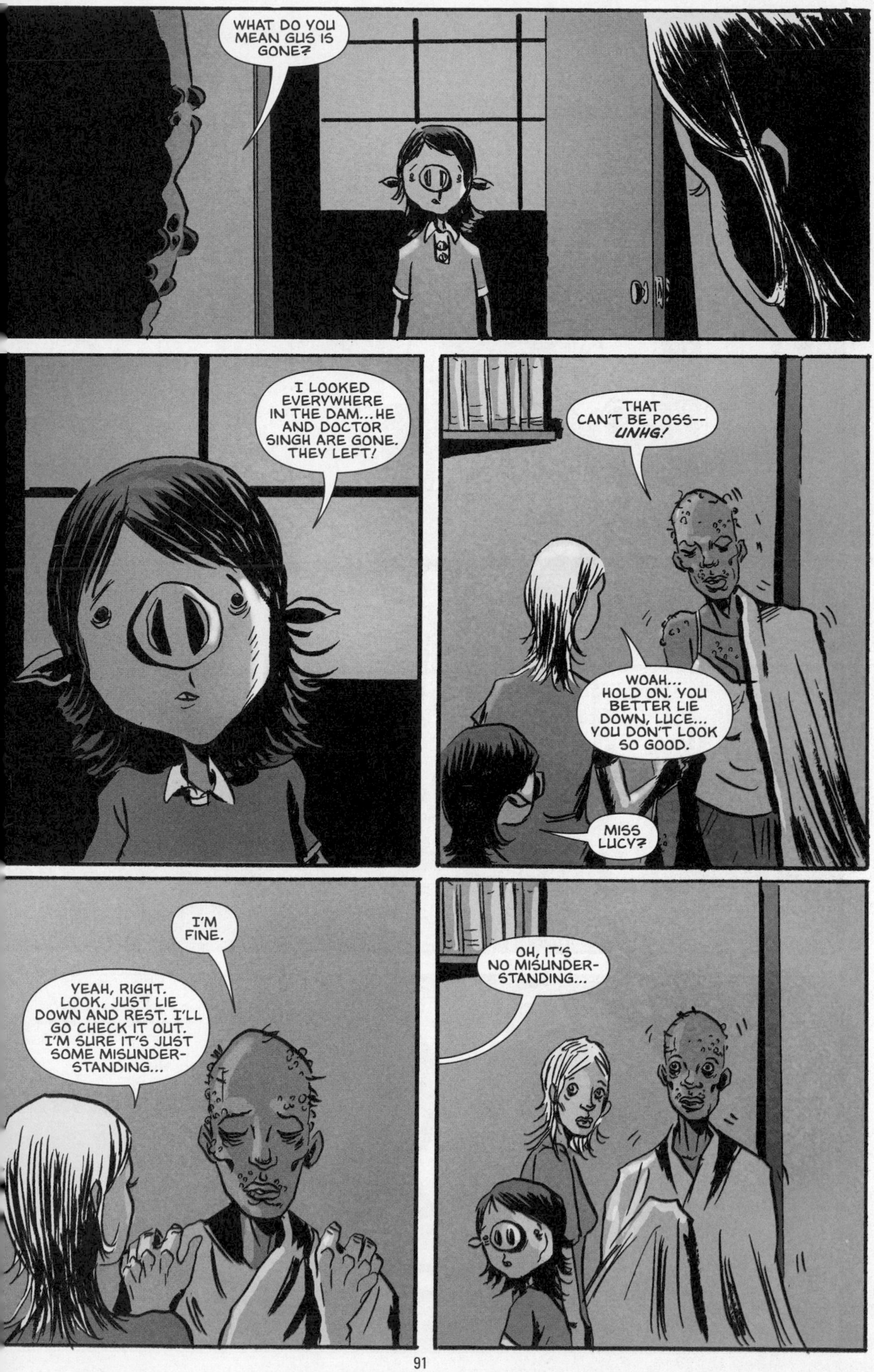
WHAT DO YOU MEAN GUS IS GONE?
I LOOKED EVERYWHERE IN THE DAM...HE AND DOCTOR SINGH ARE GONE. THEY LEFT!
THAT CAN'T BE POSS-- UNHG!
WOAH... HOLD ON. YOU BETTER LIE DOWN, LUCE... YOU DON'T LOOK SO GOOD.
MISS LUCY?
I'M FINE.
YEAH, RIGHT. LOOK, JUST LIE DOWN AND REST. I'LL GO CHECK IT OUT. I'M SURE IT'S JUST SOME MISUNDER-STANDING...
OH, IT'S NO MISUNDER-STANDING...

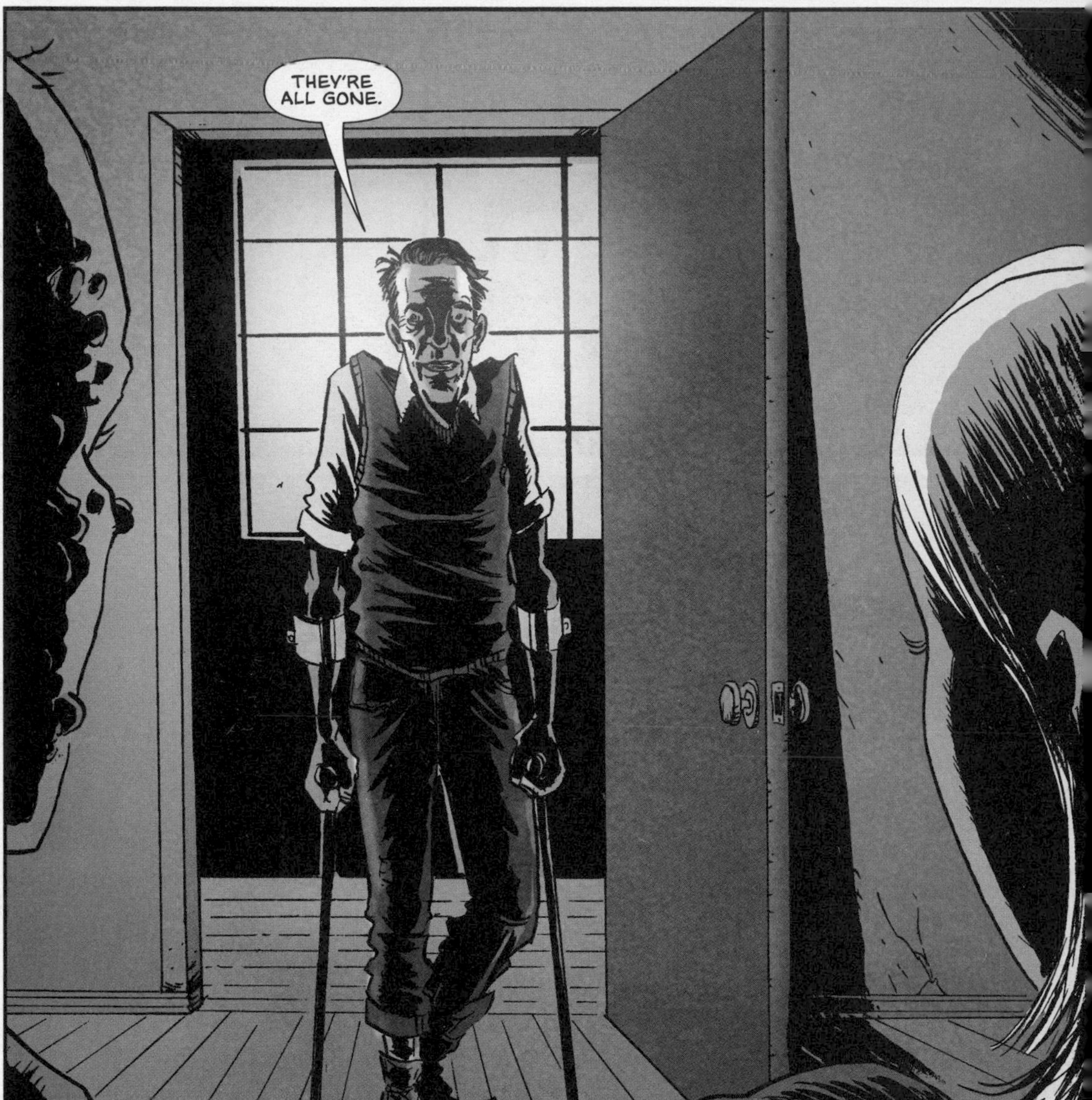
THEY'RE ALL GONE.

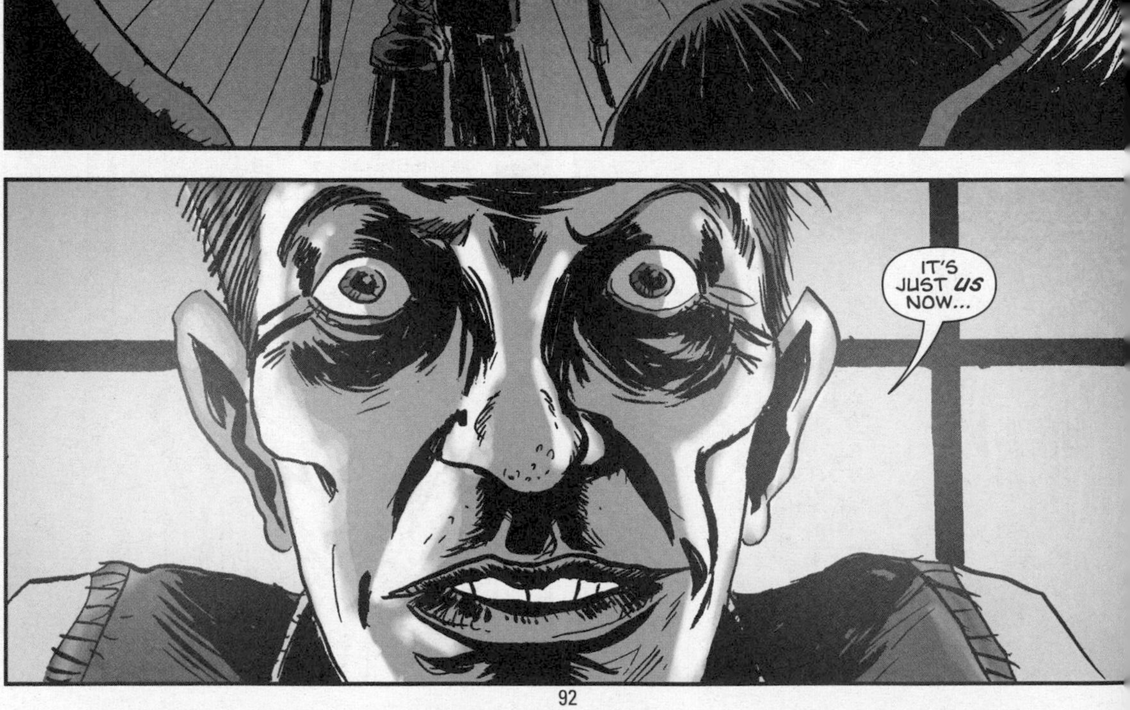
IT'S JUST *US* NOW...

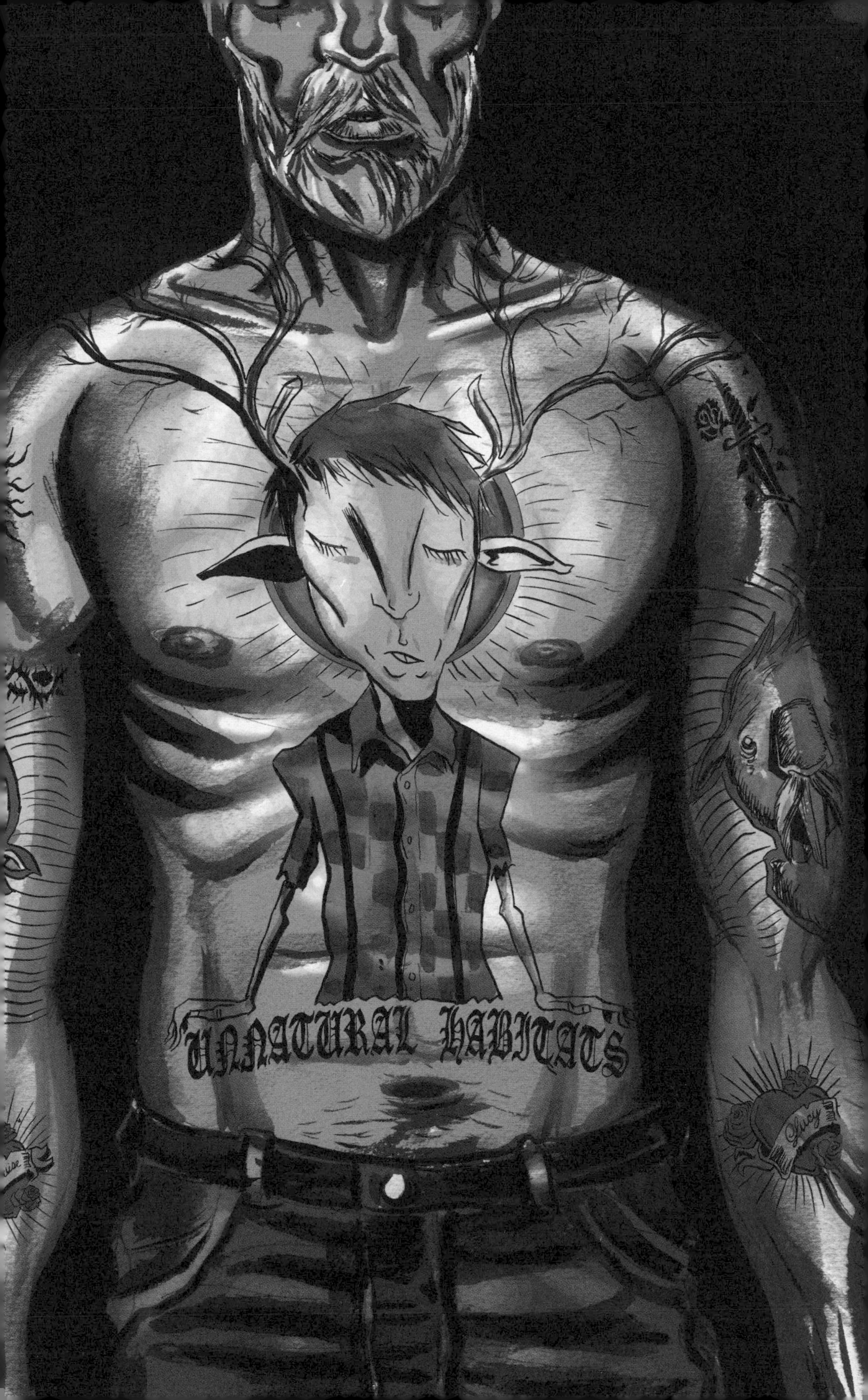
UNNATURAL HABITATS
Lucy

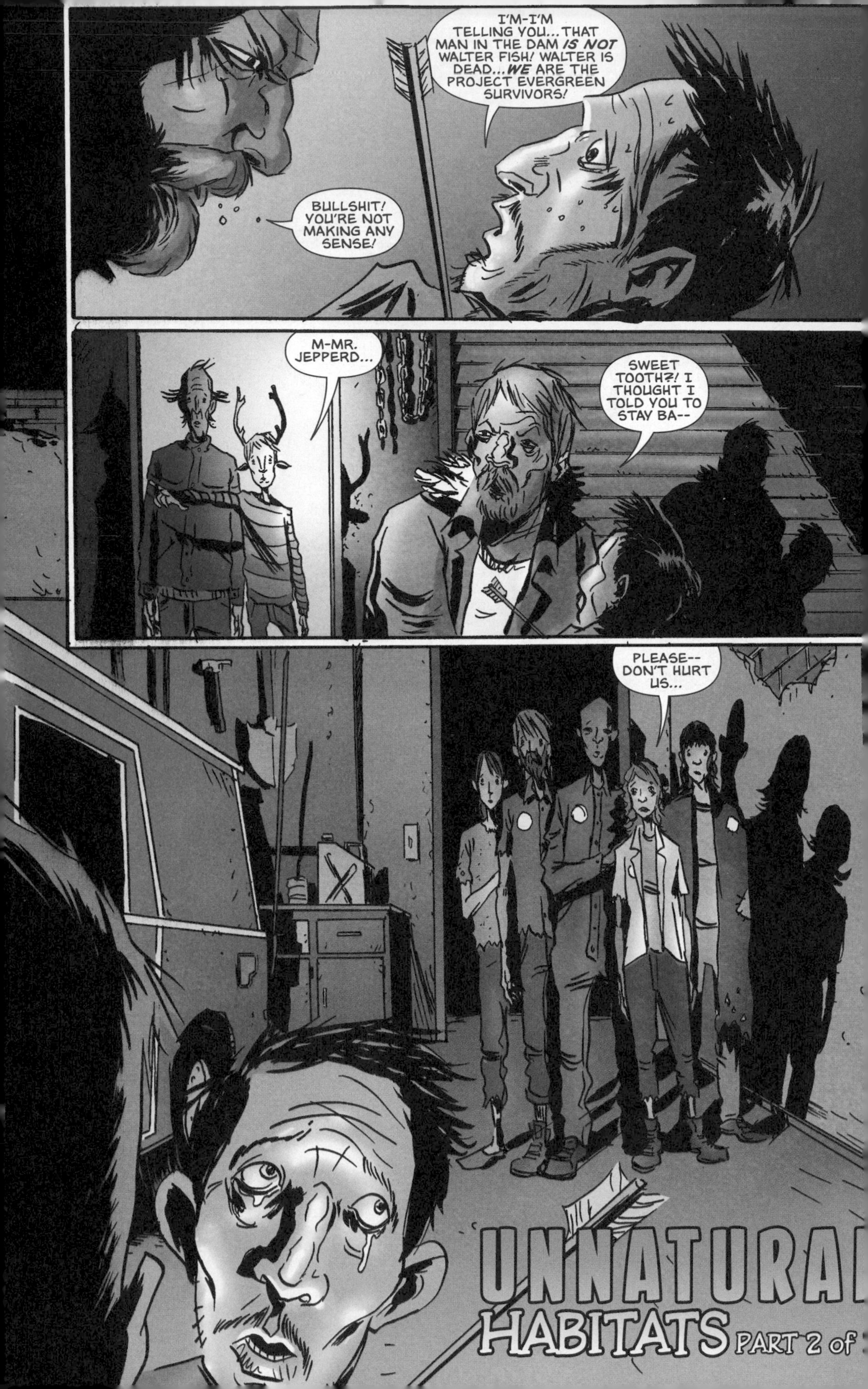
I'M-I'M TELLING YOU... THAT MAN IN THE DAM *IS NOT* WALTER FISH! WALTER IS DEAD... *WE* ARE THE PROJECT EVERGREEN SURVIVORS!
BULLSHIT! YOU'RE NOT MAKING ANY SENSE!
M-MR. JEPPERD...
SWEET TOOTH?! I THOUGHT I TOLD YOU TO STAY BA--
PLEASE-- DON'T HURT US...
UNNATURAL HABITATS PART 2 of

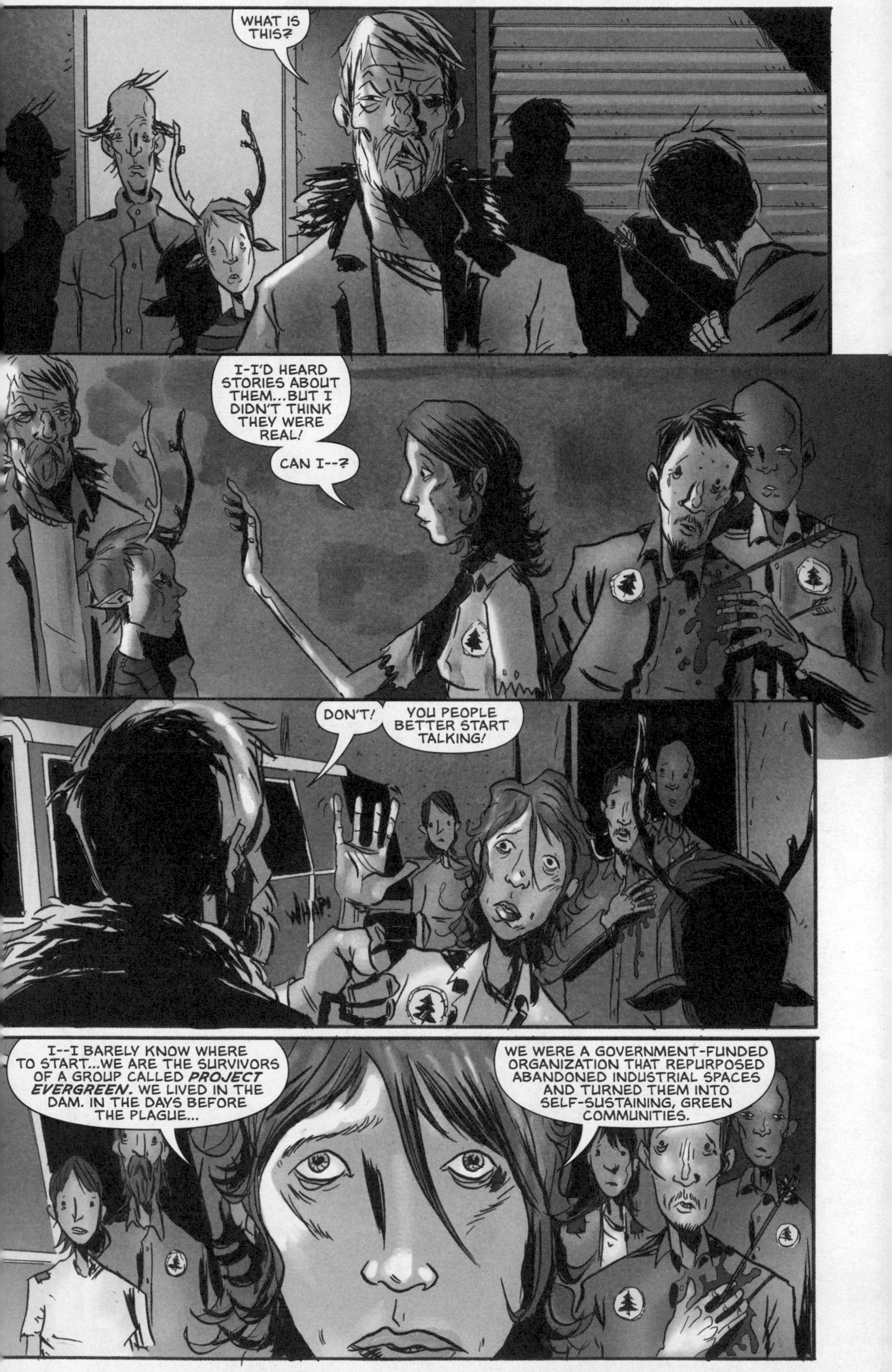
WHAT IS THIS?
I-I'D HEARD STORIES ABOUT THEM...BUT I DIDN'T THINK THEY WERE REAL!
CAN I--?
DON'T!
YOU PEOPLE BETTER START TALKING!
WHAP!
I--I BARELY KNOW WHERE TO START...WE ARE THE SURVIVORS OF A GROUP CALLED *PROJECT EVERGREEN*. WE LIVED IN THE DAM. IN THE DAYS BEFORE THE PLAGUE...
WE WERE A GOVERNMENT-FUNDED ORGANIZATION THAT REPURPOSED ABANDONED INDUSTRIAL SPACES AND TURNED THEM INTO SELF-SUSTAINING, GREEN COMMUNITIES.

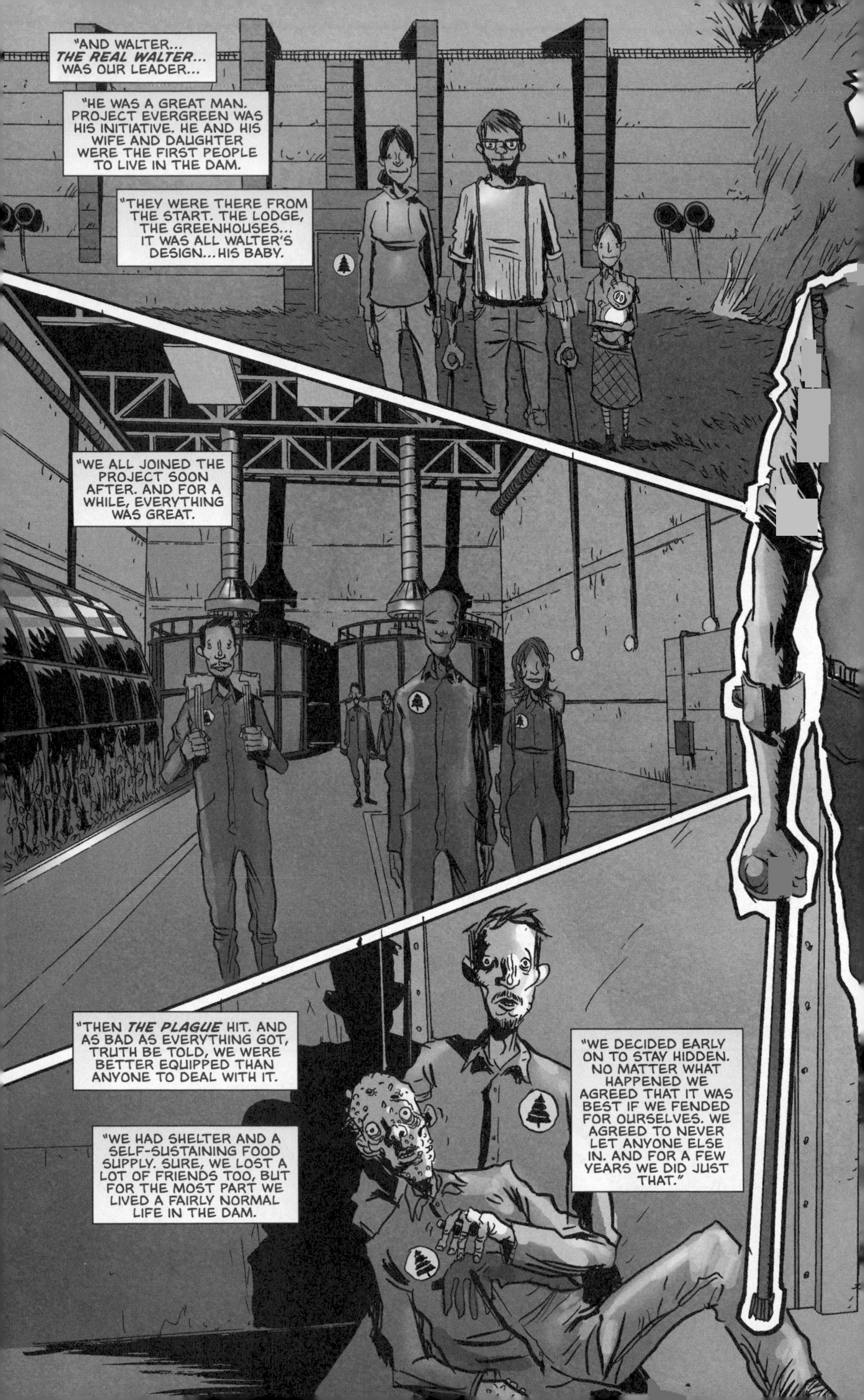
"AND WALTER... *THE REAL WALTER*... WAS OUR LEADER...
"HE WAS A GREAT MAN. PROJECT EVERGREEN WAS HIS INITIATIVE. HE AND HIS WIFE AND DAUGHTER WERE THE FIRST PEOPLE TO LIVE IN THE DAM.
"THEY WERE THERE FROM THE START. THE LODGE, THE GREENHOUSES... IT WAS ALL WALTER'S DESIGN...HIS BABY.
"WE ALL JOINED THE PROJECT SOON AFTER. AND FOR A WHILE, EVERYTHING WAS GREAT.
"THEN *THE PLAGUE* HIT. AND AS BAD AS EVERYTHING GOT, TRUTH BE TOLD, WE WERE BETTER EQUIPPED THAN ANYONE TO DEAL WITH IT.
"WE HAD SHELTER AND A SELF-SUSTAINING FOOD SUPPLY. SURE, WE LOST A LOT OF FRIENDS TOO, BUT FOR THE MOST PART WE LIVED A FAIRLY NORMAL LIFE IN THE DAM.
"WE DECIDED EARLY ON TO STAY HIDDEN. NO MATTER WHAT HAPPENED WE AGREED THAT IT WAS BEST IF WE FENDED FOR OURSELVES. WE AGREED TO NEVER LET ANYONE ELSE IN. AND FOR A FEW YEARS WE DID JUST THAT."

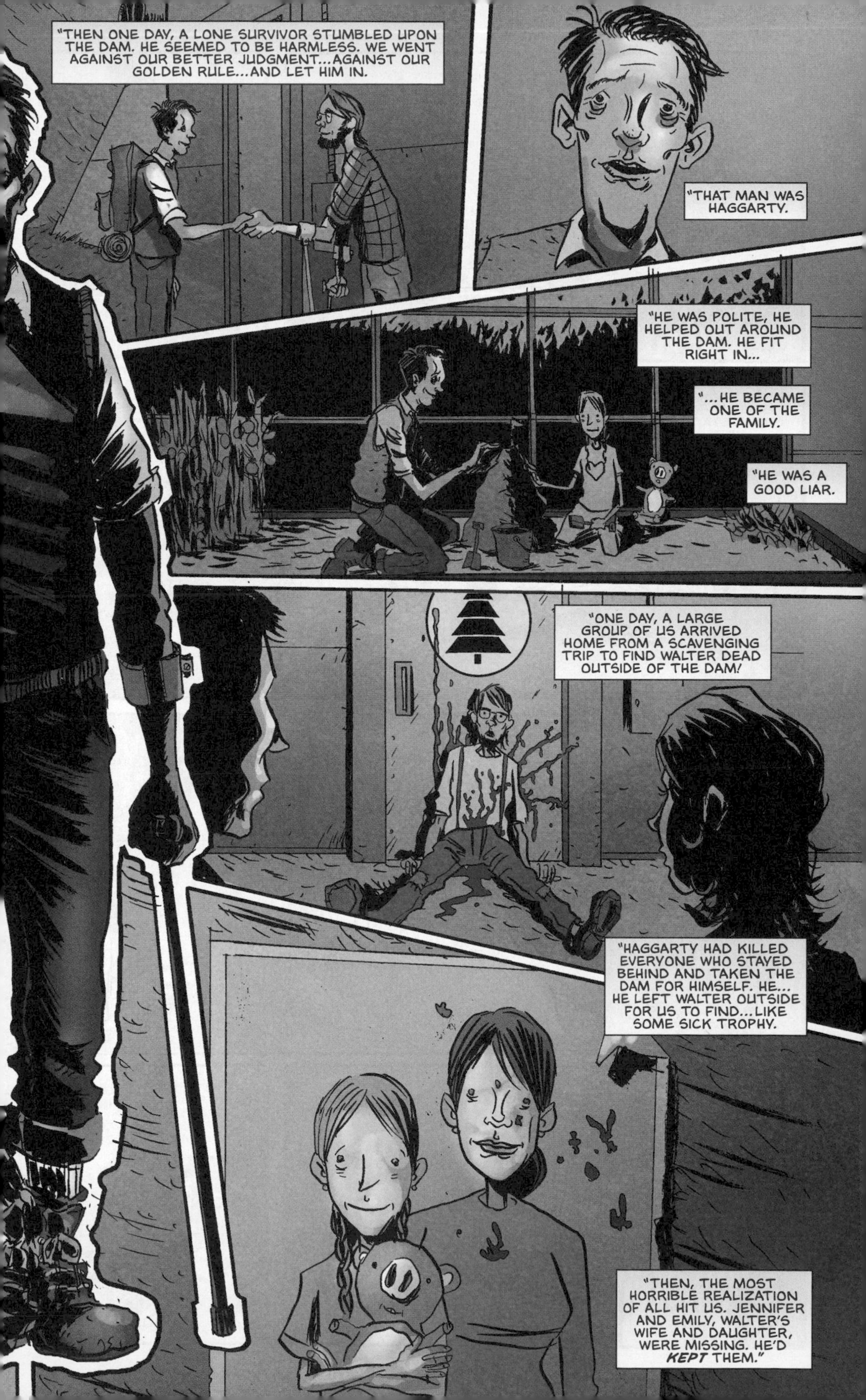
"THEN ONE DAY, A LONE SURVIVOR STUMBLED UPON THE DAM. HE SEEMED TO BE HARMLESS. WE WENT AGAINST OUR BETTER JUDGMENT...AGAINST OUR GOLDEN RULE...AND LET HIM IN.
"THAT MAN WAS HAGGARTY.
"HE WAS POLITE, HE HELPED OUT AROUND THE DAM. HE FIT RIGHT IN...
"...HE BECAME ONE OF THE FAMILY.
"HE WAS A GOOD LIAR.
"ONE DAY, A LARGE GROUP OF US ARRIVED HOME FROM A SCAVENGING TRIP TO FIND WALTER DEAD OUTSIDE OF THE DAM!
"HAGGARTY HAD KILLED EVERYONE WHO STAYED BEHIND AND TAKEN THE DAM FOR HIMSELF. HE... HE LEFT WALTER OUTSIDE FOR US TO FIND...LIKE SOME SICK TROPHY.
"THEN, THE MOST HORRIBLE REALIZATION OF ALL HIT US. JENNIFER AND EMILY, WALTER'S WIFE AND DAUGHTER, WERE MISSING. HE'D ***KEPT*** THEM."

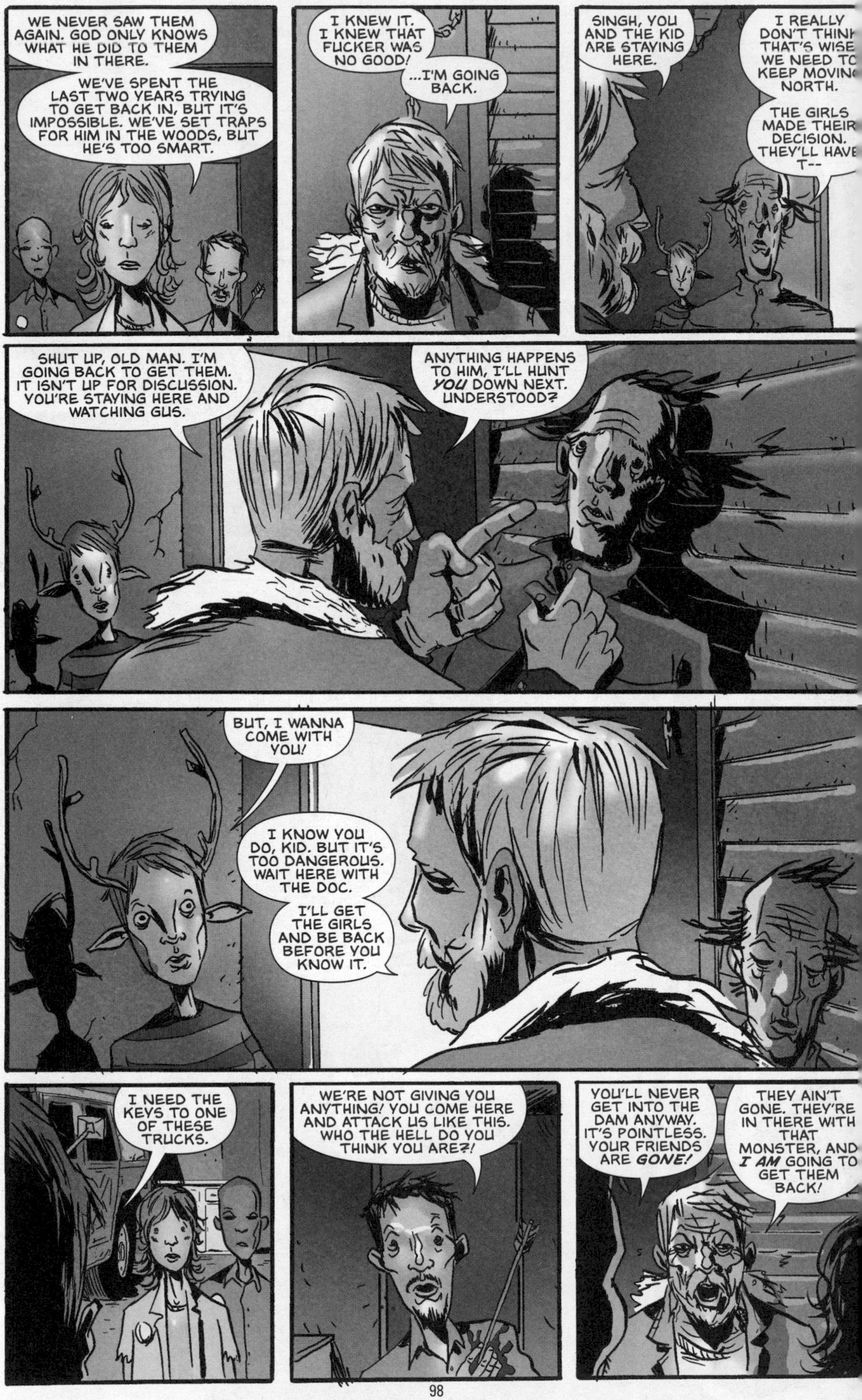

WE NEVER SAW THEM AGAIN. GOD ONLY KNOWS WHAT HE DID TO THEM IN THERE.
WE'VE SPENT THE LAST TWO YEARS TRYING TO GET BACK IN, BUT IT'S IMPOSSIBLE. WE'VE SET TRAPS FOR HIM IN THE WOODS, BUT HE'S TOO SMART.
I KNEW IT. I KNEW THAT FUCKER WAS NO GOOD!
...I'M GOING BACK.
SINGH, YOU AND THE KID ARE STAYING HERE.
I REALLY DON'T THINK THAT'S WISE. WE NEED TO KEEP MOVING NORTH.
THE GIRLS MADE THEIR DECISION. THEY'LL HAVE T--
SHUT UP, OLD MAN. I'M GOING BACK TO GET THEM. IT ISN'T UP FOR DISCUSSION. YOU'RE STAYING HERE AND WATCHING GUS.
ANYTHING HAPPENS TO HIM, I'LL HUNT *YOU* DOWN NEXT. UNDERSTOOD?
BUT, I WANNA COME WITH YOU!
I KNOW YOU DO, KID. BUT IT'S TOO DANGEROUS. WAIT HERE WITH THE DOC.
I'LL GET THE GIRLS AND BE BACK BEFORE YOU KNOW IT.
I NEED THE KEYS TO ONE OF THESE TRUCKS.
WE'RE NOT GIVING YOU ANYTHING! YOU COME HERE AND ATTACK US LIKE THIS. WHO THE HELL DO YOU THINK YOU ARE?!
YOU'LL NEVER GET INTO THE DAM ANYWAY. IT'S POINTLESS. YOUR FRIENDS ARE *GONE!*
THEY AIN'T GONE. THEY'RE IN THERE WITH THAT MONSTER, AND *I AM* GOING TO GET THEM BACK!

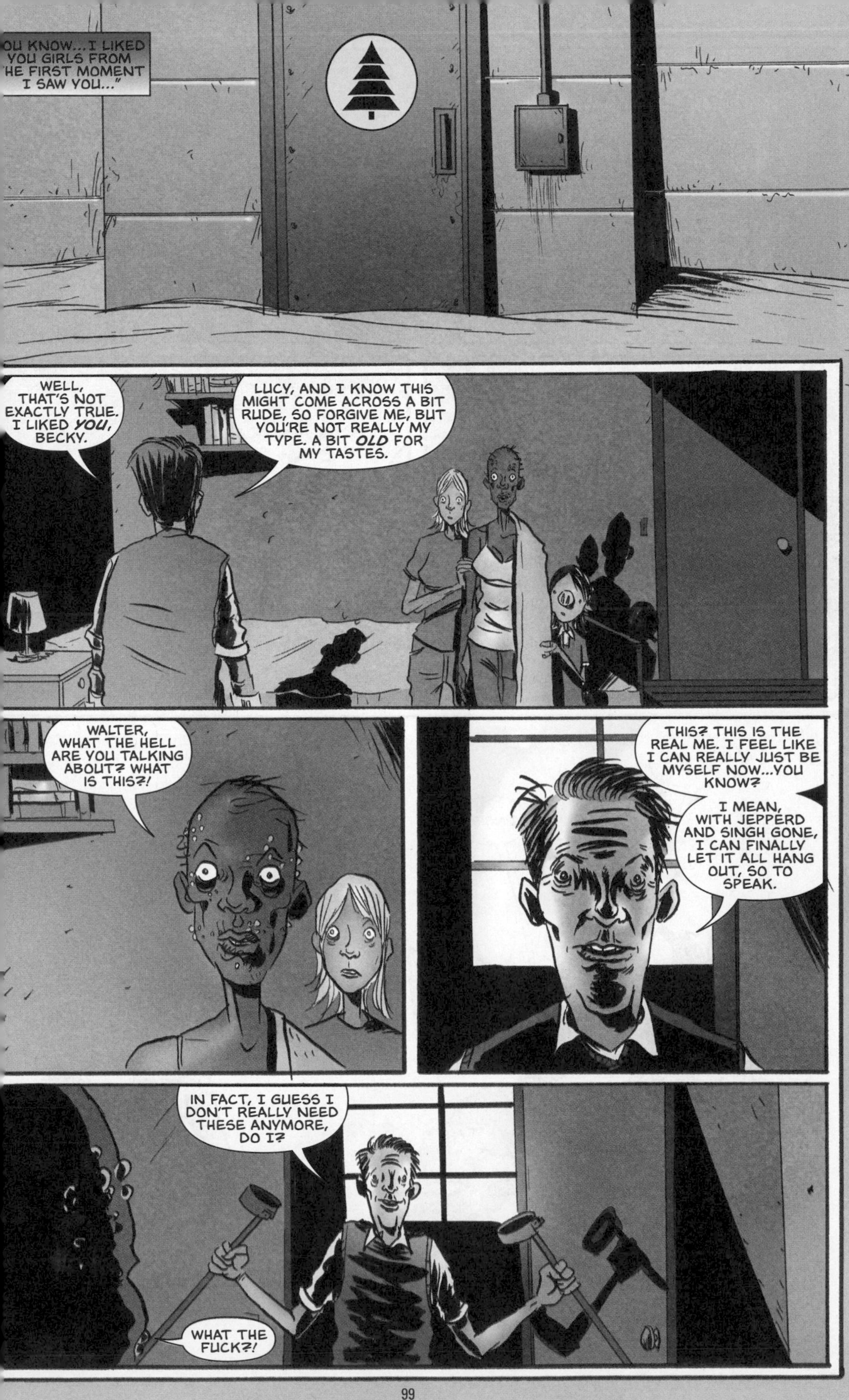
OU KNOW...I LIKED YOU GIRLS FROM HE FIRST MOMENT I SAW YOU..."
WELL, THAT'S NOT EXACTLY TRUE. I LIKED *YOU*, BECKY.
LUCY, AND I KNOW THIS MIGHT COME ACROSS A BIT RUDE, SO FORGIVE ME, BUT YOU'RE NOT REALLY MY TYPE. A BIT *OLD* FOR MY TASTES.
WALTER, WHAT THE HELL ARE YOU TALKING ABOUT? WHAT IS THIS?!
THIS? THIS IS THE REAL ME. I FEEL LIKE I CAN REALLY JUST BE MYSELF NOW...YOU KNOW?
I MEAN, WITH JEPPERD AND SINGH GONE, I CAN FINALLY LET IT ALL HANG OUT, SO TO SPEAK.
IN FACT, I GUESS I DON'T REALLY NEED THESE ANYMORE, DO I?
WHAT THE FUCK?!

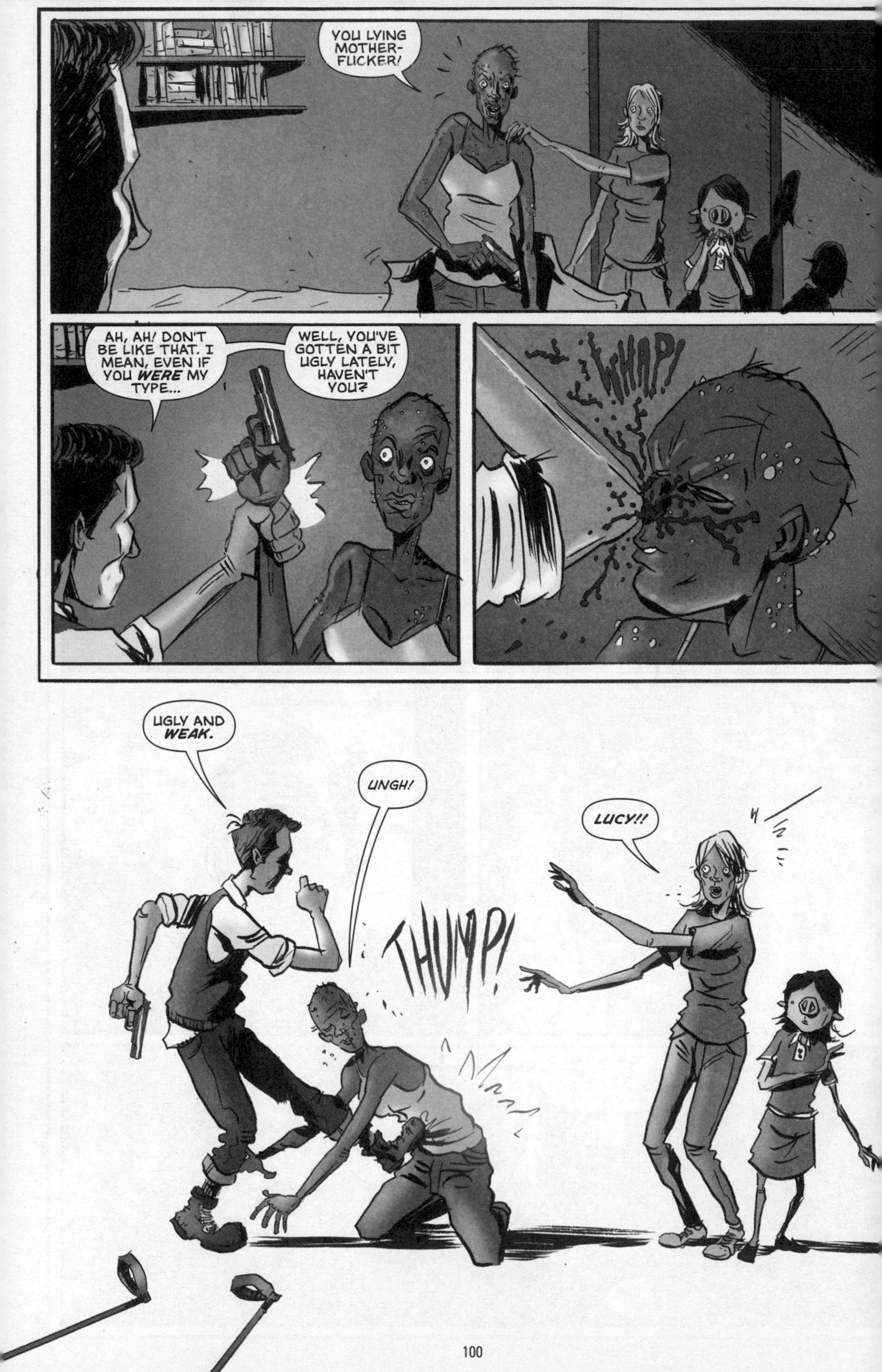

YOU LYING MOTHER-FUCKER!
AH, AH! DON'T BE LIKE THAT. I MEAN, EVEN IF YOU *WERE* MY TYPE...
WELL, YOU'VE GOTTEN A BIT UGLY LATELY, HAVEN'T YOU?
WHAP!
UGLY AND *WEAK.*
UNGH!
THUMP!
LUCY!!

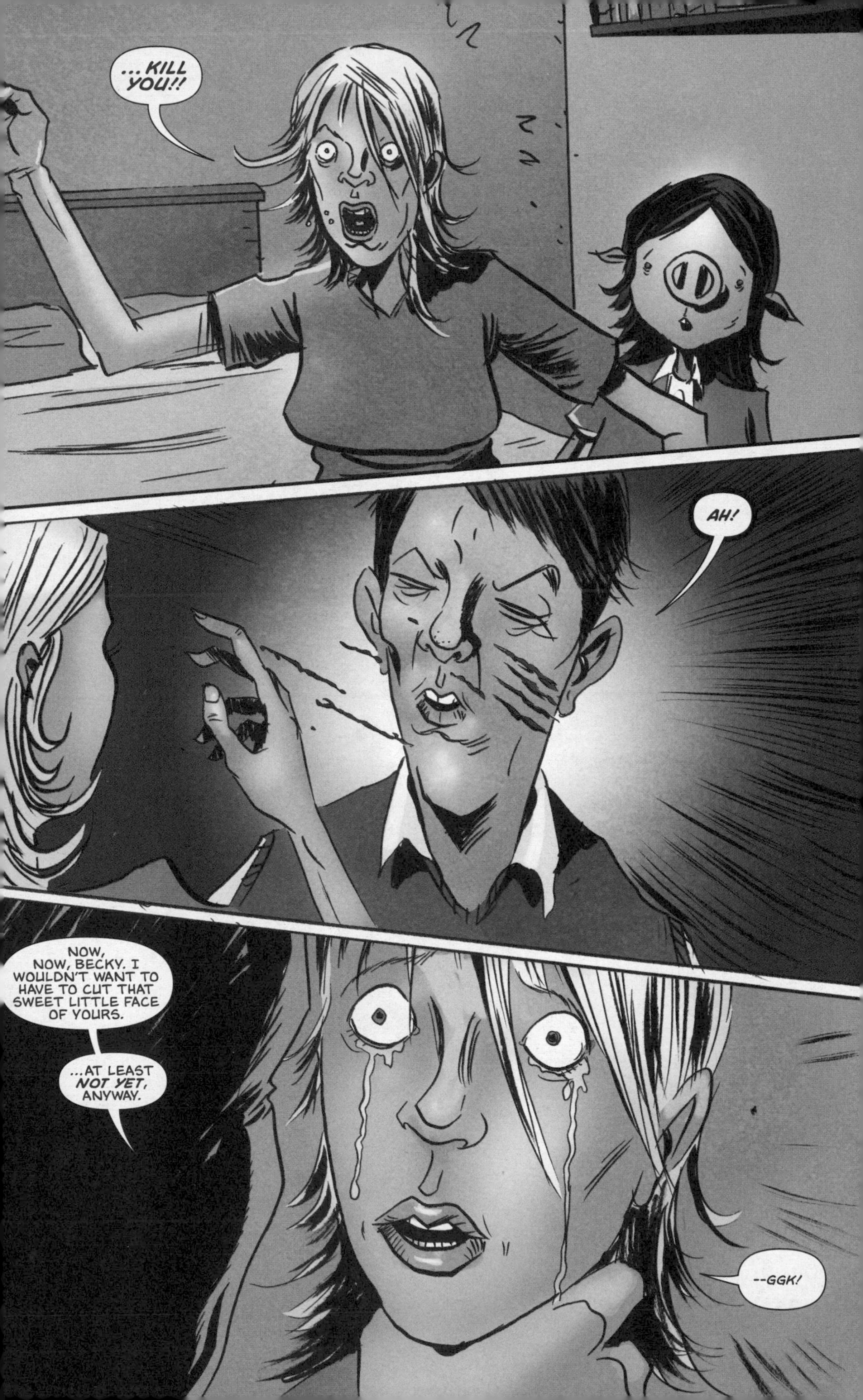
...KILL YOU!!
AH!
NOW, NOW, BECKY. I WOULDN'T WANT TO HAVE TO CUT THAT SWEET LITTLE FACE OF YOURS.
...AT LEAST NOT YET, ANYWAY.
--GGK!

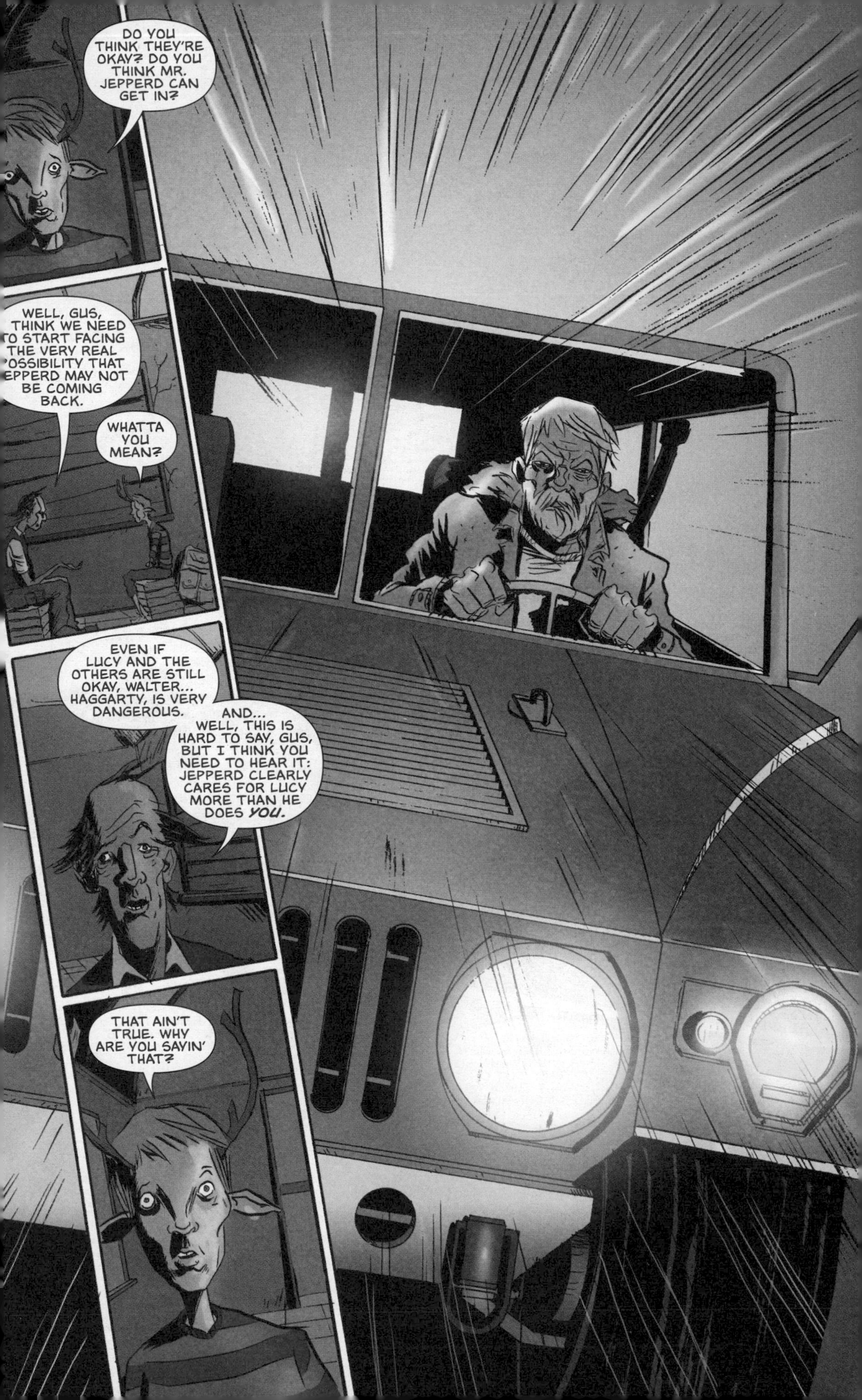
DO YOU THINK THEY'RE OKAY? DO YOU THINK MR. JEPPERD CAN GET IN?
WELL, GUS, THINK WE NEED TO START FACING THE VERY REAL POSSIBILITY THAT JEPPERD MAY NOT BE COMING BACK.
WHATTA YOU MEAN?
EVEN IF LUCY AND THE OTHERS ARE STILL OKAY, WALTER... HAGGARTY, IS VERY DANGEROUS.
AND... WELL, THIS IS HARD TO SAY, GUS, BUT I THINK YOU NEED TO HEAR IT: JEPPERD CLEARLY CARES FOR LUCY MORE THAN HE DOES YOU.
THAT AIN'T TRUE. WHY ARE YOU SAYIN' THAT?

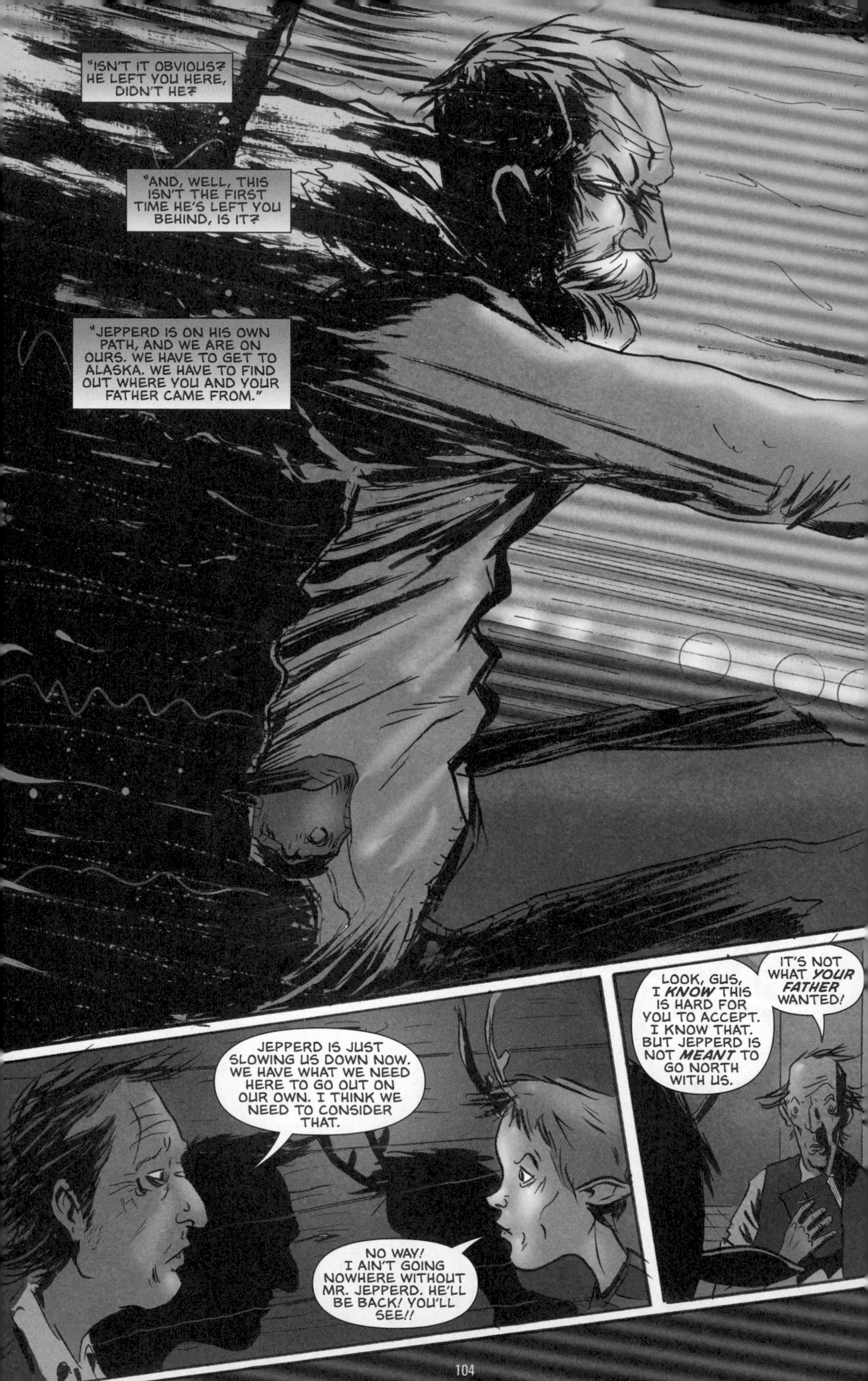
"ISN'T IT OBVIOUS? HE LEFT YOU HERE, DIDN'T HE?
"AND, WELL, THIS ISN'T THE FIRST TIME HE'S LEFT YOU BEHIND, IS IT?
"JEPPERD IS ON HIS OWN PATH, AND WE ARE ON OURS. WE HAVE TO GET TO ALASKA. WE HAVE TO FIND OUT WHERE YOU AND YOUR FATHER CAME FROM."
JEPPERD IS JUST SLOWING US DOWN NOW. WE HAVE WHAT WE NEED HERE TO GO OUT ON OUR OWN. I THINK WE NEED TO CONSIDER THAT.
NO WAY! I AIN'T GOING NOWHERE WITHOUT MR. JEPPERD. HE'LL BE BACK! YOU'LL SEE!!
LOOK, GUS, I *KNOW* THIS IS HARD FOR YOU TO ACCEPT. I KNOW THAT. BUT JEPPERD IS NOT *MEANT* TO GO NORTH WITH US.
IT'S NOT WHAT *YOUR FATHER* WANTED!

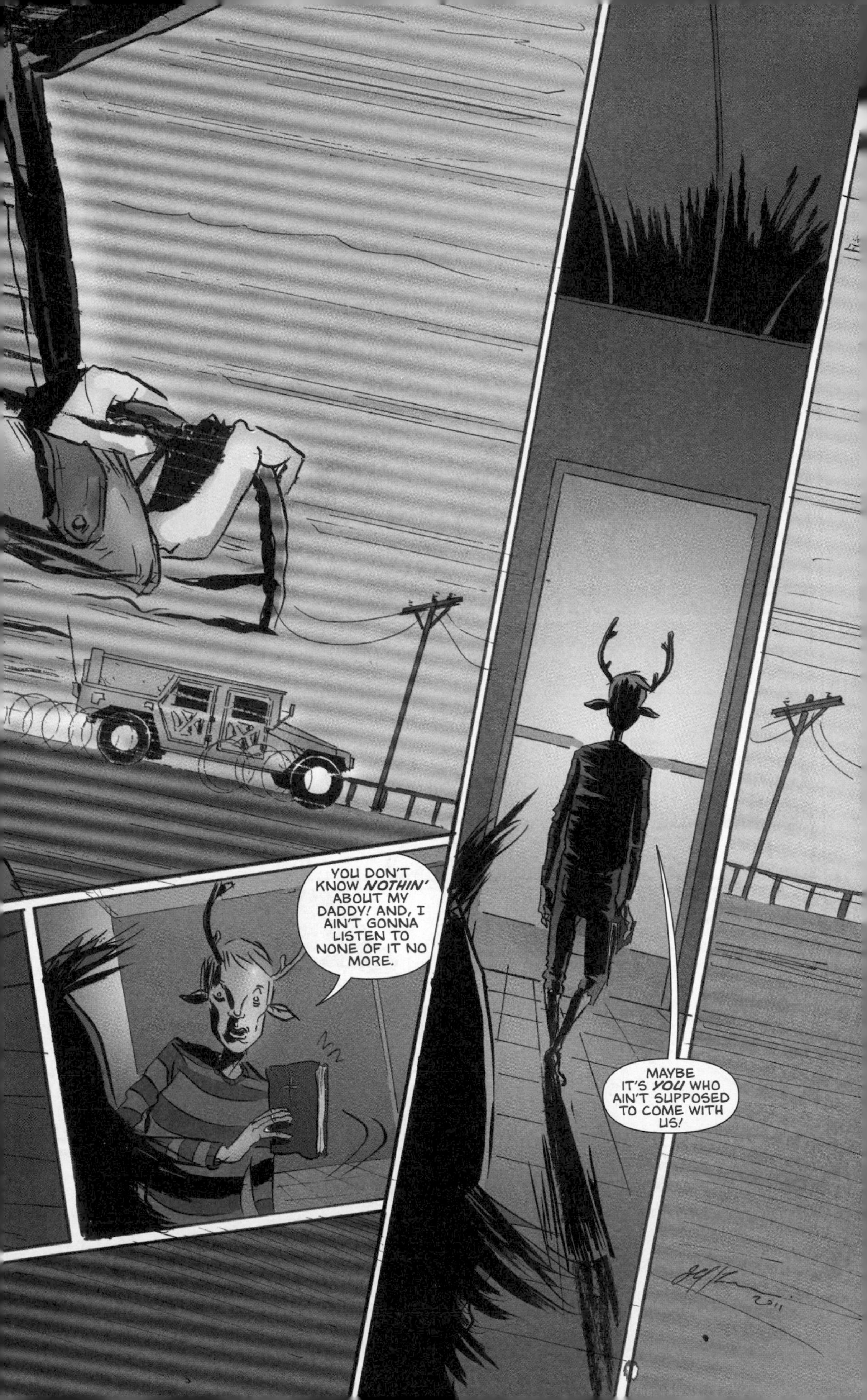
YOU DON'T KNOW *NOTHIN'* ABOUT MY DADDY! AND, I AIN'T GONNA LISTEN TO NONE OF IT NO MORE.
MAYBE IT'S *YOU* WHO AIN'T SUPPOSED TO COME WITH US!

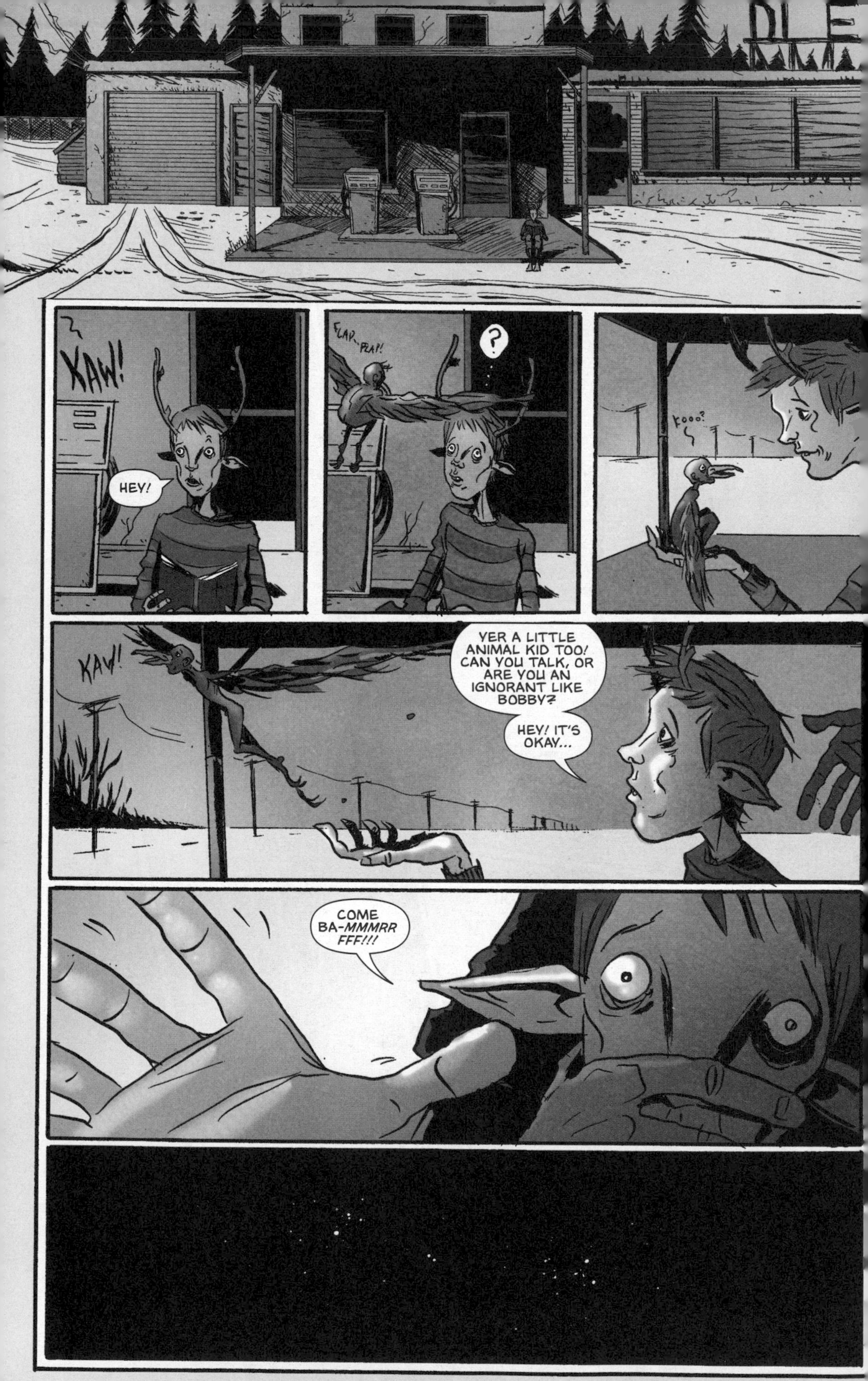
KAW!
HEY!
FLAP.. FLAP!
?
kooo?
KAW!
YER A LITTLE ANIMAL KID TOO! CAN YOU TALK, OR ARE YOU AN IGNORANT LIKE BOBBY?
HEY! IT'S OKAY...
COME BA-MMMRR FFF!!!

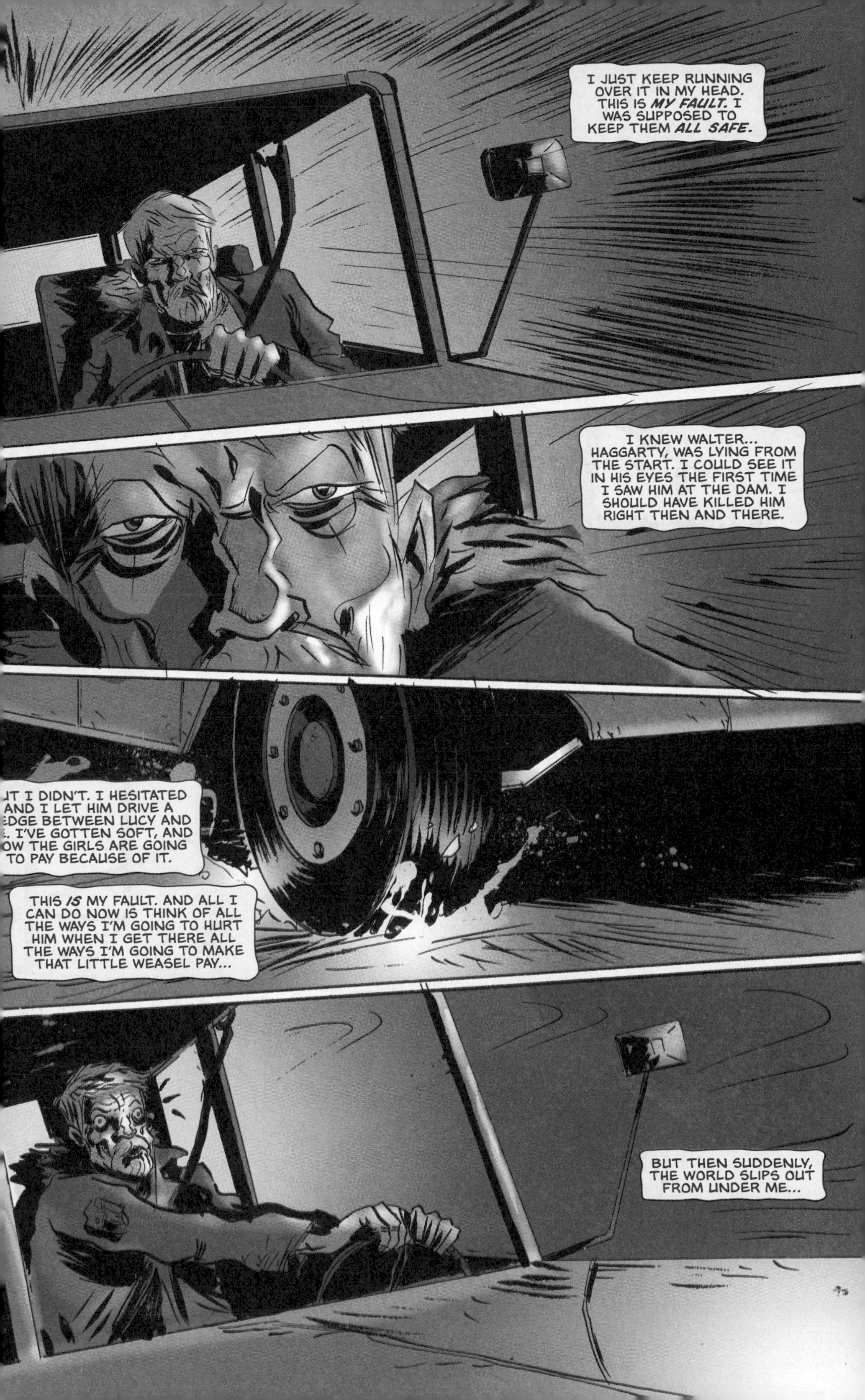
I JUST KEEP RUNNING OVER IT IN MY HEAD. THIS IS *MY FAULT.* I WAS SUPPOSED TO KEEP THEM *ALL SAFE.*
I KNEW WALTER... HAGGARTY, WAS LYING FROM THE START. I COULD SEE IT IN HIS EYES THE FIRST TIME I SAW HIM AT THE DAM. I SHOULD HAVE KILLED HIM RIGHT THEN AND THERE.
UT I DIDN'T. I HESITATED AND I LET HIM DRIVE A EDGE BETWEEN LUCY AND . I'VE GOTTEN SOFT, AND OW THE GIRLS ARE GOING TO PAY BECAUSE OF IT.
THIS *IS* MY FAULT. AND ALL I CAN DO NOW IS THINK OF ALL THE WAYS I'M GOING TO HURT HIM WHEN I GET THERE ALL THE WAYS I'M GOING TO MAKE THAT LITTLE WEASEL PAY...
BUT THEN SUDDENLY, THE WORLD SLIPS OUT FROM UNDER ME...

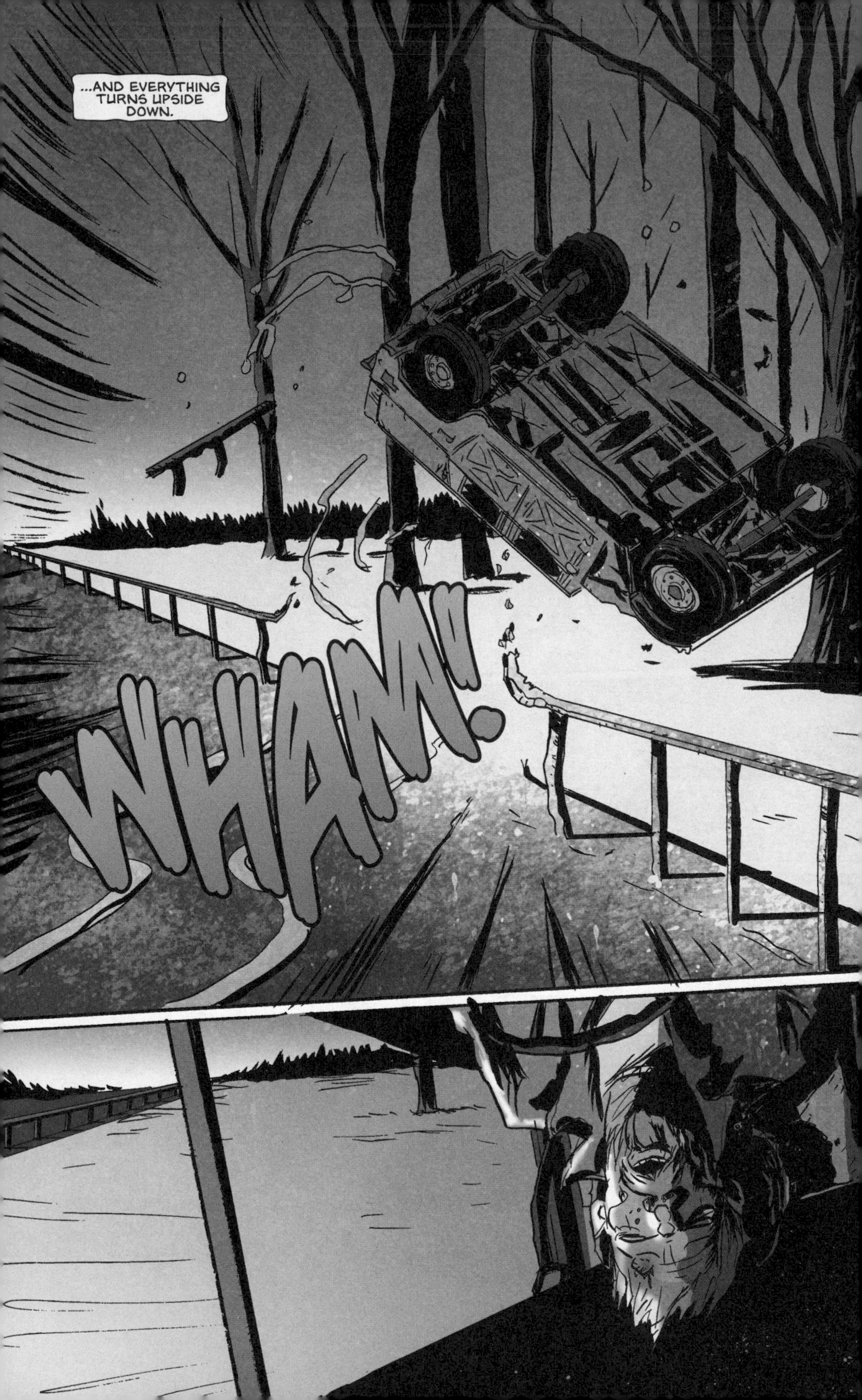
...AND EVERYTHING TURNS UPSIDE DOWN.
WHAM!

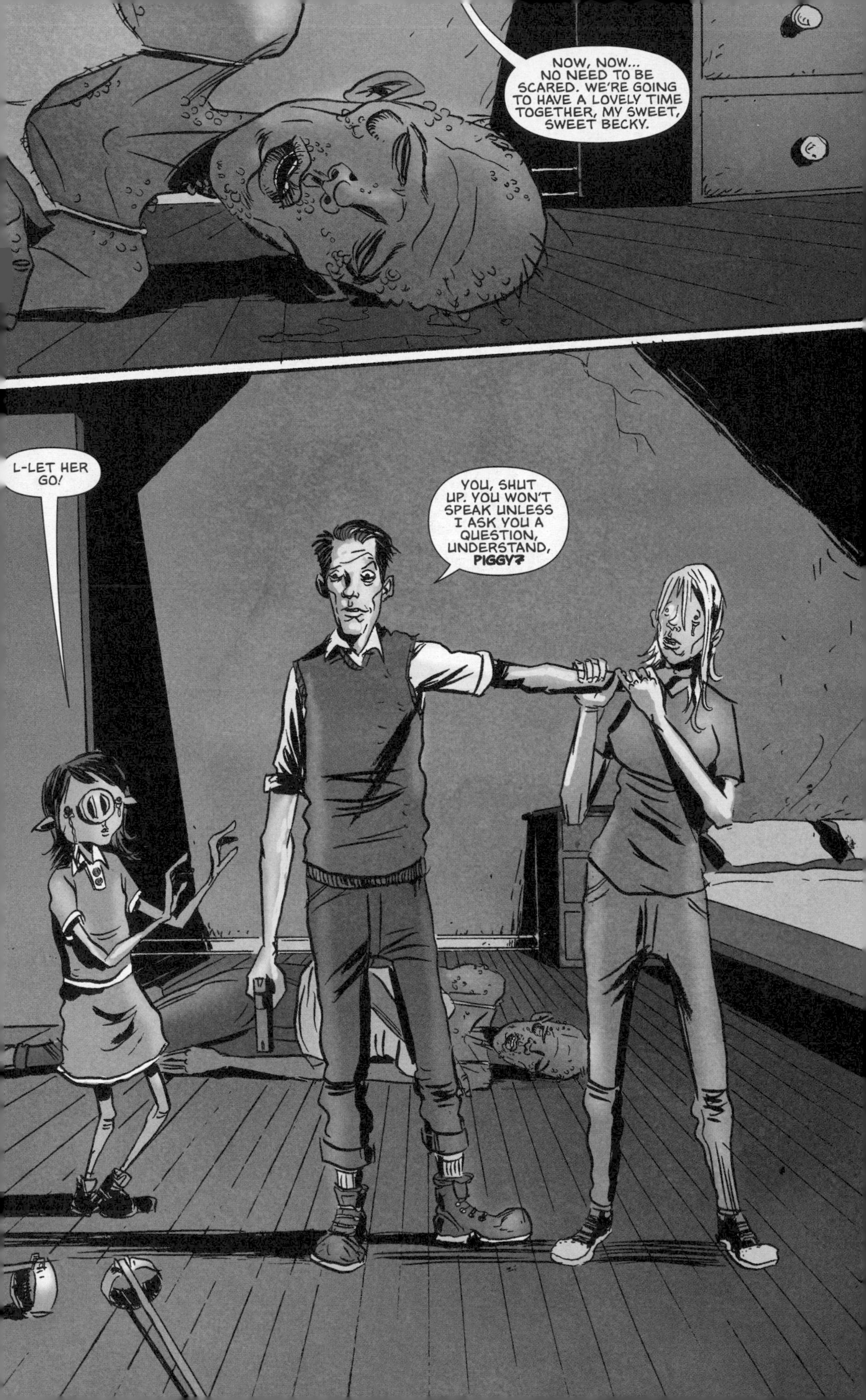
NOW, NOW... NO NEED TO BE SCARED. WE'RE GOING TO HAVE A LOVELY TIME TOGETHER, MY SWEET, SWEET BECKY.
L-LET HER GO!
YOU, SHUT UP. YOU WON'T SPEAK UNLESS I ASK YOU A QUESTION, UNDERSTAND, PIGGY?

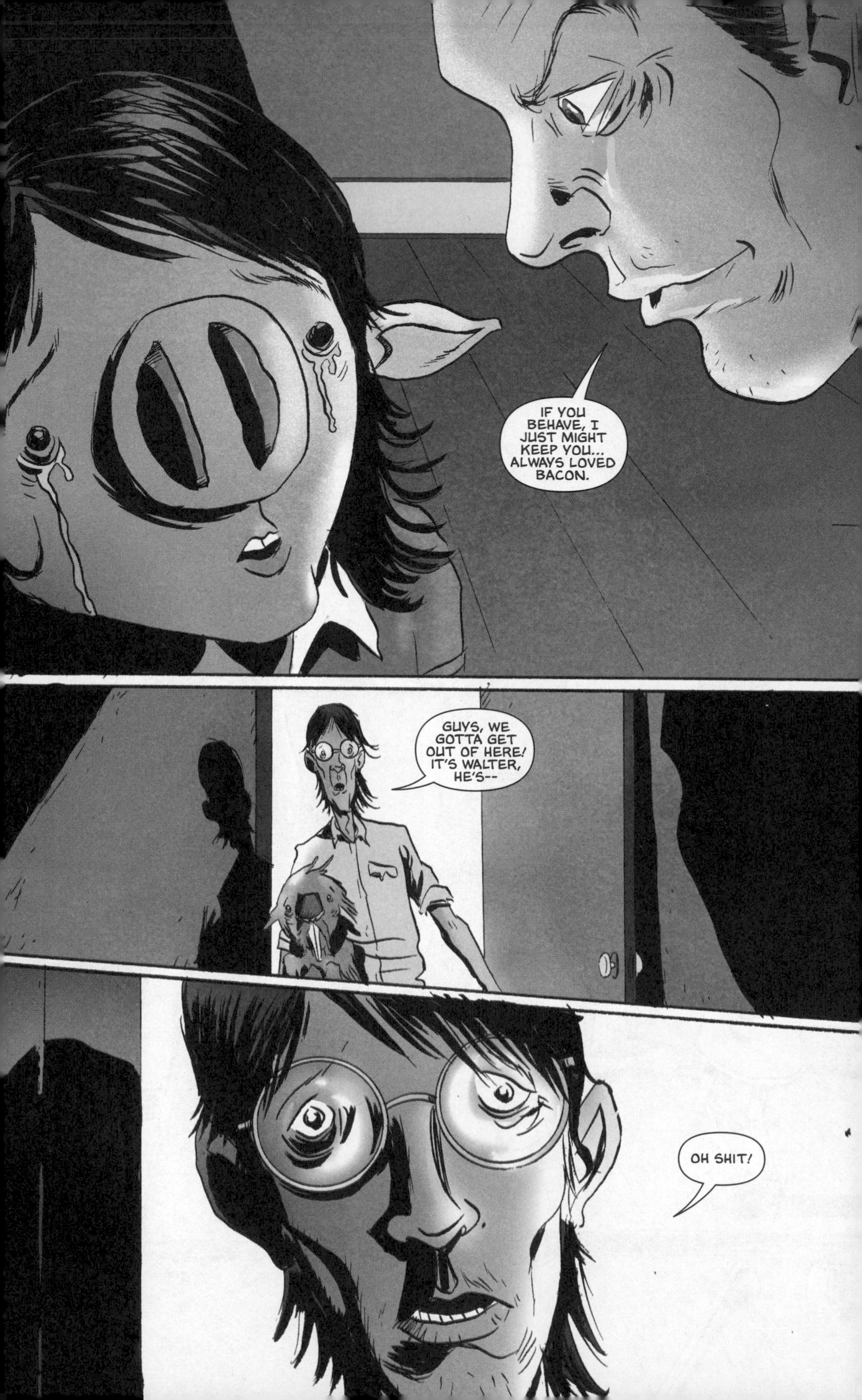
IF YOU BEHAVE, I JUST MIGHT KEEP YOU... ALWAYS LOVED BACON.
GUYS, WE GOTTA GET OUT OF HERE! IT'S WALTER, HE'S--
OH SHIT!

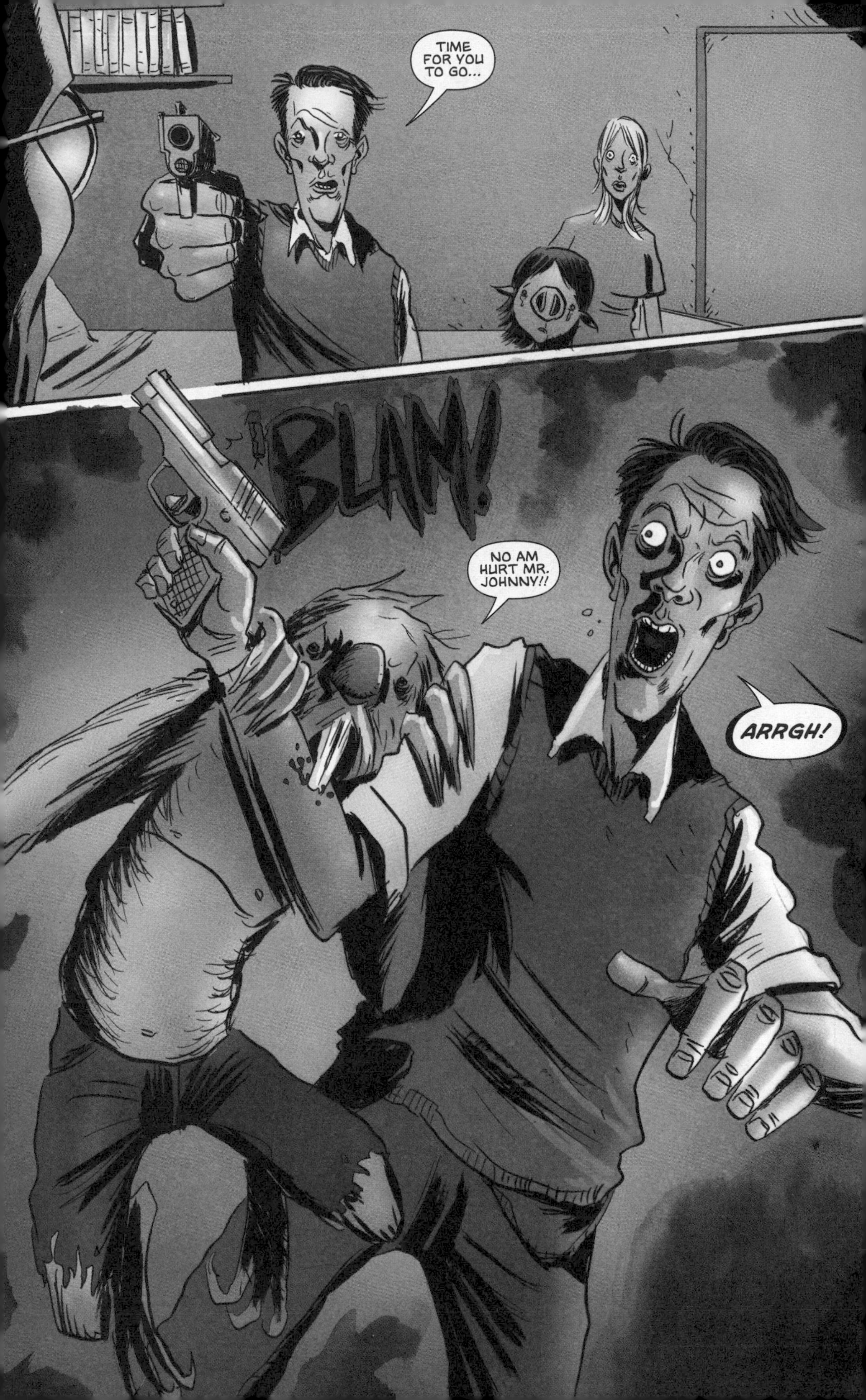
TIME FOR YOU TO GO...
BLAM!
NO AM HURT MR. JOHNNY!!
ARRGH!

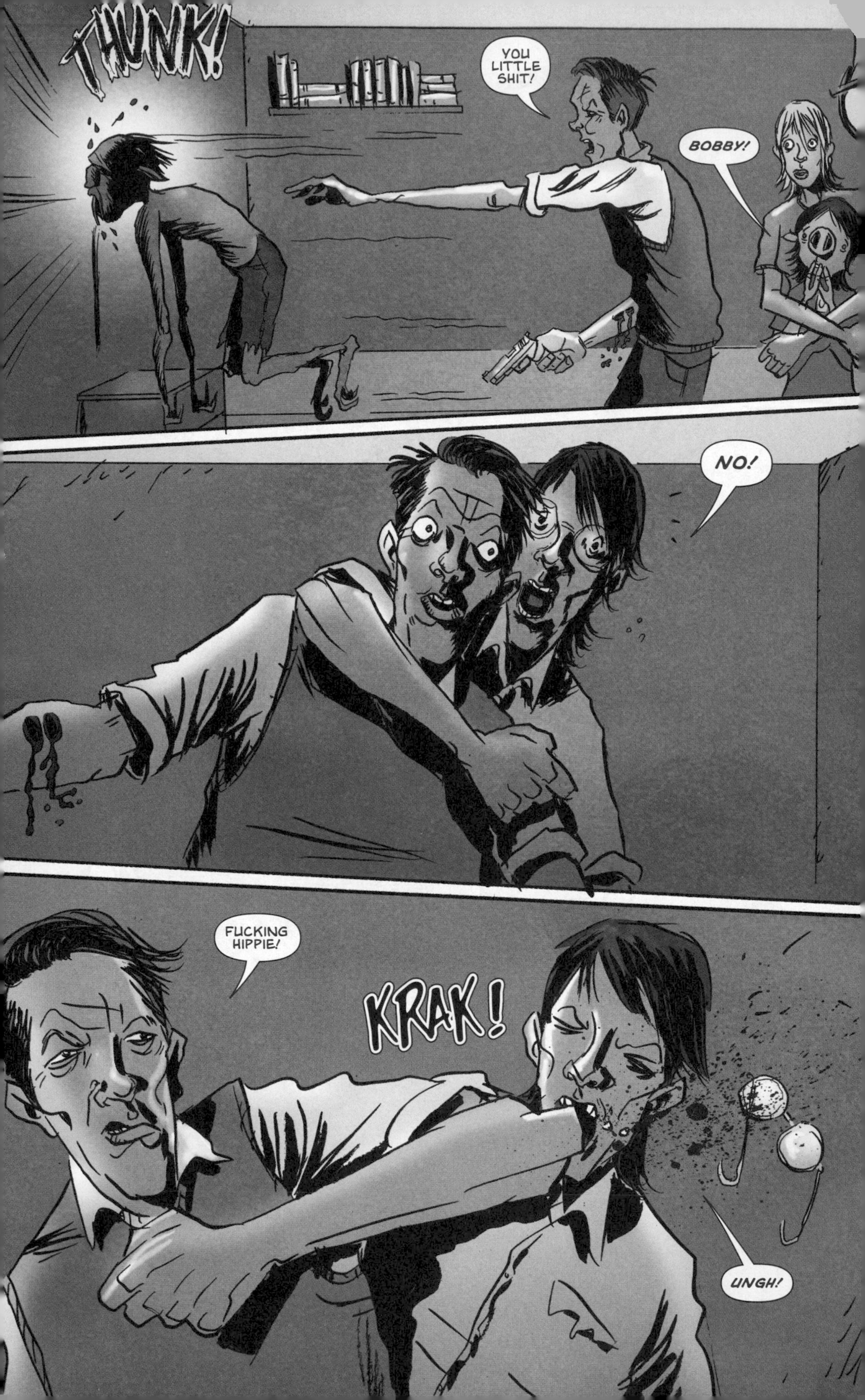
THUNK!
YOU LITTLE SHIT!
BOBBY!
NO!
FUCKING HIPPIE!
KRAK!
UNGH!

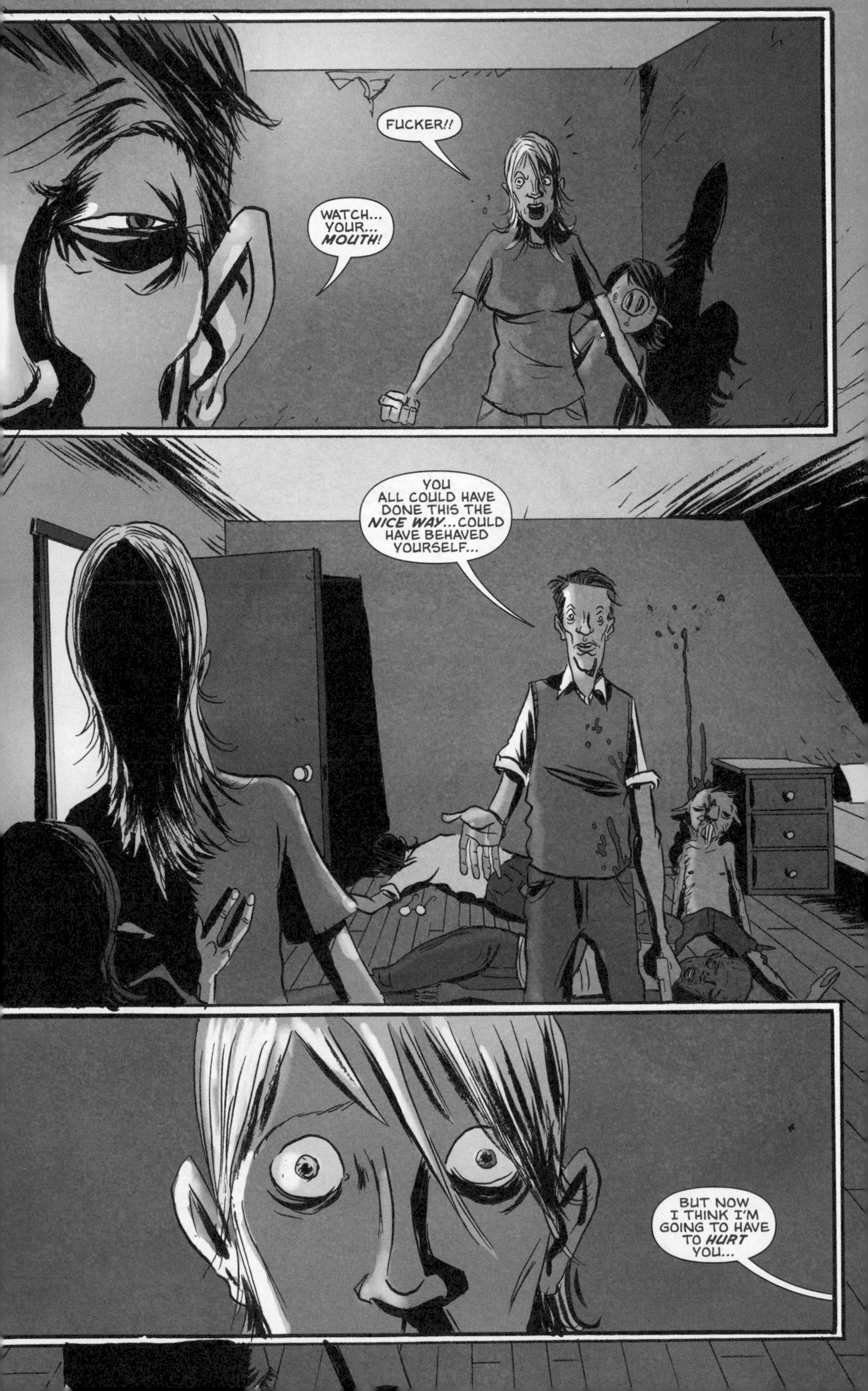
FUCKER!!
WATCH... YOUR... MOUTH!
YOU ALL COULD HAVE DONE THIS THE NICE WAY... COULD HAVE BEHAVED YOURSELF...
BUT NOW I THINK I'M GOING TO HAVE TO HURT YOU...

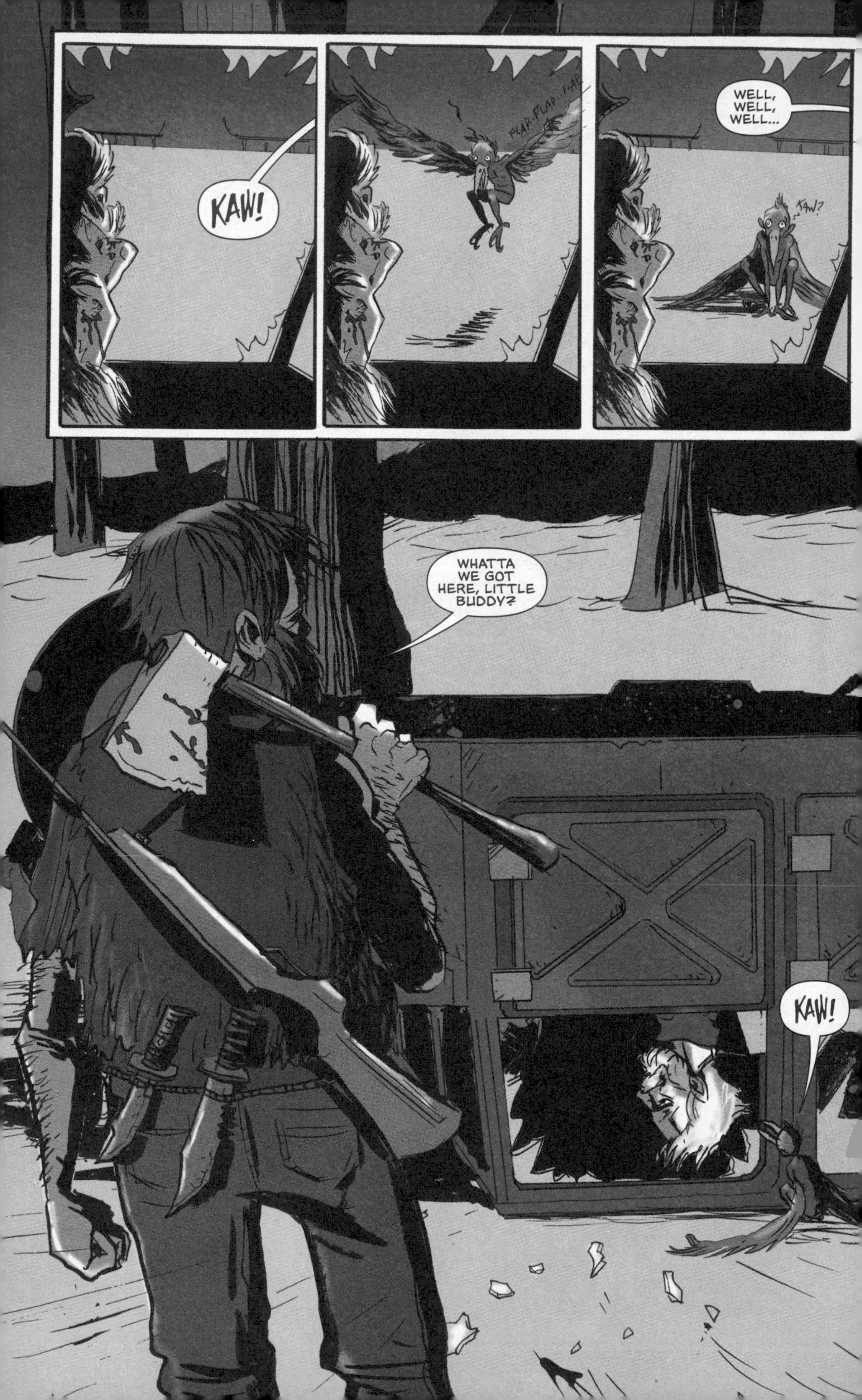
KAW!
FLAP-FLAP-FLAP
WELL, WELL, WELL...
KAW?
WHATTA WE GOT HERE, LITTLE BUDDY?
KAW!

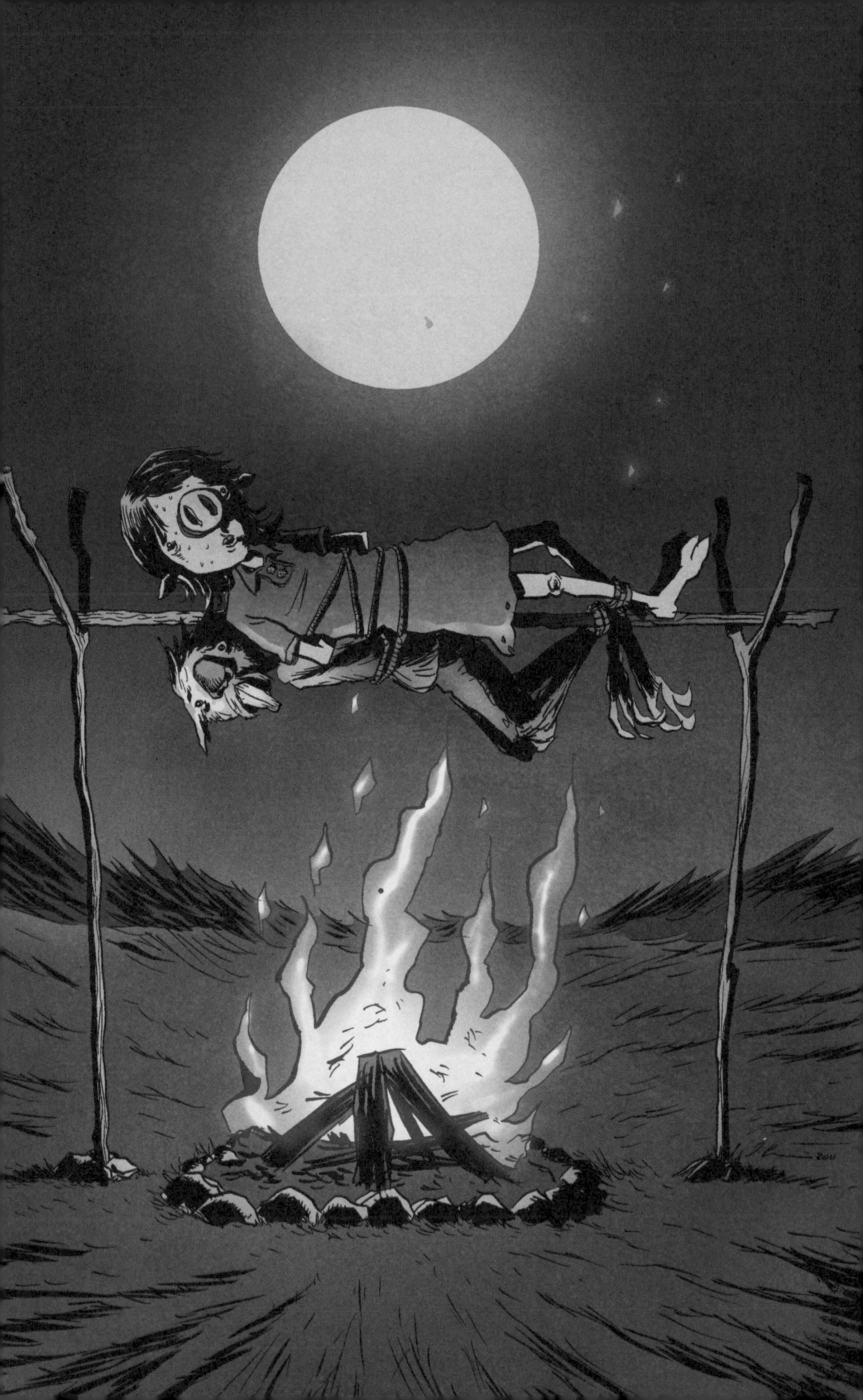
2011

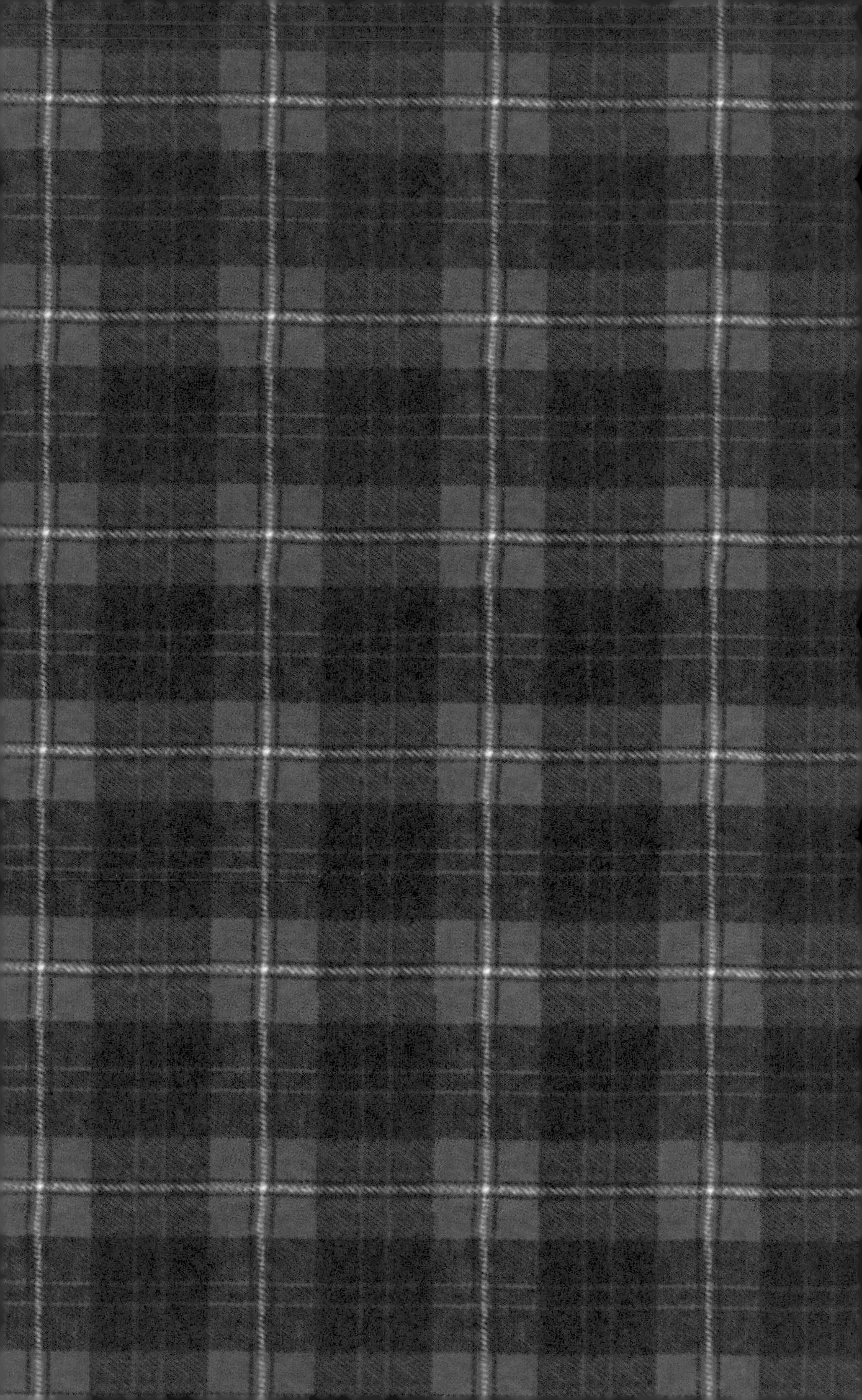

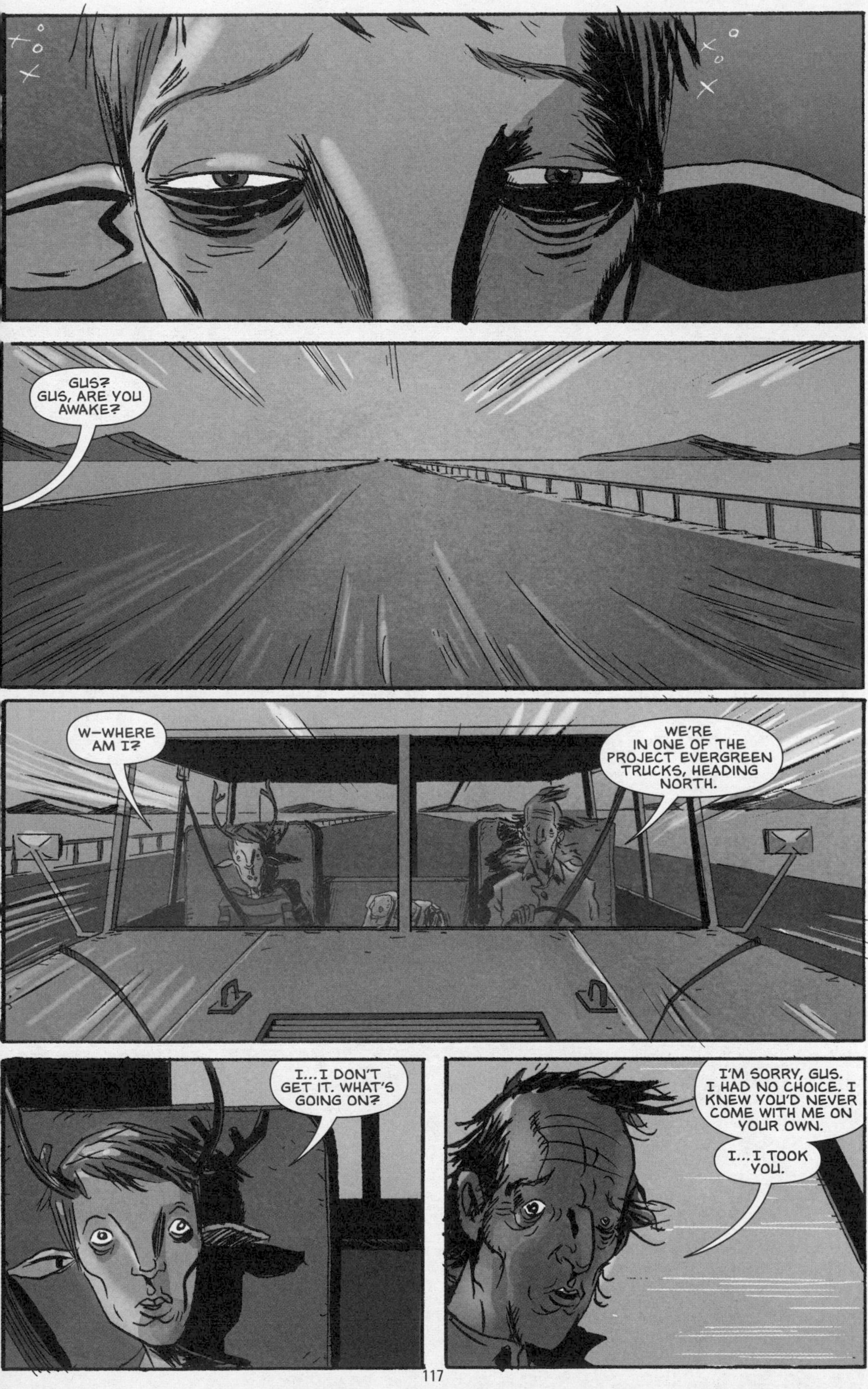
GUS? GUS, ARE YOU AWAKE?
W-WHERE AM I?
WE'RE IN ONE OF THE PROJECT EVERGREEN TRUCKS, HEADING NORTH.
I...I DON'T GET IT. WHAT'S GOING ON?
I'M SORRY, GUS. I HAD NO CHOICE. I KNEW YOU'D NEVER COME WITH ME ON YOUR OWN.
I...I TOOK YOU.

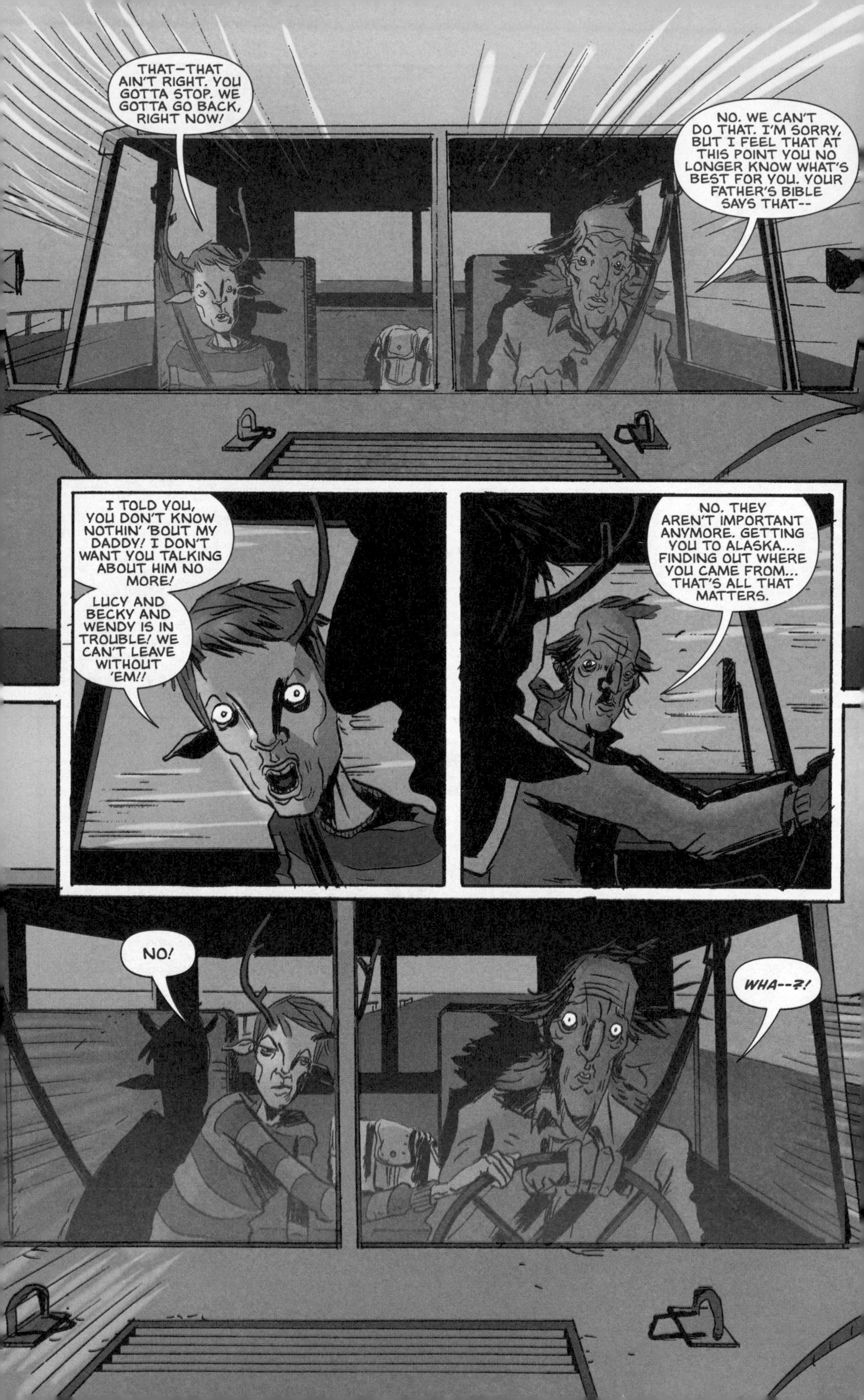
THAT—THAT AIN'T RIGHT. YOU GOTTA STOP. WE GOTTA GO BACK, RIGHT NOW!
NO. WE CAN'T DO THAT. I'M SORRY, BUT I FEEL THAT AT THIS POINT YOU NO LONGER KNOW WHAT'S BEST FOR YOU. YOUR FATHER'S BIBLE SAYS THAT--
I TOLD YOU, YOU DON'T KNOW NOTHIN' 'BOUT MY DADDY! I DON'T WANT YOU TALKING ABOUT HIM NO MORE!
LUCY AND BECKY AND WENDY IS IN TROUBLE! WE CAN'T LEAVE WITHOUT 'EM!!
NO. THEY AREN'T IMPORTANT ANYMORE. GETTING YOU TO ALASKA... FINDING OUT WHERE YOU CAME FROM... THAT'S ALL THAT MATTERS.
NO!
WHA--?!

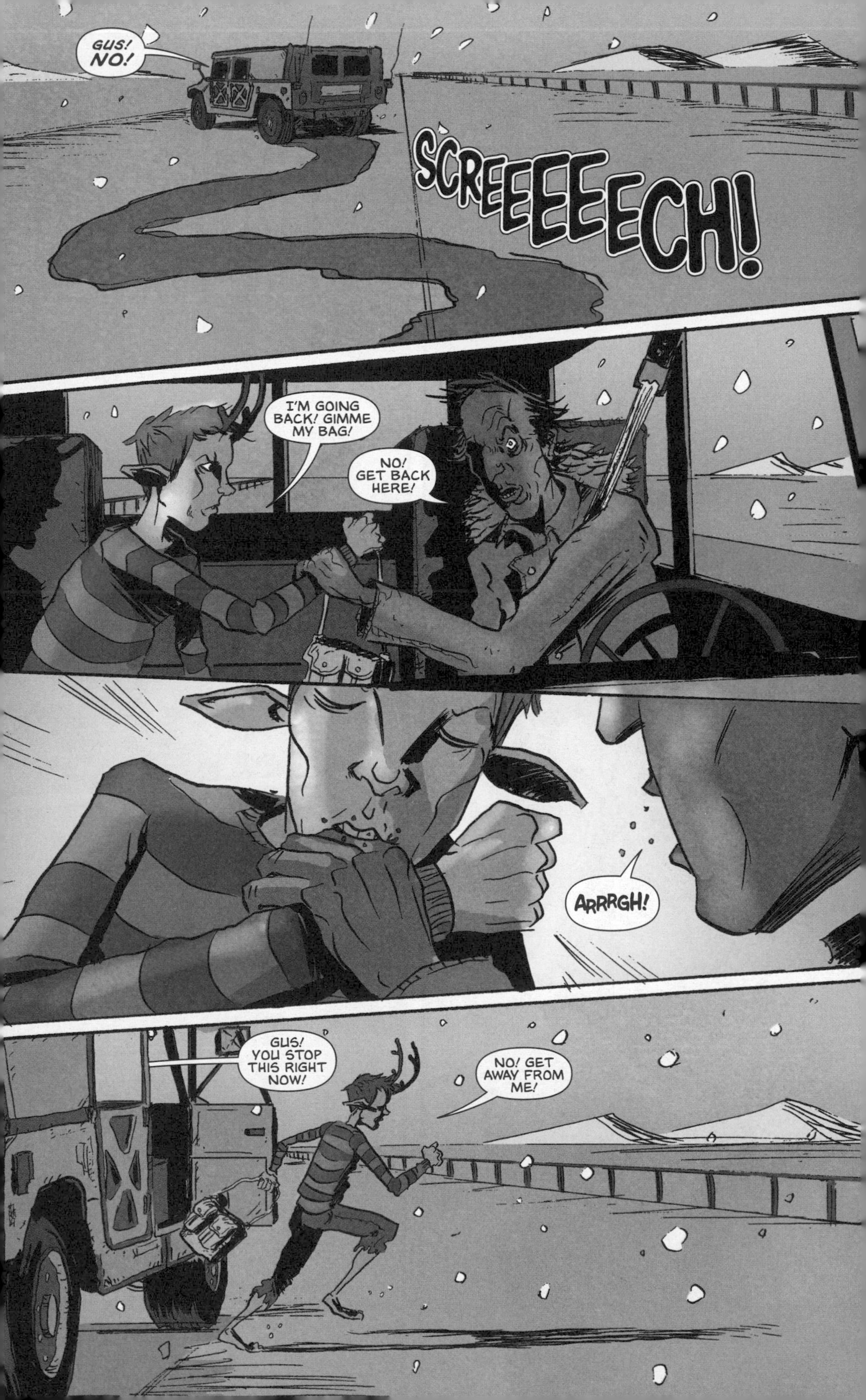

GUS! NO!
SCREEEEEECH!
I'M GOING BACK! GIMME MY BAG!
NO! GET BACK HERE!
ARRRGH!
GUS! YOU STOP THIS RIGHT NOW!
NO! GET AWAY FROM ME!

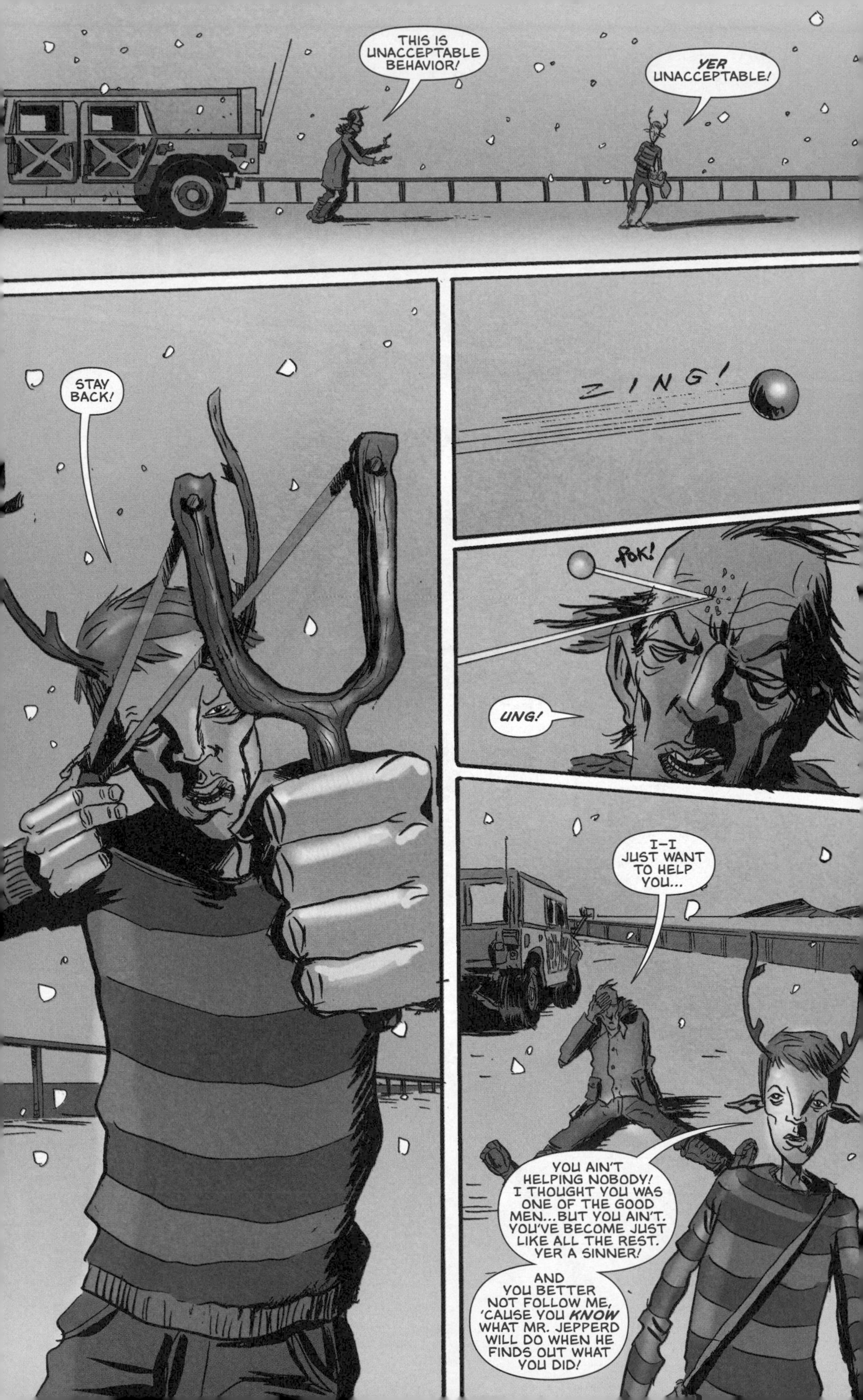
THIS IS UNACCEPTABLE BEHAVIOR!
YER UNACCEPTABLE!
STAY BACK!
ZING!
POK!
UNG!
I–I JUST WANT TO HELP YOU...
YOU AIN'T HELPING NOBODY! I THOUGHT YOU WAS ONE OF THE GOOD MEN...BUT YOU AIN'T. YOU'VE BECOME JUST LIKE ALL THE REST. YER A SINNER!
AND YOU BETTER NOT FOLLOW ME, 'CAUSE YOU KNOW WHAT MR. JEPPERD WILL DO WHEN HE FINDS OUT WHAT YOU DID!

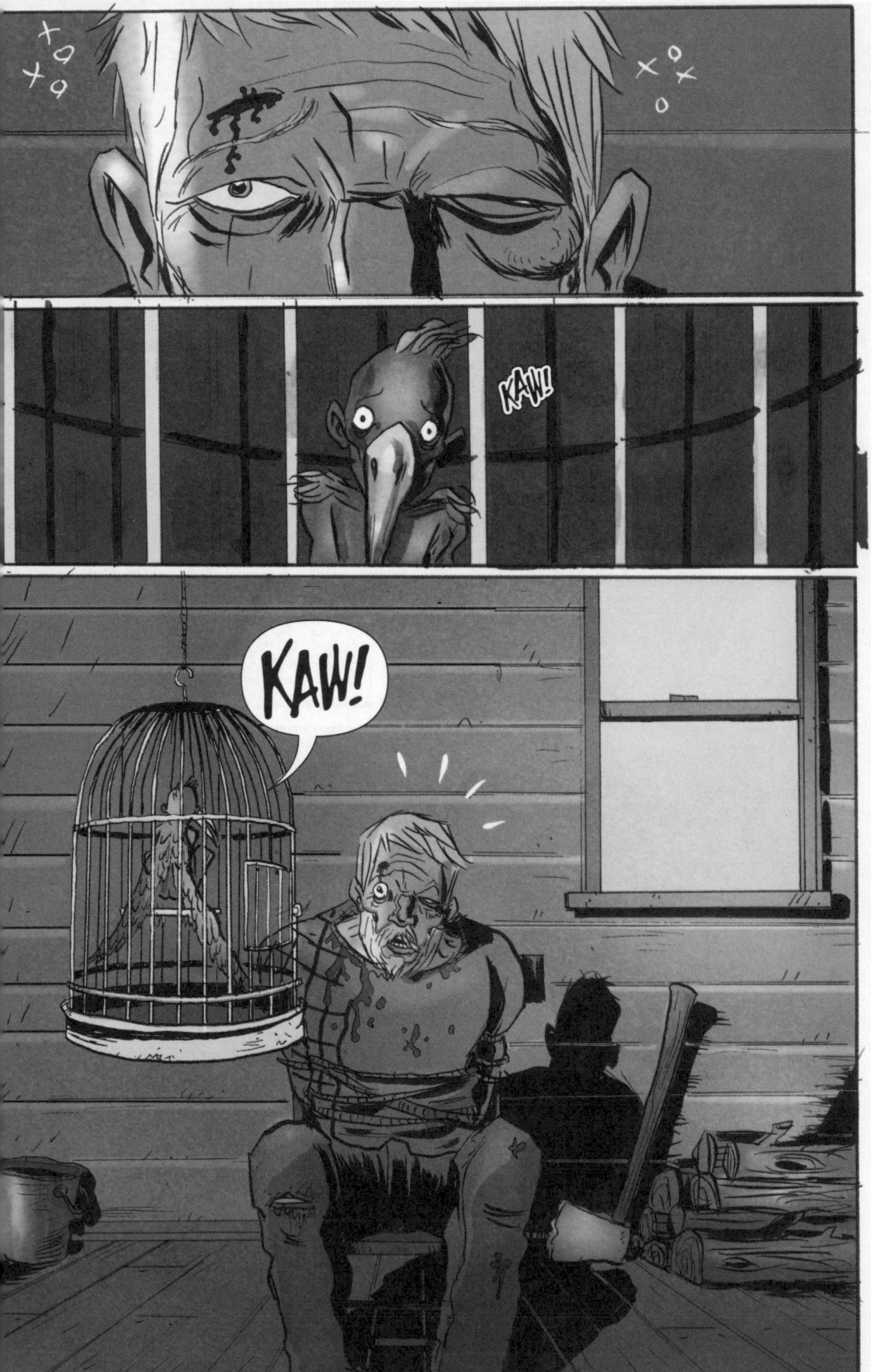
KAW!
KAW!

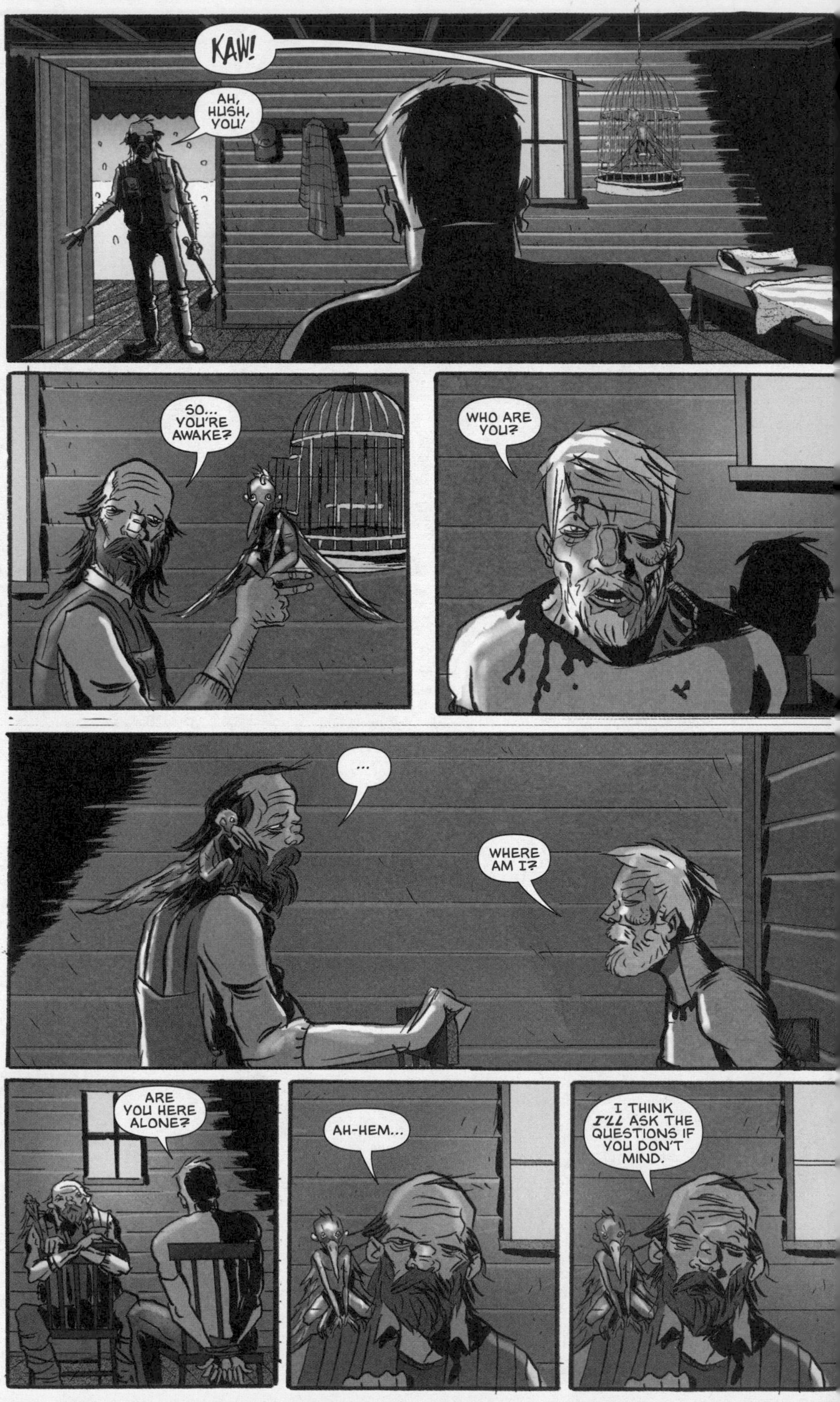
KAW!
AH, HUSH, YOU!
SO... YOU'RE AWAKE?
WHO ARE YOU?
...
WHERE AM I?
ARE YOU HERE ALONE?
AH-HEM...
I THINK I'LL ASK THE QUESTIONS IF YOU DON'T MIND.

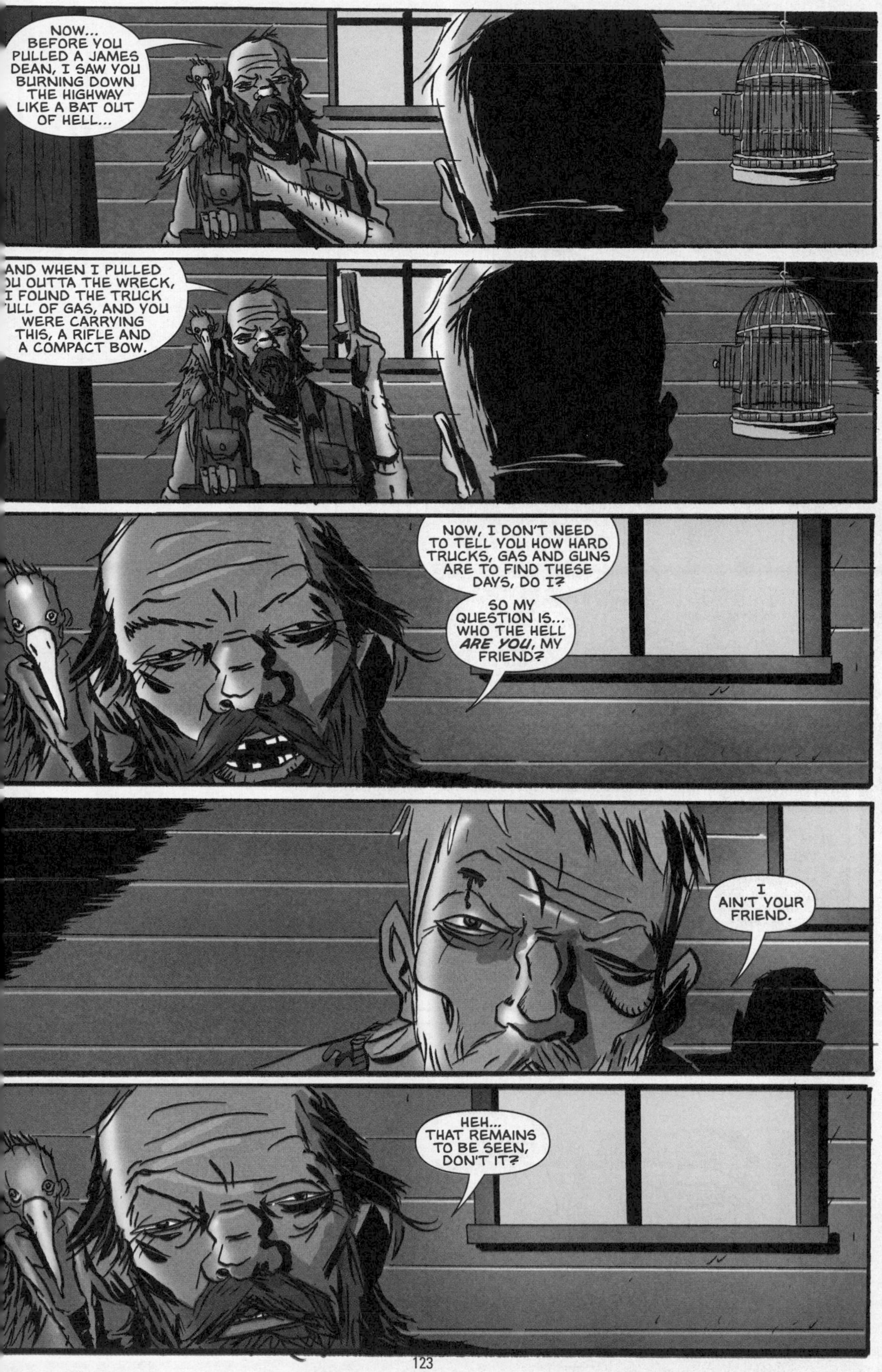
NOW... BEFORE YOU PULLED A JAMES DEAN, I SAW YOU BURNING DOWN THE HIGHWAY LIKE A BAT OUT OF HELL...
AND WHEN I PULLED YOU OUTTA THE WRECK, I FOUND THE TRUCK FULL OF GAS, AND YOU WERE CARRYING THIS, A RIFLE AND A COMPACT BOW.
NOW, I DON'T NEED TO TELL YOU HOW HARD TRUCKS, GAS AND GUNS ARE TO FIND THESE DAYS, DO I?
SO MY QUESTION IS... WHO THE HELL ARE YOU, MY FRIEND?
I AIN'T YOUR FRIEND.
HEH... THAT REMAINS TO BE SEEN, DON'T IT?

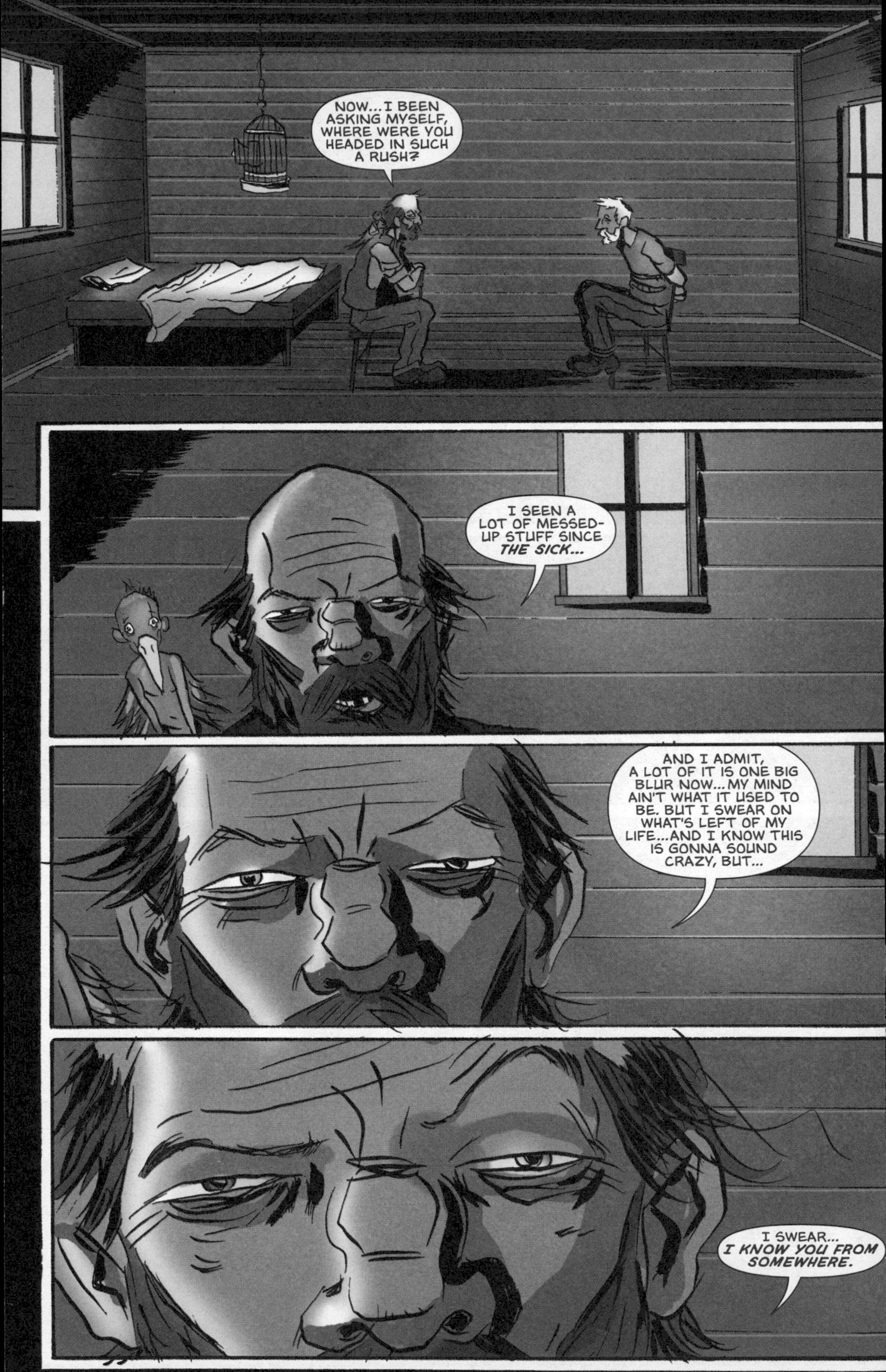
NOW... I BEEN ASKING MYSELF, WHERE WERE YOU HEADED IN SUCH A RUSH?
I SEEN A LOT OF MESSED-UP STUFF SINCE *THE SICK*...
AND I ADMIT, A LOT OF IT IS ONE BIG BLUR NOW... MY MIND AIN'T WHAT IT USED TO BE. BUT I SWEAR ON WHAT'S LEFT OF MY LIFE...AND I KNOW THIS IS GONNA SOUND CRAZY, BUT...
I SWEAR... *I KNOW YOU FROM SOMEWHERE.*

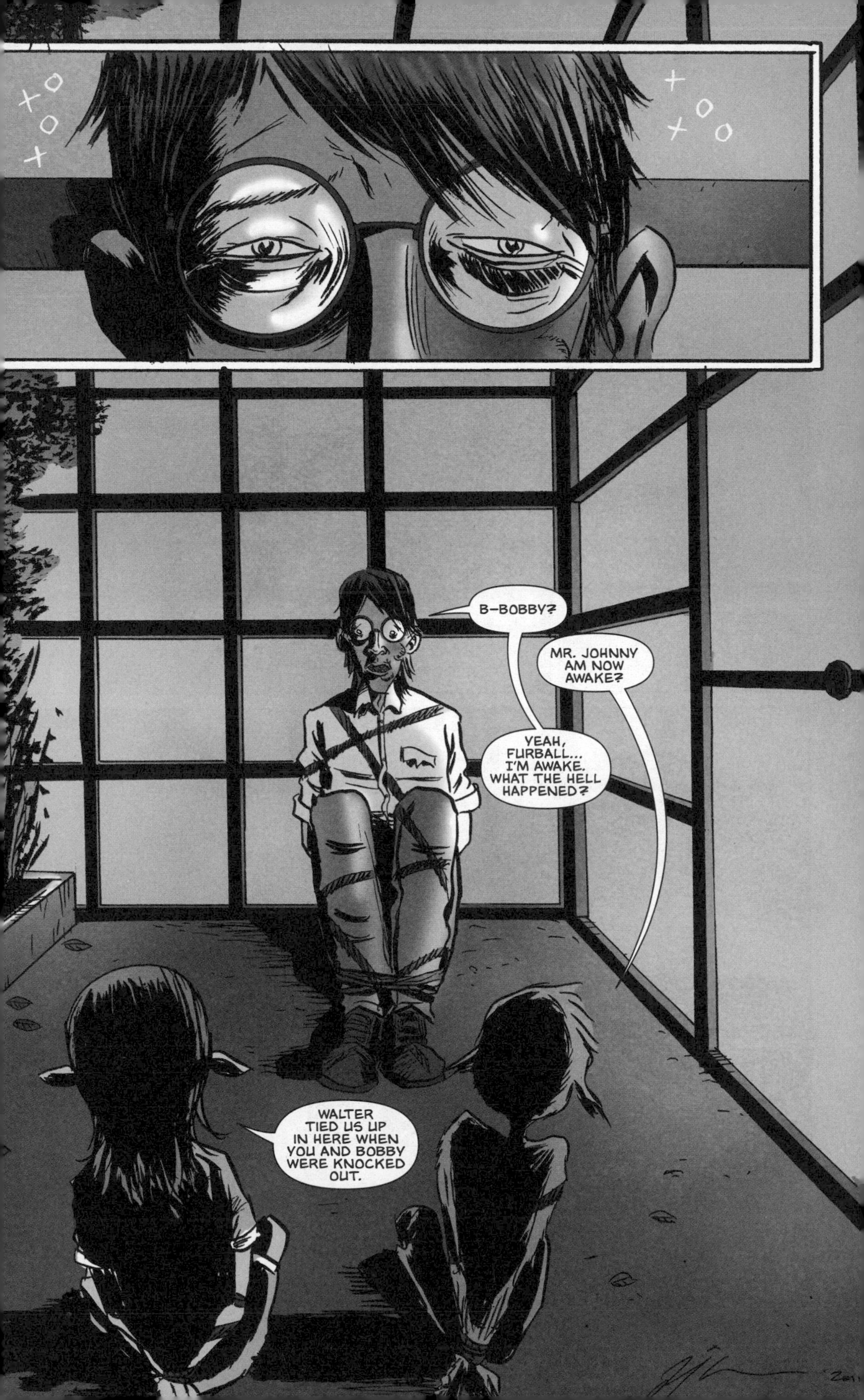
B-BOBBY?
MR. JOHNNY AM NOW AWAKE?
YEAH, FURBALL... I'M AWAKE. WHAT THE HELL HAPPENED?
WALTER TIED US UP IN HERE WHEN YOU AND BOBBY WERE KNOCKED OUT.

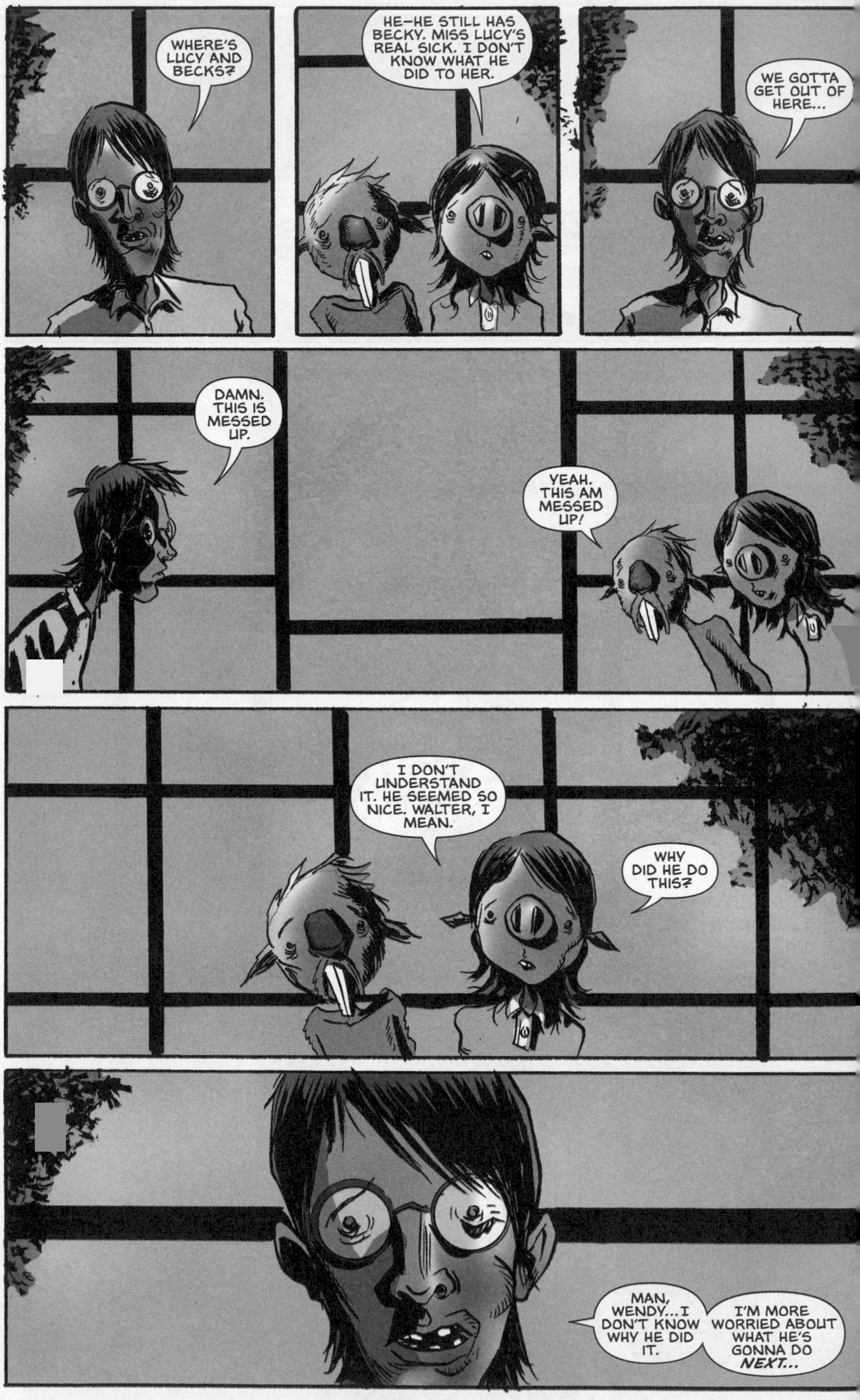
WHERE'S LUCY AND BECKS?
HE—HE STILL HAS BECKY. MISS LUCY'S REAL SICK. I DON'T KNOW WHAT HE DID TO HER.
WE GOTTA GET OUT OF HERE...
DAMN. THIS IS MESSED UP.
YEAH. THIS AM MESSED UP!
I DON'T UNDERSTAND IT. HE SEEMED SO NICE. WALTER, I MEAN.
WHY DID HE DO THIS?
MAN, WENDY... I DON'T KNOW WHY HE DID IT.
I'M MORE WORRIED ABOUT WHAT HE'S GONNA DO *NEXT...*

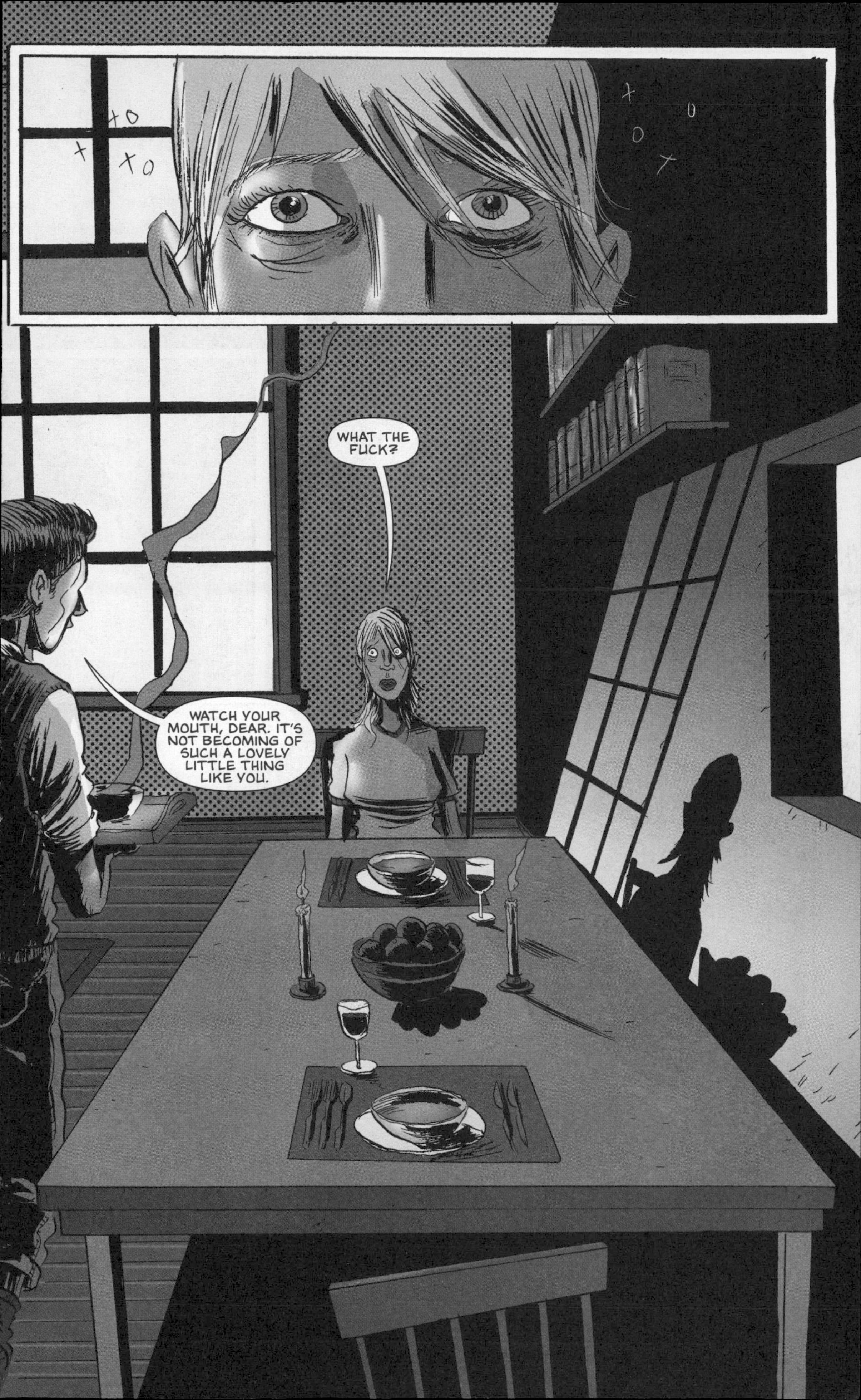
WHAT THE FUCK?
WATCH YOUR MOUTH, DEAR. IT'S NOT BECOMING OF SUCH A LOVELY LITTLE THING LIKE YOU.

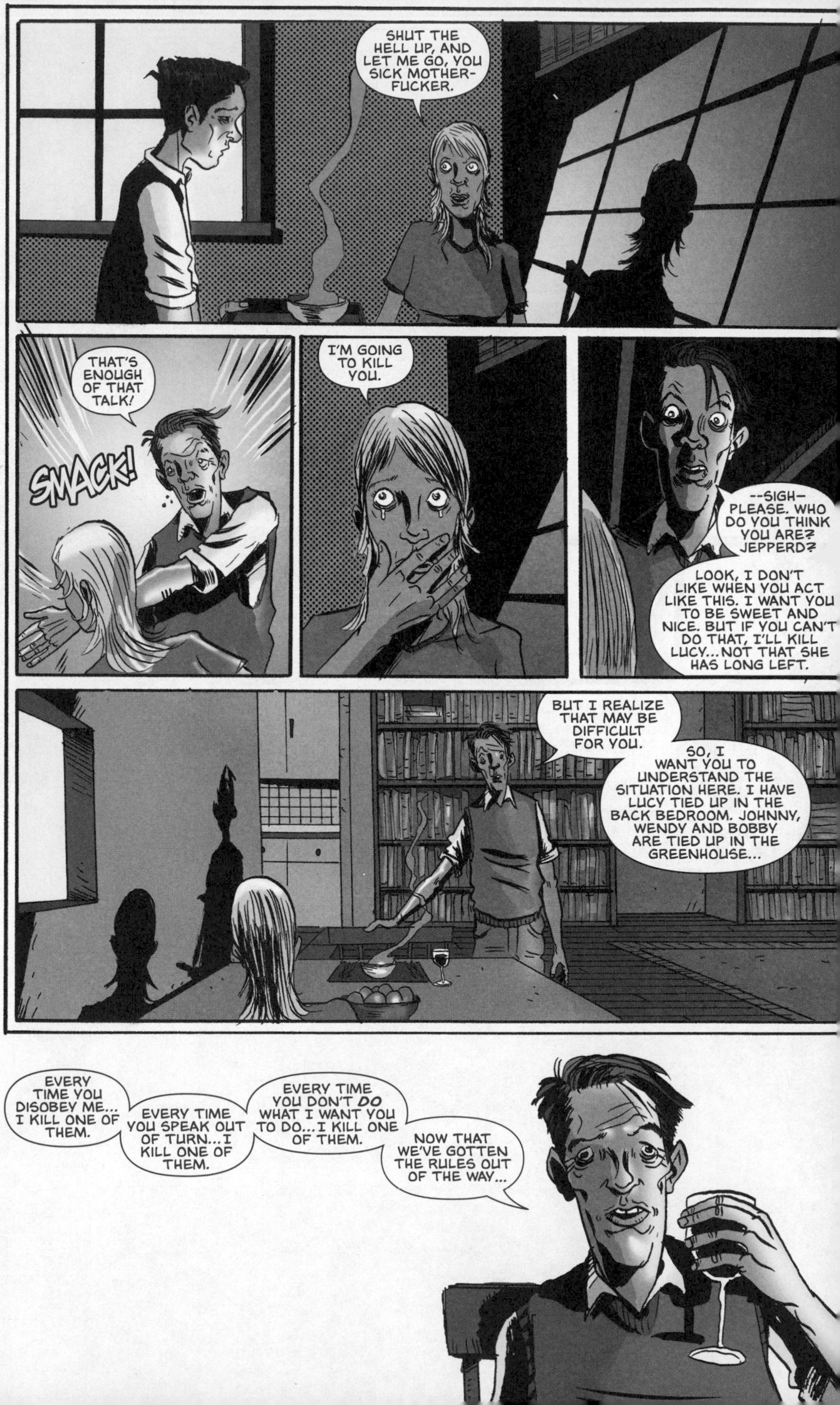
SHUT THE HELL UP, AND LET ME GO, YOU SICK MOTHER-FUCKER.
THAT'S ENOUGH OF THAT TALK!
SMACK!
I'M GOING TO KILL YOU.
--SIGH-- PLEASE. WHO DO YOU THINK YOU ARE? JEPPERD?
LOOK, I DON'T LIKE WHEN YOU ACT LIKE THIS. I WANT YOU TO BE SWEET AND NICE. BUT IF YOU CAN'T DO THAT, I'LL KILL LUCY... NOT THAT SHE HAS LONG LEFT.
BUT I REALIZE THAT MAY BE DIFFICULT FOR YOU.
SO, I WANT YOU TO UNDERSTAND THE SITUATION HERE. I HAVE LUCY TIED UP IN THE BACK BEDROOM. JOHNNY, WENDY AND BOBBY ARE TIED UP IN THE GREENHOUSE...
EVERY TIME YOU DISOBEY ME... I KILL ONE OF THEM.
EVERY TIME YOU SPEAK OUT OF TURN... I KILL ONE OF THEM.
EVERY TIME YOU DON'T *DO* WHAT I WANT YOU TO DO... I KILL ONE OF THEM.
NOW THAT WE'VE GOTTEN THE RULES OUT OF THE WAY...

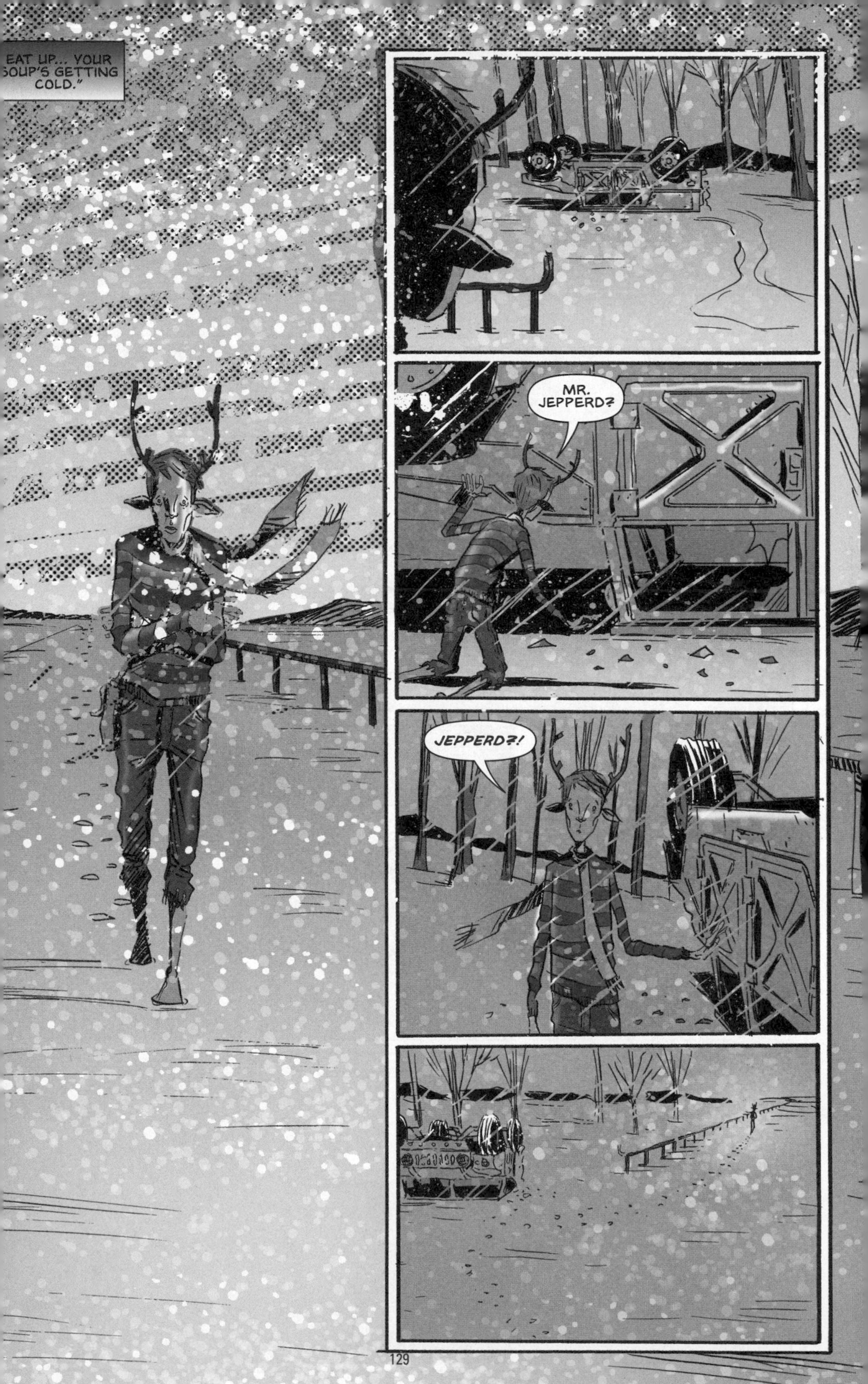
EAT UP... YOUR SOUP'S GETTING COLD."
MR. JEPPERD?
JEPPERD?!

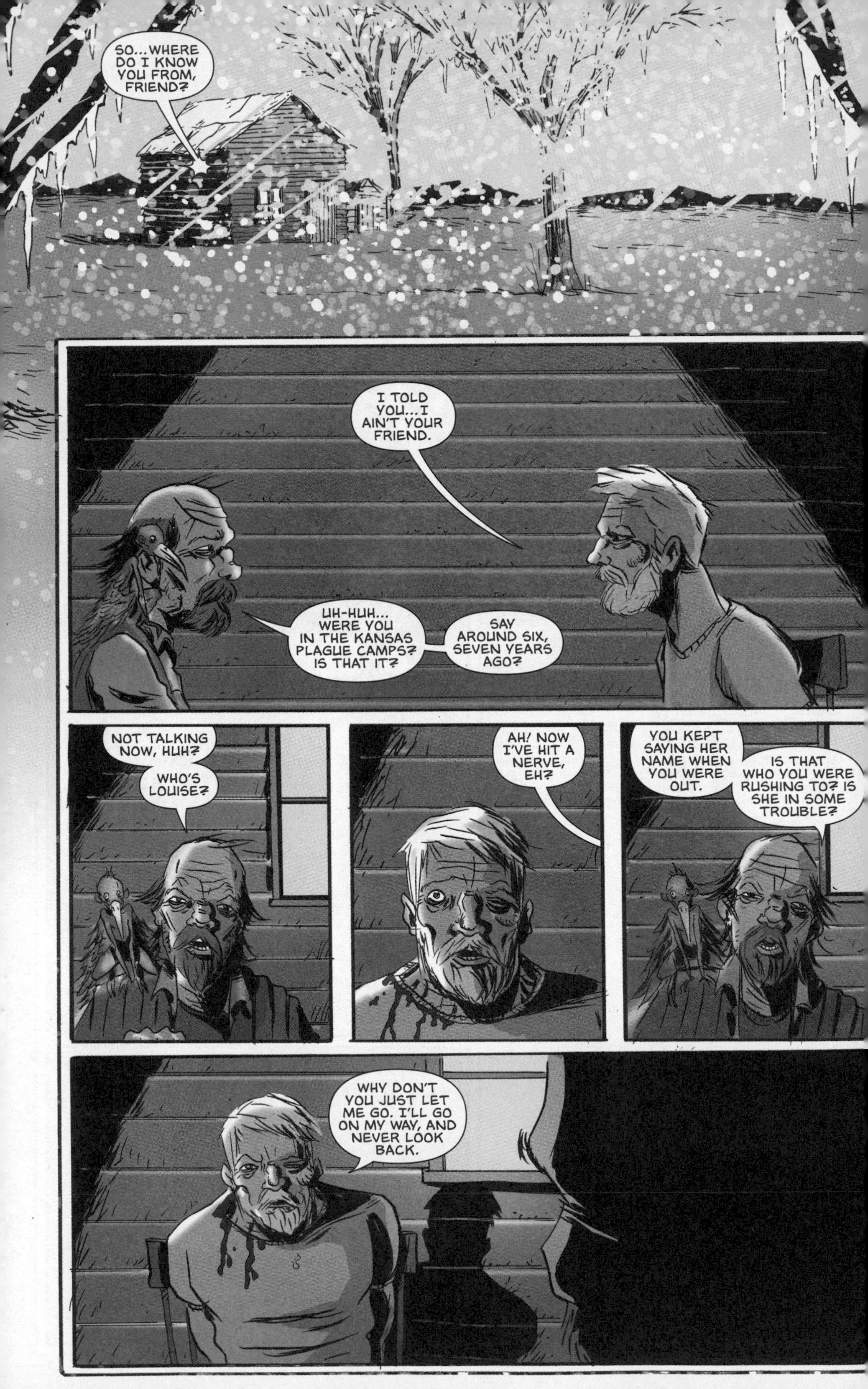
SO...WHERE DO I KNOW YOU FROM, FRIEND?
I TOLD YOU...I AIN'T YOUR FRIEND.
UH-HUH... WERE YOU IN THE KANSAS PLAGUE CAMPS? IS THAT IT?
SAY AROUND SIX, SEVEN YEARS AGO?
NOT TALKING NOW, HUH?
WHO'S LOUISE?
AH! NOW I'VE HIT A NERVE, EH?
YOU KEPT SAYING HER NAME WHEN YOU WERE OUT.
IS THAT WHO YOU WERE RUSHING TO? IS SHE IN SOME TROUBLE?
WHY DON'T YOU JUST LET ME GO. I'LL GO ON MY WAY, AND NEVER LOOK BACK.

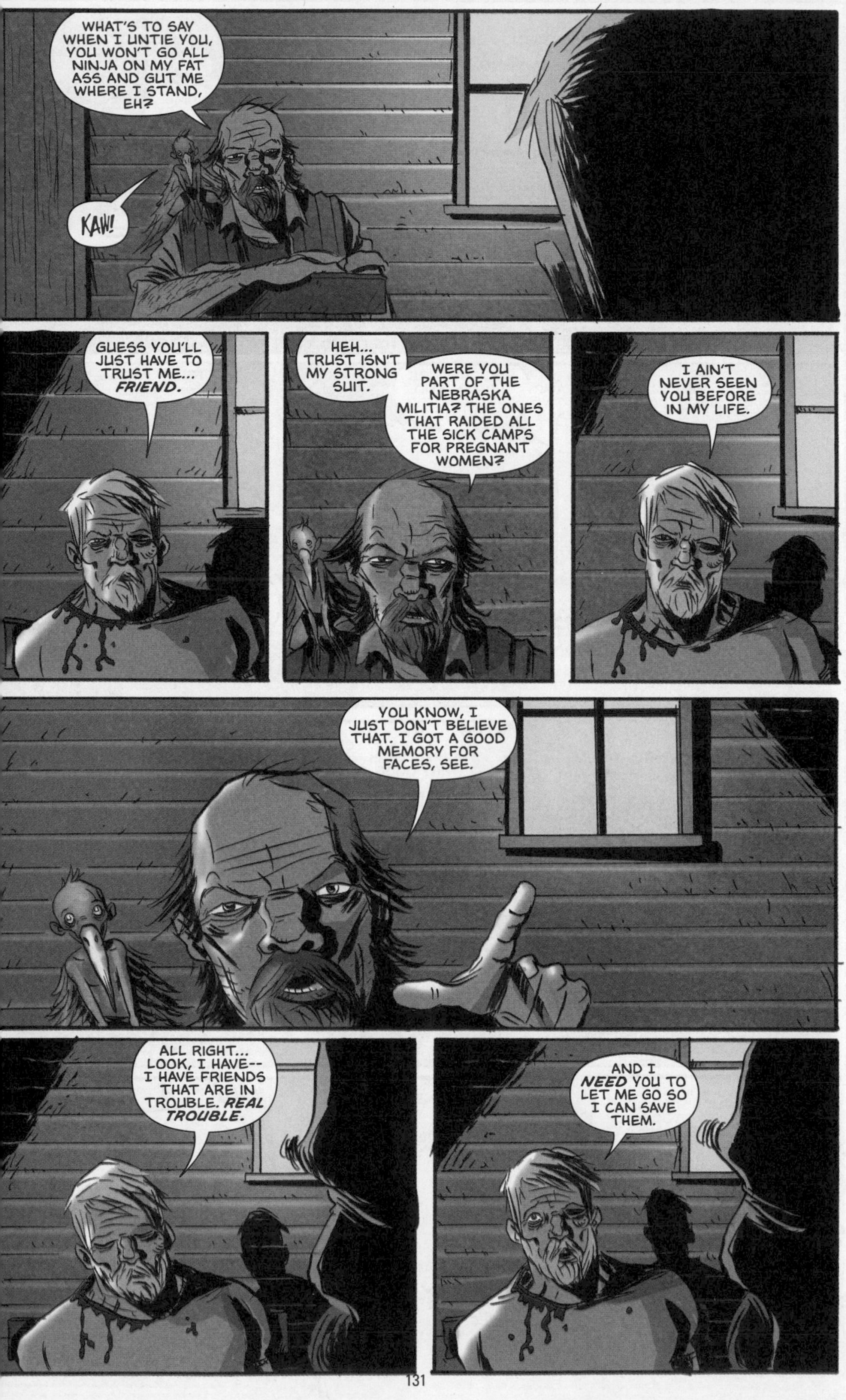
WHAT'S TO SAY WHEN I UNTIE YOU, YOU WON'T GO ALL NINJA ON MY FAT ASS AND GUT ME WHERE I STAND, EH?
KAW!
GUESS YOU'LL JUST HAVE TO TRUST ME... *FRIEND.*
HEH... TRUST ISN'T MY STRONG SUIT.
WERE YOU PART OF THE NEBRASKA MILITIA? THE ONES THAT RAIDED ALL THE SICK CAMPS FOR PREGNANT WOMEN?
I AIN'T NEVER SEEN YOU BEFORE IN MY LIFE.
YOU KNOW, I JUST DON'T BELIEVE THAT. I GOT A GOOD MEMORY FOR FACES, SEE.
ALL RIGHT... LOOK, I HAVE-- I HAVE FRIENDS THAT ARE IN TROUBLE. *REAL TROUBLE.*
AND I *NEED* YOU TO LET ME GO SO I CAN SAVE THEM.

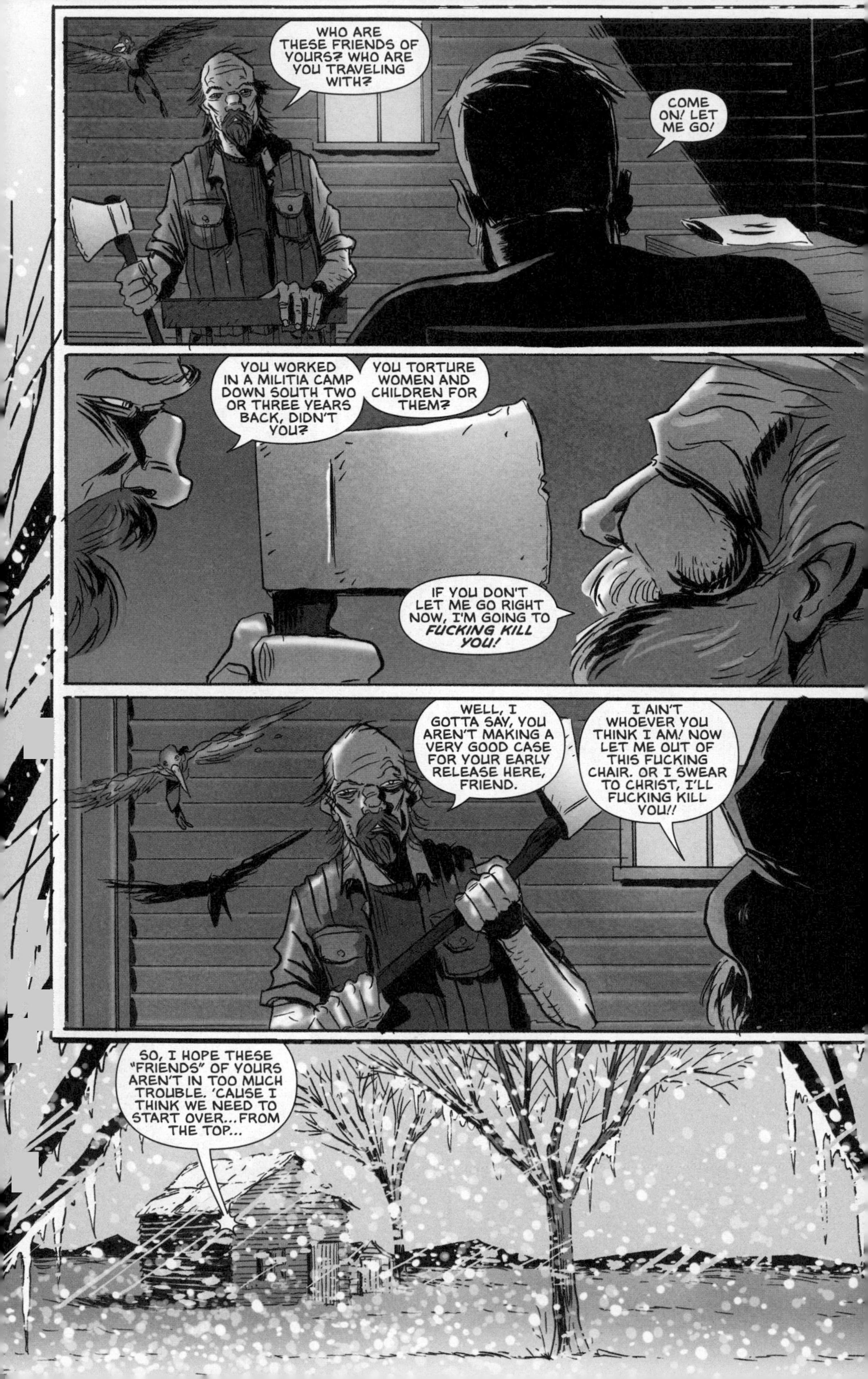
WHO ARE THESE FRIENDS OF YOURS? WHO ARE YOU TRAVELING WITH?
COME ON! LET ME GO!
YOU WORKED IN A MILITIA CAMP DOWN SOUTH TWO OR THREE YEARS BACK, DIDN'T YOU?
YOU TORTURE WOMEN AND CHILDREN FOR THEM?
IF YOU DON'T LET ME GO RIGHT NOW, I'M GOING TO *FUCKING KILL YOU!*
WELL, I GOTTA SAY, YOU AREN'T MAKING A VERY GOOD CASE FOR YOUR EARLY RELEASE HERE, FRIEND.
I AIN'T WHOEVER YOU THINK I AM! NOW LET ME OUT OF THIS FUCKING CHAIR. OR I SWEAR TO CHRIST, I'LL FUCKING KILL YOU!!
SO, I HOPE THESE "FRIENDS" OF YOURS AREN'T IN TOO MUCH TROUBLE. 'CAUSE I THINK WE NEED TO START OVER...FROM THE TOP...

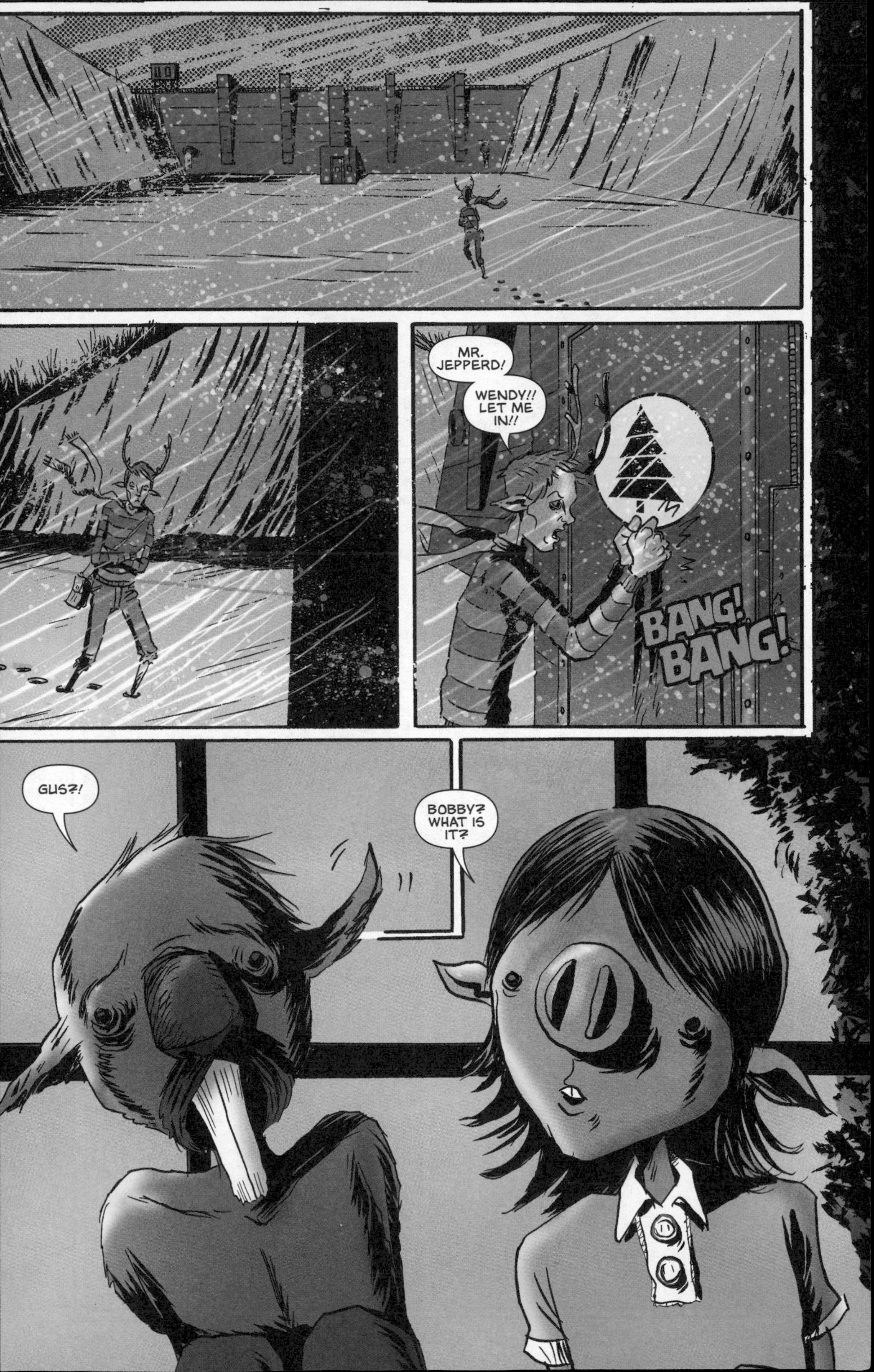
MR. JEPPERD!
WENDY!! LET ME IN!!
BANG! BANG!
GUS?!
BOBBY? WHAT IS IT?

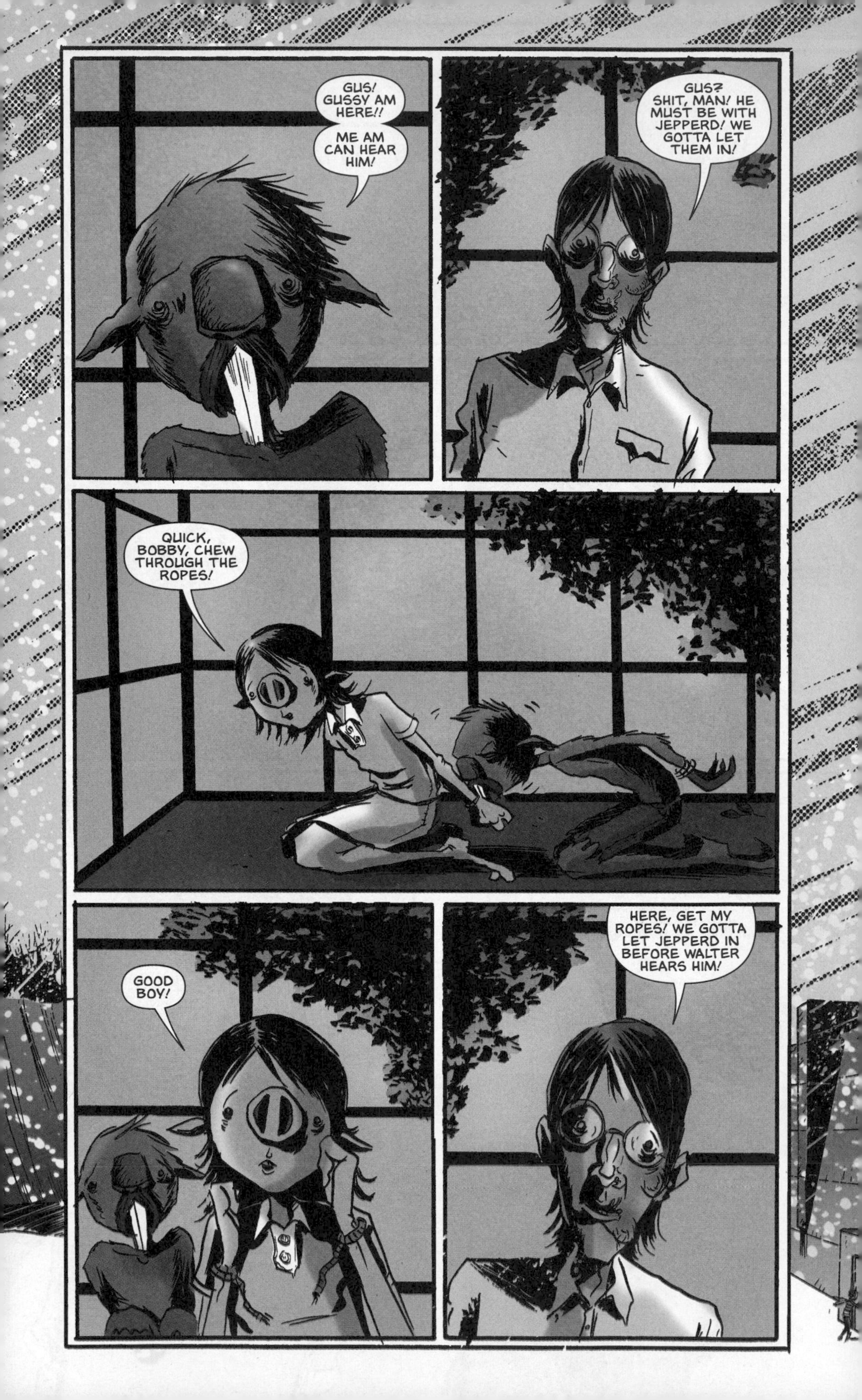
GUS! GUSSY AM HERE!!
ME AM CAN HEAR HIM!
GUS? SHIT, MAN! HE MUST BE WITH JEPPERD! WE GOTTA LET THEM IN!
QUICK, BOBBY, CHEW THROUGH THE ROPES!
GOOD BOY!
HERE, GET MY ROPES! WE GOTTA LET JEPPERD IN BEFORE WALTER HEARS HIM!

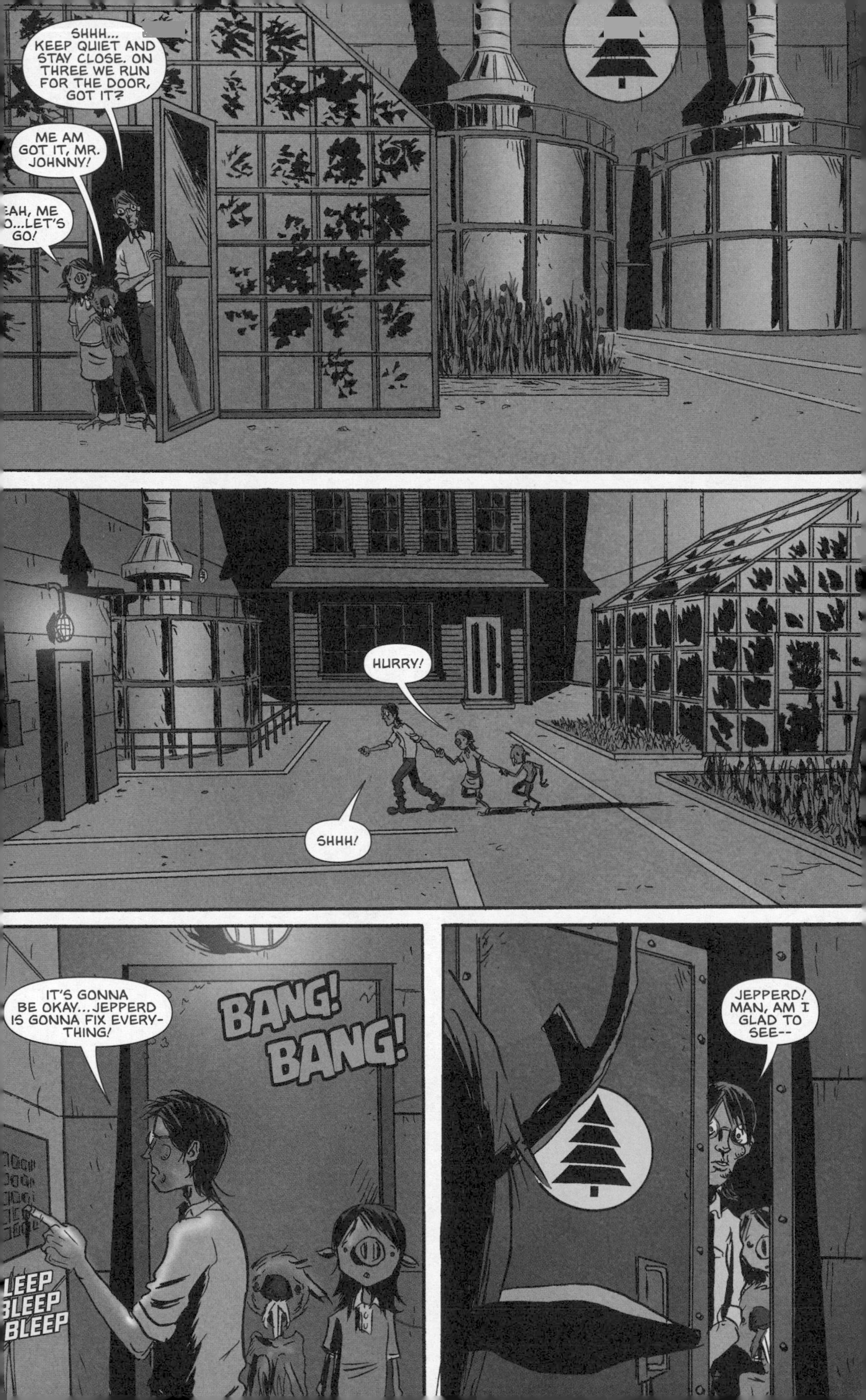
SHHH... KEEP QUIET AND STAY CLOSE. ON THREE WE RUN FOR THE DOOR, GOT IT?
ME AM GOT IT, MR. JOHNNY!
EAH, ME O...LET'S GO!
HURRY!
SHHH!
IT'S GONNA BE OKAY...JEPPERD IS GONNA FIX EVERY-THING!
BANG! BANG!
LEEP BLEEP BLEEP
JEPPERD! MAN, AM I GLAD TO SEE--

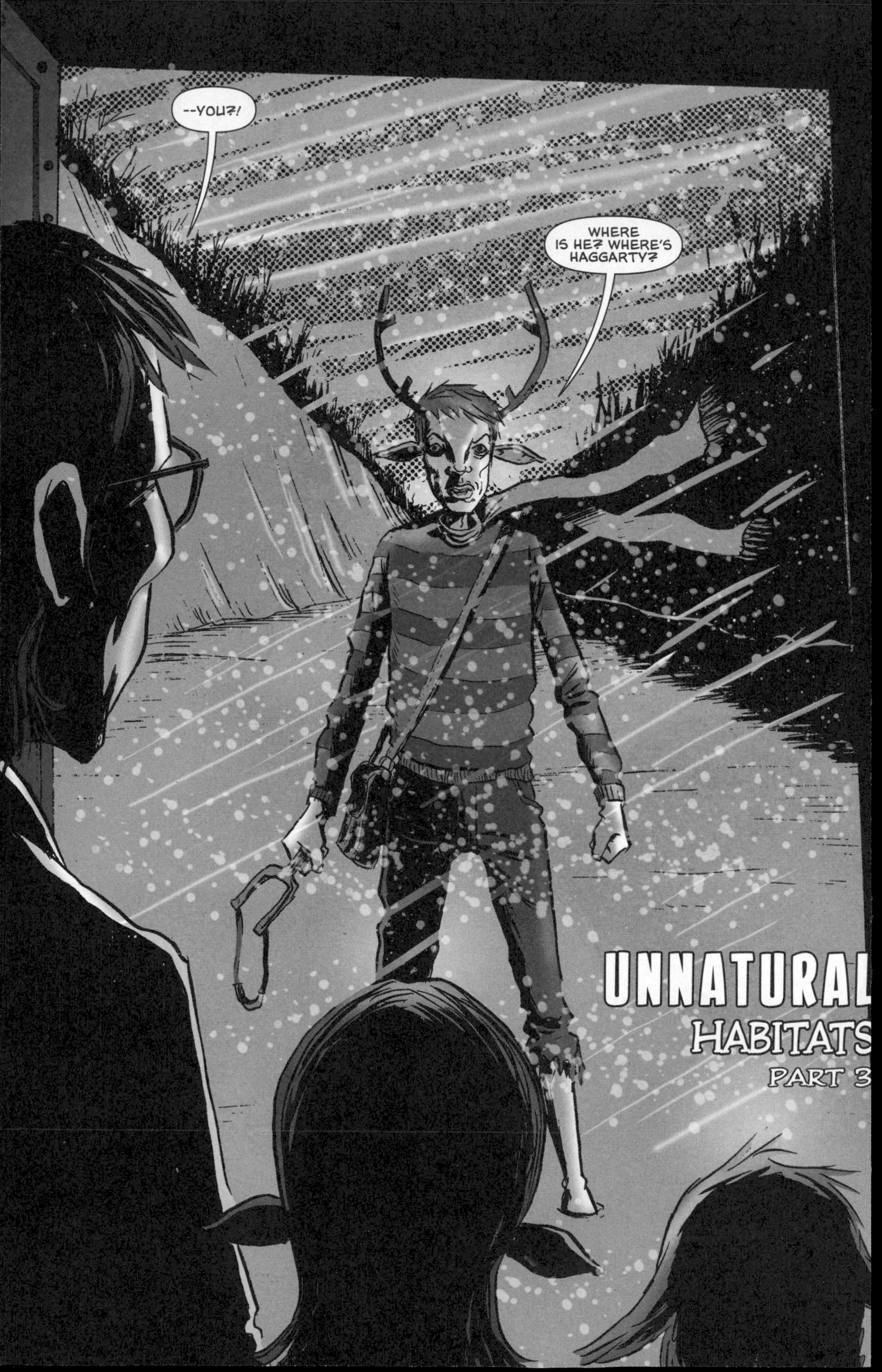
--YOU?!
WHERE IS HE? WHERE'S HAGGARTY?
UNNATURAL HABITATS PART 3

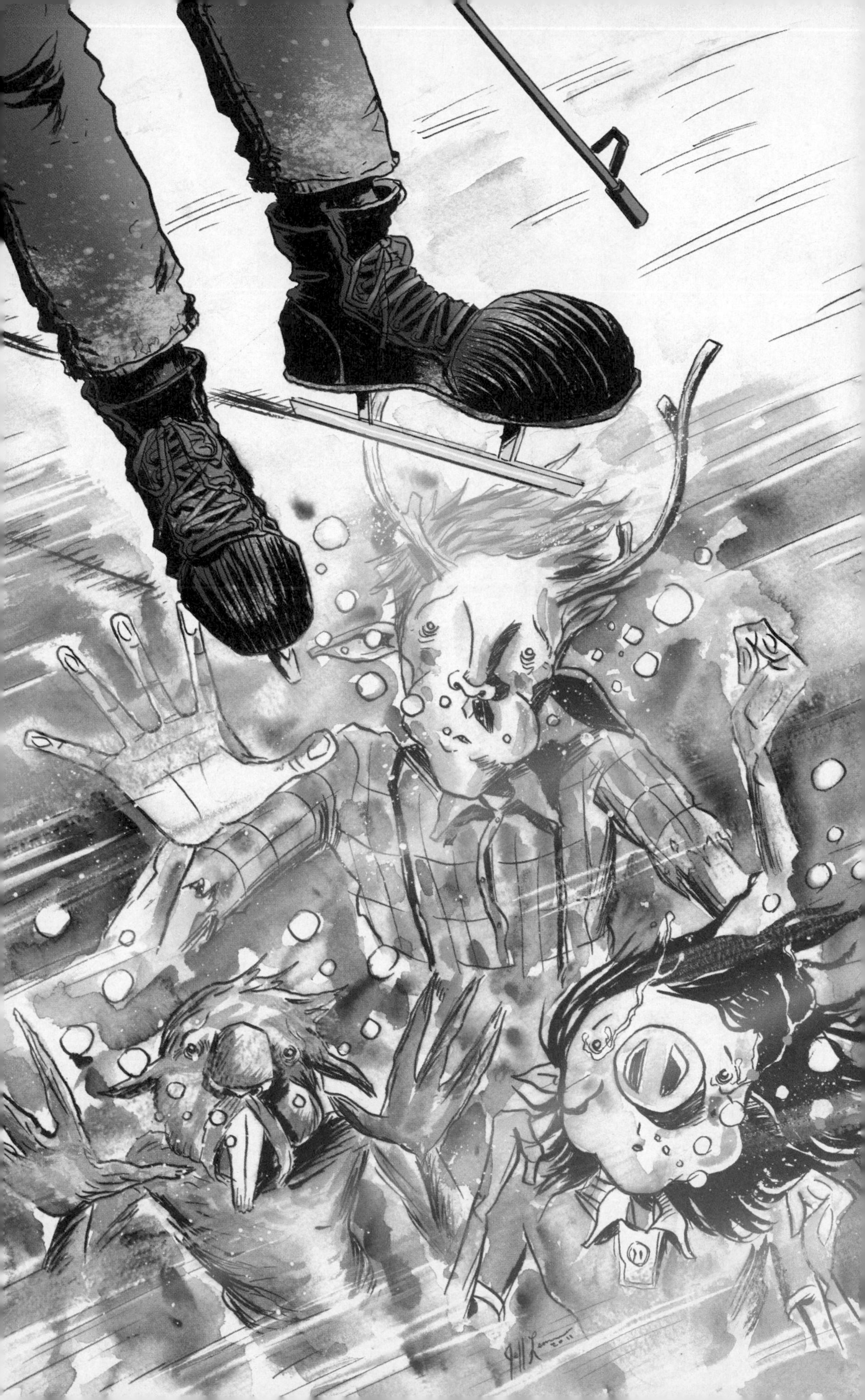

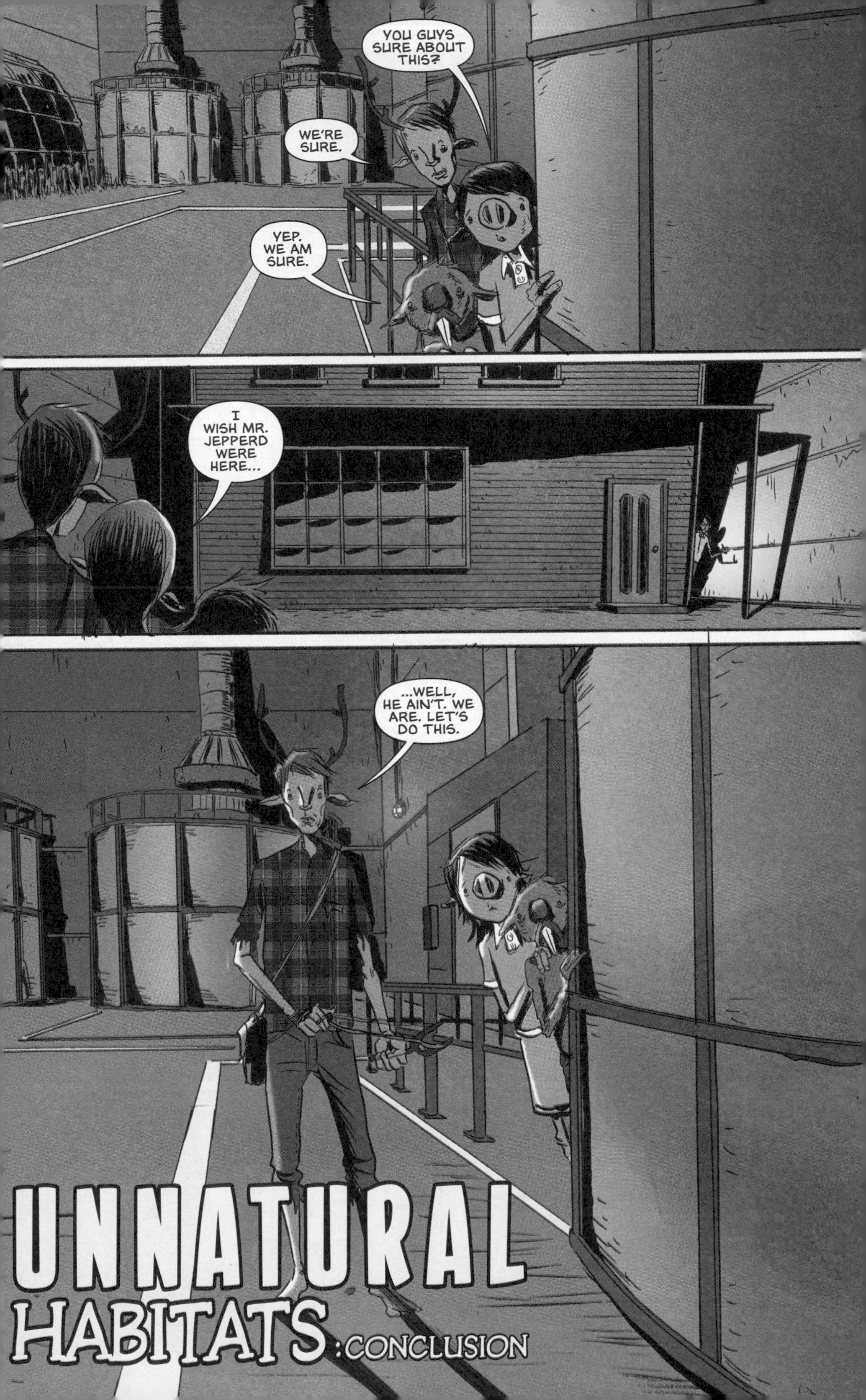
YOU GUYS SURE ABOUT THIS?
WE'RE SURE.
YEP. WE AM SURE.
I WISH MR. JEPPERD WERE HERE...
...WELL, HE AIN'T. WE ARE. LET'S DO THIS.
UNNATURAL HABITATS: CONCLUSION

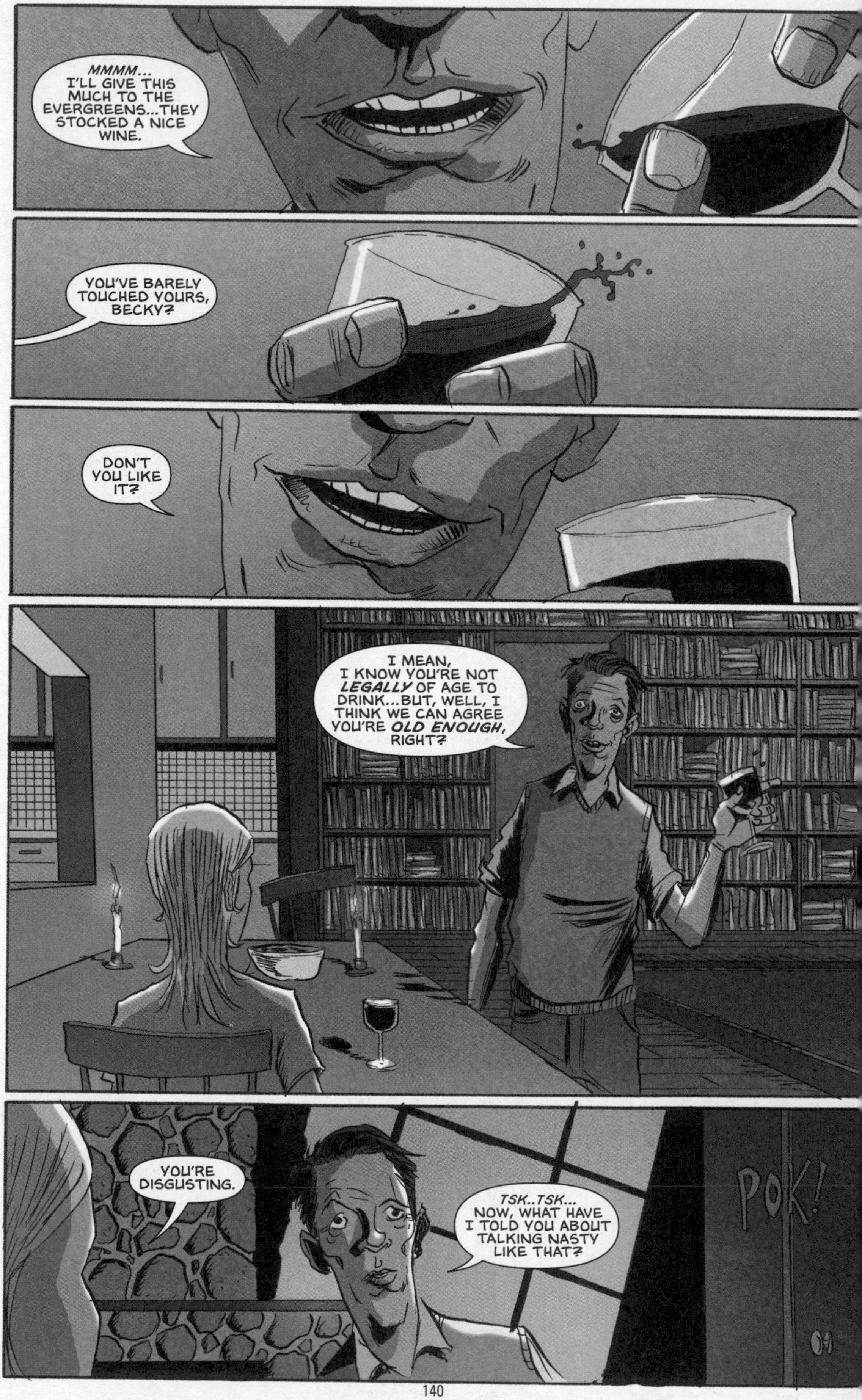
MMMM... I'LL GIVE THIS MUCH TO THE EVERGREENS...THEY STOCKED A NICE WINE.
YOU'VE BARELY TOUCHED YOURS, BECKY?
DON'T YOU LIKE IT?
I MEAN, I KNOW YOU'RE NOT LEGALLY OF AGE TO DRINK...BUT, WELL, I THINK WE CAN AGREE YOU'RE OLD ENOUGH, RIGHT?
YOU'RE DISGUSTING.
TSK..TSK... NOW, WHAT HAVE I TOLD YOU ABOUT TALKING NASTY LIKE THAT?
POK!

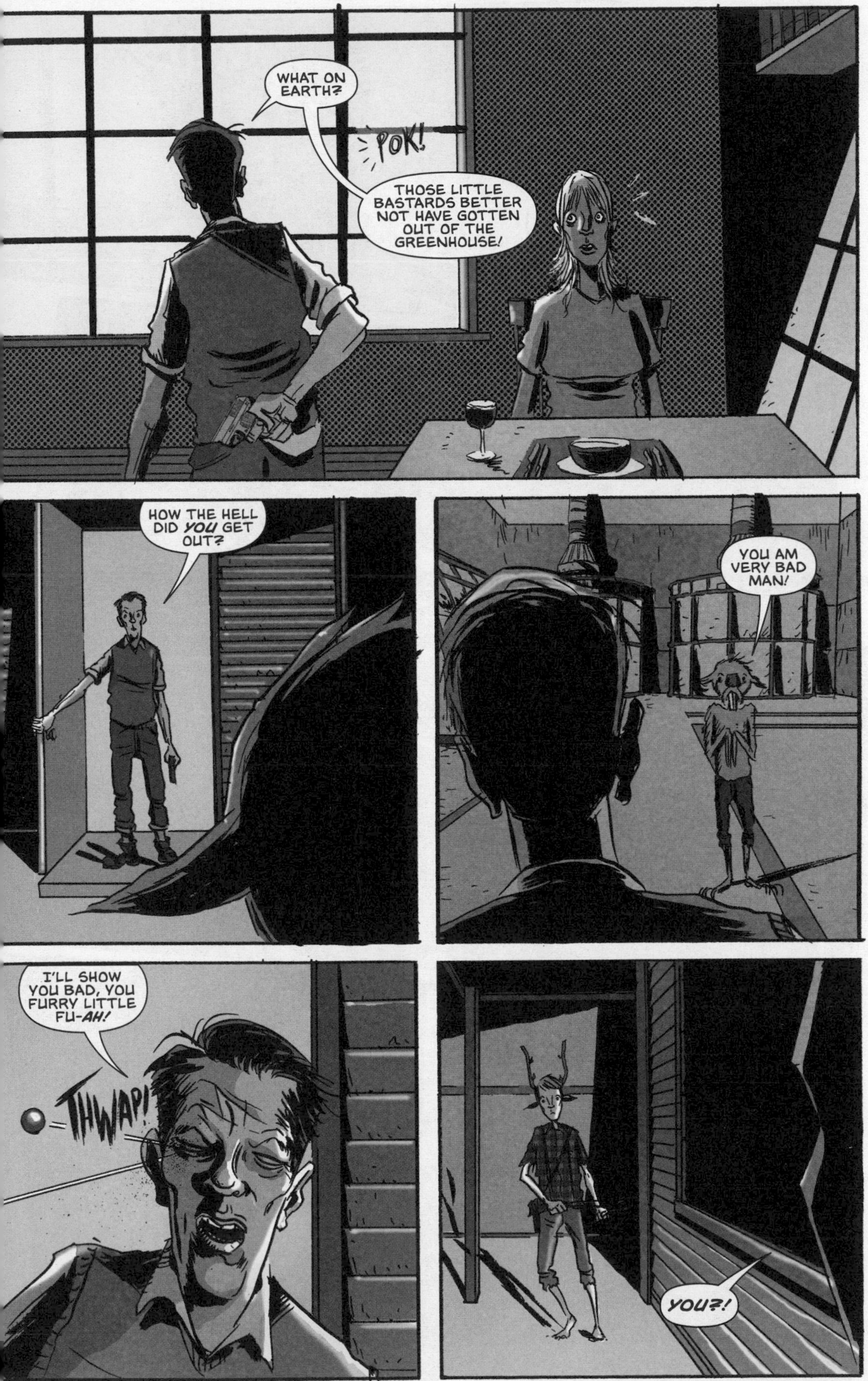
WHAT ON EARTH?
POK!
THOSE LITTLE BASTARDS BETTER NOT HAVE GOTTEN OUT OF THE GREENHOUSE!
HOW THE HELL DID *YOU* GET OUT?
YOU AM VERY BAD MAN!
I'LL SHOW YOU BAD, YOU FURRY LITTLE FU-*AH!*
THWAP!
YOU?!

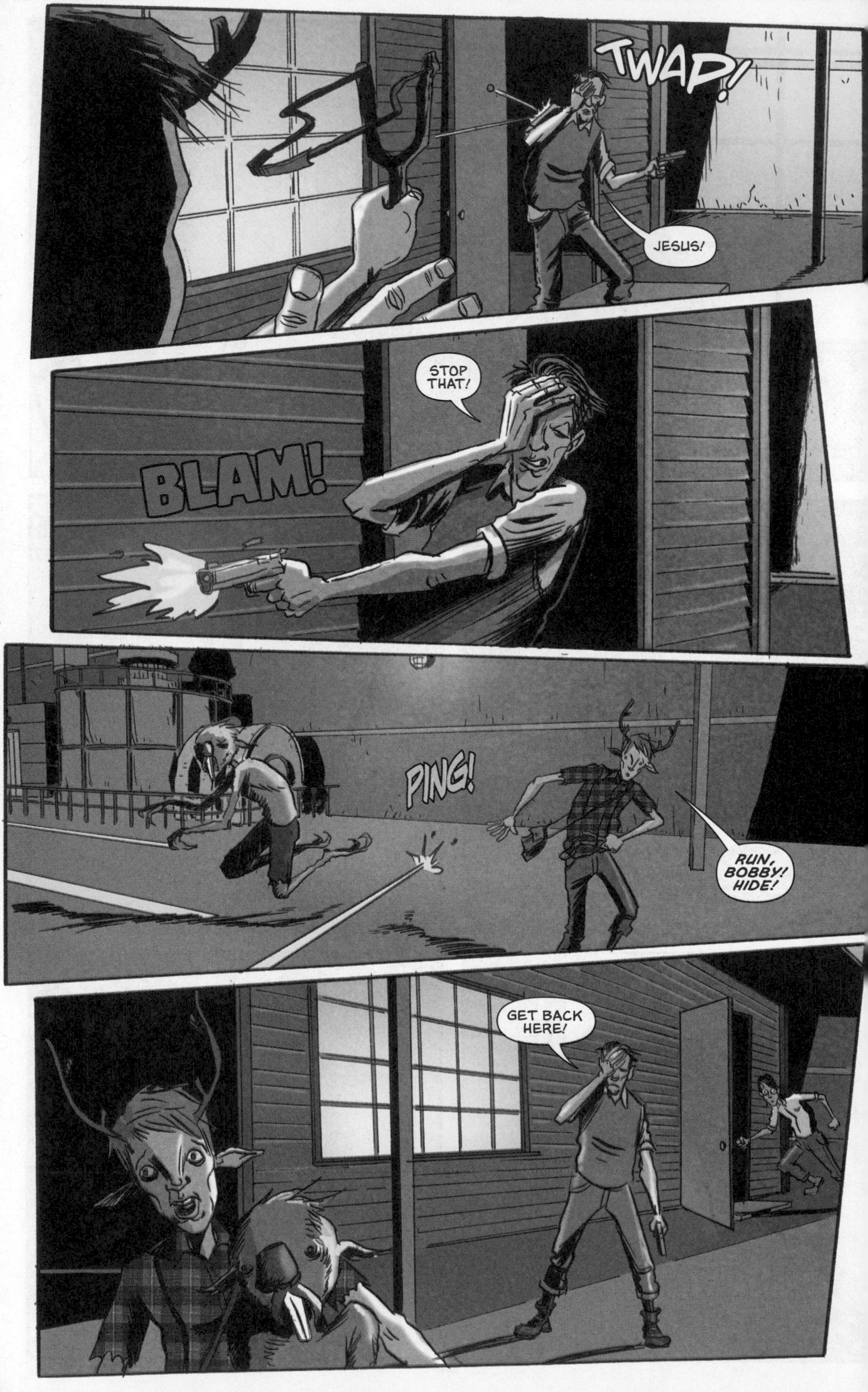
TWAP!
JESUS!
STOP THAT!
BLAM!
PING!
RUN, BOBBY! HIDE!
GET BACK HERE!

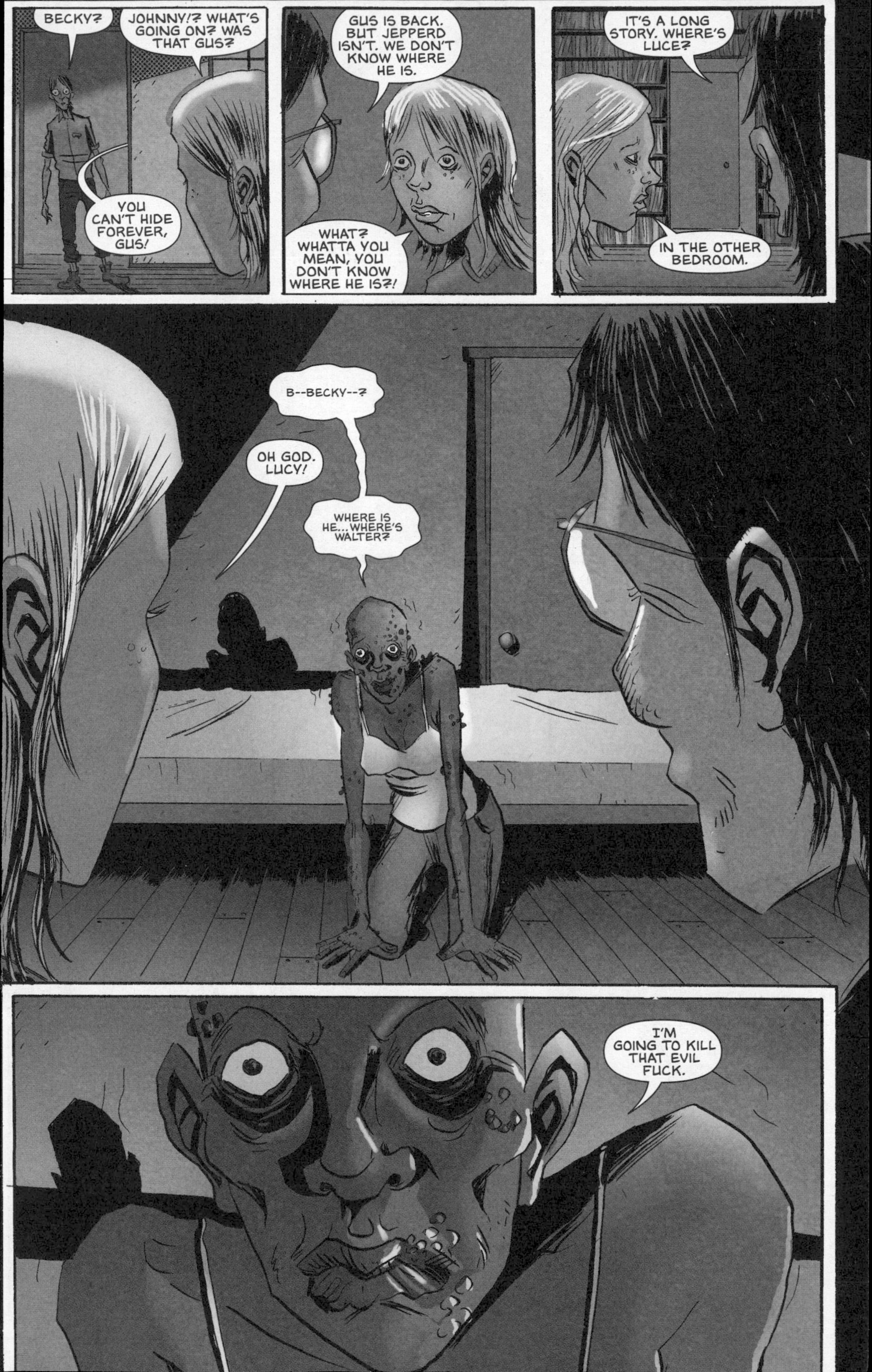
BECKY?
JOHNNY!? WHAT'S GOING ON? WAS THAT GUS?
YOU CAN'T HIDE FOREVER, GUS!
GUS IS BACK. BUT JEPPERD ISN'T. WE DON'T KNOW WHERE HE IS.
WHAT? WHATTA YOU MEAN, YOU DON'T KNOW WHERE HE IS?!
IT'S A LONG STORY. WHERE'S LUCE?
IN THE OTHER BEDROOM.
B--BECKY--?
OH GOD. LUCY!
WHERE IS HE...WHERE'S WALTER?
I'M GOING TO KILL THAT EVIL FUCK.

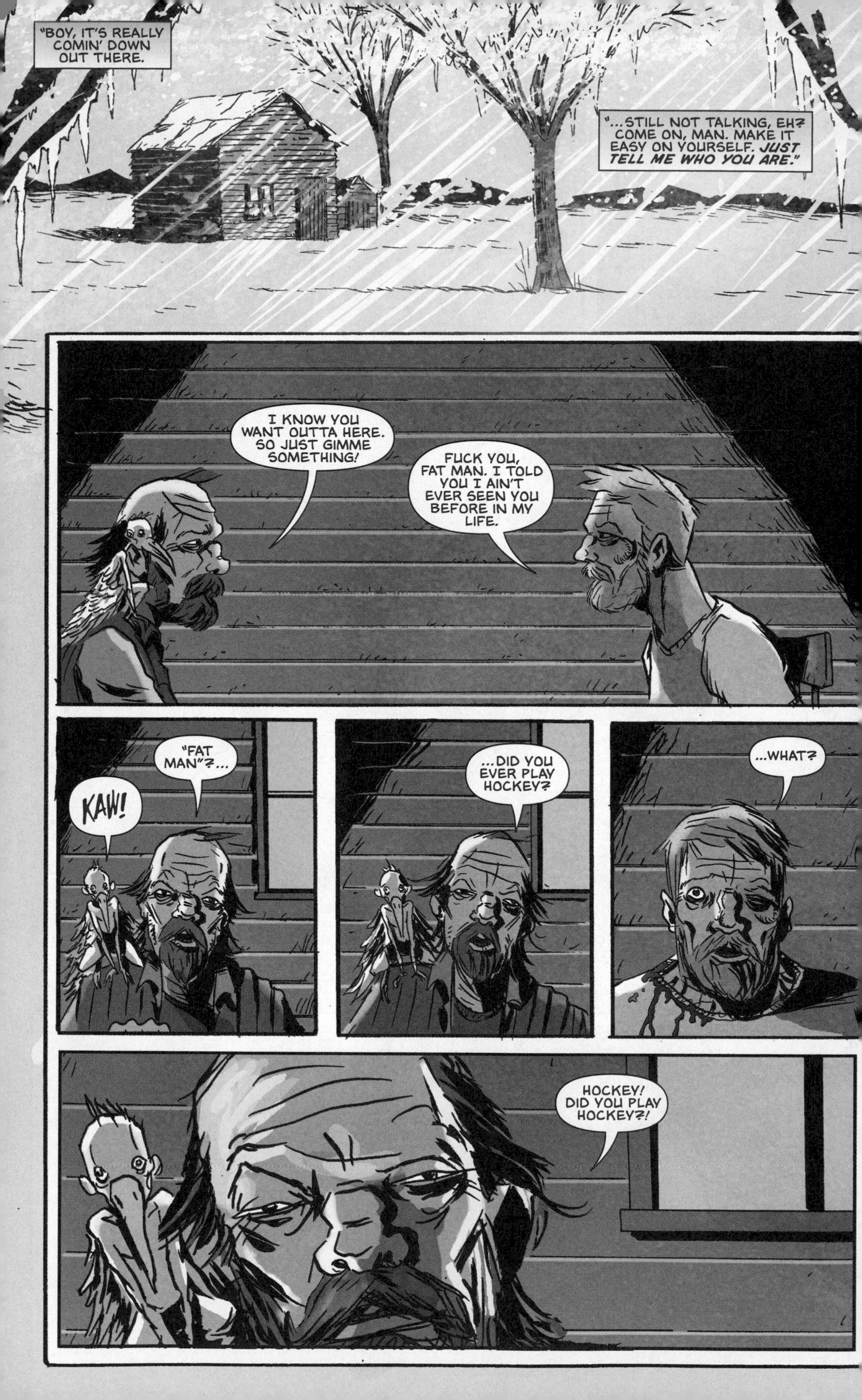
"BOY, IT'S REALLY COMIN' DOWN OUT THERE.
"...STILL NOT TALKING, EH? COME ON, MAN. MAKE IT EASY ON YOURSELF. *JUST TELL ME WHO YOU ARE.*"
I KNOW YOU WANT OUTTA HERE. SO JUST GIMME SOMETHING!
FUCK YOU, FAT MAN. I TOLD YOU I AIN'T EVER SEEN YOU BEFORE IN MY LIFE.
KAW!
"FAT MAN"?...
...DID YOU EVER PLAY HOCKEY?
...WHAT?
HOCKEY! DID YOU PLAY HOCKEY?!

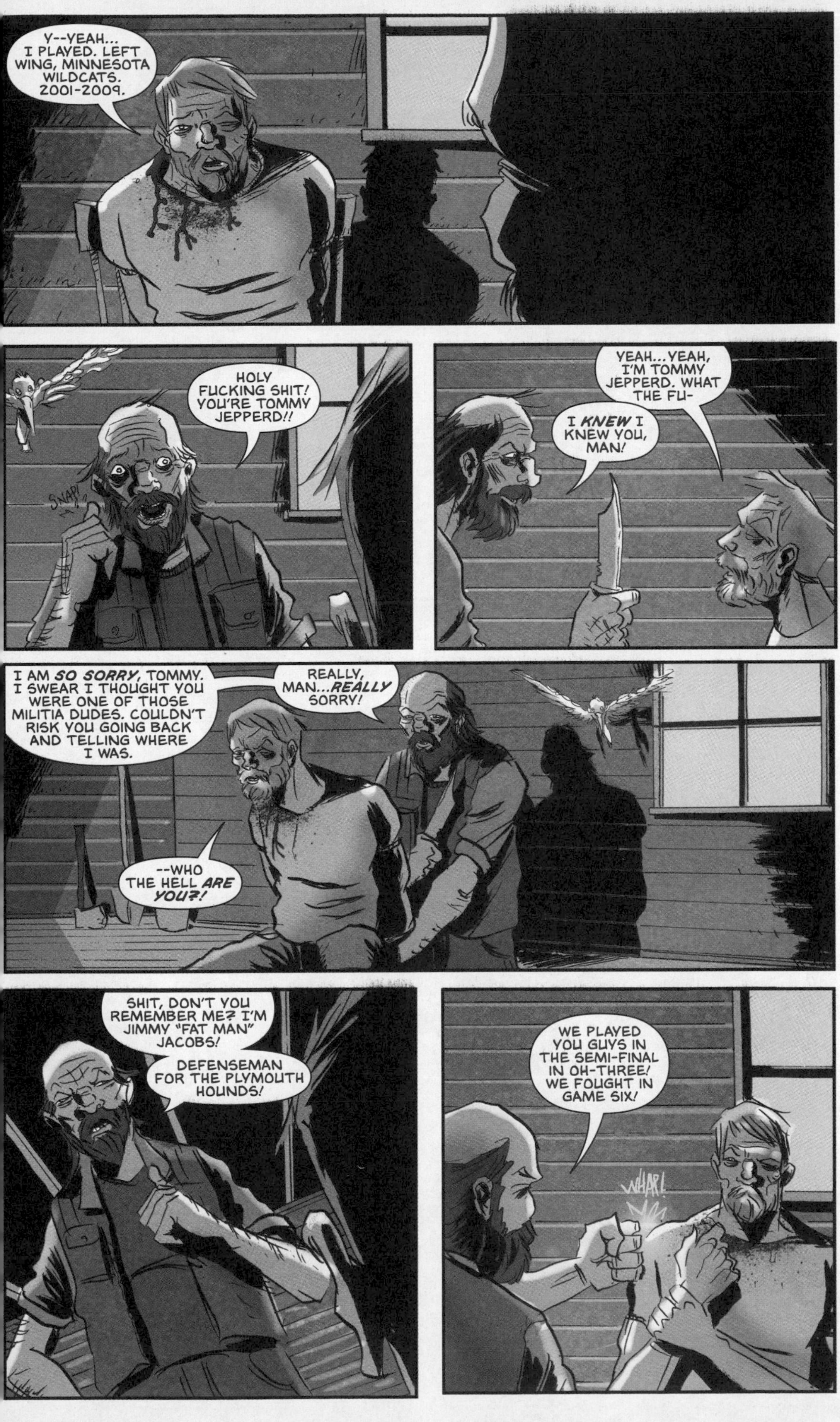
Y--YEAH... I PLAYED. LEFT WING, MINNESOTA WILDCATS. 2001-2009.
HOLY FUCKING SHIT! YOU'RE TOMMY JEPPERD!!
SNAP!
YEAH...YEAH, I'M TOMMY JEPPERD. WHAT THE FU-
I KNEW I KNEW YOU, MAN!
I AM SO SORRY, TOMMY. I SWEAR I THOUGHT YOU WERE ONE OF THOSE MILITIA DUDES. COULDN'T RISK YOU GOING BACK AND TELLING WHERE I WAS.
REALLY, MAN...REALLY SORRY!
--WHO THE HELL ARE YOU?!
SHIT, DON'T YOU REMEMBER ME? I'M JIMMY "FAT MAN" JACOBS!
DEFENSEMAN FOR THE PLYMOUTH HOUNDS!
WE PLAYED YOU GUYS IN THE SEMI-FINAL IN OH-THREE! WE FOUGHT IN GAME SIX!
WHAP!

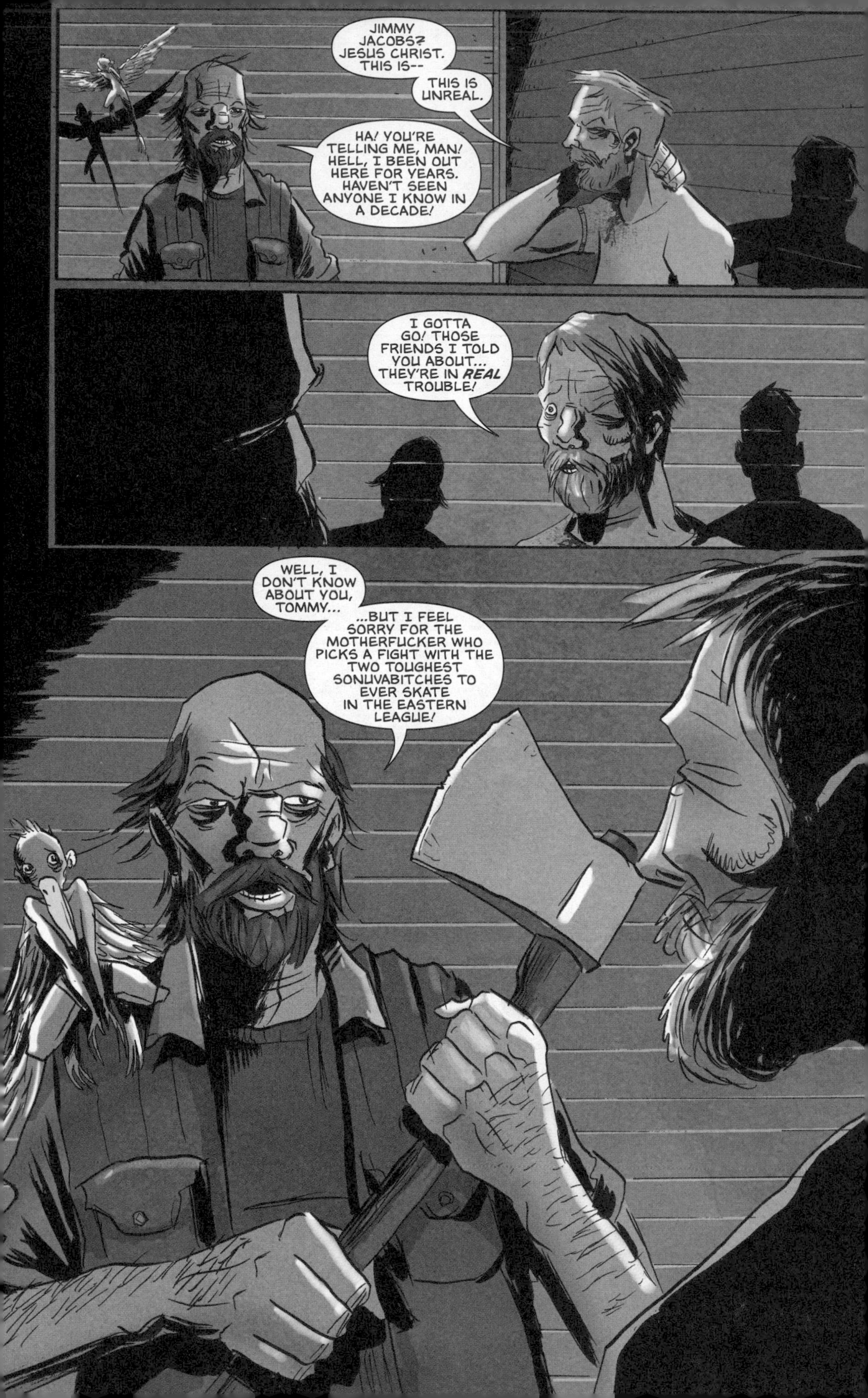
JIMMY JACOBS? JESUS CHRIST. THIS IS--
THIS IS UNREAL.
HA! YOU'RE TELLING ME, MAN! HELL, I BEEN OUT HERE FOR YEARS. HAVEN'T SEEN ANYONE I KNOW IN A DECADE!
I GOTTA GO! THOSE FRIENDS I TOLD YOU ABOUT... THEY'RE IN REAL TROUBLE!
WELL, I DON'T KNOW ABOUT YOU, TOMMY...
...BUT I FEEL SORRY FOR THE MOTHERFUCKER WHO PICKS A FIGHT WITH THE TWO TOUGHEST SONUVABITCHES TO EVER SKATE IN THE EASTERN LEAGUE!

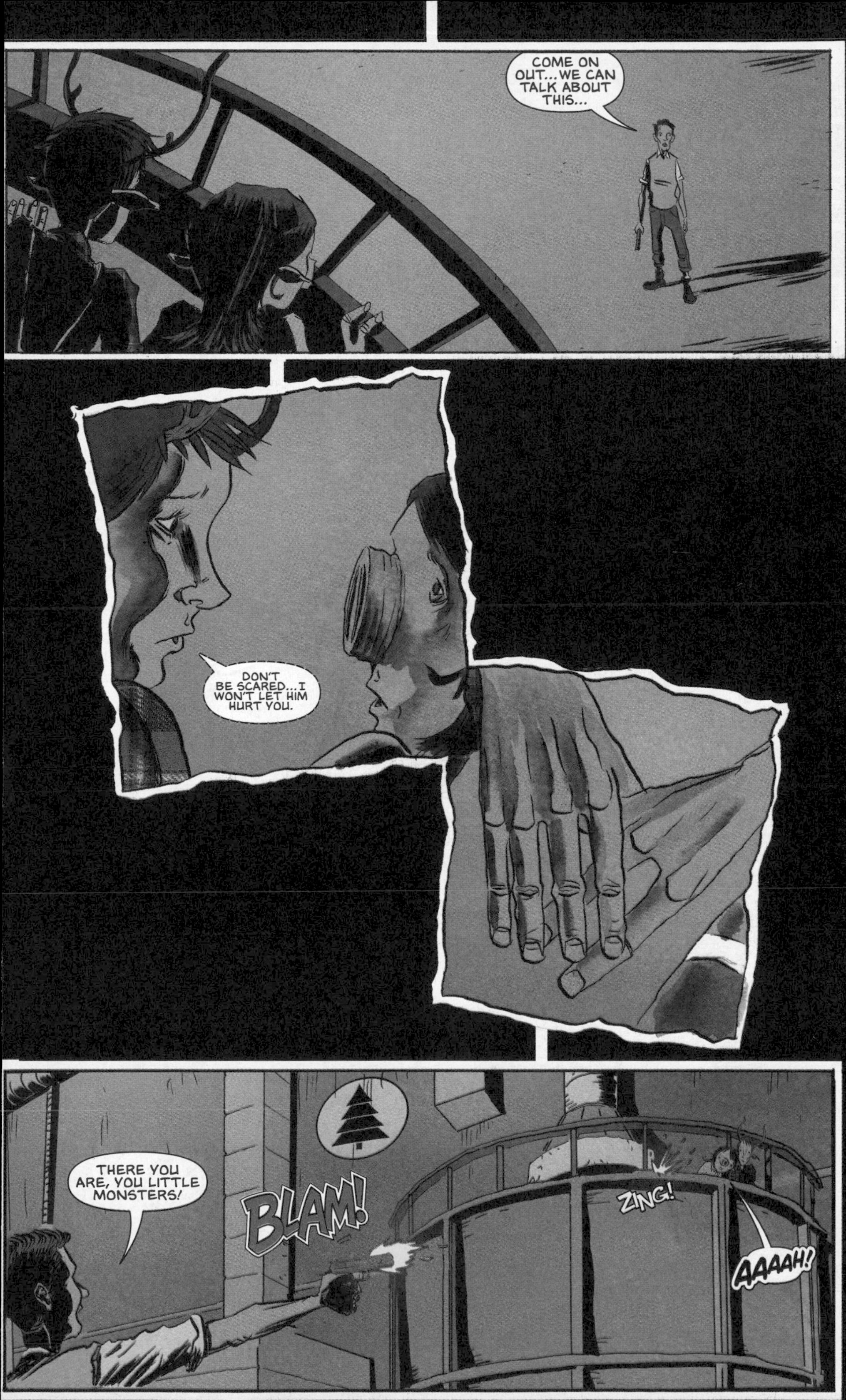
COME ON OUT...WE CAN TALK ABOUT THIS...
DON'T BE SCARED...I WON'T LET HIM HURT YOU.
THERE YOU ARE, YOU LITTLE MONSTERS!
BLAM!
ZING!
AAAAH!

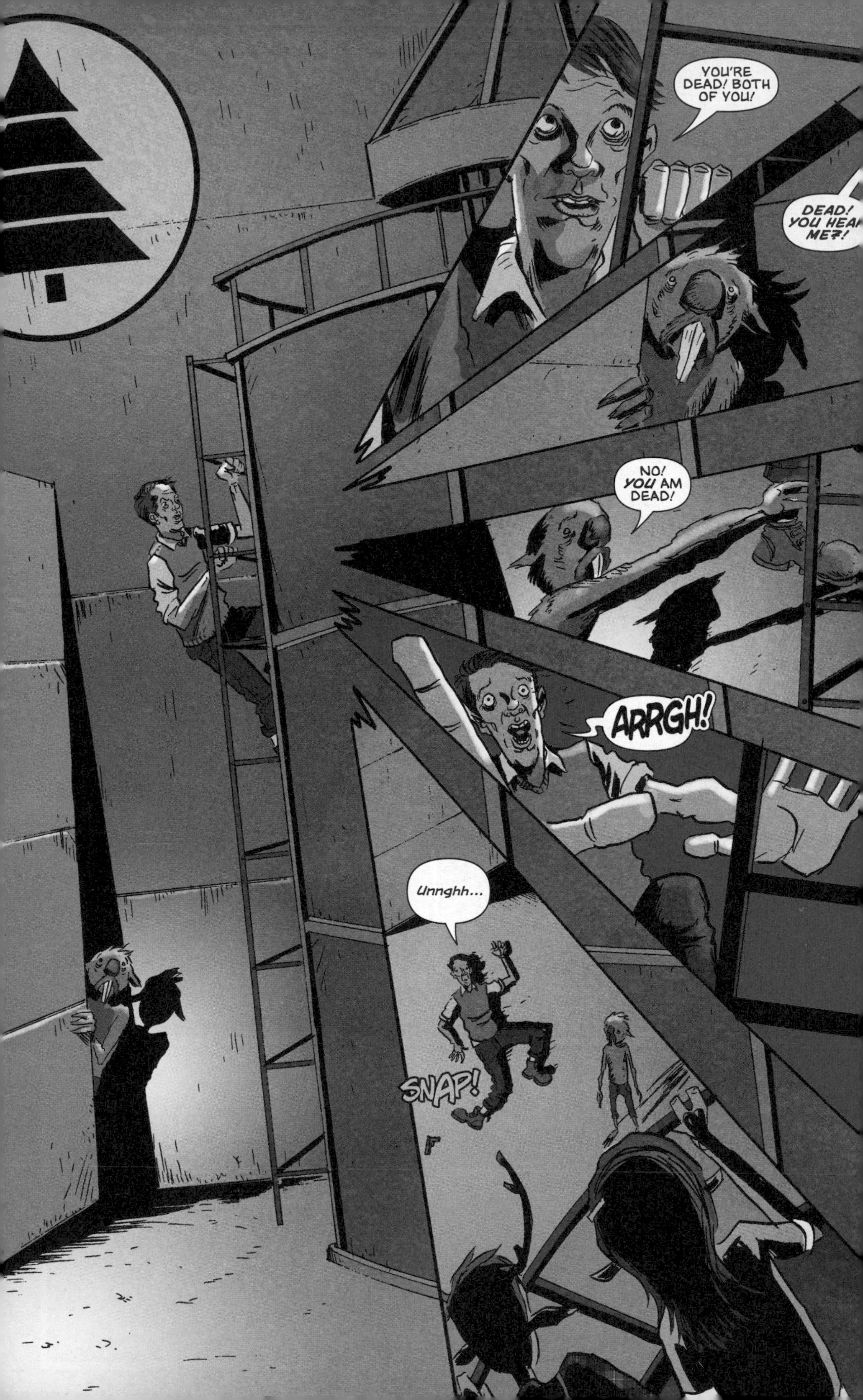
YOU'RE DEAD! BOTH OF YOU!
DEAD! YOU HEA ME?!
NO! YOU AM DEAD!
ARRGH!
Unnghh...
SNAP!

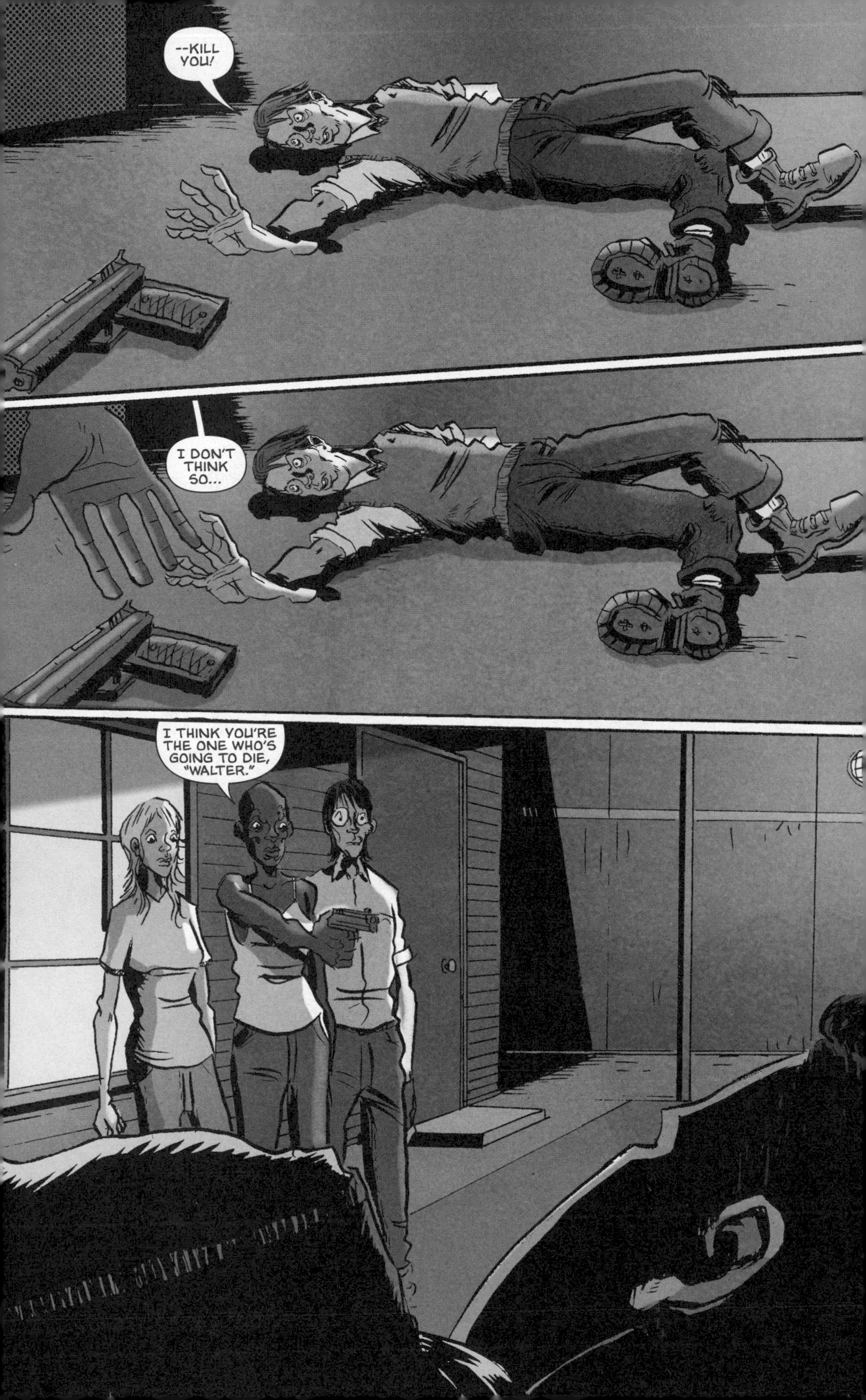
--KILL YOU!
I DON'T THINK SO...
I THINK YOU'RE THE ONE WHO'S GOING TO DIE, "WALTER."

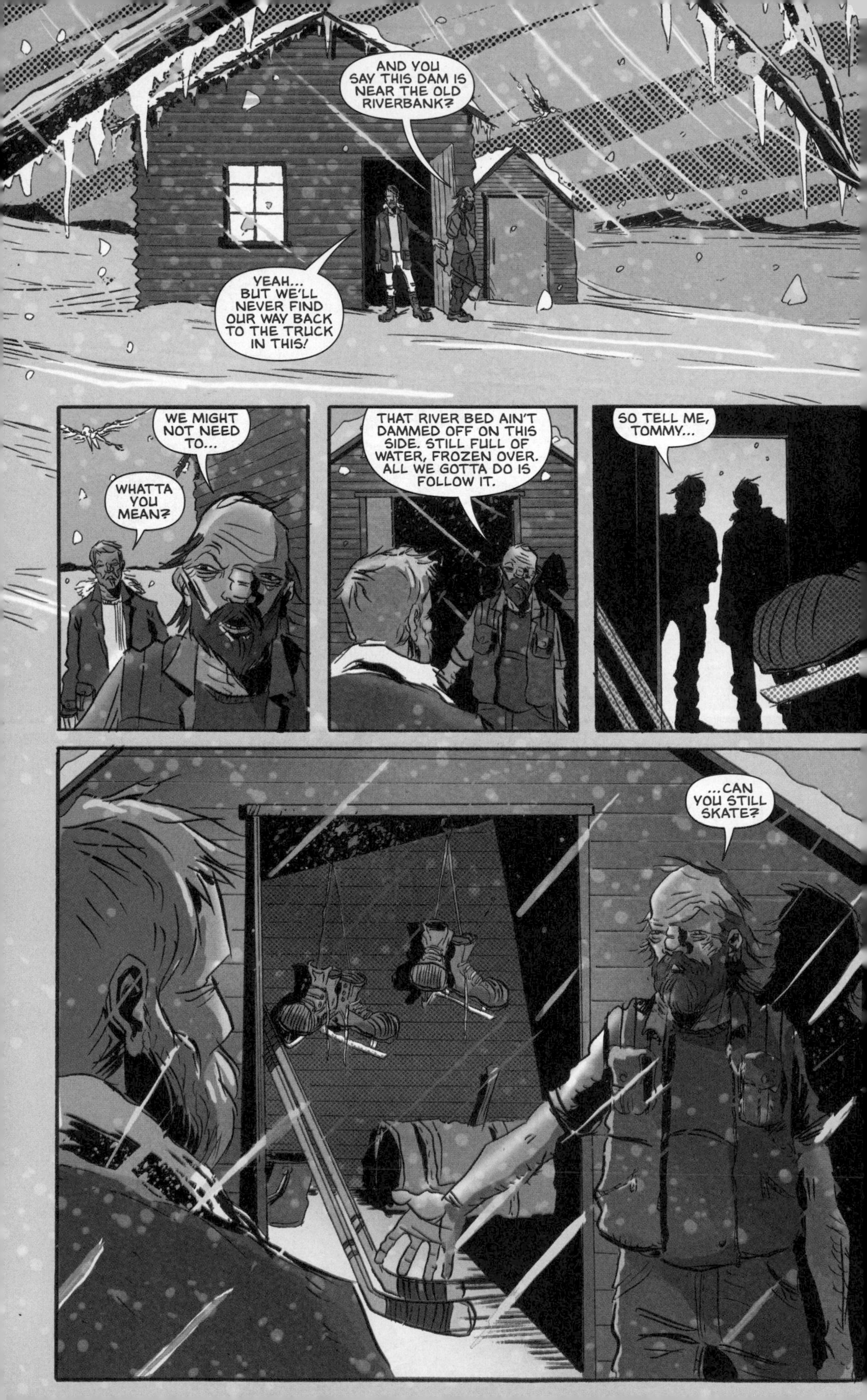
AND YOU SAY THIS DAM IS NEAR THE OLD RIVERBANK?
YEAH... BUT WE'LL NEVER FIND OUR WAY BACK TO THE TRUCK IN THIS!
WE MIGHT NOT NEED TO...
WHATTA YOU MEAN?
THAT RIVER BED AIN'T DAMMED OFF ON THIS SIDE. STILL FULL OF WATER, FROZEN OVER. ALL WE GOTTA DO IS FOLLOW IT.
SO TELL ME, TOMMY...
...CAN YOU STILL SKATE?

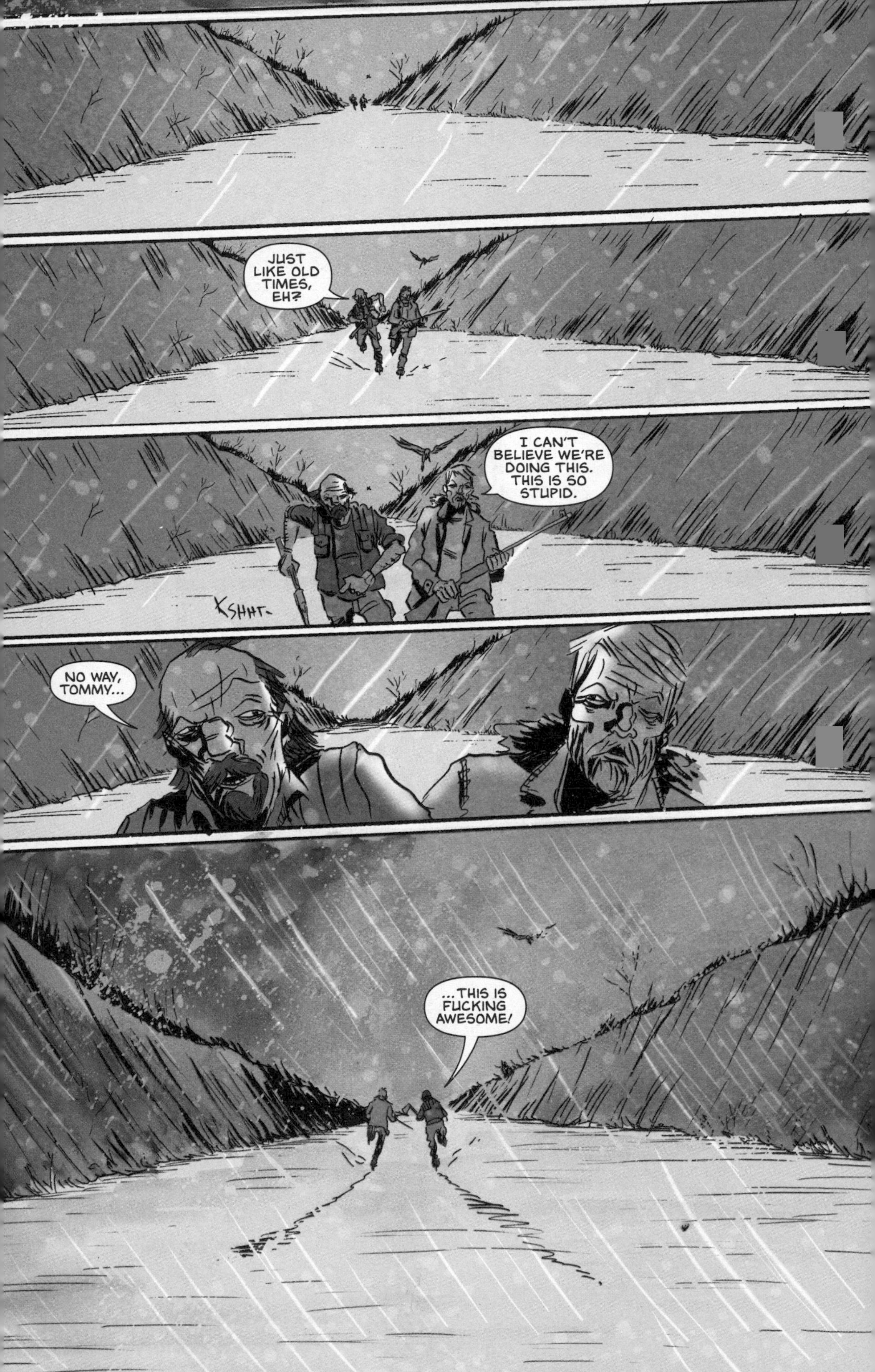
JUST LIKE OLD TIMES, EH?
I CAN'T BELIEVE WE'RE DOING THIS. THIS IS SO STUPID.
KSHHT.
NO WAY, TOMMY...
...THIS IS FUCKING AWESOME!

"P-PLEASE--"

PLEASE, DON'T SHOOT ME!

SHUT UP.

NO! STOP!

NO...THIS AIN'T RIGHT. WE CAN'T JUST KILL HIM.

GUS, STEP OUT OF THE WAY.

SWEETIE, I DON'T KNOW WHAT YOU THINK, BUT THIS MAN IS *VERY BAD.*

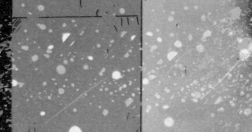

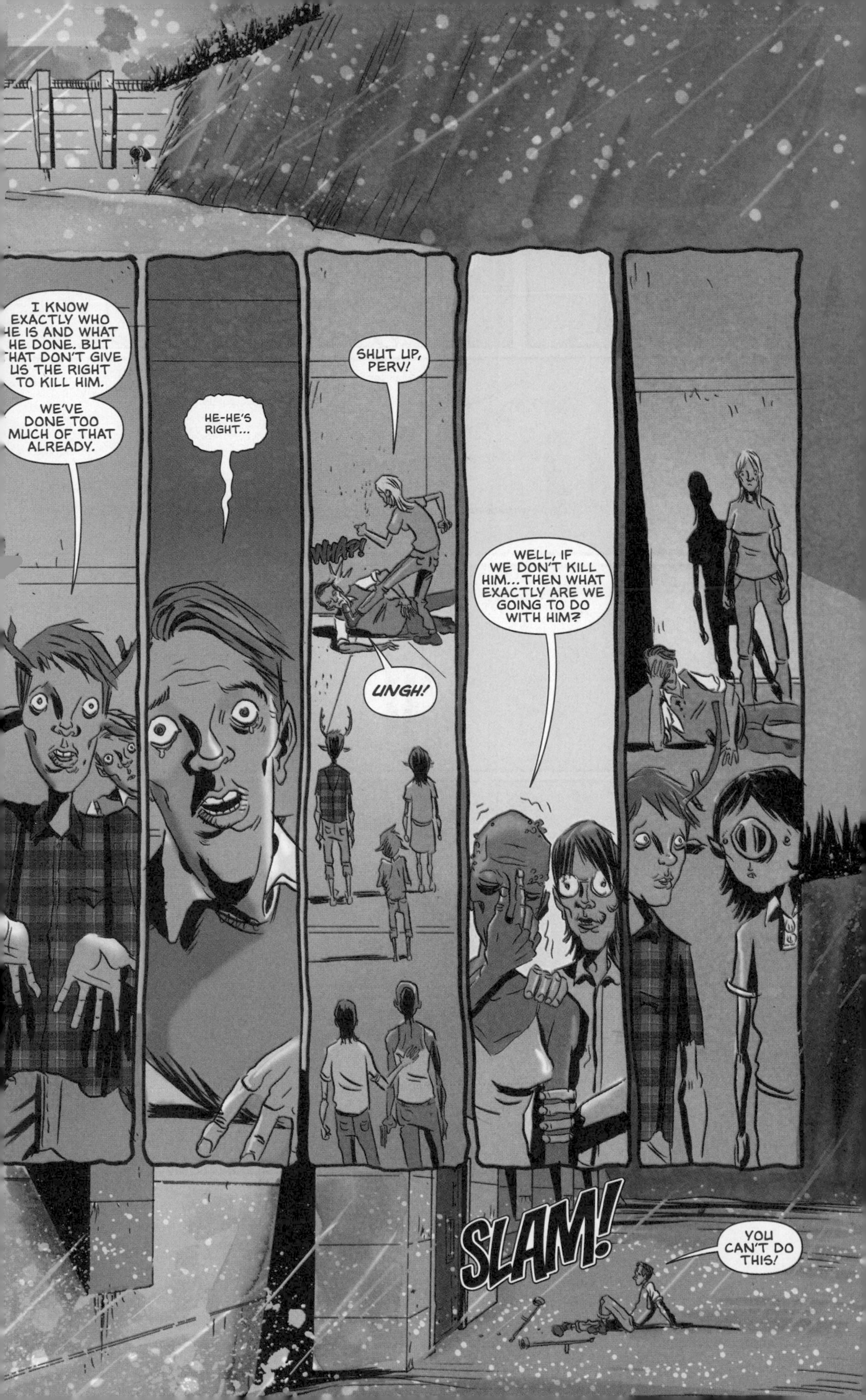
I KNOW EXACTLY WHO HE IS AND WHAT HE DONE. BUT THAT DON'T GIVE US THE RIGHT TO KILL HIM.
WE'VE DONE TOO MUCH OF THAT ALREADY.
HE-HE'S RIGHT...
SHUT UP, PERV!
WHAP!
UNGH!
WELL, IF WE DON'T KILL HIM...THEN WHAT EXACTLY ARE WE GOING TO DO WITH HIM?
SLAM!
YOU CAN'T DO THIS!

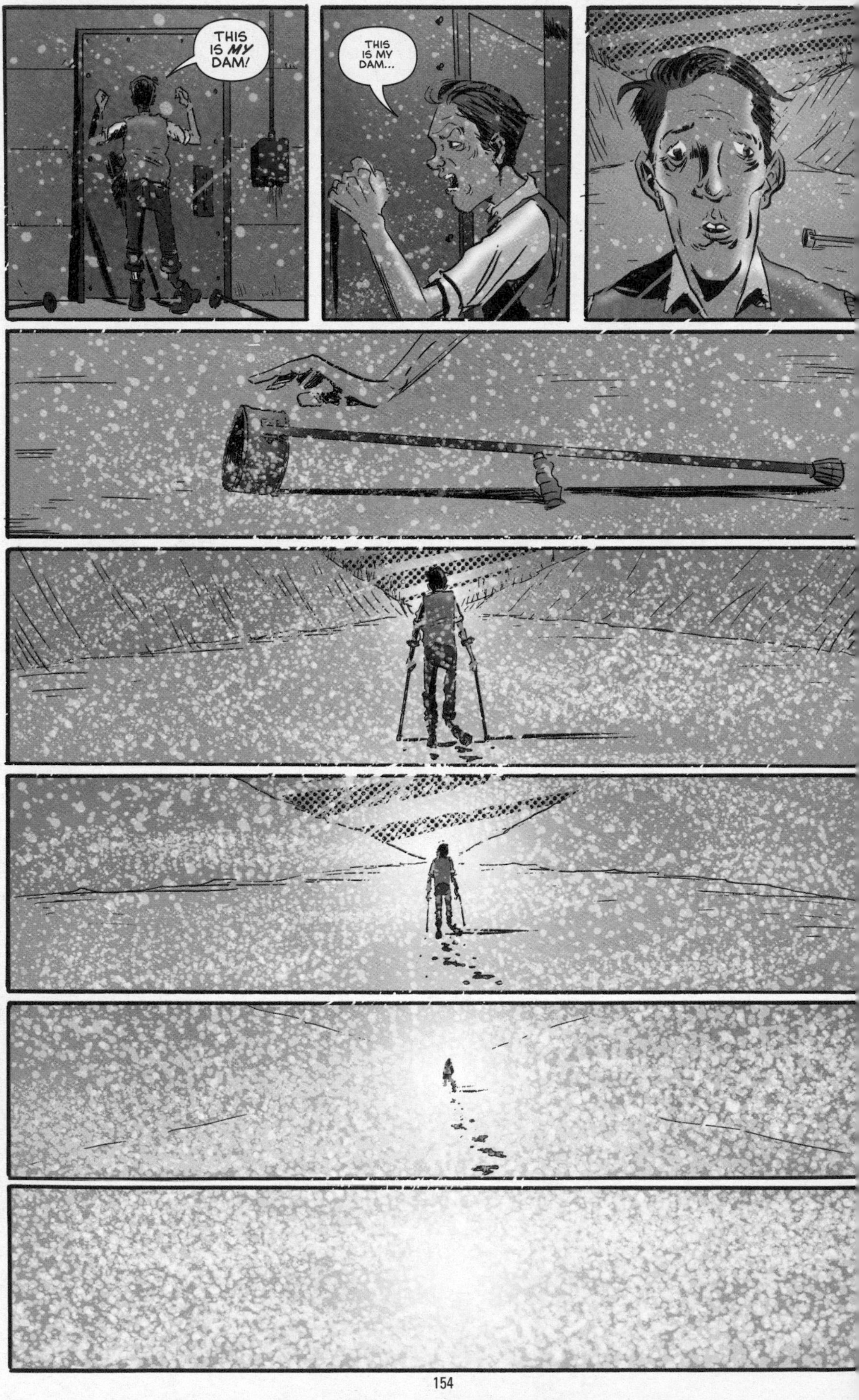
THIS IS *MY* DAM!
THIS IS MY DAM...

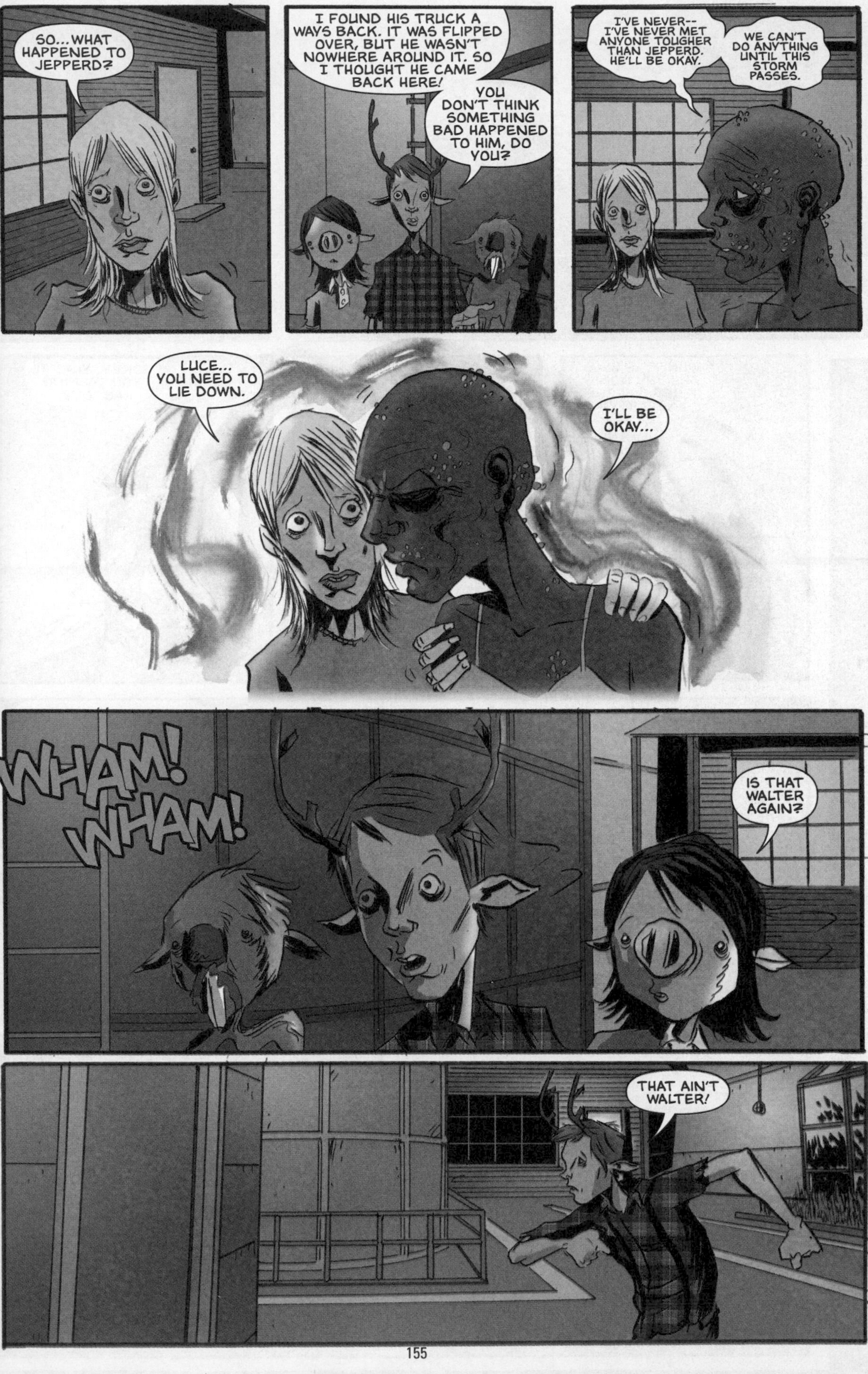
SO...WHAT HAPPENED TO JEPPERD?
I FOUND HIS TRUCK A WAYS BACK. IT WAS FLIPPED OVER, BUT HE WASN'T NOWHERE AROUND IT. SO I THOUGHT HE CAME BACK HERE!
YOU DON'T THINK SOMETHING BAD HAPPENED TO HIM, DO YOU?
I'VE NEVER-- I'VE NEVER MET ANYONE TOUGHER THAN JEPPERD. HE'LL BE OKAY.
WE CAN'T DO ANYTHING UNTIL THIS STORM PASSES.
LUCE... YOU NEED TO LIE DOWN.
I'LL BE OKAY...
WHAM! WHAM!
IS THAT WALTER AGAIN?
THAT AIN'T WALTER!

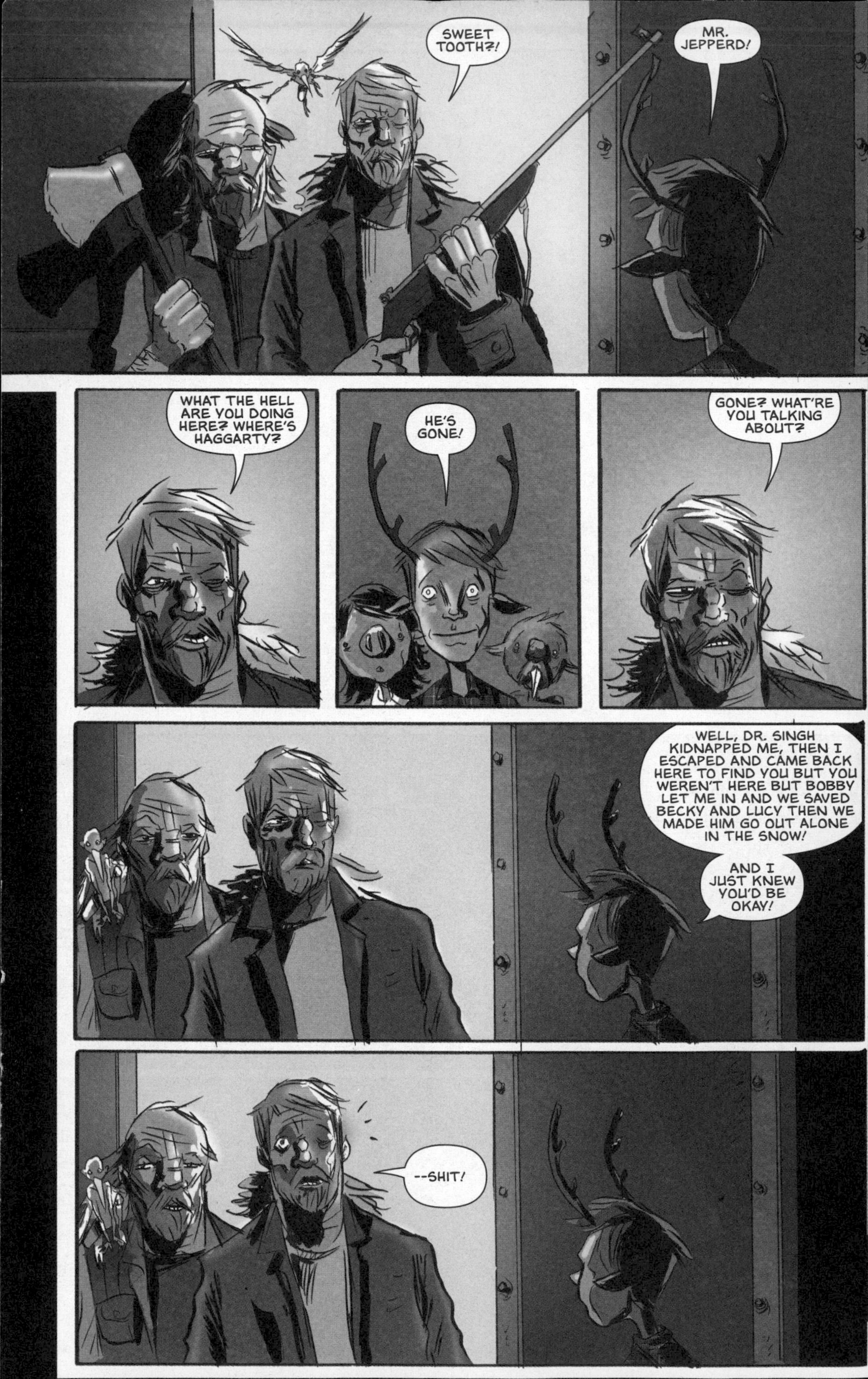
SWEET TOOTH?!
MR. JEPPERD!
WHAT THE HELL ARE YOU DOING HERE? WHERE'S HAGGARTY?
HE'S GONE!
GONE? WHAT'RE YOU TALKING ABOUT?
WELL, DR. SINGH KIDNAPPED ME, THEN I ESCAPED AND CAME BACK HERE TO FIND YOU BUT YOU WEREN'T HERE BUT BOBBY LET ME IN AND WE SAVED BECKY AND LUCY THEN WE MADE HIM GO OUT ALONE IN THE SNOW!
AND I JUST KNEW YOU'D BE OKAY!
--SHIT!

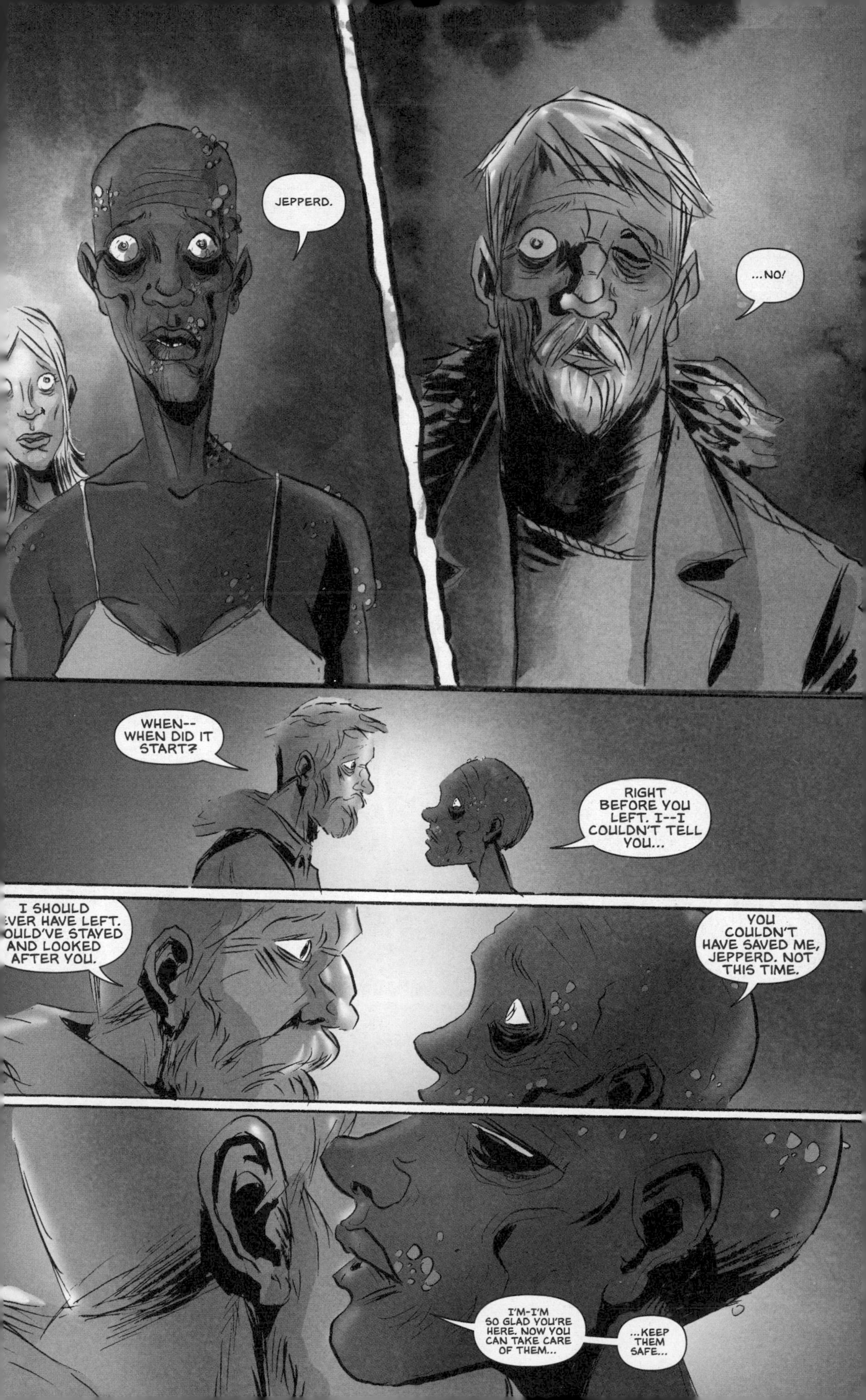
JEPPERD.
...NO!
WHEN-- WHEN DID IT START?
RIGHT BEFORE YOU LEFT. I--I COULDN'T TELL YOU...
I SHOULD EVER HAVE LEFT. OULD'VE STAYED AND LOOKED AFTER YOU.
YOU COULDN'T HAVE SAVED ME, JEPPERD. NOT THIS TIME.
I'M-I'M SO GLAD YOU'RE HERE. NOW YOU CAN TAKE CARE OF THEM...
...KEEP THEM SAFE...

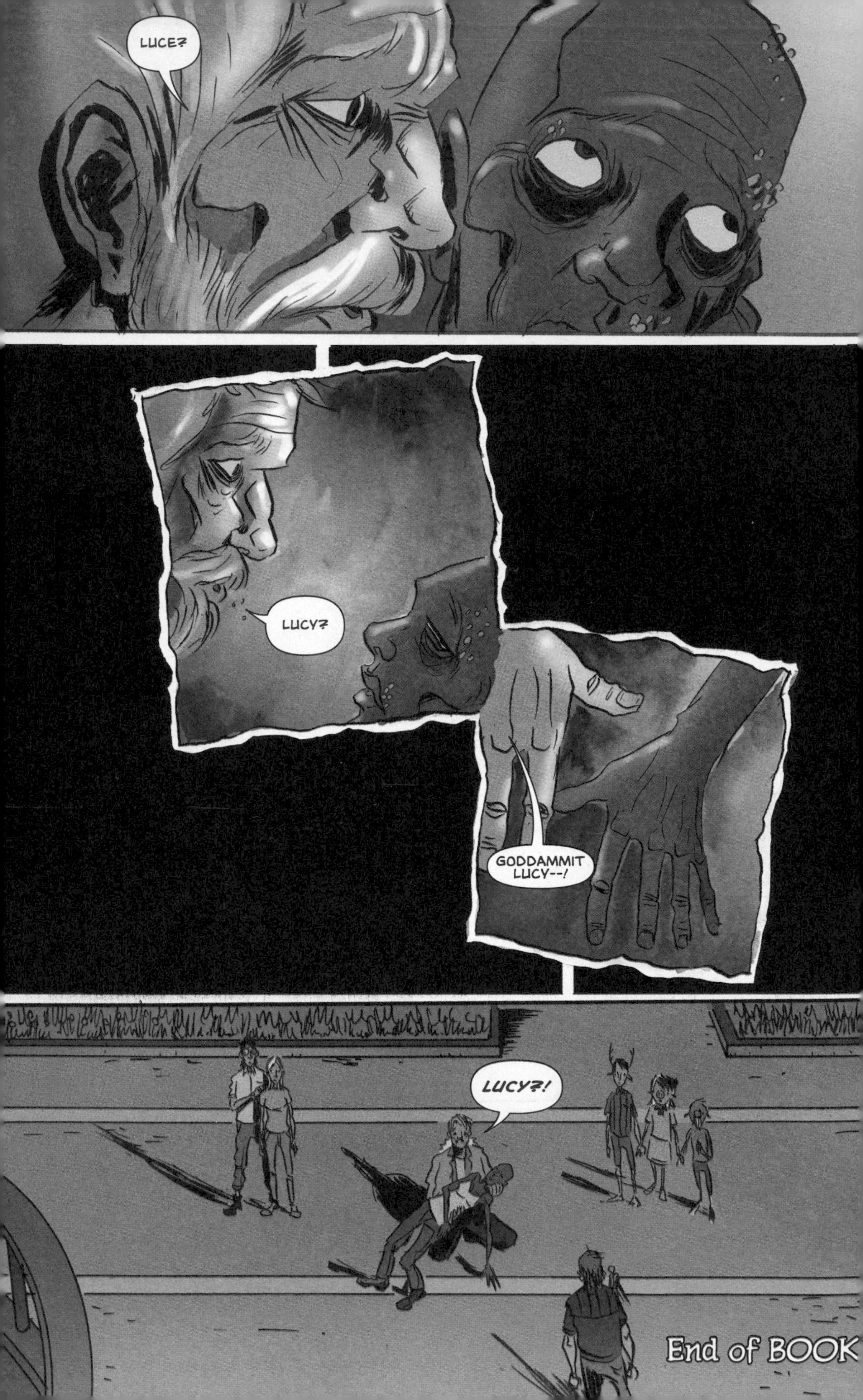
LUCE?
LUCY?
GODDAMMIT LUCY--!
LUCY?!
End of BOOK

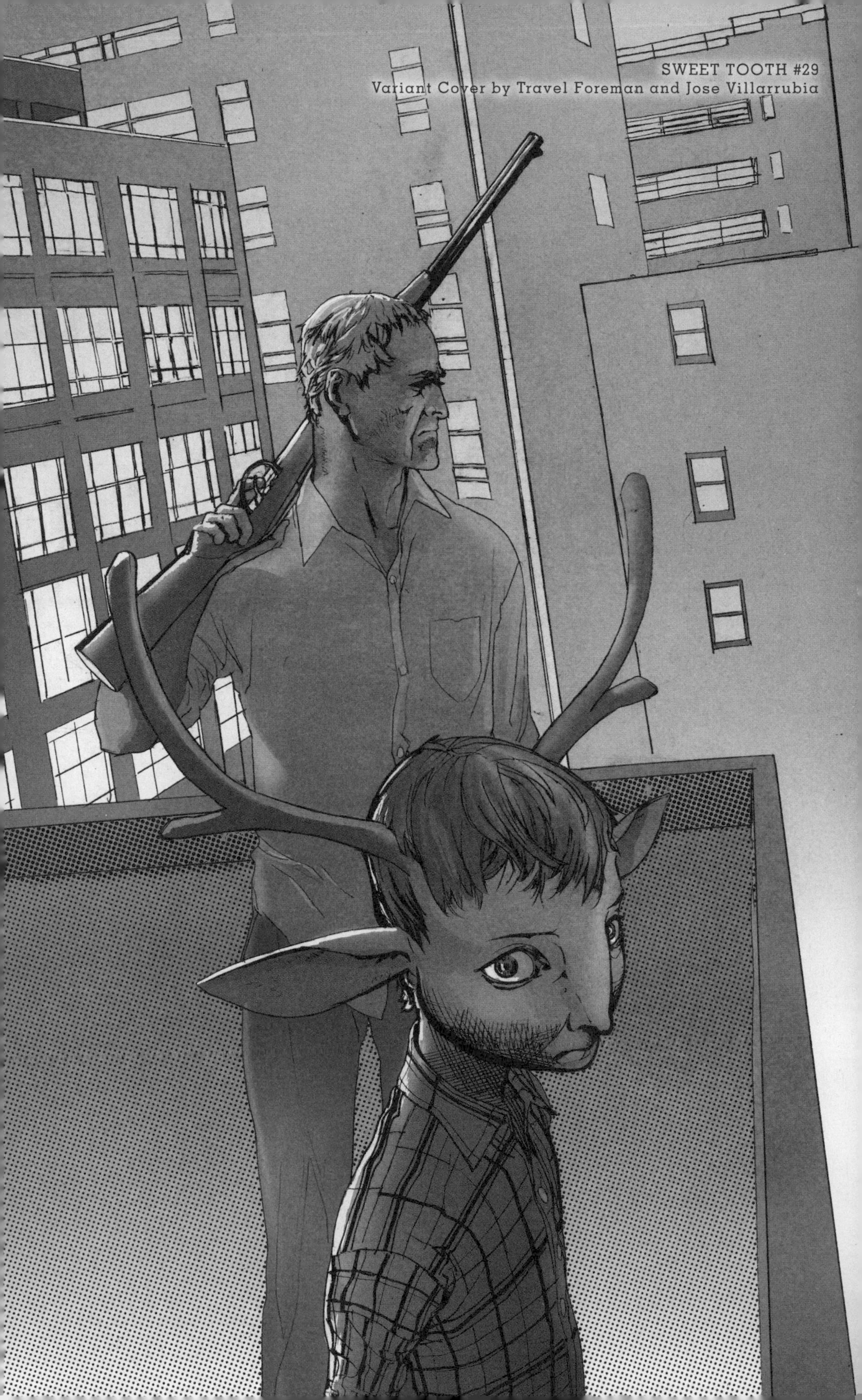

SWEET TOOTH #29
Variant Cover by Travel Foreman and Jose Villarrubia